Transforming Relationships in Forensic Psychological Practice

Transforming Relationships in Forensic Psychological Practice is first and foremost a clinicians' guide: it has been written with the aim of supporting people to develop, maintain and repair relationships within their work as forensic practitioners.

Research repeatedly finds that client perception of the therapeutic relationship is a significant factor in treatment success; however, data suggests that forensic psychologists have a poor history of trust and engagement with people in prisons. Tackling this issue head-on, this book explores key factors in working relationships across a broad range of forensic client groups, settings and tasks and reflects on specific points of tension in forensic therapeutic relationships. Drawing on the expertise of a diverse range of authors, it unpicks the challenges in building such relationships and explores factors such as neurodiversity, extremism, professional boundaries and working effectively with women and children. It outlines how productive working relationships can be developed and maintained, and highlights the essential constituent parts of that process, using both a theoretical and experiential lens. Finally, this book identifies and discusses examples of good practice from both practitioner and, in places, service participant perspectives.

Guiding practitioners to find respectful and connected solutions, while maintaining safety and appropriate professional and personal boundaries, *Transforming Relationships in Forensic Psychological Practice* is an essential resource for all professionals working in forensic settings, both qualified and in training.

Jo Shingler is a Chartered Psychologist and HCPC Registered Forensic Psychologist, currently working within STRIVE, a co-commissioned service between HMPPS and the NHS as part of the Offender Personality Disorder (OPD) pathway.

Nicola Bowes is an HCPC Registered Forensic Psychologist and Professor of Practitioner Psychology at Cardiff Metropolitan University, UK. She leads the largest university provider of forensic psychology training in the UK.

Tassie Ghilani is National Lived Experience Lead for HMPPS and a passionate advocate for system reform. She works to improve outcomes for people in prison and on probation, promote culture change and the meaningful inclusion of lived experience in justice activities.

'This timely and informative book captures the transformational journeys made by experienced forensic psychologists in a wide variety of professional settings in the UK over recent years. It highlights and reflects on the development of our thinking in how we, as a profession, relate to "others" in the criminal justice system and focuses on the needs and experiences of our diverse range of Experts by Experience. Each chapter raises specific professional issues, like equality, neurodiversity, power imbalances, terrorism, working with children, women and those subject to Indeterminate Prison sentences, all of which assist the reader to consider and understand better our therapeutic challenges in different contexts. The book also explores the unique complexities of professional boundaries in forensic settings and the need for practitioners to understand boundaries from a specifically trauma informed perspective. Of special interest for those on their professional training pathway to qualification in forensic psychology, is a chapter on managing supervision relationships and the authors offer strategies around maintaining personal wellbeing while navigating the complexities challenges of life as a trainee.

This book will inform and have relevance for both practitioners and trainees who are curious about how forensic psychology has evolved and is shaping the future and influencing our profession and wider society today.'

Dr Jacqueline Bates-Gaston, *Registered HCPC Practitioner*
Psychologist and BPS Chartered Forensic Psychologist.
Former Chief Psychologist with the Northern Ireland
Prison Service and Parole Board Psychologist
Member for England and Wales

'This remarkable collection represents a major challenge to forensic psychology's understanding how change works. According to the medical model, you target the right dosage of the right treatment to the right population, and you will reduce recidivism. The contributions in this book present a much more humble, humanistic appreciation of change as a two-way street, a co-production, a dynamic between people. It should be required reading for those wanting to make a real difference in real lives.'

Professor Shadd Maruna, *Head of Sociology, Social Policy and*
Criminology; School of Law & Social Justice,
University of Liverpool, UK

'This book addresses a neglected topic in forensic work: that of how professionals working with forensic service users can nurture relationships appropriately to benefit all parties and arrive at the best possible outcomes for all. There needs to be consideration of the individual's characteristics and background, which in forensic service users are often traumatic and disadvantageous. Power differentials inevitably impact on the professional-service user relationship. The task in hand also affects the interaction, whether this is assessment or intervention. Professionals need to think carefully about how they manage these issues and this book provides a solid basis for this purpose. Experienced professionals, academics and service users have contributed to an original and thought-provoking text that will undoubtedly benefit all professionals working with people in the criminal justice system.'

Professor Mary McMurran, *Forensic Psychologist, Clinical Psychologist. Visiting Professor Cardiff Metropolitan University, UK*

'As a chartered counselling psychologist who worked in a forensic setting, I wish this book had been written 25 years ago! As the current chief exec of the PRT, who repeatedly hears about the challenges of disempowerment and mistrust that people in prison and probation face, in relation to their contact with psychologists, this book finally addresses the elephant in the room.

Every important setting where forensic work is undertaken is covered within the chapters of this book. No stone is left unturned, no challenge minimised. This is such an honest and authentic collection of work. The fact that the resounding message from each chapter is the same, it becomes the most legitimate call to action that I have ever seen. It settles the age-old debate that the quality of the therapeutic alliance, in particular 'bond', is necessary (rather than just sufficient) in bringing about meaningful change.

I hope this becomes an essential text for all trainee practitioners in a forensic setting. It should be the book that helps them decide whether a career within a forensic setting is actually for them and if it is, how to navigate the complex challenges they are likely to face along the way.'

Pia Sinha, *CEO of the Prison Reform Trust*

'The core of psychology involves humans understanding other humans, often through a professional relationship. This book shines an essential light on that professional relationship within a forensic psychology context. The rich variety of authors' perspectives, offering voices from different seats in the assessment and therapeutic room, provides hopeful and practical direction to practitioners in the field. This book consolidates the current knowledge base around relational practice, suggests solutions to identified challenges, and is a valuable addition to the forensic psychology literature.'

Dr Sally Tilt, *Chair of Division of Forensic Psychology, British Psychological Society*

'This book provides an essential and timely resource for anyone working within the complex and often challenging field of forensic psychology. Bridging the gap between theory and frontline practice, this guide offers rich, grounded insights drawn from academics, experienced practitioners, and—crucially—those with lived experience of the criminal justice and health systems. Each chapter offers practical strategies and real-world examples that promote ethical, trauma-informed, and relationally attuned care. Thought-provoking, accessible, and deeply humane—this is not just a handbook, but a call to practice with integrity and relational courage.'

Dr Fiona Williams, *Head of Interventions Services,*
Interventions Operations and Investments,
Rehabilitation Directorate, His Majesty's Prison
and Probation Service

Issues in Forensic Psychology
Series Editors
Richard Shuker
Geraldine Akerman

The views expressed by the authors/editors may not necessarily be those held by the Series Editors or HMPPS.

Global Perspectives on Interventions in Forensic Therapeutic Communities
A Practitioner's Guide
Edited by Geraldine Akerman and Richard Shuker

Trauma-Informed Forensic Practice
Edited by Phil Wilmot and Lawrence Jones

Working with Autistic People in the Criminal Justice and Forensic Mental Health Systems
A Handbook for Practitioners
Edited by Nichola Tyler and Anne Sheeran

Challenging Bias in Forensic Psychological Assessment and Testing
Theoretical and Practical Approaches to Working with
Diverse Populations
Edited by Glenda C. Liell, Martin J. Fisher, and Lawrence F. Jones

The Journey from Prison to Community
Developing Identity, Meaning and Belonging with Men in the UK
Edited by Jo Shingler and Jennifer Stickney

Transforming Relationships in Forensic Psychological Practice
Edited by Jo Shingler, Nicola Bowes and Tassie Ghilani

For more information about this series, please visit: www.routledge.com/Issues-in-Forensic-Psychology/book-series/IFP

Transforming Relationships in Forensic Psychological Practice

Edited by
Jo Shingler, Nicola Bowes and
Tassie Ghilani

Routledge
Taylor & Francis Group

LONDON AND NEW YORK

Designed cover image: Getty Images

First published 2026
by Routledge
4 Park Square, Milton Park, Abingdon, Oxon OX14 4RN

and by Routledge
605 Third Avenue, New York, NY 10158

Routledge is an imprint of the Taylor & Francis Group, an informa business

For Product Safety Concerns and Information please contact our EU
representative GPSR@taylorandfrancis.com. Taylor & Francis Verlag
GmbH, Kaufingerstraße 24, 80331 München, Germany.

British Library Cataloguing-in-Publication Data
A catalogue record for this book is available from the British Library

ISBN: 978-1-032-89359-4 (hbk)
ISBN: 978-1-032-89354-9 (pbk)
ISBN: 978-1-003-54237-7 (ebk)

DOI: 10.4324/9781003542377

Typeset in Sabon
by codeMantra

All of the proceeds from this book will be donated to The Prison Reform Trust (PRT), an independent UK charity. Its mission is to create a just, humane, and effective penal system by reducing unnecessary imprisonment, improving prison conditions, and promoting equality and human rights. It achieves this through research, policy development, public education, and campaigning, and it supports people held in prison, their families, prison staff, and others through advice and advocacy.

Registered charity number in England and Wales is: 1035525

Contents

Contributors

Geraldine Akerman is a Consultant Forensic Psychologist, registered with HCPC and Chartered by the BPS. She has worked in prisons for 26 years, formally for HMPPS and more recently for the NHS. She is an Honorary Professor at Cardiff Metropolitan University and a visiting lecturer at the University of Birmingham. She has published widely in the areas of sexual offending, therapeutic communities and trauma-informed practice.

Louise E. Bowers is a Forensic Psychologist and Director of The Forensic Psychologist Service, UK.

With over 30 years of post-qualification experience across a range of settings, including Justice and Health, Louise has particular expertise in working with children and young people who have committed serious offences and are facing or serving long custodial sentences.

Nicola Bowes is a Forensic Psychologist and Professor of Practitioner Forensic Psychology at Cardiff Metropolitan University, UK.

Nicola is Past Chair of the British Psychological Society Division of Forensic Psychology and leads the largest university provider of forensic psychology training in the UK. She is passionate about equality, diversity and inclusion and advocates for those who feel that they don't "fit in".

Andi Brierley is a PhD student and senior lecturer at Leeds Trinity University. Drawing on 15 years in youth justice practice and his own lived experience of the criminal justice system, he has authored four books on penology and youth justice. His work focuses on desistance and lived experience professionals.

Amy Canning is a Clinical Psychologist in the UK.

Amy has been working in a specialist forensic service for autistic people and people with learning disabilities for the last decade.

Louise Coates is a Chartered Psychologist and Registered Forensic Psychologist in the UK.

Louise is currently working in private practice, providing therapy, training, supervision and staff support. She has worked within the criminal justice system for over 30 years, including community, secure mental health, youth justice, courts and prison settings, specialising in working with trauma and chronic threat.

Christopher Dean is a Chartered and Registered Forensic Psychologist, Director of Identify Psychological Services Ltd and a Senior Fellow at the Global Center on Cooperative Security, UK.

Chris has 25 years' experience in justice settings, including as a practitioner, consultant and senior manager. He has pioneered the development of innovative, evidence-based assessments, interventions, training programmes and professional guidance to prevent terrorism and violent extremism both nationally and internationally. He also publishes widely on this topic.

Karen De Claire is a Chartered Psychologist and Registered Forensic Psychologist, and Reader at Cardiff Metropolitan University, UK.

Karen has worked in prisons, secure services and the community for over 25 years, specialising in supervision, psychological risk assessment, interventions, and understanding the role of personal relationships in reducing offending and reoffending.

Sophie Ellis is a Research Manager for the Prison Reform Trust and PhD candidate at Cambridge University, UK.

Formerly in HMPPS Psychology Services, Sophie subsequently co-founded UNGRIPP to reform IPP sentencing, alongside families of those serving IPP. Her research explores imprisonment's moral dimensions, with a focus on indefinite sentences, prison psychology and the effects of law and policy on prisoners' experiences.

Tassie Ghilani is in the UK.

Tassie is a passionate leader, driving justice reform through lived experience. She champions outcomes for care leavers, women and those in custody. Her work focuses on embedding lived experience and involvement into policy to support second chances and reduce reoffending.

Kerensa Hocken is a Registered Forensic Psychologist and Principal Forensic Psychologist within His Majesty's Prison and Probation Service, UK.

Kerensa's areas of interest include Compassion Focused Therapy (CFT) in forensic settings, sexual offending and people with learning disabilities who offend. She is a co-founder of the CFT forensic special interest group within the Compassion Mind Foundation and a lead trainer for forensic CFT. She is a co-founder and former trustee of the Safer Living Foundation (SLF), a charity to prevent sexual abuse. She is a co-host of The Forensic Psychology Podcast and the BBC2 series Behind the Crime.

Jake is an autistic expert by experience who is very committed to helping professionals in both mental health and criminal justice services work more effectively with autistic people.

Jude Kelman is a Forensic Psychologist within His Majesty's Prison and Probation Service, UK.

Dr Kelman has 30 years' experience in justice settings and is the founding and Lead Psychologist for the Women's Group. She is passionate about improving outcomes for women in the criminal justice system and works hard to influence policies and practices, in order to improve the support and services available.

Tee Khan is based in the UK.

Tee's early life challenges included experiencing deprivation and school exclusion, leading to involvement in the criminal justice system. Transforming adversity into strength, Tee has rehabilitated and emerged as a passionate advocate for rehabilitation, equitable approaches to justice and criminal justice reform. Tee believes in the power of early intervention as a vital diversionary method to help at-risk youth avoid the pitfalls of the system.

Chinonso Lazz-Onyenobi is at Elysium Healthcare and His Majesty's Prison and Probation Service, UK.

Chinonso is a Forensic Psychologist registered with the HCPC. She is an EMDR-trained therapist, a Qualified Coach and a BPS-registered Clinical Supervisor. She currently works as a Senior Registered Psychologist in HMPPS. She also works in a hospital for service users sectioned under the Mental Health Act.

Monica Lloyd is an Honorary Senior Research Fellow at the University of Birmingham, UK.

Monica worked as a Forensic Psychologist in HMPPS and HM Inspectorate of Prisons, and later as an academic at the University of Birmingham where she pioneered the first dual forensic/clinical Doctorate Programme. Her expertise is in terrorist offending.

Michael McCracken is a Forensic Psychologist in the Probation Board for Northern Ireland.

Michael is a Forensic Psychologist and Senior Leader within the Probation Service in Northern Ireland. He previously worked for the Northern Ireland Prison Service. He is co-chair of the Secure Care and Specialist Services group (Forensic Managed Care Network) and champions trauma-informed practice across a variety of committees (UK and Europe).

Dakshina Raghavendra is a Registered Forensic Psychologist at Cardiff Metropolitan University, UK.

Dakshina is a Registered Forensic Psychologist, working with the Offender Personality Disorder (OPD) and NHS specialist women's OPD services in prison and secure hospitals. She is passionate about making forensic practice more inclusive, drawing on frameworks outside traditional Eurocentric models and hopes to develop more culturally sensitive approaches in practice.

Stephen Robinson is a Chartered and Registered Counselling Psychologist at Elysium Healthcare, University of Chester, UK.

Stephen is an HCPC-registered Counselling Psychologist, trained in a range of therapies including EMDR, DBT, CBT and Person Centred Therapy. Previously, he was a teacher and Special Educational Needs Co-ordinator (SENDCO). He now works in a hospital with clients sectioned under the Mental Health Act and in private practice.

Jo Shingler is a Chartered Psychologist and Registered Forensic Psychologist in the UK.

Jo is currently working within STRIVE (Core OPD & IIRMS service), a co-commissioned service between HMPPS and the NHS as part of the Offender Personality Disorder (OPD) pathway. She has worked in prisons and the community for over 30 years, specialising in psychological risk assessment, interventions, and understanding and improving therapeutic relationships in forensic settings.

Emma Stevenson is a Registered and Chartered Forensic Psychologist, and Director of The Forensic Psychologist Service, UK.

Emma has over 25 years' experience delivering forensic clinical services. She has worked across diverse settings, including prisons and secure mental health settings, with a focus on complex risk assessment, expert witness work, supervision and therapy.

Hannah Toogood is a Consultant Learning Disability Psychiatrist in the UK.

Hannah has been working in a specialist forensic service for autistic people and people with learning disabilities for the last decade.

Jason Warr is an Associate Professor in Criminology at the University of Nottingham, UK.

Jason has research interests in penology, sociology of power, narrative and sensory criminology, and the philosophy of science. His most recent book is concerned with forensic psychologists employed within the prisons of England and Wales: *Forensic Psychologists: Prisons, Power, and Vulnerability.*

Phil Willmot is a Consultant Forensic and Clinical Psychologist at Rampton Hospital, UK.

Phil is a Joint Lead Psychologist in the Men's Personality Disorder Service at Rampton Hospital. He is also a senior lecturer in Forensic Psychology at the University of Lincoln.

Acknowledgements

First and foremost, we would like to thank all of the authors and contributors who made this book possible. Every contributor brings expertise, insight and humanity to this volume, and we feel very proud and humbled to have had so many clever people contribute. We are also delighted that so many authors invited other people to contribute to their chapters – both colleagues and people with lived experience. It is a joy when people share the power, and we hope this volume embodies that principle.

We would also like to thank the people who gave up their time to give us advice and feedback throughout this journey. These include Rachael Dagnall, Martine Ratcliffe, Emma Stevenson and Jennifer Stickney. We would also like to thank the publishers, Annabel Harris and Ceri McClardy who have borne with us (and our various dramas and delays) with kindness and patience.

JS: I feel a strong need to pay tribute to all the people who have enabled me to get to a position in my life and career where people might want to listen to what I have to say. These people are too numerous to name individually! But I would like to particularly pay tribute to my parents. I am sad that neither of them is here to see this volume in print as I am so immensely proud of it. But I would not be here without their unfailing love and support, and I probably didn't tell them as often as I should have done how much that enabled me to take risks and step outside of my comfort zone.

I have worked with so many amazing people over the years. I'd like to mention "The Stepford Doctors" (you know who you are): the years we worked together are among my fondest, funniest and most irreverent memories. I also want to acknowledge my current work colleagues, the Dorset STRIVE team, who never cease to amaze me with their compassion and creativity. I feel so lucky to have found another lot of colleagues who enhance my life so much.

I also want to acknowledge all the people I have worked with over the years, who I continue to work with, in prison and the community: namely the people who have been in receipt of professional services. I continue to learn from you all, and I am so grateful for the trust you have shown me, and your willingness to allow me into your worlds. This book is for you, and by you, as without you all, it really wouldn't exist.

Finally, I want to thank the co-editors, Nic and Tassie. You are both brilliant, clever, insightful, compassionate and humble. And great company of course. What we have created together is most certainly better than the sum of the parts: teamwork really does make the dream work! Thank you both so much.

NB: I want to thank Jo and Tassie: Jo for inviting me to be part of this brilliant book which was her idea and a topic she has been such a beacon for; Tassie for joining us in this brilliant journey and making everything better, a particular talent that I think you both demonstrate more generally. I want to thank the people I have worked with in justice settings and in academia, for bearing with my rough edges and teaching me to be better at my role. Then to the amazingly patient people who have loved me, had my back and shown me how to be a better human – I thank you for the light you bring to the world and to my life. I need to especially thank my brilliant daughter for inspiring me by staying brave, compassionate and kind. I want to thank my lovely boy Dave who I miss keenly and my new lovely boy Cliff. Dogs are great at relationships. I hope that we could all aim to be more dog.

TG: Being part of this book and working with Jo and Nic has been an incredible experience. You both are such warm and kind people who have made the process genuinely enjoyable, and I've learnt so much from them along the way. I want to begin by thanking Richard Mackie and Debbie McKay: my corporate parents at a time when I was at my worst and needed support the most, two strangers who believed in me when I couldn't believe in myself, and who became people I never wanted to disappoint or let down. Rory McErlean: thank you. I wouldn't have half the career I do without you. You've taught me so much, and you've been one of the few people who have stuck by me at every point in my professional life. To my chosen family: thank you for reminding me that it's not the building blocks you start with that define you, but the ones you choose along the way and finally. This book represents something deeply real and powerful. Psychological relationships have shaped my life from childhood: once a source of oppression and silence, they are now something I can examine, understand and speak about. Contributing to this book, and reading the contributions of others, feels like finding my voice. I know this book will be a powerful tool in strengthening relational practice. To the readers: those working to build better relationships and those whose lives have been shaped by them: I hope this book helps you feel seen, heard and understood.

Foreword

Writing a book about relationships in forensic settings could be fraught with difficulties. Secure settings are not an easy place to develop relationships between those living and working in them. The transient nature of some settings means most interactions are superficial, hi and bye. However, those providing interventions in such places need to be able to interact on a deeper level. Ben Crewe and colleagues (2014) observed that some places in a prison, for example visits, and the chapel, lend themselves to deeper relationships. Furthermore, it may be easier for non-operational grades (i.e. those who are not tasked with maintaining order and control, for example prison officers) and third sector personnel to appear less authoritarian, providing individuals with a brief opportunity to remove their "masks" and express their vulnerability. However, we know people in operational roles are usually those who have the most regular contact with those living in or accessing the services, and so there needs to be consistency to prevent splitting.

Lawrence Jones (2007) reported how frequent changes of therapist and key worker can be common in some forensic services, and this can risk undermining the therapeutic alliance that is essential to many trauma-informed interventions. This also adds to the challenges that arise. Staff working in forensic settings will have had their own life experiences, which make them the people they are, sometimes a wounded healer, sometimes having a saviour complex, or just wanting to help others in any way they can. There can be complications in relationships between colleagues, which in a well-functioning setting will be resolved through discussion in reflective practice, supervision and so on. Initiatives such as restorative practice (as reported by Kathryn Rowsell and colleagues, 2024) encourage communication and restoration between individuals or groups where harm has been caused. This can help resolve conflict while providing the opportunity to discuss difficulties and learn skills essential for life. If left unresolved, such conflicts can fester and have a profound impact on the work with the individuals, repeating previous encounters, be they patients, prisoners or any justice-involved individuals. Lots of these individuals may have had fraught relationships in the past, so it can require negotiation and building of trust and ability and willingness to heal ruptures to get to that effective, professional, safe relationship. Once it happens, it will be very rewarding and enriching for both parties.

Most research into the efficacy of interventions highlights that it is the relationship, not the therapeutic model, that is important. Bill Marshall and colleagues (2005) described how being warm, empathic and directive was found to get improvements in key elements of criminogenic need that were not obtained by hostile practices. Jon Taylor wrote eloquently about the need to explore the nature and the significance of the therapeutic relationship in forensic settings. He discusses the transference-based or relationally based interventions. He reminds us that those engaging in this work may have had poor early relational experiences which could be replicated in the current settings. On this theme within this volume, Jo Shingler and Phil Willmot discuss the importance of having trauma-informed boundaries. Therefore, there is a need to address this as and when it arises. Learning from those we are there to work with is an integral part of the work and so Tassie Ghilani and Tee Khan provide invaluable insight into receiving the services of a forensic psychologist in the criminal justice system, highlighting how the relationship with the forensic psychologist can be truly transformational. Jude Kelman draws on her vast experience of working with women in prison to help us consider how gender impacts on the relationship.

This unique volume manages to weave stories of how and where relationships have flourished in various forensic settings into a rich tapestry. It considers issues such as culture, context and personal and professional boundaries. Chapter topics include working with groups who may be particularly difficult to engage with, such as children accused of serious offending and needing to undergo psychological assessments (explained beautifully by Louise Bowers); and those who are imprisoned for an indeterminate time, and the complications this may present (considered in depth by Sophie Ellis and Emma Stevenson). Using the voices of those working and living within or accessing the services, it illustrates how, by being creative and having a shared goal, so much can be achieved. It considers boundaries and how they can be maintained in order to provide a safe therapeutic environment and relational setting. The hope is that it will provide practitioners sound evidence-based examples of how to work effectively in these settings. After all, we are relational beings, and those working in or accessing the services will always benefit from safe relationships.

Hon Professor Dr Geraldine Akerman
Oxford Health NHS Trust, University of Birmingham and Cardiff
Metropolitan University, Forensic Psychology Network.

References

Crewe, B., Warr, J., Bennett, P., & Smith, A. (2014). The Emotional Geography of Prison Life. *Theoretical Criminology*, 18(1), 56–74.

Jones, L. F. (2007). Iatrogenic Interventions with Personality Disordered Offenders. *Psychology, Crime & Law, 13*(1), 69–79.

Marshall, W. L. (2005). Therapist Style in Sexual Offender Treatment: Influence on Indices of Change. *Sexual Abuse, 17*(2), 109–116. https://doi.org/10.1177/107906320501700202 (Original work published 2005).

Rowsell, K., Pegg, K., Wallis, P., & Barker, R. A. (2024). Systematic Review of Participant and Facilitator Experiences of Restorative Justice Interventions in the Forensic Secure Estate. *International Journal of Forensic Mental Health, 23*(3), 229–240. https://doi.org/10.1080/14999013.2023.2289113

Taylor, J. (2024). Psychological Interventions in Forensic Settings: The Role of the Therapeutic Relationship as a Mediator of Change. In M. P. Levine (Ed). *Trust and Psychology – Who, When, Why and How We Trust* (pp. 145–170). IntechOpen.

Introduction

Jo Shingler, Nicola Bowes and Tassie Ghilani

Relationships can be joyous, transformative, wonderful connections between us and other people, places and things. They are perhaps the most important part of our lives. At the same time, relationships can be painful, harmful and difficult to navigate. Some of us have been harmed in relationships, know the pain of broken or abusive relationships, or have experienced loss in relationships, and this can create difficulties as we navigate the consequences of those experiences. Adversity in childhood and attachment difficulties affect developmental trajectories, impacting biologically, psychologically and socially. This adversity makes it more difficult to connect with opportunities offered in terms of education, hobbies, healthy activities and interests. Attention is instead focused on surviving threats, which are difficult or impossible to escape from. Adversity in childhood is life limiting, affecting people across domains including health (where poorer outcomes are reported), progress in education, employment (with the consequent impact on financial stability and safety) and of course in terms of contact with the criminal justice system.

As forensic practitioners, whether we are psychologists or whether we come from another professional background, we are generally well aware of the trauma and relational adversity experienced by those under forensic restrictions or in receipt of forensic services. However, relationships involve us too: we contribute to and affect the nature and trajectory of our relationships, both in our personal and our professional lives. We might think that our professional relationships are immune to the impact of our own life experiences, but of course this is an illusion, a smokescreen that can prevent self-reflection and lure us towards pejorative assessments of the interpersonal styles of the people in front of us. Similarly, those of us who have not been exposed to relational challenges may find it difficult to comprehend how being exposed to those experiences impacts others. Yet our function is to connect *as* humans *with* other humans. Despite our professional façade, we are only human, and as practitioners, we have the opportunity to connect in human ways with other humans.

A positive and connected relationship between professional and service user is key in any form of therapeutic or goal-focused work. Research repeatedly finds that client perception of the therapeutic relationship is a significant

DOI: 10.4324/9781003542377-1

factor in treatment success and that it is more important than therapeutic modality or application of various therapeutic techniques (Lambert & Barley, 2001). That is, the therapeutic relationship is consistently crucial, regardless of the type, frequency or approach of psychological intervention, and regardless of the qualifications and professional background of the therapist. More specifically, professional relationships are central to a range of criminal justice outcomes, which we will elucidate shortly. Therefore, the need for a volume that specifically addresses the issue of professional relationships in a range of criminal justice settings, populations and encounters is long overdue.

When we measure the quality of therapeutic relationships, one reliable and valid measure is the "Working Alliance Inventory" (Horvath & Greenberg, 1989 (original); Hatcher & Gillaspy, 2006 (short version)). The Working Alliance Inventory (WAI) explores the alliance between a therapist and a client across three domains, "goals", "tasks" and "bond", from the perspectives of each person (therapist and client). While positive outcomes are related to all three domains, it is bond that appears to have the greatest impact on outcomes (Lo Coco et al., 2011). Bond items on the WAI relate to respecting one another, appreciating one another and feeling cared for. Bond emphasises a mutual belief between therapist and client of being liked. Most practitioners want to engage in authentic, compassionate practice, as defined by bond, but this is particularly challenging in forensic settings where there is a strong emphasis on security; on physical and environmental boundaries; where there are complex power dynamics; where deadlines and business needs have to be met; and where there are limited resources for forming or maintaining contact once an intervention or assessment has been completed. People in receipt of forensic services know when relationships are transactional, and pressures like meeting deadlines can cause psychologists to engage in activity where they "do things to" rather than "do things with" the people they work with. We know both psychologists and people held in prison experience and dislike the feeling of "ticking boxes" or being on a "production line" when completing important psychological interventions (Shingler et al., 2018). Completing emotionally and psychologically challenging tasks in this context can feel overwhelming and dehumanising; it can feel impossible to achieve good, genuine relationships with people while also managing the pressures of time and outputs. It is also difficult to talk about liking or caring for people in some forensic settings because this may clash with the organisational culture, where those things may be perceived as a threat to safety or security. In order to be effective practitioners, it is important that we preserve the autonomy of psychologists to engage in liking and caring for people while maintaining safe, professional practice. We have moved on in many places from structural security to relational security; and while this may seem a progressive move, we have always relied on relational security for organisations to run effectively. So despite concerns about security and boundaries, prisons and other closed institutions have always had person-to-person relationships at the front and centre. Moreover, if we look at foundational work around relationships, we can ask the same question posed by Donald Winnicott (1965); what does a "good enough" relationship look like in forensic psychology practice? And how can we make sure we are doing that?

There are specific issues for forensic psychologists to consider when addressing the issue of meaningful and effective professional relationships with the people they work with. Forensic psychologists have a poor history of trust and engagement with people in prison. There is consistent evidence that forensic psychologists are seen as untrustworthy yet powerful; emotionally, experientially and physically distant from people in prison; and a tool of the "system" aimed at controlling people in prison and prolonging incarceration (Crewe, 2011; Maruna, 2011; Shingler et al., 2020a; Warr, 2008). There are issues associated with the history, development and changes in the role of prison-based forensic psychology that have contributed to this state of affairs (Gannon & Ward, 2014), but the bottom line is that we face a crisis of legitimacy in the profession (Shingler, 2019). Despite this, there is good evidence that the working relationship can help to overcome some of these challenges. Effective interpersonal relationships can transform the experience of psychological risk assessment in prison, something that has been identified as an extremely stressful element of an indeterminate sentence (Attrill & Leill, 2007; Shingler et al., 2020b). It can also ease the transition between prison and community and between community and prison on recall (Shingler & Purvis, 2024; Shingler et al., 2024), both of which are turbulent and emotionally demanding experiences.

Furthermore, many other professionals who work in forensic settings face similar challenges in forming positive relationships, but where this is possible, it is associated with improved outcomes, both across different professions and contexts. Lowenkamp et al. (2014) reported that among people on probation, those working with motivational and positive probation officers had better recidivism outcomes. Warm, empathic and directive group therapists in prisons were found to get improvements in key elements of criminogenic need that were not obtained by hostile therapists (Marshall et al., 2005). People convicted of sexual offences were found to be more likely to disclose risky behaviours and feelings to community practitioners when those practitioners had the skills to build positive and effective relationships (Westwood et al., 2011). Key elements of an effective working relationship, such as openness, transparency, collaboration and trustworthiness (Shingler et al., 2018) are related to acceptance of and compliance with criminal justice sanctions (Tyler & Huo, 2002).

The focus of this book, then, is on the relationships between us, as forensic practitioners, and the people we work with in forensic settings. While there is an emphasis on the roles of forensic psychologists throughout, much of the material is equally applicable to people in other roles and from other professional backgrounds. This book explores our roles, our responsibilities, the expectations people have of us, and how these things affect the people who depend on us for assessment and intervention. Our work with people is often constrained by organisational demands or expectations, meaning that sometimes, our relationships with others are time and task limited. Over the history of the profession of forensic psychology in particular, this "transactional" form of relating has created difficulties between us and the people we work with. These types of interactions can be re-traumatising, in that professionals with power and authority appear, make demands, give little in the way of choice or autonomy, and then leave. The demands we put on people during these transactions are significant: we may be asking/expecting/requiring people to talk about very painful experiences. We expect them to be honest with us and to trust us when they have only just met us; we expect them to have faith in a system that they have not experienced as worthy of trust. When people struggle to meet these demands, we reflect this as a weakness or failure of them as individuals: perhaps we describe them as "superficially engaged", "demanding", "manipulative" or having "complex needs". It is important to acknowledge that the impact of our interactions rarely ends with us. While we may only hold a brief moment of contact, the consequences of what is said, or unsaid, can ripple across a person's wider network of support. Other professionals may be left managing the fallout from a difficult session, or worse, the person themselves may carry the weight of unresolved distress. This raises a critical challenge for us as forensic psychologists: to better understand our role within a broader system of care, and to actively contribute to more joined-up, relational approaches. Multi-agency working is not just a procedural expectation: it is a moral and relational imperative. By using our collective influence more intentionally, we can shape how people experience services, reduce harm and build greater trust in the systems meant to support them.

This book, then, is a call to action. It challenges forensic psychologists, and those working in similar roles, to reflect on the quality of their relationships with the people they serve and to ask whether our practices truly support healing, hope and rehabilitation. It's a call to change and to explore how our relationships with the people we work with can be an opportunity for safe, positive connections. Can we leave the people we work with feeling more (not less) hopeful about future professional (and human) relationships? Between us and the chapter authors, we have experienced change in the justice system and a shift towards a more rehabilitative approach. This remains a work in progress, but some of the change has been the result of psychologists implementing more procedurally just ways of working; considering the impact of stigmatisation; listening and responding to our critical friends (often criminologists) and the people who are in receipt of our services in order to try to improve environments, culture and opportunities for reconnection and recovery. We have recognised the impact of stigmatisation and the importance of focusing on strengths, holding hope for people, and helping them to hold hope for themselves.

To summarise, there is sound evidence that the relationship between people in receipt of forensic services and forensic psychologists (as well as a range of other forensic practitioners) is both crucial to positive outcomes and fraught with difficulty. If we are to address the legitimacy crisis and move beyond the view of prison-based psychologists as "the quiet ones with the power" (Shingler et al., 2020a), then the place to start is with the professional relationship. In this book, we address these issues head-on and provide guidance, information and direction for psychologists and other practitioners working in forensic settings. We explore key issues in working relationships across a broad range of client groups and tasks. We reflect on specific points of tension in forensic therapeutic relationships and challenge each other to find respectful and connected solutions, while maintaining safety and appropriate professional and personal boundaries.

In writing and editing this book, we thought carefully about the use of language. Language matters, and our use of it communicates our views and attitudes about the people we work with. We have wrestled with how to refer to people who are held in prison and who are engaged with forensic services. We wanted to use terms that reflected the individuality, value and innate humanness of everyone we work with. While individual chapter authors have made their own decisions about this, in line with their work, their roles and the focus of their chapters, we have encouraged inclusivity, respect and humanity in our use of terms. We want to use language that reduces rather than amplifies power differences. We want to discuss individuals in a way that reflects their context and their current relationship with us, rather than in a way that reduces and defines people into a specific role (e.g. "offender"). We realise that using inclusive and non-judgemental language does not solve the problems of stigmatisation, marginalisation and discrimination, but it is a step towards humanising people.

We have also been keen to co-create this book where possible: after all, a relationship needs to be looked at from both sides in order to be fully understood. In this way, we hope we have enacted power sharing, rather than just talked about it and provided a space for more perspectives and voices to be heard.

We hope that this book helps us as practitioners to talk about how and why we do things, to have conversations we might not have otherwise had and to explore how we might grow as practitioners and as a profession and improve the experiences of the people we work with. We always intended for this book to be challenging, and we have faith that our colleagues will step up to the challenge to be better and do more to combat inequality and share power.

We are delighted that so many clever and compassionate people have agreed to contribute to this book. We have learned a great deal through our discussions with all the chapter authors. We are also delighted to hear so many lived experience voices throughout the chapters. This variety of experiences and perspectives is humbling, enriching and enabling, and we all need to do more to hear the voices of those who have experienced our professional input.

For ease of reading, we have divided this volume into three parts. The first part focuses on what we see as foundational issues in our relationships in forensic settings. Part 1 is opened by the voices of Tassie Ghilani and Tee Khan, people with lived experience of forensic psychologists. Their powerful account of the impact on people when we do not take care to empathise and humanise must form the starting point in all of our journeys towards being better. Chinonso Lazz-Onyenobi and Stephen Robinson then address equality, diversity and inclusion. By focusing on disability, race and sexuality, they bring their personal insights into navigating prejudice and discrimination and how we can all learn from this. In Chapter 3, Phil Willmot and Jo Shingler explore relational boundaries in forensic relationships: if we don't get our boundaries right, then other forms of relating can feel unsafe, both for us and the people we work with. Finally, Michael McCracken reflects on his experience of working in Northern Ireland to explore the issue of "othering", a process that occurs in all forensic settings, but that was arguably intensified in Northern Ireland during The Troubles. This illuminating chapter provides guidance for us all, regardless of our workplace, to overcome the harmful effects of othering.

Part 2 leads us to examine the different needs of different groups of people within forensic settings. We absolutely accept that the chapters included here are not an exhaustive list of the range of different needs found across prisons, probation and secure hospitals. However, it is a start, and as we have read these chapters, we have found a great deal of broad applicability within them. Louise Bowers discusses working with children in forensic psychological assessment; her clinical guidance has relevance beyond this population, and we urge anyone working in an assessment context or with children in other contexts to read and digest this. Next, Jude Kelman reports on new and significant research data to explore relational issues in working with women in prison. She reflects on being truly trauma informed and how this can transform relationships. Again, the relevance and reach of her ideas are broad. Of specific interest is Jude's reflection that it was only in 2016 that women's prisons were managed separately from those for men: before this, women were expected to fit in to the management approaches designed with male prisoners in mind. Next, Amy Canning, Hannah Toogood and Jake support us to understand and work more effectively with autistic people: their chapter had an immediate impact on us and our practice, enabling us to recognise the extent to which the world is designed by and for "neurotypicals", and how this creates barriers for those who experience the world differently. In Chapter 8, Sophie Ellis and Emma Stevenson address the need for "sentence literacy" in our work, drawing our attention to the impact of indeterminate sentences on those serving them and on the need for us to actively and compassionately take account of this impact. They suggest that sentence type, especially Imprisonment for Public Protection (IPP) and other indeterminate sentences, should be viewed as a responsivity need. Finally, Christopher Dean and Monica Lloyd share their extensive and foundational experiences of working alongside those convicted of terror-related offences, at a time when there was virtually no knowledge about this group or how best to engage with them. Their bottom-up approach is the essence of a humanising and individualising approach, which has relevance for us all.

In Part 3, we turn to some of the specific tasks we engage in as forensic practitioners. We start, appropriately, at the beginning: with a focus on the next generation of forensic psychologists. Nicola Bowes, Louise Coates, Karen De Claire and Dakshina Raghavendra address how we can support people in training to build the relationships they need to work effectively: how they can learn, thrive and ultimately challenge the status quo. Next, Jo Shingler and Jason Warr share a reflective conversation about forensic psychological risk assessment. They discuss how a task that brings power issues into the sharpest focus can be done with humanity and compassion, if we are brave and insightful enough to engage in proper reflexive thinking, and challenge organisational bias and dogma. Finally, Kerensa Hocken draws on her immense knowledge of Compassion Focused Therapy to enable us all to bring a more compassionate approach to forensic relational practice.

Our volume is opened by a voice of compassion and humanity well known to everyone in the field of forensic psychology. We are so grateful to Geraldine Akerman for sharing her wisdom and experience with us and reminding us of the importance of creating safe spaces for relating. To close, we turn back to the value of listening to those who have experienced psychological services. We so appreciate Andi Brierley's time and insight and feel that it is absolutely appropriate that he should have the last word. Andi's experiences of forensic psychologists and his advice are a calling for us all to be better, more human and more humble in our work.

References

Attrill, G., & Liell, G. (2007). Offenders' view on risk assessment. In Padfield, N. (Ed.). *Who to release? Parole, fairness and criminal justice* (pp. 191–201). Cullumpton, Devon: Willan Publishing.

Crewe, B. (2011). Depth, weight, tightness: Revisiting the pains of imprisonment. *Punishment and Society, 13*(5), 509–529.

Gannon, T. A., & Ward, T. (2014). Where has all the psychology gone? A critical review of evidence-based psychological practice in correctional settings. *Aggression and Violent Behaviour, 19*, 435–446.

Hatcher, R. L., & Gillaspy, J. A. (2006). Development and validation of a revised short version of the working alliance inventory. *Psychotherapy Research, 16*(1), 12–25. https://doi.org/10.1080/10503300500352500

Horvath, A. O., & Greenberg, L. S. (1989). Development and validation of the working alliance inventory. *Journal of Counseling Psychology, 36*(2), 223–233. https://doi.org/10.1037/0022-0167.36.2.223

Lambert, M. J., & Barley, D. E. (2001). Research summary on the therapeutic relationship and psychotherapy outcome. Psychotherapy: Theory, Research, Practice, Training, 38(4), 357–361. https://doi.org/10.1037/0033-3204.38.4.357

Lo Coco, G., Gullo, S., Prestano, C., & Gelso, C. J. (2011). Relation of the real relationship and the working alliance to the outcome of brief psychotherapy. *Psychotherapy, 48*(4), 359–367. https://doi.org/10.1037/a0022426

Lowenkamp, C. T., Holsinger, A., Robinson, C. R., & Alexander, M. (2014). Diminishing or durable treatment effects of STARR? A research note on 24-month re-arrest rates. *Journal of Crime and Justice, 37*(2), 275–283.

Marshall, W. L. (2005). Therapist style in sexual offender treatment: Influence on indices of change. *Sexual Abuse: A Journal of Research and Treatment, 17*(2), 109–116.

Maruna, S. (2011). Why do they hate us? Making peace between prisoners and psychology. *International Journal of Offender Therapy and Comparative Criminology, 55*(56), 671–675.

Shingler, J. (2019). *Understanding the process of psychological risk assessment: Exploring the experiences of psychologists, indeterminate sentenced prisoners and Parole Board members.* Unpublished PhD Thesis, University of Portsmouth. https://researchportal.port.ac.uk/en/studentTheses/understanding-the-process-of-psychological-risk-assessment

Shingler, J., Sonnenberg, S. J., & Needs, A. (2018). Risk assessment interviews: Exploring the perspectives of psychologists and indeterminate sentenced prisoners in the United Kingdom. *International Journal of Offender Therapy and Comparative Criminology, 62*(10), 3201–3224.

Shingler, J., Sonnenberg, S. J., & Needs, A. (2020a). Psychologists as 'the quiet ones with the power': Understanding indeterminate sentenced prisoners' experiences of psychological risk assessment in the United Kingdom. *Psychology, Crime & Law, 26*(6), 571–592.

Shingler, J., Sonnenberg, S. J., & Needs, A. (2020b). 'Their life in your hands': The experiences of prison-based psychologists conducting risk assessments with indeterminate sentenced prisoners in the United Kingdom. *Psychology, Crime & Law, 26*(4), 311–326.

Shingler, J., & Nick, W. (2024). Recall, recovery and re-release. In Shingler, J., & Stickney, J. (Eds.). *The journey from prison to community: Developing identity, meaning and belonging with men in the UK* (pp 44–59). Abingdon, Oxon: Routledge, Taylor & Francis.

Shingler, J., & Purvis, C. (2024). "It's not just words, it's something you can feel": How therapeutic relationships can support prison-community transitions. In Shingler, J., & Stickney, J. (Eds.). *The Journey from prison to community: Developing identity, meaning and belonging with men in the UK* (pp. 155–173). Abingdon, Oxon: Routledge, Taylor & Francis

Tyler, T. R., & Huo, Y. J. (2002). *Trust in the law: Encouraging public cooperation with the police and courts.* New York: Russell Sage Foundation.

Warr, J. (2008). Personal reflections on prison staff. In Bennett, J., Crewe, B., & Wahidin, A., (Eds.). *Understanding prison staff* (pp. 17–29). Cullumpton, Devon: Willan Publishing.

Westwood, S., Wood, J., & Kemshall, H. (2011). Good practice in eliciting disclosures from sex offenders. *Journal of Sexual Aggression, 17*(2), 215–227.

Winnicott, D. W. (1965). *The maturational processes and the facilitating environment: Studies in the theory of emotional development.* International Universities Press.

Part 1
Foundations

1 The human side of forensic psychology

Tassie Ghilani and Tee Khan

At the heart of this book is one constant: the person. Throughout every chapter, no matter how complex the theory or how structured the system, we return to the human experience, to how forensic psychology is felt, interpreted and lived by those receiving it. This book is not just about what psychology *does*, but about what it *means* to the people on the receiving end. It is about impact, often unseen, sometimes unintended, but always significant.

This opening chapter is written from the perspective of people with lived experience of receiving psychological services and interventions within the criminal justice system. Our work is rooted in bringing those voices, often unheard or misunderstood, into the heart of organisations. We don't simply represent these experiences; we amplify them, ensuring that the insights of those who have lived in criminal justice systems are embedded in decision-making, policy development and practice.

We occupy a unique space, navigating the complex dynamics between people in prison and the professionals who work there. Our role is to advocate for meaningful change, not by pointing fingers, but by offering a mirror. What we share in this chapter reflects the perceptions and lived experiences of those who have received psychological interventions within the criminal justice system. It is not a claim that all practitioners behave in these ways, nor an accusation of intent or incompetence. We are not suggesting it is deliberate or that psychologists do not care. Rather, this is an honest account of how these services can *feel* to those on the receiving end, feelings that are shaped by context, history and power dynamics. By sharing these experiences, we hope to offer a perspective that supports reflection, not criticism, and helps practitioners better understand the impact their role can have, even when intentions are good.

Think of the way a child fears the boogie man: an all-encompassing, terrifying figure; when in reality, it may just be a shadow or a creaky door. The fear is real, even if the cause is misunderstood. Similarly, the emotional reactions described here are not about blame, but about the impact. By offering these reflections, we hope to give practitioners a new lens, one

DOI: 10.4324/9781003542377-3

that will help shape understanding and inform future practice, regardless of intention.

> It's hard because if you act too happy then you're seen to not be taking it seriously; you act too sad, you are depressed and can't manage the situation. Everything is game of trying to find and show the correct emotion. (Mark)

When people think of forensic psychology, they often imagine cold assessments, clinical diagnoses and risk evaluations. However, what is frequently overlooked is the deeply human experience behind these interactions: the emotions, thoughts and internal struggles of individuals who find themselves face to face with forensic psychologists. For those navigating this world, it is not simply about understanding behaviour or motivations. It is about confronting the vulnerability, mistrust and isolation that come with being examined, judged and often reduced to a case file.

For Corrie, her first experience sitting across from a forensic psychologist left a lasting impression. A child at the time, she had no understanding that this would be the first of many appointments, with different people, in various locations, at different stages of life. The room felt colder than the rest of the building, not because of its temperature, but because of the atmosphere. The tension in the air was thick, as though invisible strings were pulling at her every move. This was not just another small room; it was the place where judgements would be made about who she was: whether she was "dangerous", "broken" or perhaps even beyond help.

From the moment the psychologist looked at her, she felt as though she were under a microscope. Every twitch, every word, every pause seemed to be dissected. The psychologist was neither harsh nor unfriendly, but there was a clinical detachment that made it clear this was not a conversation between two people: it was an examination. She was expected to lay bare her life, fears and traumas, all while the psychologist took notes without ever truly meeting her eyes.

The questions asked by the psychologist cut deep, yet there was no warmth behind them. It felt as though the psychologist was waiting for a response that would confirm pre-existing assumptions. It was like playing a game with unclear rules, one that seemed impossible to win. Despite honest efforts to explain herself, it felt as though her words were not truly heard. The psychologist was listening, perhaps, but not understanding.

The most difficult part came at the end, walking out of the room with a profound sense of entrapment. Corrie couldn't shake the thought: *You think you know me, but you don't. Not really.*

The repetitive churn of psychological intervention and the constant demonstration of vulnerability...

Sitting with a forensic psychologist can feel like playing a game of chess without knowing the rules. Psychologists ask for trust and openness, but trust is a dangerous commodity in prison, something hard-earned and easily weaponised. Behind bars, vulnerability can lead to hurt or betrayal, a lesson often learned early in life. Yet, psychologists often expect it to be offered freely, as though the context doesn't matter.

The power dynamic in these interactions is undeniable. Psychologists sit across the table holding all the cards, while the individual navigates the conversation knowing that every word could influence their future. The tension this creates is constant. One misstep can feel catastrophic, threatening any progress made. For some, the pressure leads to withdrawal or rebellion: responses born not from defiance, but from fear and self-preservation. Sadly, these behaviours often reinforce the very stereotypes that professionals already hold, deepening the cycle of mistrust.

These encounters can leave individuals feeling more trapped than ever: not just physically, but emotionally. To break this cycle, the system must recognise the weight of these interactions and the damage that can be done when they are handled without care. Mistrust doesn't come from nowhere; it grows in the spaces where people feel unseen, unheard and misunderstood. If left unaddressed, the cost is not just missed opportunities; it is the quiet, growing isolation of those who most need support.

Psychologists often talk about risk, treating the person before them as though they are a ticking time bomb that must be defused. Every word spoken, every action, is scrutinised: not for its meaning to the individual, but for its implications in the psychologist's assessments. These sessions rarely feel like opportunities for understanding; instead, they are exercises in classification and risk management.

One of the most challenging aspects is recognising the significant influence these psychologists hold over an individual's future. They are the ones who participate in meetings, compile reports and provide input that shapes decisions about parole, freedom and life beyond the prison walls. It is difficult not to feel judged unfairly when so much of one's fate rests in the hands of someone who may not fully understand the person behind the file.

> No matter how hard I work to change, it sometimes feels like they're just waiting for me to slip up. (Charlie)

The aftermath of sessions with a forensic psychologist often leaves individuals grappling with unresolved emotions. Psychologists delve into past traumas, pain and experiences which people would rather leave buried, yet when the session ends, the psychologists disappear. There is no follow-up, and there is no concern for how the individual manages the emotional turmoil stirred up during the session. People are left to process the aftermath alone.

Distrust in forensic psychology develops gradually, like a slow burn that eventually ignites into a roaring fire. For many, it begins long before encountering a psychologist in prison. It originates in childhood, where individuals are often labelled "problematic" or "difficult" by teachers, social workers and other authority figures. These labels persist, and by the time individuals enter the criminal justice system, they are entrenched not only in the minds of professionals but also in the minds of the individuals themselves, forming part of how they see and define their own identity.

A major factor contributing to this distrust is the repetitive cycle of recounting traumatic stories to various professionals. Each new psychologist, social worker or probation officer requests the same narrative, forcing individuals to relive their worst experiences repeatedly. Over time, these stories lose their personal connection and become detached, clinical accounts. This process makes individuals feel as though their lives are reduced to case files being passed between professionals. The lack of continuity in care, with no cohesive or sustained support, erodes trust. It becomes difficult to believe anyone truly cares when no one stays long enough to see things through (or when questions are asked in order to inform an assessment, not in order to offer any actual tangible help). This constant turnover breeds scepticism: why trust someone who might be gone in a few months? Why open up when the next professional could have an entirely different perspective?

The inherent power dynamic also plays a significant role. Psychologists wield considerable influence within the prison system, assessing risk, making parole recommendations and shaping decisions that can determine someone's future. This power creates vulnerability, as individuals are acutely aware that their words might be misinterpreted or taken out of context, potentially constructing an inaccurate picture that could follow them for years. Previous experiences of being let down by the system only deepen this mistrust. Many have participated in interventions that promised change but failed to deliver, such as rehabilitation programmes or parole hearings that ended in disappointment. These cumulative let-downs make it harder to believe that the system (or the psychologists within it) truly have their best interests at heart.

Hindsight often provides clarity. Looking back, individuals can reflect on their experiences and recognise that certain relationships were less positive than they initially seemed, or identify areas in themselves that required development. However, in the moment, especially when receiving a diagnosis, the experience is overwhelming and frightening. It can trigger denial and resistance, as the label feels defining and restrictive, boxing individuals in and challenging their sense of self.

In such moments of fear and denial, the approach taken by a psychologist is crucial. Instead of reinforcing a diagnosis as a defining characteristic, a more effective strategy involves gently guiding individuals towards understanding it themselves. Rather than directly highlighting negative patterns of behaviour, which can feel accusatory and increase resistance, psychologists can foster self-awareness by asking thoughtful questions, encouraging reflection and creating a safe space for individuals to explore their behaviours and their impact without feeling judged. Reaching these realisations independently is far more empowering and lasting than being told what is wrong. It becomes an act of self-discovery rather than something imposed from the outside.

This approach respects an individual's autonomy and dignity, recognising them as the expert on their own life. It builds trust and nurtures a collaborative relationship where the goal is not merely diagnosis and treatment but empowering individuals to understand and change negative patterns. Ultimately, this process can lead to profound, meaningful transformation that feels self-driven, rather than externally enforced.

The way it feels to us...

For many individuals who have been through the system, working with psychologists often feels like an endless cycle of judgement. It is not just about actions or past mistakes; it often feels like psychologists are evaluating who a person is at their core. The focus on fitting individuals into models, diagnoses and risk assessments frequently comes across as dismissive of the real, personal stories behind those labels.

There is a sense of helplessness in these interactions. People sit across from psychologists, answering questions while fully aware of the power dynamics at play. Psychologists hold the authority to determine whether someone is progressing or has "changed". Yet, this power often feels disconnected from an understanding of what it is truly like to live within the system. Sometimes, decisions are based not on what has been done but on the potential for what *might* happen again. This disconnect can be deeply frustrating. Even when individuals work hard to turn their lives around, they remain tethered to their past through risk factors or profiles in their files. For many, it feels as though freedom remains just out of reach, as they are forever defined by their worst moments.

Walking into a room with a forensic psychologist often brings an unspoken tension. The formal setting, the clinical tone and the dynamic of being judged before even speaking can feel stifling. Psychologists may not intend to appear judgemental, but for someone accustomed to being judged by society, the legal system and even those meant to help, defensiveness becomes second nature.

One of the most challenging aspects is the feeling of being psychoanalysed rather than genuinely listened to. Many feel as though psychologists approach sessions with a mental checklist, aiming to categorise rather than connect. The invasive nature of this scrutiny can make individuals feel less like a person and more like a specimen under a microscope. The lack of genuine connection often leads to guarded responses, with individuals saying what they think psychologists want to hear to end the session. Being honest feels too risky when the outcome seems predetermined. This isn't about manipulation – it's a functional, often unconscious survival strategy in an environment where vulnerability can be punished and power dynamics are ever-present.

Trust is another major barrier. Psychologists often assume it will be freely given simply because of their position or title, but trust is not automatic, it must be earned over time. Unfortunately, many enter sessions expecting immediate vulnerability, which can create immense pressure and discomfort. Interactions often feel clinical and obligatory rather than genuine attempts to connect. The sterile environment, the notepad and the structured conversations contribute to the feeling of being just another file in the psychologist's workload.

Adding to the frustration is the sense that psychologists often approach sessions with preconceived ideas. Having read an individual's file, they seem to arrive with conclusions already formed, asking questions that feel more like confirmation of their assumptions than attempts to understand. This reinforces the perception that individuals are judged not for who they have become but for who they were at their lowest. Even significant personal progress can feel invisible under the weight of these assumptions.

The lack of accessibility to psychologists further exacerbates the problem. Scheduled appointments, often brief and formal, are the only points of contact. Building trust is nearly impossible when interactions are infrequent and limited to tick-box exercises. This creates the impression that psychologists are fulfilling a procedural obligation rather than genuinely seeking to help.

Cold and detached behaviour from psychologists often leaves individuals feeling alienated. Sitting across from someone who appears more interested in analysing than understanding can make it incredibly difficult to form meaningful connections. This impersonal approach strips away any sense of humanity from the interaction, reducing individuals to problems to be solved rather than people with complex emotions and needs.

For individuals who have grown up in environments where trust is a luxury, encountering a psychologist who is overly kind or "soft" can be unsettling. Such behaviour can seem disingenuous, raising suspicions about hidden motives. People conditioned to expect confrontation or manipulation may interpret warmth as a potential trap, questioning whether kindness is a tactic to elicit vulnerability for ulterior purposes. This suspicion is often rooted in survival mechanisms developed in environments where showing vulnerability was dangerous.

Gentleness can also feel alien when it contrasts sharply with the harsh realities individuals are accustomed to. Being treated with compassion may evoke feelings of weakness or exposure, making it challenging to navigate an unfamiliar dynamic. It is not that these individuals reject kindness outright but rather that they struggle to process it when it is offered.

What works best in these situations is an approach that combines empathy with straightforwardness. Individuals need psychologists who are honest, consistent and clear in their intentions, demonstrating care without appearing manipulative. A balanced approach, compassionate yet grounded in reality, can help bridge the gap between mistrust and genuine connection. Such an approach reassures individuals that psychologists care without avoiding difficult truths.

Ultimately, it is this balance of kindness, clarity and consistency that creates a foundation for trust. For those who have spent their lives in environments where trust was dangerous and kindness was rare, such an approach can pave the way for meaningful and transformative relationships.

The power of language: words that define or destroy

Language matters. It shapes how people see themselves and how they are seen by others. For those who have been through the system, reading what has been written about them, in psychological reports, case files or care records, can have a lifelong impact. Words don't just describe; they define. And when those words are cold, clinical or cruel, they can reinforce the very shame, hopelessness and isolation people are already battling.

Michelle, now 27, described the moment she read her own care file. In black and white, it stated that at just 12 years old, she was "prostituting herself to grown men" and that she was "troubled and beyond help". Those words didn't just reduce her to her trauma: they erased all nuance, all context and all humanity. She wasn't a child being exploited; she was labelled as someone complicit in her own abuse. The impact of reading that language, years later, was devastating. It made her feel blamed, dehumanised and stripped of the right to a future not defined by her past.

Psychological language, when used carelessly, can become another form of violence, silent but searing. Descriptions like "manipulative", "resistant" or "high risk" can stick to a person's identity like glue, even when they've changed. These labels often fail to capture the reasons behind behaviour: the survival mechanisms born from trauma, the fear behind the withdrawal or the desperation behind the aggression. What professionals write may follow someone for years, impacting everything from parole decisions to the way officers treat them. People aren't just reading these words; they're internalising them.

If psychologists want to build trust, they must be accountable for the words they use. Language should not pathologise pain or punish vulnerability. It should reflect complexity, acknowledge progress and never lose sight of the person behind the behaviour. A report isn't just a document; to the person it describes, it can feel like a verdict. That's the power of language. And used with care, it can be the first step towards healing rather than harm.

Trust is earned not given, why is it so hard to build it...

Some psychologists take the time to look beyond the case file, beyond the risk assessments, and genuinely listen to the person in front of them. They treat individuals as human beings, not just as inmates. These rare interactions feel different. Conversations with these psychologists are not about ticking boxes or fitting someone into a psychological profile. Instead, they are about understanding who the individual is and where they come from. These moments of connection bring hope: hope that change is possible and that there are people within the system who genuinely want to help. While rare, such experiences suggest that forensic psychology can be about more than control and judgement; it can also be about healing.

Creating an environment that fosters trust and connection is not about following a checklist or adhering strictly to professional guidelines. It is about treating people as individuals first and clients second. One of the most powerful things a psychologist can do is approach each person with a genuine desire to understand who they are beyond the labels and reports. This means setting aside preconceived notions and allowing individuals to show who they are now, rather than being defined by their worst mistakes.

Consistency is crucial in building trust, and it takes time. However, this can be challenging in a system where psychologists frequently change. When psychologists stay involved beyond initial assessments and are present throughout the process, it creates a sense of reliability. Knowing that the person sitting across from them will not disappear in a few months makes it easier for individuals to open up and engage. Progress will not always be immediate or linear. There will be setbacks, outbursts and moments that seem like failures. In these times, it is essential for psychologists to persevere and not give up at the first hurdle. Change is messy, and individuals need to feel that their psychologist will not abandon them when things become difficult.

Acknowledging the negative experiences individuals have had with the system is also essential. Many have been let down by promises made but not kept. When psychologists recognise this history and validate it, it can help rebuild eroded trust. Efforts such as holding focus groups, gathering feedback and adapting practices based on what individuals share show that their voices matter and that the system is willing to change for the better. The environment where sessions take place also plays a significant role in fostering trust. Sterile, confined spaces can feel intimidating, whereas more relaxed settings (even something as simple as taking a walk during a session) can encourage openness and honest communication.

Sensitivity to individual dynamics is equally important. For instance, male psychologists may unintentionally trigger trauma responses in women with specific histories. Being aware of such factors and assigning professionals accordingly can make individuals feel safer and more comfortable. Addressing inappropriate behaviour assertively and immediately also reinforces the idea that the space is safe and respectful. Offering practical, realistic advice tailored to each person's circumstances further demonstrates genuine consideration for their well-being.

Ultimately, individuals need to feel heard, understood and respected. They need to be seen as more than the sum of their mistakes, recognised as people capable of change. When psychologists approach their work with empathy, listen without judgement and invest in the people they work with, it can make an immeasurable difference.

The loss of a trusted psychologist, however, can be devastating. For many individuals, trust is not something that comes easily. A lifetime of broken promises and abandonment by those who were supposed to care has instilled deep scepticism. Many struggle with attachment disorders, carrying the weight of betrayal that began long before entering the criminal justice system. For these individuals, trusting a psychologist with their deepest fears and regrets is an extraordinary risk. When that trust is reciprocated, it can provide a rare sense of safety in an otherwise hostile world.

When that connection is abruptly taken away, it feels like a betrayal of the fragile trust that took so long to build. Starting over with someone new is not just difficult, it is emotionally agonising. It reinforces every reason why individuals were hesitant to trust in the first place and reminds them that relationships, no matter how promising, can be temporary. This cycle of opening up only to be abandoned deepens the scars of mistrust and makes it harder to believe in the sincerity of others.

For someone with a history of attachment disorders, losing a trusted psychologist is not merely a setback; it confirms a long-held belief that trust is dangerous and that no one stays. The result is often a retreat into isolation, with walls rebuilt thicker and higher than before. This makes it nearly impossible for the next professional to break through, perpetuating a cycle of mistrust and reinforcing the belief that keeping others at a distance is safer than risking emotional harm again.

The unintentional consequences of every interaction...

When someone has been through the system, they quickly learn to keep their guard up. Trust becomes fragile, and after being broken enough times, it can feel nearly impossible to rebuild. Sitting across from a forensic psychologist, there may be a faint hope, perhaps this time will be different. But when the encounter goes wrong, it is more than just a bad experience. It can feel like a profound betrayal, reinforcing the belief that trusting others is too great a risk.

A negative encounter with a psychologist is not merely a missed opportunity; it leaves lasting scars. When psychologists dismiss feelings, judge individuals based on their worst moments or speak at them rather than with them, it solidifies the perception that people in power are not there to help but to control and label. This experience can make individuals feel as though they have been boxed into an identity they cannot escape.

The effects of these interactions can be devastating. Instead of fostering openness, they lead to withdrawal. Individuals learn to say what they think the psychologist wants to hear, engaging at a superficial level to avoid deeper vulnerability. Why risk being hurt again if previous attempts to trust have only led to pain? By keeping their guard up, they also cut themselves off from the possibility of real change, perpetuating a cycle of isolation.

This sense of betrayal extends far beyond the psychologist in question. It influences how individuals view the entire system. If one professional has let them down, what assurance is there that others will not do the same? Mistrust spreads, making individuals more guarded, more suspicious and less willing to give anyone a genuine chance. This not only stalls their progress but also hinders their potential for rehabilitation and diminishes any hope for a better future.

Negative experiences with psychologists also foster resentment. Psychologists are no longer seen as allies but as obstacles, representatives of a system designed to oppress rather than support. This can lead individuals to act out, not from a desire to disrupt but as a way of reclaiming some sense of control. Unfortunately, such actions often reinforce the negative labels imposed on them, creating a vicious cycle of misunderstanding and misrepresentation.

The consequences of these encounters are far-reaching. They are not confined to a single moment but ripple through every aspect of an individual's life, shaping how they view themselves, how they interact with others, and whether they can ever truly believe in the possibility of change. The most damaging consequence is often the loss of hope: a deep sense of being let down by a system that was meant to help.

When distrust takes hold, it becomes a cycle that is hard to break. Individuals may comply with psychologists' expectations, saying what is required to avoid conflict, but this compliance is not progress. It is a defence mechanism. Genuine feelings and issues remain buried, and psychologists never see the full picture because trust has been eroded. The result is that assessments and reports are based on half-truths, perpetuating a distorted understanding of the individual.

This cycle of silence and compliance extends beyond psychologists, affecting relationships with parole boards, correctional officers and even peers. Individuals present a version of themselves they believe others want to see, wearing a mask to avoid further judgement. This self-protective behaviour stifles growth, hinders rehabilitation and leaves individuals in a state of limbo, unable to move forward or heal fully.

Negative encounters with forensic psychology services create a ripple effect that can last long after the session ends. Judgemental or detached interactions often lead to defensive behaviour, making authentic engagement nearly impossible. The vulnerability required to open up is met with coldness or misjudgement, discouraging any future attempts to share. Such interactions can also trigger stress and anxiety, reinforcing feelings of being reduced to past mistakes.

How to make the change in practice…

What if the system could be different? What if individuals were seen not just as risks to be managed but as people to be understood? Imagine if forensic psychologists took the time to build genuine trust and connect on a human level. The potential impact of such an approach could be transformative.

Trust does not happen overnight; it is built slowly through consistent, respectful interactions. When a psychologist demonstrates genuine interest in the person sitting in front of them, beyond the file and past mistakes, it opens the door to meaningful change. But this connection must extend beyond the appointment itself. What happens after the session ends? How does the individual cope with the emotions stirred up, and who supports them in managing their distress? Practitioners must recognise the ripple effects of their work and consider how their interventions might inform and prepare other staff, such as prison officers, to better support individuals during these moments of vulnerability.

This is where self-reflection becomes critical. Do you, as a psychologist, truly consider the broader impact of your sessions? Are you equipping the system around the individual to handle the emotional aftermath? It is not enough to assume you are already doing this; it requires an honest evaluation of your practice. Challenge yourself to ask, "What else could I do?" Could you engage in debriefs with staff or share insights about how best to support individuals after difficult appointments? Could you see beyond your role to create a bridge between therapeutic intervention and day-to-day support?

The answers to these questions lie in embracing humility and a willingness to learn. No matter how experienced or insightful you believe yourself to be, there is always room to grow. What if every session were not merely an assessment but a conversation that informed a wider network of care? If psychologists truly listened, without judgement or preconceived notions, and considered the individual as part of a broader system, they could transform not only lives but also the environment in which those lives are lived.

Conclusion

> You never know the difference you might make. But know this: it could be everything. (Arabella)

Picture walking into a room where every detail of your life, every mistake and every moment of pain, is laid bare before someone you've never met. In that moment, you might wonder what they see. Are you just another case file, another problem to solve? Or do they see the complexity of your story, the weight of your struggles and the flicker of hope you carry despite it all?

For those who have lived through the system, moments of connection (or disconnection) with a psychologist leave a lasting impact. What might feel like a routine conversation to one person can feel monumental to another. The way a psychologist frames a question, the tone of their voice or the act of listening without judgement can resonate long after the session ends. It can be the difference between feeling understood and feeling dismissed, between hope and despair.

The person on the receiving end of these interactions may experience a ripple effect that the psychologist never sees. A kind word, a moment of genuine empathy or a small gesture of understanding can shift the trajectory for someone who feels lost in the system. It's easy to overlook the power psychologists hold: not in their assessments or authority, but in the way they make someone feel during that brief time together.

Each individual, sitting across from a psychologist, carries a story, often filled with pain, regret and a longing to be seen as more than their worst moments. Taking the time to listen, to engage not only with their past but also with their potential, creates a space where change can begin. The immediate impact may not always be visible, but a psychologist's presence, approach and willingness to connect can plant seeds that grow long after the session ends.

In rooms where lives are laid bare and futures hang in the balance, even the smallest act of humanity can make an immense difference. These are the moments remembered long after the doors close. For those who have walked this path, these interactions are often the strength to believe in something better.

As psychologists move forward in their work, they may not always know how their words will land or how their actions will resonate, but they will. Words linger, actions echo, and they can shape a person's journey in ways that may never be fully understood. Every interaction is an opportunity to leave a mark: to either reinforce the walls someone has built or help tear them down.

2 Privilege, power and practice

Navigating protected characteristics in therapeutic spaces

Chinonso Lazz-Onyenobi and Stephen Robinson

Introduction

While protected characteristics are relevant across many settings, prisons and secure environments create unique challenges for individuals who fall into these groups. Foucault (1977) observes that prisons are microcosms of wider society but with heightened power imbalances and systemic discrimination. Understanding how protected characteristics shape an individual's (service users[1] and practitioners) experience of prison and secure environments is critical for practitioners aiming to create a rehabilitative, inclusive and psychologically safe space. Practitioners play a key role in providing the raw ingredients needed to create a purposeful, safe and reflective space for service users to develop their insight and reduce risk to self and others. We would argue that practitioners need to focus on establishing a purposeful therapeutic relationship including therapeutic jurisprudence in which the therapeutic relationship supports procedural justice and self-determination (Howieson, 2023). Kastrani et al. (2015) note that the therapeutic relationship is not just an interpersonal experience, but rather that it is influenced by social constructs such as gender, race, disability and other protected characteristics: "In that way the therapeutic environment acts as a mirror of society. Thus, awareness ... of the ways that gender and social identities enter the therapeutic relationship is a prerequisite for effective and ethical practice" (p. 90). Within the therapeutic relationship, it is important to consider our own identity and how this can influence the therapeutic process (Heilbrun et al., 2021). This process includes understanding the intersection between our own privileges and disadvantages, as well as that of the service user. One way to do this is through the consideration of the protected characteristics of the Equality Act (2010). These are: age, disability, gender reassignment, marriage and civil partnership, pregnancy and maternity, race, religion or belief, sex, and sexual orientation. It is well documented that the coverage of these characteristics may not be addressed in depth within therapeutic training (Ho et al., 2023; Naz et al., 2019). In light of this, the authors argue that it is imperative for practitioners to cultivate a nuanced understanding of each relevant characteristic, critically evaluate their own biases and assumptions

DOI: 10.4324/9781003542377-4

and consider how these elements may facilitate or impede the development of a robust therapeutic alliance. This includes recognising the role of intersectionality, where overlapping identities and experiences (such as disability, race, gender or socioeconomic status) can compound barriers or shape the therapeutic dynamic in complex ways.

The term "intersectionality" was originated by Kimberle Crenshaw in 1989 to describe how systems of oppression overlap for Black women who face racism and sexism. This term has been expanded to include the way various social identities, such as race, gender and socioeconomic status, overlap and interact, creating unique experiences of oppression or privilege (Morrison et al., 2022). It is of note that socioeconomic status is not a protected characteristic in the Equality Act 2010 but regarded as an important part of an individual's social identity (Michaeloudis et al., 2023). By acknowledging and working with these intersections, practitioners can provide more nuanced, individualised and effective interventions that resonate with service users' lived experiences. Protected characteristics do not stand alone, and it is important for the reader to consider the interplay of different characteristics as well as the intergenerational impact that disadvantage has for minoritised groups in our society.

Within therapeutic settings, the importance of cultural competency can significantly enhance the quality of care provided (Hunter et al., 2021). By understanding the unique challenges faced by individuals belonging to different protected groups, practitioners can tailor their approaches to meet specific needs, thereby fostering a sense of safety and trust. Moreover, the strength of the therapeutic alliance is positively influenced by the professional's ability to acknowledge, hold and respect the service user's multiple identities. Positive therapeutic alliance is linked to better service user engagement and overall improved treatment outcomes regardless of therapeutic modality (Flückiger et al., 2018). In building a safe and positive therapeutic relationship, we argue that there is a need for practitioners to be aware of, and sensitive to, service users who may have several protected characteristics (Wang et al., 2021). Therapeutic sensitivity enhances rapport and empowers service users to share what they feel is important for them. It is the responsibility of the practitioner to sensitively provide equitable care to all service users (Morrison et al., 2022). It is also a requirement of our regulatory body as practitioner psychologists, the Health and Care Professions Council (HCPC), where the Standards of Proficiency (SOPs: HCPC, 2023) have been revised to require practitioners not just to understand the importance of inclusive practice, but to take action to challenge barriers to inclusion (HCPC, 2023). That means that all practitioner psychologists are required to be able to: recognise protected characteristics and consequences of barriers to inclusion, including for socially isolated groups (SOP 5.5) and actively challenge these barriers, supporting the implementation of change wherever possible (SOP 5.6). As practitioner psychologists it may be helpful to ask ourselves what we are doing to actively challenge the barriers to inclusion.

In this chapter, literature and personal reflections will be provided alongside anonymised and adapted service user narratives, to illustrate how three of these characteristics (disability, race and sexual orientation) impact all of us in different ways as part of the therapeutic relationship. The characteristics focused on have personal ties to the authors, and so we felt able to speak to these from both our professional understanding and our lived experience. The other protected characteristics are of equal importance, and the reader is strongly advised to explore the literature around those remaining characteristics. We hope that this chapter will challenge practitioners to "do the work" of increasing their understanding of their own privilege and biases. We hope that the guidance in this chapter will help promote inclusivity and support learning that addresses the unique intersectional needs of what makes us and each person we work with unique and valued human beings. This learning can then be used to enhance therapeutic alliance.

Disability

Disability means:

> The individual has (1) a physical or mental impairment, and (2) the impairment has a substantial and long-term adverse effect on the person's ability to carry out normal day-to-day activities.
>
> (Para 6.1 a&b)

The World Health Organization (WHO) has estimated that one-sixth of the global working population has some form of disability. It is well documented that this population experience significant challenges in various aspects of their professional and personal lives compared to individuals who are not disabled (World Health Organization & World Bank, 2011). As therapists, we are invited to consider the emotional and psychological impact on individuals who, despite their efforts and capabilities, find their professional and personal aspirations hindered by systemic barriers rather than personal limitations.

As reflective practitioners, and in line with HCPC standards, we are encouraged to critically examine our own professional environments, including therapeutic settings. Consider the following questions:

- Are you familiar with your organisation's policy on disability and inclusion in the workplace?
- How accessible is this policy, both in terms of locating it and understanding its implications?
- How does the lived experience within your organisation reflect the values and commitments outlined in the policy?

These reflections are not only relevant to our clients' experiences but also to our responsibilities as practitioners committed to equity, inclusion and ethical practice.

Within the therapeutic space, practitioners need to pay attention to the individual needs or adjustments that service users may require to mitigate barriers to accessing the service being provided. Personal circumstances change as can the nature and characteristics of the disability, and it is therefore important to regularly review the needs of the service user within the therapeutic space and, where possible, adapt or reasonably adjust sessions so the service user can feel seen and heard (Royal College of Speech and Language Therapists, 2023). For example, enlarging visual resources for visually impaired service users or knowing how to work with a signer within the therapeutic space are just two of many potential reasonable adjustments within the practitioner's control. The importance of establishing a safe alliance through collaboration, empathy and mutual understanding is imperative to service user growth regardless of whether they have a disability or not. However, it is particularly important when working with people with a disability who may face additional barriers impacting their level of engagement (Cameron et al., 2020). However, the practitioner's definition of safe may be very different to that of the service user, for instance, a bright colourful room may be inviting to one service user but overwhelming and feel unsafe to another.

> **Personal reflection (Stephen):** Within a context of working in private practice and working within a mental health hospital setting, I have taken time in supervision and through attending CPD around the experiences of disabled therapists and disabled former service users of what it means to be psychologically safe. Whilst uncomfortable sharing, I reflect that there have been times when I have used my value judgements as to what a safe environment is. For instance, my therapy space in private practice is visually appealing (for me anyway), I have chosen the colours I like, laid the room out how I see as appropriate and felt that I always gave the service user the most comfortable chair. I have the incense burner on, dim the lights and I am ready to go. However, whilst these adaptations create a safe therapeutic space for me, it doesn't mean that my service users feel the same, something I learned from experience when a service user[2] asked, "Is it OK if we can turn off the oil burner, it's making me feel sick and I am struggling to breathe". I got up and turned off the oil burner as soon as they asked. They then thanked me and shared that they had been "plucking up the courage to ask as they did not want to offend me". Later I could not help but kick myself and reflected this in supervision. I'm creating the right conditions for me but what about the service users I work with, do I even ask them if they are OK with certain smells or items in the room? I work with some service users who are neurodiverse and have sensory difficulties, how do they

feel about the chair they are sitting in and the environment from a multi-sensory perspective? Now I ask the service user (both in private practice and within the mental health hospital) if they are OK with the therapeutic space and if there is anything I need to adapt which could get in the way of developing our relationship.

Individuals with disabilities often hesitate to request necessary adjustments due to fears of being perceived as burdensome or different. This reluctance is influenced by societal attitudes that can lead to feelings of shame and anxiety when advocating for one's needs. Research has shown that employees with psychiatric disabilities frequently experience fear and anxiety that negatively affects their willingness to seek adjustments often due to concerns about anticipated discrimination or non-inclusive workplace cultures (Dong et al., 2021). Similarly, autistic individuals may struggle to identify and request appropriate workplace adjustments, fearing they may be labelled as "troublesome" or "unreasonable" (Crompton et al., 2022).

> **Personal Reflection (Stephen):** As a Counselling Psychologist, it is a course requirement to engage in at least 40 hours of personal therapy. I did the online trawl and found someone whom I thought was suitable. Before I met them, I must admit I was nervous, I wondered if they would like me, what would I wear, what impression they would have of me, what would the room look like, where would I sit.... I hyper-focused on this when I should have been writing essays and working through that never ending to-do list. If I'm feeling like this and I know what therapy is, how must it feel for others who are just experiencing this for the first time? Upon reflection, the experience made me appreciate the courage required to meaningfully engage in the therapeutic process.

Service users with disabilities can often experience anxiety regarding initial contact with practitioners. They can come into the room with various value judgements based on their lived experiences. For example, for a service user who has Crohn's disease may be anxious about where the bathroom is within the therapeutic space, and they may spend hours ruminating on what to say if they need to go during the session. In considering how these barriers can be reduced, the practitioner may not be able to fully prepare their environment to meet the needs of the service user. However, it is important to discuss during the initial contracting process if the service user has any specific needs that need to be brought to the practitioner's attention and discuss how these can be managed so they are able to focus on the content within the session. Consider the therapeutic relationship as building a house; there is no point putting all the effort into the decoration if the foundations are unstable. Therefore, it is paramount that practitioners explore, and continue to review, service user needs and adaptations, as failing to adequately prepare service users can lead to this metaphorical house crashing down (Cameron et al., 2020).

The importance of "getting it" regarding disability

The relationship should be built on a foundation of respect and understanding, where practitioners actively listen and validate service users' experiences (Forber-Pratt et al., 2019). Validation is crucial as service users with disabilities face more stigma, marginalisation and discrimination than individuals who are not disabled (Forber-Pratt et al., 2019). Practitioners must ensure that they are employing adaptive strategies to accommodate specific needs. This may involve using visual aids, sign language interpreters or adapting the environment, so the service user can access the therapeutic space (such as the use of ramps). Such adaptations not only facilitate better engagement but also demonstrate commitment to meeting the service user's needs (Wills et al., 2018).

When we think about disability in the therapeutic space, physical disability is not always actively discussed or considered in the same way as other aspects such as neurodiversity. When discussed, it is likely to be in the form of physical adjustments to be made or resources required to support the practicalities of the therapeutic environment. While this is important, other aspects require attention too. "*Disablism* is a set of assumptions (conscious or unconscious) and practices that promote the differential or unequal treatment of people because of actual or presumed disabilities" (Campbell, 2008). Wang et al. (2024) found that individuals with disability experience microaggressions, such as not being directly addressed in a group discussion. Other attitudinal concerns can also be shown, including individuals being trained from childhood to not stare at individuals with visible disabilities (Campbell & Patel, 2024), which can result in a level of dismissal or invisibility of those with physical disabilities. Concerns such as these led Campbell and Patel (2024) to highlight how common it is for individuals with disabilities to feel invisible. When they are not experiencing invisibility, those with physical disability can be viewed by able-bodied individuals as having impairments that go beyond the physical and include emotional and cognitive abilities (Campbell & Patel, 2024) without any evidence to back this up. In this context, it is essential to consider both visible and non-visible disabilities, as these can significantly impact an individual's daily life and access to services. Non-visible disabilities, such as neurological conditions, mental health disorders and energy-limiting conditions, may not present with obvious external signs but can have profound effects on a person's well-being (Hunt, 2024a). The invisibility of these conditions often leads to stereotypes and judgements, with individuals being unfairly labelled as lazy or unmotivated, thereby devaluing their experiences (Campbell & Patel, 2024). Furthermore, research suggests that women are more frequently affected by certain disabilities, reinforcing the need to examine how gender bias influences perceptions and support systems (Hunt, 2024a).

Disabilities exist on a spectrum, meaning that even among individuals with the same diagnosis, the manifestations and needs can differ significantly

(Parent Center Hub, 2018). Society often assumes that unless a disability presents in its most extreme form, it is neither impactful nor recognisable. This misconception may similarly influence practitioners' perspectives, sometimes leading to a one-size-fits-all approach that does not adequately address individual needs (Washington University, 2023). However, two individuals with the same disability may require entirely different adjustments. For instance, one person with a neurological condition may benefit from a structured and predictable environment, while another may need flexibility in their schedule to manage their symptoms effectively (Job Accommodation Network, 2020). Practitioners must critically examine their biases and ensure they approach each case with an understanding of intersectionality and individual differences.

Some societies tend to prioritise values such as individualism and independence, which can marginalise those who do not fit within this framework, including individuals with disabilities (Owens, 2015). This societal context can lead to the perception that people with disabilities are not compatible with mainstream expectations of productivity and self-sufficiency (Nario-Redmond et al., 2019). Consequently, practitioners must recognise these structural challenges and the pressures and stressors faced by those with both visible and non-visible disabilities. Doing so can foster an understanding of how certain practices (such as wellness programmes that emphasise self-reliance) may inadvertently reinforce the ideals of individualism and fail to consider the diverse experiences of individuals with disabilities (Brown, 2002).

To support the development of therapeutic relationships, practitioners are encouraged to reflect on their own perceptions of disability and consider how these views may influence their interactions with both service users and colleagues (Hunt, 2024b; Ingham, 2018). Gaining a deeper understanding of various physical conditions, both visible and invisible, is essential, not only in terms of their impact on service users but also on colleagues. This education should be undertaken alongside insights from individuals with lived experience of disabilities to ensure a fuller and more accurate perspective (Ingham, 2018). Additionally, practitioners should be cautious about making assumptions regarding colleagues with physical disabilities, particularly in relation to their professional success. Campbell and Patel (2024) highlight that counsellors with disabilities often encounter presumptions about their capabilities, which can be both limiting and unhelpful. Instead of making assumptions, practitioners should engage in open conversations to understand an individual's personal experiences, needs and preferences. This approach fosters a more inclusive and supportive working environment, strengthening both professional relationships and the therapeutic space.

Regardless of whether the service user has a visible or invisible disability, the goal of creating a relationship is to empower service users to navigate their challenges effectively while fostering a sense of agency and autonomy. By employing a person-centred approach that values and validates the service user's voice and experiences, practitioners can help service users build resilience and achieve meaningful outcomes (Cooper & Frearson, 2017). In relation to practitioners providing reasonable adjustments, paragraphs 20–22 of the Equality Act outline the duty to make reasonable adjustments, what failure to comply looks like and the regulations. All practitioners should reflect on these sections and explore through supervision and appropriate Continuous Professional Development (CPD), how these points could impact the practitioner, the service user and the overall quality of the relationship.

Race

A summary of the Equality Act's definition of race is a reference to a person of a particular racial, ethnic or national group (see Para 9, 1–6).

A more thorough definition of race is: "Race may be characterized as the phenotypical expression of one's identity, while ethnicity can be thought of as being the expression of one's cultural identity. Race and ethnicity are both social constructions" (Williams & La Torre, 2022, p. 267).

Race, ethnicity and culture are fundamental components of an individual's identity, shaping their values and worldview (Williams et al., 2012). This worldview serves as a lens through which individuals interpret meaning and relevance, directly influencing the therapeutic process (Carter & Forsyth, 2009). Consequently, the cultural backgrounds of both practitioner and service user can affect the language and communication within the therapeutic space, potentially leading to misunderstandings if colloquialisms or cultural references are not mutually understood (Heilbrun et al., 2021).

In the context of the criminal justice system, it is imperative to address the disproportionate representation of people of colour. Recent data indicates that while people of colour constitute approximately 16% of the general population in England and Wales, they represent 27% of the prison population (Ministry of Justice, 2020). This overrepresentation is influenced by factors such as intergenerational offending and socioeconomic disadvantages (Ministry of Justice, 2025). Studies have shown that prisoners often come from backgrounds marked by social exclusion, including experiences of poverty and familial criminal history, which can perpetuate cycles of offending across generations (Cabinet Office, 2022).

The lived experiences of people of colour within the criminal justice system are further compounded by feelings of victimisation and targeted discrimination (Robertson & Wainwright, 2020). Long (2022) highlighted that women's experiences, specifically Black women's experiences in the criminal justice system, are not always considered when discussing targeted discrimination and victimisation, despite this forming part of their experience. Discriminatory policing practices, such as disproportionate stop-and-search measures, contribute to a pervasive sense of mistrust and perceived racial bias among some communities (Shankley & Williams, 2020). This mistrust is exacerbated by systemic inequalities, including disparities in sentencing and access to quality legal representation, which can lead to harsher outcomes for people of colour compared to their White counterparts (Sentencing Academy, 2020).

As practitioners, it is crucial to recognise how our own cultural backgrounds and potential biases may influence our interactions with service users from diverse ethnicities. Engaging in self-reflection and seeking to gain cultural competence can help mitigate the impact of these biases on the therapeutic process. By fostering an environment of cultural humility and understanding, practitioners can work more effectively with service users who have experienced racism, acknowledging the unique challenges they face within the criminal justice system and in society at large.

When individuals are from different cultural backgrounds, their cultural expressions may not always be understood. This may be due to the behaviours of minority groups being considered through dominant cultural perceptions, which in the case of the authors of this chapter would be the UK. This can be more prevalent with Black men, where their forms of expression and interactions may be considered aggressive or linked to criminality (Newberry, 2010). Newberry (2010) went on to indicate that such misunderstandings may result in discomfort in exploring issues of race and ethnic identity. This is linked to the rarity in clinical practice of service users being asked how they identify, which can lead to errors when race and ethnicity are assigned to them (Hicks, 2004; Naz et al., 2019). This could result in a fractured relationship when working with service users, as not discussing aspects of their identity could result in biases. As such, the nuances of an individual's identity may be missed, for example being Black British and having Trinidadian heritage will be experienced differently from being Black British and having Nigerian heritage. This bias is not always conscious, and Maharaj et al. (2021) noted that implicit attitudes are often outside conscious awareness and can be activated automatically, influencing human behaviour. A dichotomy therefore forms when race is not seen or discussed in the therapeutic relationship. This is at a disadvantage to both the service user and the practitioner.

To mitigate identity bias, Heilbrun et al. (2021) emphasised the importance of cultural competence, which includes understanding societal stereotypes and the systemic responses to people of colour. This involves recognising how legislation, institutional policies and interpersonal interactions can perpetuate biases. Practitioners must also be aware that reviewing such policies may evoke internal conflict, especially if they too are negatively impacted by the same systems. This is where intersectionality becomes crucial, as it highlights how overlapping identities can result in compounded disadvantages (Williams & La Torre, 2022).

Understanding historical contexts, such as the enduring effects of colonialism and imperialism, is imperative in comprehending how certain groups are perceived and treated today. This historical awareness provides a foundation for practitioners to appreciate the lived experiences of service users. Service users often report increased comfort and trust when working with culturally informed practitioners who value their cultural contexts and integrate their values and belief systems into therapy (Comas-Díaz, 2006). Leite and Peluso (2018) found that service users' perceptions of a practitioner's cultural competence are positively correlated with therapy satisfaction.

Moreover, cultural expressions can vary significantly; for instance, individuals from certain backgrounds may use expressive hand gestures or speak with a raised voice when passionate. These behaviours, while normative in their cultures, can be misinterpreted as aggression in different cultural contexts. Such misinterpretations can lead to biased assessments, where individuals are unjustly perceived as higher risk and consequently subjected to harsher treatments within psychological and criminal justice settings (Hareli et al., 2013).

Additionally, mental health remains a taboo subject in various cultures and religions, making it challenging for individuals to discuss their struggles openly (Codjoe et al., 2023; Cogan et al., 2023). This stigma can hinder relationship-building between practitioners and service users, as individuals may fear judgement or misunderstanding. In some cultures, seeking mental health support is associated with shame, leading individuals to suffer in silence rather than accessing necessary services (Modir et al., 2019). In some cultures, mental health issues are viewed in a more holistic manner that accounts for the mind, body and spirit (The Psyche Sphere, 2025). This holistic approach could support de-stigmatisation in these cultures, providing a different perspective on mental health. This reinforces the need for exploring the cultural background of the service user to develop an appropriate therapeutic approach that caters to the individual.

By actively engaging in self-reflection and striving for cultural competence, practitioners can create a more open and supportive therapeutic environment. This approach fosters meaningful connections and facilitates effective interventions tailored to the unique cultural contexts of each service user.

Personal reflection (Chinonso): Service user T[3] reported from their experience, "they [practitioners] should ask me about my experiences including being Black and being a man". He stated this will allow them to "know my story". This suggests that viewing the individual as a whole including acknowledging cultural and racial identity, especially in environments and situations in which they are the minority, is beneficial for progress in developing supportive relationships with professionals. There have been occasions in which I have known younger Black and Asian service users to refer to older service users from the same background as "uncle", which has at times been seen as a form of manipulation by some staff that are typically not from that culture. Whilst the environment matters, the culture of those individuals is also important to consider, in regard to the way such situations are viewed.

Another way to ensure race is considered in the therapeutic relationship is the development of goals and themes early in the therapeutic process that would allow the service user to bring up issues that are linked to race, ethnicity and culture (Maharaj et al., 2021). In doing this, the practitioner is creating open communication and a space in which the service user can bring more of themselves to the therapeutic process.

> **Personal reflection (Chinonso):** Service user T indicated that exploring how this aspect of his identity may have influenced his experiences, supported him in developing openness and allowed him to bring more of himself to the therapeutic space. He stated this allows practitioners to "look at me as a whole person to help me open up". However, this is only supportive if the practitioner is open to being uncomfortable and challenging their own biases/reactions as what may be said could be a trigger especially if they are part of the group that has caused harm to the service user.

In consideration of being part of a group that may have caused harm, Drustrup (2021) reflected on how White people not acknowledging racism can impact their psyche and emotionality. This results in a willingness to continue inflicting harm on others and not truly understanding themselves as they do not acknowledge the impact race (being racialised as White) has on them. This can be linked to Miserocchi (2014) noting,

> White individuals often see themselves as cultureless and unbiased because of the institutionalized invisibility of Whiteness, which makes it difficult to become aware of oppression and privilege and one's participation in that dynamic. For White therapists, these blind spots could lead to unintentional oppression of service users, potentially harming them.
>
> (p. 1)

This blindness may then be used as the standard when working with individuals from other racial groups (Kinouani, 2023). This can result in silence around racism which when brought to a therapeutic relationship can be seen by the service user as agreeing with or condoning harmful ideologies and practices. This, as mentioned above, results in a therapeutic space that is potentially harmful to the service user and can hinder full participation in the therapeutic process. This can be linked to research showing that Black service users have a preference for Black practitioners, due to aspects such as a level of familiarity associated with racial identity, resulting in greater ease when developing a therapeutic relationship (Goode-Cross & Grim, 2016).

> **Personal reflection (Chinonso):** Service user T reported the preference for "a Black, preferably African, female therapist" when asked,

citing familiarity and not having to explain elements of himself to the practitioner. Some of the Black service users I have worked with have highlighted experiencing racism and microaggressions from other staff members. When I enquired about them sharing this with other practitioners and/or other staff members who can support them that are not Black, they mentioned they spoke to me as they felt I would understand their perspective. The main aspect was about not having to explain why they believed certain actions were racially charged.

Another important aspect to consider is that practitioners of colour, due to structural and interpersonal racism and racial hierarchy, may internalise racism and inferiority (Maharaj et al., 2021). It is of note that practitioners of colour may experience discomfort in discussing race with service users with a different racial identity, especially those racialised as White (Gavel, 2012), which can result in missed opportunities to explore racial or cultural dynamics and feelings of anxiety. This can play a role in the therapeutic relationship if service users are consciously or unconsciously aware of this.

Attention should be paid to racism as a stressor at work, which impacts the well-being of Black practitioners and contributes to burnout (Shell et al., 2022). Individuals racialised as White are unlikely to feel this same racial stress due to the structure of society in which they are racially comfortable (Kinouani, 2023). As noted above, this can translate into the therapeutic space and result in blind spots, making it more challenging to support and understand colleagues from a different racial background. Support in supervision and with colleagues who create a supportive space that allows for these issues to be brought to light can aid healing for the practitioner and allow for greater cultural and racial development for the White practitioners. A supportive space in this context should also be seen as a space to be accountable, acknowledge the systemic challenges faced by colleagues and to challenge one's own biases. Options to support this process include exploring other therapeutic modalities, for example, teaching/learning about African Psychology and encouraging use in practice; as well as having knowledge about issues linked to racial identity, multiple identities and systemic discrimination faced by individuals who are not racialised as White (Good-Cross & Grim, 2016). Practitioners who can discuss race and racial trauma within the supervision space are likely to be more open and confident in broaching this topic with service users, further highlighting the importance of such discussions in supervision to support therapeutic practice. Being open to the discomfort of such conversations develops the practitioner's skills, especially as service users are encouraged to sit in their discomfort to support the therapeutic process. In essence, we learn to follow our own advice.

As Good-Cross and Grim (2016) highlighted, Black practitioners (and practitioners from other cultural and racial backgrounds) are not monolithic in character or experience. This is the same for service users of colour. Therefore, this should be taken into consideration when exploring this chapter and the literature in general.

To summarise, to support your development as a culturally and racially competent and informed practitioner, you may want to reflect on these questions in supervision:

- What is your identity and worldview (your cultural, racial, social identity), and how does this create privilege and bias for you?
- How do you invite service users to raise their identity and worldview within your sessions?
- What are you doing to improve your cultural competence?
- What action are you taking to address the disproportionate representation of people of colour in justice and health services?
- How are you considering the harm that has been experienced by service users because of discrimination and unjust systems and structures?

The HCPC SOPs (HCPC, 2023) and the British Psychological Society practice guidelines (2017) require practitioners to consider a service user's protected characteristics. Therefore, these reflective questions and those throughout this chapter can support embedding this approach into practice.

Sexual Orientation

The Equality Act 2010 defines sexual orientation as a person's sexual orientation to persons of the same sex, persons of the opposite sex or persons of either sex (see Para 12.1).

This characteristic is diverse and quickly evolving (some would argue devolving depending on what part of the world the reader is from). While some countries have laws which protect their lesbian, gay, bisexual, transgender, queer, intersex, plus (LGBTQI+) community, at the time of writing this chapter, there are 64 countries where being part of the LGBTQI+ community can result in imprisonment and in 12 of those nations, the death penalty is either mandated or optional to the courts.

Within a UK context, the Equality Act may protect LGBTQI+ individuals in all areas of their life; however, the reality of this can feel very different. For instance, a Stonewall survey (Bachman & Gooch, 2023) of over 5,000 LGBTQI+ participants in the UK found that:

- 52% participants had experienced depression in the last year
- 13% of LGBTQI+ individuals aged 18–24 had attempted to end their life by suicide. This increased to 46% for transgender participants
- 41% of non-binary participants engaged in self-harm behaviours

- 19% LGBTQI+ participants had not disclosed their identity to healthcare professionals. This figure increased to 41% for bisexual males and 29% for bisexual women
- 13% of LGBTQI+ individuals had seen or experienced discriminatory behaviour of healthcare staff

Training for practitioners working with LGBTQI+ service users is somewhat limited (Ho et al., 2023), and it is not uncommon for practitioners to have "blind spots" when it comes to understanding the complexity and diversity within the LGBTQI+ community. Having said that, it is the responsibility of the practitioner to increase their understanding through engaging in CPD, exploring in supervision and through personal development and not to just rely on service users to educate them.

Therapy and the LGBTQI+ community

The above statistics demonstrate the disproportionate distress that is present in the LGBTQI+ community. Historically, the relationship between the therapeutic and LGBTQI+ communities has been somewhat problematic. To provide context, until 1967, it was illegal in the UK to be gay and therapy rooms, like many other places, were not necessarily safe spaces for the LGBTQI+ community. Homosexuality was viewed as a mental health disorder in diagnostic manuals until 1990 (Cochran et al., 2014). In addition to viewing homosexuality as a disorder or mental illness, it was also commonplace for conversion therapy to be used to "cure homosexuality". Some countries, including the USA, still allow this unethical and harmful practice to continue. When the UK was close to making conversion therapy illegal, the UK government excluded people who identify as transgender due to different considerations when it came to the transgender population such as ensuring therapeutic support for those with gender dysphoria was not impacted (House of Lords, 2024); the UK government are continuing work in this area (UK Parliament, 2025). This highlights that within the LGBTQI+ community, practitioners need an appreciation of the unique challenges faced by this community with therapy and therapists. Therapists and psychological organisations were instrumental in making changes to diagnostic manuals and have been united in their efforts to ban conversion therapy since 2015, perhaps more recently demonstrating some allyship with the LGBTQI+ community.

Trust and safety within the therapeutic environment are paramount to successful outcomes. However, with the history of this community being pathologised and criminalised, it is not unexpected that navigating themes associated with shame, internalised homophobia, rejection and feelings of exclusion are common presentations for service users. A practitioner's ability to demonstrate sensitivity towards the unique challenges this community has faced, and still faces, can help provide the practitioner with a useful context in empathising with their narrative.

Personal reflection (Stephen): I grew up in the 1980s when the infamous gravestone image with "AIDS" written on it was thrusted into our homes. It terrified me. This led to thoughts that being gay means you are going to die soon and increased my feelings of shame. Also, Section 28 was part of my schooling. The discussion of gay relationships was non-existent. I later learnt that coming out is not just a one-time event: every time I changed job or met new people, I had to assess the environment and decide. It's exhausting. No wonder this community often experiences mental health difficulties such as anxiety, depression, substance abuse.

The therapeutic alliance is a critical factor in the effectiveness of therapy, particularly for LGBTQI+ service users who may have experienced discrimination, stigma or trauma related to being part of the LGBTQI+ community (Alessi et al., 2019). This includes bisexual service users, who often share how they do not feel part of either the gay or heterosexual community, leading to further marginalisation (Dodge et al., 2016).

> **Personal reflection (Stephen):** As a gay man who works within healthcare settings, there have been several times when I have read reports by other professionals who describe the person they are writing about as "homosexual" or that they are in a "homosexual relationship". This makes me shudder as this term has connotations with disorder, medicalisation and being abnormal. I wonder how the service user would feel or even if they have had the opportunity to challenge this.

LGBTQI+ individuals face considerable ostracisation from society, which is only magnified within the prison system. The experience of being incarcerated as an LGBTQI+ person is shaped by multiple intersecting factors, including gender, sexual orientation and institutional policies. Each experience is unique; the common thread is the heightened vulnerability and complexity of needs that require a nuanced understanding and support. For gay men in prison, openly expressing their identity remains taboo, often forcing individuals to conceal their sexuality to avoid mockery, abuse or even targeted violence from both peers and staff (Why Me? 2024). The hypermasculine environment of male prisons often reinforces rigid norms around gender and sexuality, leaving little room for LGBTQI+ individuals to seek support or build connections without fear of reprisal. In contrast, the experience of LGBTQI+ women in prison is markedly different (Barrow Cadbury Trust, 2021). While same-sex relationships between female prisoners are more visible and, at times, even encouraged by peers, they are often viewed negatively by prison staff, who may perceive them as manipulative or disruptive rather than as genuine expressions of identity and connection (Why Me? 2024). Relationships between women in custody are frequently a source of conflict, sometimes escalating into violence, which further shapes institutional attitudes towards LGBTQI+ prisoners in the female estate. These differing experiences underscore the need for prison psychologists and staff to develop a deeper awareness of the unique pressures facing the different LGBTQI+ individuals in custody. Without this understanding, institutional responses risk reinforcing harmful stereotypes and exacerbating the marginalisation of an already vulnerable population (Urban Institute, 2023).

When working with LGBTQI+ people, therapists are encouraged to create space for conversations that explore not only identity but also the broader sociocultural context in which that identity has developed. Affirmative practice involves more than acceptance: it requires genuine curiosity, cultural humility and a commitment to understanding the unique lived experiences of everyone. To support this process, therapists might reflect on and sensitively explore the following questions to deepen their understanding of a client's identity and environment:

- Have you, and if so, when did you come out?
- Are there areas of your life, such as work or family, where you have not come out, and how do you feel about that?
- Do people in your life accept you for who you are, and how do you know?
- Do you accept yourself?
- Are there aspects of yourself where you carry shame or guilt, and if so, where do you feel this comes from?
- How do you feel about sharing this part of yourself within these sessions?
- When did you come to terms with being LGBTQI+?
- How did you manage that process?

These questions are not intended to pathologise or intrude, but to centre the client's narrative, support identity development and build a therapeutic relationship rooted in safety, affirmation and trust (Nieder et al., 2020).

More personal reflections to consider:

- What barriers do you feel they may bring, and how would you hold and explore them?
- How do you feel when you see two people of the same sex holding hands in the community?
- How do you feel when you see an individual who identifies as trans?

With these examples, the practitioner may wish to consider where their response comes from, the historical conditions of worth or value judgements which were imposed on them when growing up and what they can do to challenge possible unhelpful judgements, so they are able to sit in the world of the service user.

Reflective points

Through the three protected characteristics discussed, we have reviewed literature and developed some questions to help practitioners explore how they can create purposeful therapeutic spaces that are equitable and inclusive. To support this work, we have identified two interventions as starting points that we will briefly outline, that could be used in supervision to identify CPD needs that are linked to diversity, equity and inclusion.

Social GRRRAAACCEEESS

No, the above is not a typo, nor us resting our heads on the keyboard! GGRRAAACCEEESSS stands for "gender, geography, race, religion, age, ability, appearance, class, culture, ethnicity, education, employment, sexuality, sexual orientation and spirituality" (Burnham, 2018). This is a useful framework to understand how different aspects of social identity can result in power and privilege differences. To illustrate, two hypothetical examples are provided. Consider the perspective of David, the White, cis, straight male who is 50 years old, has been to university, is able-bodied, employed, considers themselves middle class, married with three children and a practising catholic. They live in the suburbs of the South East of the UK.

- What comes up for you in terms of power and privilege?
- What can you as a practitioner relate to?
- What comes up for you in terms of the challenges and or pre/judgements you may have?
- How will you hold them within the therapy room?

Now consider Emma, a mixed-race gay female in her 20s who got excluded from school, is on benefits because she is registered disabled, considers herself an atheist and comes from the North West in the UK.

- Would you respond to David the same way as Emma? If not, why not?
- What comes up for you in terms of power and privilege with regards to Emma?

The purpose of this model is to help practitioners consider visible and invisible differences and helps to plan how to engage with a variety of service users in the most anti-oppressive way.

The Johari Window

The Johari Window was developed by Luft and Ingham in 1955 and used as a tool to demonstrate and enhance the awareness of personal relationships. It is also an effective tool for self-development (Luft & Ingham, 1955). There are some useful diagrams available online.[4] The Johari Window model enables us to think about four elements of ourselves and our relationships with others and to think about the differences between how we see ourselves and how others see us. The four elements are as follows:

Window One: "The Arena": things that are "known to self and known to others". We reveal a great deal about ourselves, including by the way we speak or dress; whether we choose to wear a wedding ring; our race and any visible disabilities are also revealed. Reflection on what we reveal and on what people might conclude about us by what they see can help us understand a bit more about how we are perceived by others.

Window Two: "The Blind Spot" where others know things about you that you do not. Thinking about this window is useful in increasing our self-awareness. It also prompts us to ask for feedback from the people we work with (colleagues and service users), so we can learn more about how we are experienced.

Window Three: "The hidden area", or "The façade". This is where you know things about yourself, but you do not share these with others. Consider why you choose not to share. Is it because if you do, you may feel exposed, vulnerable or it is not appropriate? Appropriate self-disclosure can be used to reduce this area.

Window Four: "The unknown" window where others do not know aspects of you, and you don't either. Through self-discovery, shared discovery and through the observations of others, this window reduces. This window is a powerful tool to take supervision to self-explore.

You can use the Johari Window model to explore aspects of your identity that are shared and not shared with your service users, and reflect on how they may experience you as an individual. This enables discussion about ourselves and our biases, what we choose to share and hide, and what others see in us that we may not be aware of.

> **Reflection (Chinonso & Stephen):** We all have prejudices, the key thing is to be aware of them and to explore this in personal therapy, supervision or through CPD. Leave your prejudices outside the door and if you can't, should you be working with this group?

Conclusion

This chapter aimed not only to introduce the reader to three key protected characteristics under the Equality Act (2010) but also to encourage deeper reflection on how these characteristics shape experiences within society and the criminal justice system. More importantly, it has sought to challenge us all, both as individuals and practitioners, to critically examine our unconscious biases and the ways they may manifest in our professional practice. The nuanced needs of individuals with protected characteristics have too often been ignored, dismissed or misunderstood by society and institutions that struggle to adapt to those who do not fit into the perceived norm. This absence of belonging and institutional inflexibility can leave individuals feeling unseen and unsupported, reinforcing systemic barriers rather than dismantling them.

While this chapter focused on specific characteristics that are particularly pertinent to the authors, this does not diminish the significance of other protected characteristics, nor does it suggest that work in those areas is complete. Practitioners are encouraged to use this discussion as a starting point: an opportunity to reflect on their therapeutic approach and consider whether it enhances or impedes inclusivity within their practice. If those reading this chapter were asked to write a chapter about those other characteristics, what considerations would they have? What may overlap and what may be unique? We hope that this chapter has provided the reader with an appreciation for the courage it takes for service users to share their narratives, their stories and their lives with us. And how we may respectfully respond to this by recognising and addressing our own biases, including bringing unconscious bias to awareness, as an essential step towards mitigating blind spots and ensuring our practice does not reinforce exclusionary norms. Engaging in CPD that challenges the dominant "cis, White, neurotypical, heteronormative" lens is a powerful tool in broadening perspectives and improving practice. Ultimately, practitioners must remain vigilant, reflexive and open to understanding how protected characteristics shape the lived experiences of those they support. Creating an environment where service users feel heard, valued and appropriately challenged is a requirement of our regulatory body as psychologists, not an optional extra. It is fundamental to effective and ethical practice.

Useful resources

Disability

- HYPERLINK "https://www.rcot.co.uk/explore-resources/learning-disabilities-neurodiversity" Learning disabilities & neurodiversity | RCOT – a good resource about learning disability and neurodiversity.
- HYPERLINK "https://hdsunflower.com/uk/insights/category/invisible-disabilities" Hidden disabilities – includes information about disabilities that are not visible.

Race

- HYPERLINK "https://racereflections.co.uk/" Rethinking inequality, injustice and oppression – great resource for exploring race and inequality.
- HYPERLINK "https://www.runnymedetrust.org/" The Runnymede Trust – a resource that explores structural racism in Britian.
- HYPERLINK "https://raceequalitymatters.com/" Race Equality Matters – a good resource about tackling racial inequality in the workplace.

LGBTQI+

- The Queer Mental Health Workbook by Dr Brendan Dunlop – a useful resource in explaining specific issues and interventions which are related to the LGBTQI+ community.
- https://lgbtplushistorymonth.co.uk/ includes lots of useful resources for developing awareness of the LGBTQI+ community.

- https://notaphase.org – great resource for developing awareness of the trans community.
- https://lgbt.foundation – great website where resources are available for the LGBTQI+ – there is a useful link for healthcare professionals.

Notes

1 In this chapter, service user refers to people detained in prisons and secure hospitals.
2 This service user gave consent for this example to be used.
3 This service user agreed to share their experience to give insight from a service user perspective for this chapter.
4 For example, https://thedecisionlab.com/reference-guide/psychology/johari-window.

References

Alessi, E., Dillon, F., & Horn, R. (2019). The therapeutic relationship mediates the association between affirmative practice and psychological well-being among lesbian, gay, bisexual, and queer service users. *Psychotherapy*, 56(2), 229–240. https://doi.org/10.1037/pst0000210

Bachmann, C. L., & Gooch, B. (2023). LGBT in Britain: Health report (pp. 1–12). Stonewall. https://files.stonewall.org.uk/production/files/lgbt_in_britain_health.pdf

Barrow Cadbury Trust. (2021). *LGBT+ people in prisons: Experiences in England and Scotland*. https://barrowcadbury.org.uk/wp-content/uploads/2023/11/LGBT-People-in-Prisons-Full-Report-16-FEB-21-WEB-1.pdf

British Psychological Society. (2017). *Practice guidelines* (3rd ed.) [PDF]. British Psychological Society. https://doi.org/10.53841/bpsrep.2017.inf115

Brown, S., (2002) "What Is Disability Culture?", Disability Studies Quarterly 22(2). doi: https://doi.org/10.18061/dsq.v22i2.343

Burnham, J. (2018). Developments in Social Graces: Visible–invisible and voiced–unvoiced. In I.-B. Krause (Ed.), Culture and reflexivity in systemic psychotherapy: Mutual perspectives (pp. 139–160). Routledge. https://doi.org/10.4324/9780429473463-7

Cabinet Office. (2022, July 4). *A complete guide to GFiE – Prison leavers and lived experience*. GOV.UK. https://gfie.blog.gov.uk/2022/07/04/a-complete-guide-to-gfie-prison-leavers-and-lived-experience/

Cameron, S., Swanton, J., & Dagnan, D. (2020). Conceptualising the therapeutic alliance: Exploring the relevance of Bordin's model for adults with intellectual disabilities. *Advances in Mental Health and Intellectual Disabilities*, 14(5), 169–179. https://doi.org/10.1108/amhid-11-2019-0034

Campbell, F. K. (2008). Refusing able (ness): A preliminary conversation about ableism. *M/C Journal, 11*(3), 1–7.

Campbell, B. T., & Patel, J. M. (2024). Perspectives on disability: Exploring issues faced by counsellors in the therapeutic relationship. *Journal of Psychological Research, Behavioral Science, and Sociology, 12*(3), 20–33.

Carter, R. T., & Forsyth, J. M. (2009). A guide to the forensic assessment of race-based traumatic stress reactions. *The Journal of the American Academy of Psychiatry and the Law, 37*(1), 28–40.

Cochran, S. D., Drescher, J., Kismodi, E., Giami, A., García-Moreno, C., & Reed, G. M. (2014). Proposed declassification of disease categories related to sexual orientation in ICD-11: Rationale and evidence from the working group on sexual disorders and sexual health. *Bulletin of the World Health Organization, 92*(9), 672–679. https://doi.org/10.2471/BLT.14.135541

Codjoe, L., N'Danga-Koroma, J., Henderson, C., Lempp, H., & Thornicroft, G. (2023). Pilot study of a manualised mental health awareness and stigma reduction intervention for Black faith communities in the UK: ON TRAC project. *Social Psychiatry and Psychiatric Epidemiology, 58*(11), 1687–1697.

Cogan, N. A., Liu, X., Chin-Van Chau, Y., Kelly, S. W., Anderson, T., Flynn, C., ... Corrigan, P. (2023). The taboo of mental health problems, stigma and fear of disclosure among Asian international students: Implications for help-seeking, guidance and support. *British Journal of Guidance & Counselling, 52*(4), 697–715. https://doi.org/10.1080/03069885.2023.2214307

Comas-Díaz, L. (2006). Cultural variation in the therapeutic relationship. In C. D. Goodheart, A. E. Kazdin, & R. J. Sternberg (Eds.), *Evidence-based psychotherapy: Where practice and research meet* (pp. 81–105). Washington, DC: American Psychological Association.

Cooper, R., & Frearson, J. (2017). Adapting compassion focused therapy for an adult with a learning disability—A case study. *British Journal of Learning Disabilities, 45*(2), 142–150. https://doi.org/10.1111/bld.12187

Crenshaw, K. (1989). Demarginalizing the intersection of race and sex: A black feminist critique of antidiscrimination doctrine, feminist theory and antiracist politics. *University of Chicago Legal Forum, 1*, 139–167.

Crompton, C. J., Ropar, D., Evans-Williams, C. V. M., Flynn, E. G., & Fletcher-Watson, S. (2022). Autistic adults' views and experiences of requesting and receiving reasonable adjustments in the UK. *Plos One, 17*(8), e0272420. https://doi.org/10.1371/journal.pone.0272420

Dodge, B., Herbenick, D., Friedman, M. R., Schick, V., Fu, T. J., Bostwick, W., Bartelt, E., Muñoz-Laboy, M., Pletta, D., Reece, M., & Sandfort, T. G. (2016). Attitudes toward bisexual men and women among a nationally representative probability sample of adults in the United States. *Plos One, 11*(10), e0164430. https://doi.org/10.1371/journal.pone.0164430

Dong, S., Eto, O., & Spitz, C. (2021). Barriers and facilitators to requesting accommodation among individuals with psychiatric disabilities: A qualitative approach. *Journal of Vocational Rehabilitation, 55*(1), 207–218. https://doi.org/10.3233/JVR-211157

Drustrup, D. (2021). Talking with White service users about race. *Journal of Health Service Psychology, 47*(2), 63–72.

Equality Act 2010, c. 15. (2010). *Equality Act 2010.* Retrieved from https://www.legislation.gov.uk/ukpga/2010/15/contents [legislation.gov.uk]

Flückiger, C., Del Re, A. C., Wampold, B. E., & Horvath, A. O. (2018). The alliance in adult psychotherapy: A meta-analytic synthesis. *Psychotherapy, 55*(4), 316–340. https://doi.org/10.1037/pst0000172

Forber-Pratt, A. J., Mueller, C. O., & Andrews, E. E. (2019). Disability identity and allyship in rehabilitation psychology: Sit, stand, sign, and show up. *Rehabilitation Psychology, 64*(2), 119–129. https://doi.org/10.1037/rep0000256

Foucault, M. (1977). *Discipline and punish: The birth of the prison* (A. Sheridan, Trans.). Penguin Books. (Original work published 1975)

Goode-Cross, D. T., & Grim, K. A. (2016). "An unspoken level of comfort": Black therapists' experiences working with Black service users. *Journal of Black Psychology, 42*(1), 29–53.

Gavel, M. (2012). *Opening a can of worms: African American therapists' attitudes about broaching race with White clients* (Master's thesis, Missouri State University). MSU Graduate Theses/Dissertations. https://bearworks.missouristate.edu/theses/2048

Hareli, S., Kafetsios, K., & Hess, U. (2013). A cross-cultural study on emotion expression and the learning of social norms. *Frontiers in Psychology, 4*, 15. https://doi.org/10.3389/fpsyg.2013.00015

HCPC. (2023). *Practitioner psychologists.* www.hcpc-Uk.org. https://www.hcpc-uk.org/standards/standards-of-proficiency/practitioner-psychologists/

Heilbrun, K., Kavanaugh, A., Grisso, T., Anumba, N., Dvoskin, J., & Golding, S. (2021). The importance of racial identity in forensic mental health assessment. *The Journal of the American Academy of Psychiatry and the Law, 49*(4), 478–487.

Hicks, J. W. (2004). Ethnicity, race, and forensic psychiatry: Are we color-blind? *Journal of the American Academy of Psychiatry and the Law Online, 32*(1), 21–33.

Ho, J. K. Y., O'Rouke, C., Laville, A., Chellingsworth, M., & Callaghan, P. (2023). Clinician experiences on training and awareness of sexual orientation in NHS talking therapies services for anxiety and depression. *The Cognitive Behaviour Therapist, 16*, e24.

House of Lords. (2024). *Conversion therapy prohibition (Sexual orientation and gender identity) Bill [HL].*

Howieson, J. A. (2023). A framework for the evidence-based practice of therapeutic jurisprudence: A legal therapeutic alliance. *International Journal of Law and Psychiatry, 89*, 101906.

Hunt, J. (2024a). Toward the emancipation of "medically unexplained" and energy-limiting conditions: Contesting and reimagining psy through the lens of feminist disability studies. *Feminism & Psychology, 35*(2), 1–19. https://doi.org/10.1177/09593535241267091

Hunt, J. (2024b). Will psychology ever 'join hands' with disability studies? Opportunities and challenges in working towards structurally competent and disability-affirmative psychotherapy for energy limiting conditions. *Medical Humanities, 50*(4), 728–739.

Hunter, J., Majd, I., Kowalski, M., & Harnett, J. E. (2021). Interprofessional communication—a call for more education to ensure cultural competency in the context of traditional, complementary, and integrative medicine. *Global Advances in Health and Medicine, 10*, 1–9. https://doi.org/10.1177/21649561211014107

Ingham, E. (2018). The (physically) wounded healer: The impact of a physical disability on training and development as a counselling psychologist: A case study. *The European Journal of Counselling Psychology, 7*(1), 31–46.

Job Accommodation Network. (2020). *Workplace accommodations: Low cost, high impact.* Retrieved from https://askjan.org/publications/Topic-Downloads.cfm?pubid=962628

Kastrani, T., Deliyanni-Kouimtzi, V., & Athanasiades, C. (2015). Greek female service users' experience of the gendered therapeutic relationship: An interpretative phenomenological analysis. *International Journal for the Advancement of Counselling, 37*, 77–92.

Kinouani, G. (2023). *White minds: Everyday performance, violence and resistance.* Policy Press.

Leite, R. O., & Peluso, P. (2018). The effects of racial and ethnic differences or similarities on the therapeutic alliance. *FAU Undergraduate Research Journal, 7*, 46–46.

Long, L. J. (2022). Black women and white criminal (in) justice. In S. A. Tate & E. Gutiérrez Rodríguez (Eds.), *The Palgrave handbook of critical race and gender* (pp. 307–324). Springer International Publishing. https://doi.org/10.1007/978-3-030-83947-5_20.

Luft, J., & Ingham, H. (1955). The Johari window, a graphic model of interpersonal awareness. In *Proceedings of the Western Training Laboratory in Group Development*. University of California, Los Angeles.

Maharaj, A. S., Bhatt, N. V., & Gentile, J. P. (2021). Bringing it in the room: Addressing the impact of racism on the therapeutic alliance. *Innovations in Clinical Neuroscience, 18*(7–9), 39.

Michaeloudis, M., Karaaslan, B., & Nyoka, T. C. (2023). *Social Class: The next protected characteristic?* Retrieved from Social Class: The next protected characteristic? - RFB Legal.

Ministry of Justice. (2020). *Ethnicity and the criminal justice system statistics 2020* (Table 1.Q.7). Ministry of Justice. https://www.gov.uk/government/statistics/ethnicity-and-the-criminal-justice-system-statistics-2020

Ministry of Justice. (2025). *Intergenerational offending: A narrative review of the literature. Ministry of Justice.* Retrieved from https://assets.publishing.service.gov.uk/media/685ea617c2633bd820a92b71/Final_report_Intergenerational_offending_-_A_review_of_the_literature.pdf

Miserocchi, K. M. (2014). *The effect of therapist white privilege attitudes on service user outcomes and the therapist-service user relationship.* University of Kentucky.

Modir, S., Alfaro, B., Casados, A., & Ruiz, S. (2019). *How cultural stigma impacts those seeking mental health services.* CHOC Children's Health. https://health.choc.org/understanding-the-role-of-cultural-stigma-on-seeking-mental-health-services/

Morrison, T., Wayne, M., Harrison, T., Palmgren, E., & Knudson-Martin, C. (2022). Learning to embody a social justice perspective in couple and family therapy: A grounded theory analysis of mfts in training. *Contemporary Family Therapy, 44*(4), 408–421. https://doi.org/10.1007/s10591-022-09635-8

Nario-Redmond, M. R., Kemerling, A. A., & Silverman, A. (2019). Hostile, benevolent, and ambivalent ableism: Contemporary manifestations. *Journal of Social Issues, 75*(3), 726–756. https://doi.org/10.1111/josi.12337

Naz, S., Gregory, R., & Bahu, M. (2019). Addressing issues of race, ethnicity and culture in CBT to support therapists and service managers to deliver culturally competent therapy and reduce inequalities in mental health provision for BAME service users. *The Cognitive Behaviour Therapist, 12*, e22.

Newberry, M. (2010). The experiences of Black and Minority Ethnic (BME) prisoners in a therapeutic community prison. In E. Sullivan & R. Shuker (Eds.), Grendon and the emergence of forensic therapeutic communities: Developments in research and practice (pp. 305–316). Wiley.

Nieder, T. O., Güldenring, A., Woellert, K., Briken, P., Mahler, L., & Mundle, G. (2020). *Ethical aspects of mental health care for lesbian, gay, bi-, pan-, asexual, and transgender people: A case-based approach. Yale Journal of Biology and Medicine, 93*(4), 593–602. https://doi.org/10.1007/something

Owens, J. (2015). Exploring the critiques of the social model of disability: The transformative possibility of Arendt's notion of power. *Sociology of Health & Illness, 37*(3), 385–403.

Parent Center Hub. (2018). *Supports, Modifications, and accommodations for students*. Retrieved from https://www.parentcenterhub.org/accommodations/

Robertson, L., & Wainwright, J. P. (2020). Black boys' and young men's experiences with criminal justice and desistance in England and Wales: A literature review. *Genealogy, 4*(2), 50. https://doi.org/10.3390/genealogy4020050

Royal College of Speech and Language Therapists. (2023). *Position paper on learning disabilities*. Retrieved from https://www.rcslt.org/speech-and-language-therapy/learning-disabilities/

Sentencing Academy. (2020). *Disproportionality in sentencing for Black, Asian and minority ethnic defendants*. Sentencing Academy. https://www.sentencingacademy.org.uk/disproportionality-in-sentencing-for-black-asian-and-minority-ethnic-defendants/

Shankley, W., & Williams, P. (2020). Minority ethnic groups, policing and the criminal justice system in Britain. *Ethnicity, Race and Inequality in the UK, 51*, 51–70.

Shell, E. M., Hua, J., & Sullivan, P. (2022). Cultural racism and burnout among Black mental health therapists. *Journal of Employment Counseling, 59*(3), 102–110.

The Psyche Sphere. (2025, March). *Cultural differences in the perception of mental illness. The Psyche Sphere*. Retrieved from https://thepsychesphere.com/cultural-differences-in-the-perception-of-mental-illness/

UK Parliament. (2025). *Written questions, answers and statements*. Retrieved from Written questions and answers - Written questions, answers and statements - UK Parliament.

Urban Institute. (2023). *Gender-responsive programming in women's prisons*. Urban Institute. https://www.urban.org/sites/default/files/2023-04/Gender-Responsive%20Programming%20in%20Womens%20Prisons.pdf

Wang, C., Huey, S., & Pan, D. (2021). Therapeutic alliance mediates the effect of directive treatment on subsyndromal depression for Asian and European American students. *Journal of Psychotherapy Integration, 31*(3), 291–301. https://doi.org/10.1037/int0000247

Wang, K., Ostrove, J. M., Manning III, R. B., Fodero, S., Ash, S. L., Whang, J., ... & Lowe, S. R. (2024). Ableism in mental healthcare settings: A qualitative study among US adults with disabilities. *SSM-Qualitative Research in Health, 6*. Article 100498. https://doi.org/10/10.1016/j.ssmqr.2024.100498

Washington University. (2023). *Disability stigma and your patients*. Retrieved from https://agerrtc.washington.edu/info/factsheets/stigma

Why Me? (2024). *LGBTQ+ people in the criminal justice system - Reflections during pride month*. Retrieved from https://why-me.org/2024/lgbtq-people-in-the-criminal-justice-system-reflections-during-pride-month/

Williams, M. T., Chapman, L. K., Wong, J., & Turkheimer, E. (2012). The role of ethnic identity in symptoms of anxiety and depression in African Americans. *Psychiatry Research, 199*(1), 31–36. https://doi.org/10.1016/j.psychres.2012.03.049

Williams, M. T., & La Torre, J. (2022). *Clinical supervision in delivering cognitive behavior therapy across race, ethnicity, and culture*. American Psychological Association, 256–287.

Wills, S., Robbins, L., Ward, T., & Christopher, G. (2018). Significant therapy events with service users with intellectual disabilities. *Advances in Mental Health and Intellectual Disabilities, 12*(5/6), 173–183. https://doi.org/10.1108/amhid-07-2018-0033

World Health Organization, & World Bank. (2011). *World report on disability*. World Health Organization.

3 A trauma-informed approach to boundaries in forensic settings

From "that's wrong", to "what's going on between us?"

Phil Willmot and Jo Shingler

Introduction

Forensic psychology's approach to professional boundaries has tended to focus on the ethical perspective. The literature has guided us in how to keep ourselves safe from attempts at boundary crossings by clients and how to avoid over-involved boundary transgressions that can cause significant harm (e.g. Gabbard, 2017; Gutheil & Brodsky, 2011). While ethical practice is, of course, important, examining boundary issues purely through an ethical lens overlooks the psychological aspects of relational patterns – both our own and those of our clients – and closes off opportunities to change relational patterns. In this chapter, we will present the literature which supports the need to understand the psychology of boundary issues in forensic psychological work. Our perspective is that taking a trauma-informed, formulation approach to boundary issues provides greater opportunity for learning and growth, without compromising ethical practice. We will discuss how to integrate a trauma-informed formulation approach into our work and discuss some principles by which we can monitor our own boundary-related behaviour with our clients across forensic settings. To start though, we will briefly outline the reasons why we think a chapter like this has a place in a book about relational practice.

We begin with some definitions.

Although we will come to critique it later, we start with the widely used definition from Gutheil and Brodsky (2011), who defined *therapeutic boundaries* as "the edge of appropriate behaviour at a given moment in the relationship between patient and therapist, as governed by the therapeutic context and contract" (p. 18).

Gutheil and Gabbard (1993) defined two other relevant concepts. A *boundary crossing* is a deviation from regular therapeutic activity that is harmless, non-exploitative and possibly supportive of therapy, for example allowing a session to over-run with a patient who is highly distressed. In contrast, a *boundary violation* is harmful or potentially harmful both to client and therapy because it involves abusing the therapeutic relationship to exploit the client.

DOI: 10.4324/9781003542377-5

Our professional relationships with our clients are different from other relationships on a number of dimensions (see Austin et al., 2006):

- The power we hold in relation to the other person.
- The flow of information (from them and to us) is not reciprocal.
- The purpose of the relationship: we are meeting the needs either of the individual we are working with (e.g. in therapy or stabilisation/psycho-educational work) OR of the institution/system (e.g. in a psychological risk assessment). We never prioritise our own needs.

Therefore, the way we manage our relationships is central to our ability to meet the goals of the task we are undertaking. Consequently, our awareness of the intersubjective space (i.e. the uniqueness of the relationship that is created between two individuals) has to remain in the foreground.

The authors of this chapter work in very different forensic settings. JS works in a community forensic service; PW works in a high secure psychiatric hospital. In writing this chapter, we have discussed the very different physical and relational environments in which we work, and this has enabled us to identify several core principles that we believe apply across all forensic settings.

In forensic settings, in prison, hospital and the community, we often work with people who have trouble managing relational boundaries. We must therefore keep in mind that the management of boundary crossings and violations is the responsibility of the professional, not of the client. This position brings specific challenges in forensic settings, where clients are often labelled as "boundary pushers". Take this extract from a report as an example:

> ... my concern would be if X were to become overfamiliar with their keyworker and start to blur boundaries.

This extract clearly places the responsibility for the blurring of boundaries with X, the client. Yet it is our responsibility as the professional to maintain our awareness of boundary issues and to notice behaviours by clients that push at our boundaries, thereby enabling us to maintain the safe space both for ourselves and our clients. This is not to say we are responsible for our clients' behaviour, nor for their "boundary pushing". However, we are responsible for our responses and for ensuring these are compassionate, based on psychological formulation, and that they provide opportunity for learning and growth: we will explore these issues in more depth later. There is a risk in forensic practice that we blame and label clients for not respecting relational boundaries, despite the evidence that boundaries are disrupted by trauma (see below). Our view is that it is more helpful, respectful and therapeutic to formulate clients' boundary crossings, or attempts at boundary crossings, in the context of their relational experiences, and to formulate our own responses and the consequences of these responses within the relational dyad. In this chapter, we will reflect on how we might do that in practice.

As a caveat, though, our focus on clinician behaviour and attitudes around boundaries does not remove responsibility from companies, organisations and professional bodies for providing guidance, support and supervision to clinicians working with people with challenging presentations in challenging contexts (see Evershed, 2011 for some advice for these groups).

Finally, in writing this chapter, we wrestled with the question of how to refer to the people we work with in forensic psychological practice (we realise this is a well-trodden path). We prefer "people" or "individuals", in order to keep the humanity of the people we work with front and centre. However, this risks masking the clear and present power dynamics within forensic psychological relationships, something we cannot shy away from if we are to manage our boundaries effectively and compassionately. We have therefore opted for consistency with the broader literature on relational boundaries (which is largely related to relationships in psychotherapy) and used "client", in order to keep in our collective minds, for the duration of this chapter anyway, the particular nature of relationships in our work.

The unique challenges of maintaining good relational boundaries in forensic populations

Crime and antisocial behaviour are, by definition, boundary violations, and our forensic clients have all violated boundaries, often repeatedly and in many different ways (Aiyegbusi & Kelly, 2012).

Managing boundaries in forensic services is uniquely challenging for a number of reasons. Firstly, rates of childhood adversity are high among forensic populations (Malvaso et al., 2022; Reavis et al., 2013) Children learn to regulate themselves and their boundaries with others through their attachment relationships with their carers (Fonagy & Target, 1997). Experiences of childhood abuse and neglect impact on the child's sense of identity and boundaries. It should therefore be expected that survivors of childhood maltreatment may struggle to regulate relational boundaries.

Secondly, power dynamics in forensic settings are complex and nuanced. Professional codes of practice and ethical guides stress the power differential that exists between professional and client, particularly when the client is detained in prison or hospital. However, as Boyle (2022) has pointed out, there are various forms of power (e.g. economic power, interpersonal power, social capital), and while practitioners may hold many types of power, forensic clients may hold considerable coercive power that is manifested in their anti-authority attitudes and ability to coerce others and subvert formal power structures. Therefore, the "boundary line" is more challenging to identify and navigate: if we want people to engage with us, then we need to be able to negotiate rules and expectations, including boundaries. If we stick to an inflexible definition of what is professionally acceptable, we are likely to trigger anti-authority patterns and alienate people. However, if we allow ourselves to be entirely led by our clients, we firstly put ourselves at risk of boundary crossing and secondly miss opportunities for people to learn about appropriate boundaries in relationships.

Thirdly, when compared to therapeutic relationships in similar health or social care settings, relationships in forensic settings can be long-lasting and intense. Long-term prisoners may be in daily contact with some prison officers for many years, and similar patterns may apply with long-term forensic patients and health care professionals. Especially in services for people with personality difficulties, the longevity, consistency and strength of the relationship is central to effective practice (Critchfield & Benjamin, 2006). In such circumstances, professional and client may get to know each other very well and boundaries may shift considerably.

Finally, the relationship between forensic professional and forensic client is multi-faceted. Professionals have a duty of care towards the people they look after. They also have a duty to rehabilitate and to protect the public, which may involve challenging antisocial behaviour and attitudes, reporting on risk, restricting their clients' liberty and in some settings, physically restraining them. Front line custodial and healthcare staff may be engaging in all of these activities with the same person in the same day. This means that our boundaries must be dynamic and individualised, if we are to be effective.

The impact of childhood trauma on boundaries

Maltreatment of any kind, but particularly in childhood, involves violation of physical and/or psychological boundaries. Studies have consistently found that survivors of all forms of childhood abuse and neglect prefer greater interpersonal distance when being approached by others (Hautle et al., 2024; Lüönd et al., 2022), whether friends or strangers (Haim-Nachum et al., 2022). Similar patterns have been found with war veterans diagnosed with posttraumatic stress disorder (Bogović et al., 2016), suggesting that trauma at any stage of life may disrupt relational boundaries.

Child sexual abuse involves a clear violation of the victim's boundaries; a number of studies have investigated the impact of child sexual abuse on the boundaries of (mainly female) adult survivors. Davis and Petretic-Jackson (2000) identified three patterns of boundary behaviours in intimate relationships among adult survivors. One involved fear of intimacy and mistrust of others, with sexual relationships tending to be casual and transient and the survivor ending the relationship if it became intimate. A second pattern involved the active avoidance of intimacy and sexuality, while the third pattern involved a need to be in a relationship, regardless of the risks or consequences, making the survivor vulnerable to repeated abuse.

DiLillo and Damashek (2003) reviewed studies of the parenting characteristics of mothers who had survived childhood sexual abuse. They reported that some survivor mothers tended to regard their child as a friend, rely on them for emotional support and struggle to set limits for their child. Conversely, other survivor mothers regarded themselves as less skilled as parents and some were reluctant to engage in physically intimate activities such as changing nappies or bathing their child. Relatedly, Musetti et al. (2012) found that adolescents with a history of childhood emotional neglect were more likely to develop emotionally detached relationships with their parents.

To summarise, the above studies highlight the clear yet complex impact of childhood neglect and abuse on the ability to maintain effective relational boundaries.

Another source of information on the impact of child sexual abuse on boundaries comes from accounts of adult survivors in therapy. Kia-Keating et al. (2010) examined the relational challenges faced by adult male survivors of child sexual abuse and the processes by which they improved their ability to seek and maintain healthy relationships in adulthood. Kia-Keating et al. identified four themes (setting boundaries, managing anger, learning to trust and developing intimacy) of which "setting boundaries" was described as "perhaps the most important" (p. 676). Most of the men's learning about boundaries came from therapy and involved both learning to understand and define boundaries and experiencing a relationship in which boundaries were maintained.

Harper (2006) investigated perceptions of boundaries among therapists and male and female adult survivors of child sexual abuse. Participants perceived boundary decisions as central to therapy, and Harper stressed the importance of discussing boundary decisions with these clients so that they understand them and develop a sense of agency in relation to boundaries.

Finally, Schneiderman et al. (2023) studied the narratives of adults who had experienced childhood maltreatment of various kinds, had been under the care of children's services, and reported positive psychosocial well-being as adults. Participants described four themes in their recovery process; seeing themselves in a good light, moving forward, coping with life and meaning making. One element of coping was learning to set boundaries in relation to abusive family members and risky behaviours.

These studies clearly illustrate how effective therapy for survivors of relational trauma allows them to experience a relationship in which healthy boundaries are maintained and to learn about the processes and dynamics of relationship boundaries, thereby enabling them to manage their own interpersonal boundaries more effectively.

Over-involvement and under-involvement

Scott (1993) drew on Systems Theory and Psychodynamic Theory to develop a theory of human boundaries. She refers to *personal space boundaries (PSBs)* as the permeable, flexible and "dynamic lines of demarcation between an individual's internal (body, mind, and spirit) and external environments" (p. 12). *Boundary permeability* is defined as "the degree to which an individual makes themselves available for interaction with others and open to change"; *boundary flexibility* is "the degree to which an individual is able to change their level of permeability in response to internal or external needs or threats". People contract their boundaries in response to threat or expand them when they feel safe or comfortable. Boundaries thereby act as a "filtering device to protect individuals" from overload, threat or intrusion or violation (Scott, 1993, p. 12). Childhood abuse can trigger a loss of trust and a sense of powerlessness and vulnerability, as well as an inability to manage the permeability or flexibility of boundaries (Geanellos, 2003). Consequently, boundaries can become "like brick walls or filmy netting; that is, too closed or too open" (p. 189). People who are unable to open their personal boundary to others may appear aloof or rude and may miss social cues and opportunities for intimacy; they may be isolated, with few friends. Conversely, people who open their boundaries indiscriminately may be experienced by others as overbearing or intrusive and put themselves at risk of further harm.

These patterns appear similar to what Daniels (2008) and Hamilton (2010) describe as under-involvement and over-involvement in professional relationships. Daniels described a continuum ranging between under-involvement (being overly distant, for example, avoiding individuals, being disinterested in them or treating them harshly) and over-involvement (being overfamiliar), while Hamilton (2010) described a similar continuum ("the boundary see-saw", p. 187) between under-involvement (emotionally cold, formal, judgemental and controlling) and over-involvement (placating, indulging, overly accepting, self-sacrificing, emotionally close, wanting to give unconditional care or to "rescue" patients).

Professionals have been more concerned about over-involvement and its potential for boundary violations. This is arguably because of the more obvious and extreme consequences of over-involvement. Examples of over-involvement may be widely reported, particularly if they involve sexual boundary violations, with widespread distress caused to the client, the professional, the organisation in which the over-involvement occurred and the wider professional group to which the "offending" professional belongs.

In contrast, under-involvement is less likely to lead to complaints and disciplinary action and may often go unnoticed. It is perhaps not surprising, therefore, that organisations pay more attention to preventing over-involvement than to preventing under-involvement. However, it has been argued (Daniels, 2008; Peternelj-Taylor, 2002) that under-involvement should be taken seriously, and the literature on the links between childhood adversity and later difficulties in managing boundaries suggests that under-involvement and over-involvement by professionals are ethically equivalent. Examples of potentially harmful under-involvement, or "withholding", might include adhering rigidly to a session plan when the client is in crisis, ignoring or dismissing a client's expression of distress, or assuming that because a client is quiet and does not ask for help, they do not want or need help. Under-involvement is the opposite of a respectful, human-to-human approach (Shingler et al., 2017) that shows someone that they matter (Stickney & Lowenstein, 2024). If we are not experienced as human in ourselves, then we are unable to engage with people on a human level and we risk losing legitimacy (Shingler, 2018). For clients who have experienced childhood neglect, under-involved caring can re-traumatise and reinforce core beliefs that they are unworthy of care or that others cannot be relied upon to care for them, and can perpetuate unhelpful patterns of relating to others.

Summary

We draw several conclusions from this review of the literature:

- People learn about boundaries through relationships, particularly early attachment relationships. Experiences of abuse or neglect within these relationships can affect relational behaviour, in particular (for the purposes of this chapter) the navigation of interpersonal boundaries. Trauma can impact on the ability to tolerate closeness (leading to under-involvement and detachment in relationships). It can also lead to enmeshment and a need for closeness (leading to over-involvement and inability to tolerate perceived abandonment).
- Trauma can affect professionals and their relational boundaries, as well as clients.
- Relational under-involvement and over-involvement are equally damaging to personal and professional relationships.

Professional relationships provide a good (and in some cases the only) opportunity for clients to learn about relational boundaries and to learn new patterns of engagement. As discussed above, forensic clients are disproportionately likely to have experienced relational trauma and consequently are more likely to have had their relational boundaries disrupted. Some clients may tend towards under-involvement, presenting as cold, withdrawn or aloof, while others may tend towards over-involvement, presenting as over-friendly, flirtatious or intrusive. Some clients may swing between these two presentations (de Zulueta, 2006). Equally, as professionals, we bring our own tendencies towards under- and/or over-involvement to our therapeutic relationships. These tendencies will interact with those of our clients. We therefore face two equal and opposite traps: responding dismissively to the client who appears withdrawn or aloof, and responding warmly to the client who is intrusive and over-friendly, both of which might be the natural response to such presentations outside the professional setting, but which risk reinforcing those patterns of behaviour. Instead, both over-involved and under-involved clients need the opportunity and space to reflect upon and learn about boundaries and to experience an appropriately boundaried relationship. Relatedly, as professionals, we need to have good insight into our own boundary patterns and be able to identify within ourselves patterns that indicate or precipitate under- or over-involvement. Navigating boundaries in our forensic practice is as much about formulating our own relational boundaries as it is about those of the person with whom we are working.

A trauma-informed approach to boundaries

We have a challenge in how we think about boundaries. We have tended to think of our own boundaries primarily through an ethical lens, in terms of whether a particular behaviour is "appropriate" or "inappropriate". Unfortunately, that perspective often infects the way we think about our clients, so that we label and dismiss their "inappropriate" behaviours as "manipulative", "grooming", "splitting" or "pushing boundaries" or as "detached", "avoidant" or "unmotivated" without seeking to understand why they keep behaving in that way. Consequently, boundaries become a shameful taboo subject both for practitioners and for clients and we avoid discussing them, while feeling annoyed and frustrated that the problem persists! Once we recognise that difficulties in managing boundaries are often a response to trauma, we can avoid unhelpful stigmatising responses and respond just as we would to any other trauma response, by formulating with the client the need that behaviour originally met and discussing how to meet that need more effectively now. Good awareness of our own boundary patterns allows us to also pay attention to our responses to our clients and to examine the interaction between our boundaries. To adapt a popular slogan of trauma-informed practice, we need to move from "That's wrong" to "what's going on between us?"

For children who grow up with a secure attachment to their carers the attachment relationship reliably provides both safety and connection (Bowlby, 1969). However, children who grow up with abusive or neglectful care may be unable to achieve both needs simultaneously: connection to an abusive or neglectful carer carries the risk of physical or psychological harm, while avoiding or maintaining superficial relations with that carer preserves the child's safety at the expense of emotional connection. We propose a reframing of interpersonal boundaries as "a dynamic balance between the fundamental human needs for safety and for connection with others".

A trauma-informed definition of professional boundaries

At the start of this chapter, we mentioned Gutheil and Brodsky's (2011) definition of therapeutic boundaries as "the edge of appropriate behaviour at a given moment in the relationship between patient and therapist, as governed by the therapeutic context and contract". This is a definition that emphasises the dynamic and context-specific nature of therapeutic boundaries. However, as we have noted, the word *appropriate* reflects an ethical rather than a trauma-informed psychological framing of boundaries. Additionally, the term "appropriate" is usually poorly defined, making it difficult to apply it meaningfully to our practice. We would therefore propose adapting the definition of Gutheil and Brodsky as follows:

> Therapeutic boundaries are defined as behaviours that balance both parties' need for connection and safety at a given moment in the relationship between client and therapist, as governed by the therapeutic context and contract.

This definition emphasises that the professional is not an impassive automaton in therapeutic relationships, but that both parties have their own feelings, needs and vulnerabilities. While the needs of the client should take precedence, this does not mean that the needs of the professional should be completely ignored or suppressed. Indeed, it has been argued that doing so increases the risk of boundary violations (Gabbard, 2017). Particularly in forensic settings, professionals need to be mindful of their own physical and psychological safety as well as the safety of their clients. When we refer to the professional's need for connection, we are primarily referring to the fact that in many models of therapy, a safe, secure and containing therapeutic relationship is an essential element of treatment. However, we should also acknowledge that the need for connection to others is a fundamental human need that therapists cannot and should not "switch off" when they enter the therapy space.

We will now go on to discuss how to manage boundaries within forensic professional relationships. We will discuss how to understand and formulate problematic boundary behaviour in the light of our revised definition of boundaries and how a formulation-based approach enables us to respond with compassion, humanity and support for change; and how to identify and manage our own personal and professional boundaries in order to maintain safety and effectiveness.

Identifying and managing boundaries in forensic psychological work

As clinicians and supervisors, we spend time reflecting on boundaries in our practice, but there is little explicit guidance in the literature about how to identify one's own boundaries. Relatedly, aside from serious boundary violations (such as sexual contact between professional and client; and the giving and receiving of items of high monetary value), there is little agreement on what constitutes an appropriate professional boundary, and likewise, what constitutes a boundary crossing (Evershed, 2011). This is probably because, as noted above, the literature generally agrees that professional boundaries must be flexible and adaptable and that boundaries differ across contexts, across theoretical models, across individual professionals and across different clients. While most organisations have policies on professional boundaries, there is, paradoxically, a view that boundaries cannot be defined or mandated by rules or guidance and must be responded to in the moment and discussed, reflected on and refined in professional supervision. As Gutheil and Brodsky (2011) note:

> In the unpredictable give-and-take between patient and therapist, most rules eventually break down or prove inadequate.
>
> (p. 32)

This makes the identification of our own personal boundaries challenging. We need to reflect on our boundaries in our work in order to keep ourselves safe; to enable us to continue practising in challenging circumstances; to enable us to hold and contain others' distress while minimising the impact on ourselves and our health; and to ensure that we work appropriately within a team, sharing information and supporting and/or challenging our colleagues as needed. We also need to keep the people we work with safe, and create a warm, empathic and understanding space in which clients can make themselves vulnerable in order to process and overcome trauma and learn new skills. We need to provide a model of relational boundaries that people can apply to other relationships in their lives: a model of respectful, kind and human relating that does not harm or subjugate either party. As noted above, victims of childhood abuse often do their learning about relational boundaries in therapy. While we might not define all (or even any) of our work as forensic practitioners as "therapy", we still have opportunities in our professional contact with clients to provide learning opportunities about relational boundaries, so it is an important area for us to consider. While we are in agreement that professional relational boundaries cannot be mandated or manualised, we do think we can provide guidance that might help us to formulate boundary issues, identify our personal relational boundaries and navigate boundary issues in our professional practice. The next section is aimed at facilitating reflective discussion about these areas.

Responding to boundary crossings

We need to think about how we use boundary crossing as a means of providing a learning opportunity about appropriate relational boundaries. This may require us to shift in our practice, to use supervision to help us to do this safely and meaningfully, and to avoid stepping into our own safety seeking behaviour when a client attempts to cross our boundaries – namely by withdrawing/withholding, activating our "under-involved" mode. It is our responsibility as professionals to notice and formulate boundary crossings and formulate a psychologically informed response that provides an opportunity for the client to learn about relational boundaries, possibly using the following questions to help us:

- What was the person's experience of relationships in their formative years? How did these experiences affect their relational boundaries? How are those patterns playing out now?
- How do I feel in my relationship with X? What is triggered in me by their behaviour within our professional relationship? What can I learn about them from this?
- What learning opportunities does X need to enable them to have a corrective boundary experience?
- How should I act to maintain my own professional boundaries, keep myself safe, at the same time as enabling learning and growth in the individual?

Below, we have provided composite examples from our own clinical practice that illustrate how we have approached boundary formulation. It is important to note that our examples below are about *formulating the relationship* – not purely formulating the client. We cannot meaningfully understand boundary issues without paying attention to our own relational tendencies within the specific context. Readers will therefore notice that, in the examples, we have attended both to the experiences and tendencies of our clients and of ourselves.

Box 1   Formulating relational boundaries in an in-patient setting

Background: John is the youngest of five children. He has a different father from his siblings, and while they all maintained regular contact with their father, John has never met his own father. Growing up, he was often made aware of this and felt different and excluded by his elder siblings. This was made worse by the fact that, as the youngest child, he received more care and attention from his mother, which sometime led to resentment by his siblings.

By the time John was 14, all his siblings had left home. When his mother was diagnosed with breast cancer, John took on much of the responsibility for caring for her over the next three years, leaving school at 15 without any qualifications to be at home with her until she eventually died when John was 17.

After his mother's death John became increasingly withdrawn and isolated. He was diagnosed with depression and began drinking heavily and abusing prescribed medication. After several attempts to kill himself, he was admitted to a mental health unit. He quickly recovered and was discharged but relapsed almost immediately and was readmitted. A cycle developed where he would be admitted, his mental health would improve and he would be noted to become overly attached and emotionally dependent on one particular (usually female) member of staff. He would protest when efforts were made to discharge him or limit his access to that member of staff. This cycle repeated until he took a member of staff hostage after she told him she was being moved to a different ward.

As a result of that incident, at the age of 21, John is now detained under the Mental Health Act in a medium secure hospital with a diagnosis of borderline personality disorder. He regards himself as different from the other patients as he is "not a criminal" and instead prefers to associate with staff. Because he is quite prosocial and friendly he is generally well liked by staff, though he is noted to "have his favourites" who he will monopolise. Some staff regard him as "overfamiliar and a bit creepy". When the ward is busy or short-staffed he can become demanding and angry if he feels his needs are not being met.

John's relational boundaries are over-involved: he seeks connection and support from people he sees as caring towards him to avoid feelings of vulnerability and isolation.

My natural position is probably towards the under-involved side of the boundaries see-saw, so I notice myself feeling uncomfortable and sometimes irritated that he always seems to seek me out to talk to and that my sessions with him tend to over-run. I know that trying to impose tighter boundaries may well draw an angry response from him which could either damage our relationship or mean I have to spend even more time with him trying to reassure him.

What can I learn about John's experiences and presentation? John needs to feel connected to others to feel safe. Without that sense of connection he feels abandoned, isolated and helpless, because experience has taught him that he is unable to cope without the support of others. John needs opportunities to tolerate being alone, to develop confidence in his own ability to be independent and trust that others are reliable and will keep him in mind when they are not with him. I need to create opportunities for him to tolerate not having his needs met immediately and to recognise that he can cope.

To maintain my boundaries, I need to distinguish between my personal emotional response to John, which is to feel slightly "smothered" by his constant attention and want to withdraw, and what I think John needs, which is to have clear boundaries and to not need my support all the time. I also need to be mindful of the risk of going too far the other way on the boundaries see-saw and of responding to his angry protests by trying to placate and reassure him which, in behavioural terms, is likely to be a positive reinforcer for his protest behaviour. Finally, I must avoid the temptation to pass the problem onto somebody else (most likely a nursing colleague who, unlike me, doesn't have the option of avoiding John).

Box 2   Formulating relational boundaries in a community setting

Background: Amy's background was one of cruelty and emotional deprivation. She was harshly punished with violence for minor transgressions; she was locked in her bedroom alone as a punishment. She witnessed significant violence both within and outside of the home, as family members were involved in crime and antisocial behaviour. She was placed in care where she witnessed sexual abuse of her peers. She was aggressive from an early age and reflects that her aggression protected her from being sexually victimised.

Amy reported no childhood experiences of being cared for, protected or valued. People either exploited and abused her or were indifferent to her, ignoring her or shutting her away.

Amy served a prison sentence for a violent crime. For most of her sentence she refused to engage with professionals, speaking to prison staff only when she absolutely had to.

Amy's relational behaviour is mistrusting and suspicious because of her childhood mistreatment. She is unable to show vulnerability for fear of being exploited; she keeps a distance from people and does not allow anyone to get close. She guards her personal information and her privacy tightly. She resents people asking questions about her life.

Amy's relational boundaries are under-involved: this approach protects her from harm.

How do I feel in my relationship with Amy: I sit more towards the over-involved end of the boundary see-saw. At times I feel on edge with Amy, feeling that any mis-step on my part will result in her ending our therapeutic relationship. I can feel that sessions are superficial and repetitive and at times I question how helpful they are to her. I think that if I suggested we ended our sessions she would not try to persuade me otherwise – she would accept it without any overt expression of loss or fear of abandonment. This puts me at risk of trying to move closer to her psychologically, in order to try harder to connect – she would likely find this aversive and withdraw further.

What can I learn about Amy's experiences and presentation: Her response to others is "keep a distance or put yourself at risk" – this is physical as well as relational, she finds it difficult being in crowded spaces and does not like it when people walk too closely past her in the street. Amy is used to not being noticed; she is used to saying "I'm fine" and this being accepted. People have not been motivated to connect with Amy in her life.

Amy needs opportunities to feel safe in connection, to learn that showing vulnerability does not lead to harm, and also to experience the benefits of connection. I need to create opportunities for her to show a little vulnerability, and for this to be safe and beneficial.

To maintain my boundaries, I need to remain awake to my desire for connection and to Amy's fear of connection – if I move too close to the centre of the boundary see-saw, it will cause her to back off. However, I also need to be mindful of Amy's distance – I must not judge myself as incompetent because she seems dismissive at times – I must not respond to her dismissiveness with rejection, and suggestion that we terminate intervention. This is what she has been used to, and this would reinforce her under-involved approach. I need to use supervision to keep myself relationally balanced with Amy – not stepping too close, yet not withdrawing prematurely.

It may help us when formulating our own boundary-related behaviour to return to the unique nature of forensic psychological relationships: the power imbalance; the lack of reciprocity in information sharing; the prioritisation of the client's needs. Contemplating these things may allow us to begin to explore and clarify our own personal limits. How do we feel about the power we hold? How do we feel about the imbalance of shared information? How well are our own needs being met currently in our lives? The better we are at self-care and the more effectively our needs are met in our personal lives, the less vulnerable we are to boundary crossings (Gutheil & Brodsky, 2011). Therefore, if we have struggles in our personal lives or if we have experienced an emotionally distressing event, we may want to alter our limits to keep ourselves safe. This brings us to our final discussion: how we navigate our relational boundaries in the context of our forensic psychological practice. As we have already noted, this area does not lend itself to rules, guidelines or manualisation. Our relationships with our clients are as unique as we are, and as they are. We have therefore focused on a set of principles by which we can regulate and reflect on boundary-related behaviour in our work.

Principle #1: Define and remain within your own, individual, intersubjective, collaborative therapeutic frame

Gutheil and Brodsky (2011) discuss the "therapeutic frame": namely the containment of the therapeutic role within a framework that defines the nature of the space and the relationship. The therapeutic frame can consist of the location, timing, duration of appointments; agreement on goals, methods and purpose of contact. It allows the client to be clear about the therapist's motives and to feel safe in the therapeutic space. The frame is created by the therapist and the client in a way that makes sense for their uniqueness as two individuals within their unique context. Frame can be altered by mutual discussion and agreement. We need to set limits within the therapeutic frame in order for the client to learn about appropriate relationships and boundaries. Returning to our conceptualisation of our own therapeutic frame within a specific professional relationship can provide a model for reflecting on and managing boundary issues. When you face a boundary dilemma, go back to your role, purpose and goals: is your proposed action (or the action you have already taken) helpful in the context of your role, goals, purpose? If not, then why are you proposing it? What is pulling you towards wanting to do it? If you have done it, and it is not appropriate, what was going on that pulled you towards that course of action? Clarity about the therapeutic frame enables us to respond more effectively and consistently to requests and demands (from both clients and other professionals).

Principle #2: Formulate our own reactions and responses to clients and how these affect our relational boundaries

We need to remain aware of our own feelings, thoughts and urges within our professional encounters with clients. We need to use supervision and reflective practice to understand how the relational dynamic has created our reactions. We need to reflect on what it is about the client, their patterns, their relational behaviour that triggers our emotional reactions and how our emotions underpin behavioural urges and responses, and we need to use reflective time to understand our reactions. It can be helpful to think:

- Would I do this/have I done this with another client?
- If yes, then what is different about this specific person that is making me question my behaviour?
- If not, why not? What is different about this situation that is making me want to behave differently?

We need to notice urges to cross boundaries, either by stepping closer to the individual or by any desire to withdraw, to punish or to reject the client. Use supervision or reflective team discussion to explore this reaction and identify what has triggered it.

We all have a natural position on the spectrum between over-involvement and under-involvement (on the "boundary see-saw", Hamilton, 2010), where we feel most comfortable. This is probably shaped by our own experiences and attachment styles. Unless that position is at either extreme of that spectrum, then it is neither right nor wrong. Don't feel ashamed or defective because your natural position is different to your colleagues. Therapeutic relationships need to provide corrective boundary experiences, and part of that is clients learning that we all have slightly different relational boundaries. What is important is that we adjust our position to suit the needs of our clients: that our boundaries are both flexible and permeable at times in order to provide that corrective experience.

Principle #3: Focus on providing a corrective boundaries experience to the client

As with other aspects of our work, start by developing a collaborative formulation of the client's boundary behaviour. Avoid stigmatising terms like "pushing boundaries" or "manipulation". Aim for a shared understanding of how early attachment experiences have shaped current patterns of behaviour and boundaries. Be explicit about how the therapeutic relationship should offer a safe base for testing out different approaches to boundaries (notice the balance of safety and challenge here – the safe space enables the testing of relational behaviours, Linehan, 1993). For clients who tend towards avoidance and under-involvement, interactions should empathically and sensitively challenge their avoidance. For patients with a more intrusive or needy style who tend towards over-involvement, interactions should sensitively and empathically explain and enforce clear boundaries and encourage them to tolerate and manage feelings of rejection or loneliness. For clients who switch between over-involvement and under-involvement, interactions should focus on maintaining consistent boundaries.

Principle #4: Only engage/intervene in a way that is primarily for the benefit of the client

The question of "cui bono?": "for whose benefit?" should be central to our boundary discussions and reflections (Gutheil & Brodsky, 2011). All of our therapeutic interventions and planned activities should be for the benefit either of the person we are working with or for the "system" (e.g. if we are directed to produce a psychological risk assessment for a parole board): contact with a client should never be about meeting our own needs. If we find ourselves acting in our own interests, then we are crossing a boundary in a way that is likely to be unhelpful in the longer term, even if our behaviour is seemingly appropriate. Self-disclosure is a behaviour that can often be aided by consideration of "cui bono?": if I share this information about myself, will it benefit the client? An example of this might be describing the steps we took to overcome a specific problem in our lives. We can model good problem solving. However, sharing a current problem we are experiencing is more likely to be about our need to offload/be validated, than it is to be about supporting or enabling change in the client.

Of course, there may be times when we must act to protect our own safety, which may be detrimental to the client. For example, we may decide to end a session early or put the phone down on someone if they are being abusive or aggressive. There is an argument that this is an opportunity to model effective relational boundaries: *I will not continue to engage with you if you shout at me*, and we would of course have attempted to soothe and support the individual to self-regulate ahead of any termination decisions. The issue of "cui bono?" is more to do with our therapeutic interventions: if we find ourselves asking questions or sharing personal information that does not serve the therapeutic purpose, then we need to stop and use reflective supervision to understand our decision-making.

Principle #5: Adopt a whole team approach to boundaries. Avoid "splitting"

Forensic clients are often accused of "splitting" teams; that is, of behaving differently towards different team members in order to "manipulate" or subvert. If we are tempted to blame a client in this way, we should ask ourselves, "who are the professionals in this situation? Why are we allowing this to happen?" If, for example, we have a client who demands a lot of time and care in order to feel safe and connected, we should not be surprised if they start to idolise and monopolise the colleague who gives them lots of attention. Nor should we be surprised if they are hostile and dismissive towards the colleague who does not. By blaming the client for this, we are simply reinforcing old and unhealthy ways of managing boundaries. Remembering principle 2, it is also not helpful either to blame the first colleague for being "too soft" or to blame the second colleague for being "too strict". Instead, teams need to have a shared formulation of the client's boundary behaviour and to be honest with each other about their own boundary styles. This enables colleagues to support each other, avoids colleagues becoming isolated or burnt out and, most importantly, maintains safe practice alongside providing clients with corrective boundary experiences. Reflective practice offers a valuable opportunity for teams to discuss and explore these issues.

Principle #6: Be open, reflective, curious and humble about boundaries

Boundaries in forensic settings are perhaps uniquely complex and dynamic, and practitioners should start from a position of recognising that, no matter how wise or experienced, none of us will get them right all the time. The act of reflecting and openly discussing boundary issues is essential to maintaining healthy boundaries. If you are unsure whether to speak or act in a certain way, then ask yourself, "How do I feel when I contemplate discussing this behaviour in supervision/a team meeting/ward round?" An urge not to discuss something or a self-narrative that convinces you it is not necessary is probably information that you absolutely should discuss it in supervision.

We may be more inclined to reflect on relationships where we are concerned about crossing boundaries, but it is equally important to reflect on therapeutic relationships that feel safe and predictable. Use supervision to understand the nature of a "safe" relationship. Creating a safe space is crucial if people are to address painful issues, but is the safety preventing psychological growth? Linehan (1993) describes how therapists need to create imbalance in the therapeutic relationship in order for growth to occur. If we stay within a safe space that is never challenged, we miss opportunities for growth. If a relationship feels safe and predictable, ask yourself what function it is serving and possibly begin to think about what you are avoiding or fearful of as a professional. Henretty and Levitt's (2010) advice suggests that if we wait until we are in a boundary crisis before we discuss these issues, then we are too late: a boundary issue may arise without warning, and we need to be as prepared as possible via regular reflective discussion about boundaries.

Being open, reflective and curious can help to foster a healthier team culture around boundaries. Sharing our struggles (e.g. "I find my sessions with X always over-run", or "does anybody else find it hard to interact with Y?") will often elicit similar experiences from colleagues and provide an opportunity to formulate what is happening and how to respond in a coordinated way. It also signals that uncertainty and openness about boundary issues are normal and healthy.

There may be times when we have to intervene to challenge the boundary behaviour of colleagues where it is clearly unsafe or unprofessional. There will be other times when we see colleagues behave in ways that make us uncomfortable (perhaps because we would not behave in that way), but where we don't know enough to immediately call it out. We need to reflect on our feelings about colleagues' boundary behaviour – just because we wouldn't do something, doesn't automatically make it a damaging boundary crossing. Perhaps our colleague has different limits to us; perhaps they are more comfortable with a closer connection than we are – something that should be discussed openly in supervision. Ideally, if we are concerned or unsure about a colleague's behaviour, we should approach the colleague sensitively and discuss it with them. A general culture of regular reflective practice will make these (potentially awkward) conversations easier. If it is impossible to discuss issues directly with the colleague, then the next step is a reflective conversation with their line manager.

Boundaries in context

The literature is clear that boundaries cannot be mandated or reduced to a set of guidelines. Context is everything. We mean context in its widest possible sense here: the physical setting; the nature of the relationship (duration, function, purpose); the traits and states of the individuals within the relationship; and the nature of the service within which the relationship exists.

To illustrate the application of our principles, we return to the two composite cases we introduced earlier. We do not provide these examples to demonstrate right or wrong ways of working. We provide them, along with our observations on the six principles of good professional boundaries, as examples of reflective decision-making. As you read them, perhaps use the opportunity to reflect: would you do what we did or not? Why do you think our course of action was right or wrong? What would you do differently and why? How would you formulate these situations from a boundary perspective?

Box 3   Navigating professional boundaries in a high secure service

Background: It's a busy day on the ward. Two patients had a fight last night and are in seclusion. The ward is still tense, and patients are nervous. On top of that, it's ward round day, and there are hardly any regular staff on duty. I know John will be unsettled by the ward dynamics and will want to talk to me because none of the nurses he gets on with are around. As I walk onto the ward, I find myself avoiding eye contact with John because I know he will want to engage me in a trivial (to me) conversation that I don't have time for. I'm also conscious of the knowing looks shared between the other patients whenever John comes to talk to me, which makes me more determined not to meet his eye.

How we engaged with the boundary principles

#1: Define and remain within the therapeutic frame: my role is to enable John to regulate his own emotions and to act independently. This

---

entails him tolerating being alone and trusting that people who are supposed to care for him do so unconditionally (i.e. because they care, not because he demands it) when necessary.

#2: Only engage for the benefit of the service user: John needs opportunities to experience relationships with clear boundaries that still provide reliable and consistent care and connection. That means being able to tolerate times when that connection is absent, knowing that that absence is only temporary.

#3: Be open, reflective, curious and humble about boundaries. I'm conscious of the twin dangers of avoiding John and reinforcing his belief that carers can't be relied upon and of "rescuing" him because he is distressed. I'm not always able to find the balanced middle way, especially in situations like this where I have to think on my feet. So it's important to reflect on my decisions and actions both with my supervisor and with colleagues on the ward who will be left to pick up the pieces if I misjudge this situation.

#4: Focus on providing a corrective boundaries experience: Rather than waiting for John to approach me, I go straight over to him, ask how he is and acknowledge that he must be feeling distressed at the moment. By taking the initiative and approaching him, I'm demonstrating care without him needing to ask for it. I also have more control over the conversation. This allows me to remind him that I'm busy today because of the ward round and then to ask him how he can take care of himself, bearing in mind that none of his favourite staff are around. I also offer (again, before he asks, demonstrating unconditional care) to check in with him just before the evening meal (so that there is a definite end time).

#5: Formulate our own responses: I notice my own reactions to John and my urge to avoid him. That's partly because I'm busy and don't have time for a long conversation and partly because I know from my formulation that "rescuing" John is not actually helping him in the long term. I also notice that the urge is shaped by what colleagues and other patients will think of me and my ability to manage boundaries if I get drawn into a conversation with John. Simply being aware of that urge to avoid helps me not to do it.

#6: Adopt a whole team approach to boundaries: It is likely that once I leave, John will approach other people to seek support. Because there are a number of staff on duty who don't know John, it is likely that his attempts to seek support will either be met with a "dismissive" (to him) response that the person is too busy, or he'll find someone who'll agree to listen to him until they get fed up and tell him they're too busy. I therefore need to alert the team to this danger so that everyone is taking a consistently compassionate yet boundaried approach with him.

Box 4   Navigating professional boundaries in a community forensic service

Background: As a result of difficulties with benefits and accommodation, Amy finds herself in emergency accommodation with little money. Amy's lack of access to basic food provisions is undermining her (already fragile) ability to regulate her emotions. Her under-involved relational style means that she will not show vulnerability by asking for help. She was offered foodbank vouchers by her probation officer, but she declined, saying she could cope.

How we engaged with the boundary principles

#1: Define and remain within the therapeutic frame: my role is to support improvements in self-regulation and to build supportive professional relationships. My role is also to support building trust, enabling Amy to feel visible, cared about and that she matters. Taking steps to meet her basic needs is consistent with these therapeutic aims.

#2: Only engage for the benefit of the service user: Our formulation of Amy as an under-involved individual suggests that being offered practical help and support will expose her vulnerability and therefore could be aversive to her – causing her to reject services and withdraw into a place of safety. However, if Amy is to make progress, she needs to learn to make her boundaries more permeable, to let people in, even a little bit, and learn that this can be beneficial and rewarding. If we can make it safe for her to accept help, it could be therapeutically beneficial for Amy going forward – if it increases her ability to ask for and accept help from professionals. There are also clear immediate benefits to Amy – meeting her basic needs will allow her to manage her emotions more effectively.

#3: Be open, reflective, curious and humble about boundaries: I notice thoughts about wanting to rescue Amy and being the person who got through to her where others had failed. I need to think about whether I am prioritising my own needs over Amy's. I reflect on the extent to which it would feel like an achievement if Amy accepted help from me – am I doing this for my benefit or for Amy's benefit? I need to discuss these issues and my planned intervention in reflective supervision.

#4: Focus on providing a corrective boundaries experience: I agree with the team that I will buy Amy a bag of basic food provisions (using service funds) without her asking and give it to her in my next session. This intervention clearly challenges Amy's relational boundaries. She looks uncomfortable and reluctant to accept the food. I can see she feels threatened and vulnerable and that she wants to with-draw. However, Amy and I have discussed this relational pattern and she recognises it in the here and now: the inability to trust people, the tendency to keep people at arm's length, a strong need for independence. Amy has previously identified that she needs to get better at accepting help, so I present this to her as an opportunity to practice this skill. Amy accepts the donation but also insists on reimbursing the service when she receives her next benefit payment – perhaps to feel more comfortable with it, to restate the relational boundary, and to restate her independence. I accept this given that the corrective boundary experience has occurred through the acceptance of help.

#5: Formulate our own responses: Acknowledging my beliefs of "wanting to rescue" or "wanting to be special" enables me to remain within my therapeutic frame – it enables me to stay awake to opportunities for boundary crossings and how Amy's learning, not my desire to rescue, is the priority. I remain clear on the rationale of the intervention and how it provides an opportunity for experiential learning. As a result of this situation, I have become more in tune with my desire to rescue and therefore more able to challenge this when it arises.

#6: Adopt a whole team approach to boundaries: Amy has been working with several members of our team. We keep in mind the importance of Amy learning to accept help from various sources (professionals or friends). Our formulation of Amy's under-involved style enables us to be more persistent when she is in need. Rather than accepting a response of "I'm fine", we can challenge that in the context of our shared (with Amy) formulation of her tendency to remain detached. It also keeps us awake to oblique requests for help – for example, Amy will say, "I've got a GP appointment on Friday" – we have learned that this is her way of asking someone to go with her. Our shared formulation enables us to notice and reinforce the skill of asking for help, which otherwise could be easily missed.

Conclusion

In this chapter, we have explored how we understand and navigate relational boundaries in forensic psychological practice. Our experience in different forensic settings has allowed us to focus on key principles in navigating boundaries and reflect on how these principles can be applied across settings.

A trauma-informed formulation approach provides us with the most effective way of understanding and responding to boundary issues in our work. We need to move away from blaming and judging clients for their boundary transgressions ("that's wrong") and towards understanding them ("what's going on between us?"). Of course, we may still need to take corrective steps to keep ourselves safe as practitioners, but we take steps from a place of compassionate understanding that provides the best opportunity for change and growth. A focus on the ethics of boundary issues has perhaps prevented us from thinking about boundaries as a response to relational trauma that needs to be understood.

We cannot realistically understand our clients' boundary issues without having a good understanding of our own relational patterns. Throughout this chapter, we have explicitly discussed formulating *the relationship* and not just *the client*. When a boundary issue makes us feel uncomfortable or uncertain (or too comfortable), this is information about the relationship between us and the client: each relationship is unique and needs to be understood and formulated with this in mind.

With the exception of clear ethical breaches, boundaries cannot be mandated by guidance and rules. The boundaries within each relationship are unique. Using the principles from this chapter can assist practitioners to reflect on the importance and value of relational boundaries and how we work with these within forensic practice.

References

Aiyegbusi, A., & Kelly, G. (2012). *Professional and therapeutic boundaries in forensic mental health practice*. Jessica Kingsley.

Austin, W., Bergum, V., Nuttgens, S., & Peternelj-Taylor, C. (2006). A re-visioning of boundaries in professional helping relationships: Exploring other metaphors. *Ethics & Behavior*, 16(2), 77–94. https://doi.org/10.1207/s15327019eb1602_1

Bogović, A., Ivezić, E., & Filipčić, I. (2016). Personal space of war veterans with PTSD – some characteristics and comparison with healthy individuals. *Psychiatria Danubina*, 28(1), 0–81.

Bowlby, J. (1969). *Attachment. Attachment and loss (vol. 1)*. Basic Books.

Boyle, M. (2022). Power in the power threat meaning framework. *Journal of Constructivist Psychology*, 35(1), 27–41. https://doi.org/10.1080/10720537.2020.1773357

Critchfield, K.L., & Benjamin, L.S. (2006). Principles for psychosocial treatment of personality disorder: Summary of the APA Division 12 Task Force/NASPR review. *Journal of Clinical Psychology*, 62(6), 661–674. https://doi.org/10.1002/jclp.20255

Daniels, T.A. (2008). *Boundary violations in forensic inpatient facilities: Survey tool development and survey results* (Unpublished doctoral dissertation). University of Saskatchewan.

Davis, J.L., & Petretic-Jackson, P.A. (2000). The impact of child sexual abuse on adult interpersonal functioning: A review and synthesis of the empirical literature. *Aggression and Violent Behavior*, 5(3), 291–328. https://doi.org/10.1016/S1359-1789(99)00010-5

de Zulueta, F. (2006). Inducing traumatic attachment in adults with a history of child abuse: Forensic applications. *British Journal of Forensic Practice*, 8(3), 4–15. https://doi.org/10.1108/14636646200600015

DiLillo, D., & Damashek, A. (2003). Parenting characteristics of women reporting a history of childhood sexual abuse. *Child Maltreatment*, 8(4), 319–333. https://doi.org/10.1177/1077559503257104

Evershed, S. (2011). The grey areas of boundary issues when working with forensic patients who have a personality disorder. In P. Willmot & N. Gordon (Eds.) *Working positively with personality disorder in secure settings: A practitioner's perspective* (pp. 127–146). Wiley-Blackwell.

Fonagy, P., & Target, M. (1997). Attachment and reflective function: Their role in self-organization. *Development and Psychopathology, 9*(4), 679–700. https://doi.org/10.1017/S0954579497001399

Gabbard, G.O. (2017). Sexual boundary violations in psychoanalysis: A 30-year retrospective. *Psychoanalytic Psychology, 34*(2), 151–156. https://doi.org/10.1037/pap0000079

Geanellos, R. (2003). Understanding the need for personal space boundary restoration in women-client survivors of intrafamilial childhood sexual abuse. *International Journal of Mental Health Nursing, 12*(3), 186–193. https://doi.org/10.1046/j.1440-0979.2003.00288.x

Gutheil, T.G., & Brodsky, A. (2011). *Preventing boundary violations in clinical practice.* Guilford Press.

Gutheil, T.G., & Gabbard, G.O. (1993). The concept of boundaries in clinical practice: Theoretical and risk-management dimensions. *The American Journal of Psychiatry, 150*(2), 188–196. https://doi.org/10.1176/ajp.150.2.188

Haim-Nachum, S., Sopp, R., Lüönd, A., Afzal, N., Åhs, F., Allgaier, A., Arevalo, A., Asongwe, C., Bachem, R., Balle, S.R., Belete, H., Mossie, T.B., Berzengi, A., Capraz, N., Ceylan, D., Dukes, D., Essadek, A., Fares-Otero, N.E., Halligan, S.L. ... Pfaltz, M.C. (2022). Childhood maltreatment is linked to larger preferred interpersonal distances towards friends and strangers across the globe. *Translational Psychiatry, 14*(1), 339–348. https://doi.org/10.31234/osf.io/nvejb

Hamilton, L. (2010). The boundary see-saw model: Good fences make for good neighbours. In A. Tennant & K. Howells (Eds.) *Using time, not doing time* (pp. 181–194). Wiley Blackwell.

Harper, K. (2006). Negotiating therapeutic boundaries with childhood sexual abuse survivors: Choices in decision-making. *Stress, Trauma, and Crisis, 9*(2), 95–117. https://doi.org/10.1080/15434610600683791

Hautle, L.L., Kurath, J., Jellestad, L., Lüönd, A.M., Wingenbach, T.S., Jansson, B., & Pfaltz, M.C. (2024). Larger comfortable interpersonal distances in adults exposed to child maltreatment: The role of depressive symptoms and social anxiety. *British Journal of Psychology, 115*(4), 599–615. https://doi.org/10.1111/bjop.12705

Henretty, J.R., & Levitt, H.M. (2010). The role of therapist self-disclosure in psychotherapy: A qualitative review. *Clinical Psychology Review, 30*(1), 63–77. https://doi.org/10.1016/j.cpr.2009.09.004

Kia-Keating, M., Sorsoli, L., & Grossman, F.K. (2010). Relational challenges and recovery processes in male survivors of childhood sexual abuse. *Journal of Interpersonal Violence, 25*(4), 666–683. https://doi.org/10.1177/0886260509334411

Linehan, M.M. (1993). *Cognitive-behavioural treatment of borderline personality disorder.* The Guilford Press.

Lüönd, A.M., Wolfensberger, L., Wingenbach, T.S.H., Schnyder, U., Weilenmann, S., & Pfaltz, M.C. (2022). Don't get too close to me: Depressed and non-depressed survivors of child maltreatment prefer larger comfortable interpersonal distances towards strangers. *European Journal of Psychotraumatology, 13*(1), 2066457. https://doi.org/10.1080/20008198.2022.2066457

Malvaso, C.G., Cale, J., Whitten, T., Day, A., Singh, S., Hackett, L., Delfabbro, P.H., & Ross, S. (2022). Associations between adverse childhood experiences and trauma among young people who offend: A systematic literature review. *Trauma, Violence, & Abuse, 23*(5), 1677–1694. https://doi.org/10.1177/15248380211013132

Musetti, A., Grazia, V., Manari, T., Terrone, G., & Corsano, P. (2021). Linking childhood emotional neglect to adolescents' parent-related loneliness: Self-other differentiation and emotional detachment from parents as mediators. *Child Abuse & Neglect, 122*, 105338. https://doi.org/10.1016/j.chiabu.2021.105338

Peternelj-Taylor, C. (2002). Professional boundaries: A matter of therapeutic integrity. *Journal of Psychosocial Nursing and Mental Health Services, 40*(4), 22–29. https://doi.org/10.3928/0279-3695-20020401-10

Reavis, J.A., Looman, J., Franco, K.A., & Rojas, B. (2013). Adverse childhood experiences and adult criminality: How long must we live before we possess our own lives? *The Permanente Journal, 17*(2), 44–48. https://doi.org/10.7812/TPP/12-072

Schneiderman, J.U., Mennen, F.E., Molina, A.C.P., & Cederbaum, J.A. (2023). Adults with a child maltreatment history: Narratives describing individual strengths that promote positive wellbeing. *Child Abuse & Neglect, 139*, 106133. https://doi.org/10.1016/j.chiabu.2023.106133

Scott, A. (1993). A beginning theory of personal space boundaries. *Perspectives in Psychiatric Care, 29*(2), 12–21. https://doi.org/10.1111/j.1744-6163.1993.tb00407.x

Shingler, J. (2018). *Understanding the process of psychological risk assessment: Exploring the experiences of psychologists, indeterminate sentenced prisoners and Parole Board members* (Doctoral dissertation, University of Portsmouth).

Shingler, J., Sonnenberg, S.J., & Needs, A. (2017). Risk assessment interviews: Exploring the perspectives of psychologists and indeterminate sentenced prisoners in the United Kingdom. *International Journal of Offender Therapy and Comparative Criminology, 62*(10), 3201–3224.

Stickney, J., & Lowenstein, J. (2024). "They spoke to me like I was a human, so I behaved like a human": Mattering, hope and release from prison. In J. Shingler & J. Stickney (Eds.) *The journey from prison to community* (pp. 174–191). Routledge.

4 Dismantling distance

From watch towers to words – how the Northern Ireland Prison Service rehumanised the "other" in custody by moving from systems of control to spaces of empathy and connection

Michael McCracken

Northern Ireland is an area with a prominent history of sectarian divide. The reverberations and legacy of years of civil unrest is still very much being felt today. During the Troubles and in subsequent years, 32 prison staff were murdered, and personal security for prison staff became a primary concern. Staff were taught to be vigilant against being conditioned by prisoners, and the way to keep safe was to reveal nothing about yourself. The psychology of "othering", attributing negative characteristics to others that sustain a sense of "them and us", occurs throughout many criminal justice and health care systems but was arguably amplified in the context of Northern Ireland. There was considerable resistance to the idea that prison staff should relate to prisoners, as for many, it felt inherently unsafe to do so. The political landscape has and is changing in Northern Ireland. It took time for the predominant focus of the prison service to move away from security and towards rehabilitation, but the Northern Irish Prison Service (NIPS) I left in 2022 was a different place than when I joined in 2008. It changed very much for the better for those in our care. This chapter will explore lessons that can be learnt from NIPS' transformation and from forensic psychologists and their ways of working in this challenging context. It will consider how they have managed to build and sustain relationships across divides. In my career, I have worked in various prisons throughout the United Kingdom and Ireland, and I see lessons from Northern Ireland that have relevance for forensic practitioners everywhere.

Context

Northern Ireland is a part of the United Kingdom in the north-east of the island of Ireland. It is home to 1.9 million people, and today, 45.7% of the population identify as Catholic and 43.5% of the population identify as Protestant (NISRA, 2022). There is a long history of residential, cultural and educational segregation of the two religious groups.

DOI: 10.4324/9781003542377-6

The recent political history of Northern Ireland has been dominated by "The Troubles". The Troubles refer to the violent sectarian conflict that lasted in Northern Ireland from 1968 to 1998. The origins of the conflict are complex, but the conflict was largely divided along religious lines: Protestants made up the majority of the unionist/loyalist section of the community supporting the union between Northern Ireland and the United Kingdom, and Catholics made up the majority of the nationalist/republican section of the community supporting a united Ireland separate from the United Kingdom.

Some of what is described in the following paragraphs makes for uncomfortable reading. The Troubles were difficult for everyone, and there is no hierarchy of harm, no monopoly on suffering and hurt. We are a society that is still processing the conflict and how it affects us.

Some 3,720 people were killed during the conflict, and more than 40,000 people were wounded, with an estimated 39% of the population of Northern Ireland reporting that they experienced a conflict-related traumatic event in their lives (Commission for Victims and Survivors, 2011).

Today in Northern Ireland, the troubles are over for many, though not all, of the population. However, it bears the scars from the conflict and faces many legacy issues. One in four children in Northern Ireland is living in poverty, levels of personal debt are higher than elsewhere in the United Kingdom, and Northern Ireland has one of the highest levels of multiple deprivation anywhere in the United Kingdom. There is a high prevalence of mental health problems with one in five of the adult population having a probable mental illness, and almost half of 11–19-year-olds report having experienced at least one adverse childhood experience (Office of the Mental Health Champion, 2023). There is ongoing intergenerational transmission of conflict-related trauma (Fargas-Malet & Dillenburger, 2016). Northern Ireland has high levels of domestic abuse, with 31,043 incidents reported to police between 1 October 2023 and 30 September 2024 (Police Service of Northern Ireland (PSNI), 2024a) and 1,548 sectarian-motivated hate incidents and crimes reported during that same period (PSNI, 2024b).

In Northern Ireland, forensic psychologists are employed in the prison service, probation service and healthcare. Prison and probation services operate independently of each other. Like other parts of the United Kingdom, the prison population in Northern Ireland has been increasing, with the overall average daily prison population increasing by 11.4% during 2023/2024 to 1,877. The male population increased from 1,607 to 1,787, while the female population increased from 78 to 90 (DOJ, 2024).

The NIPS was created in December 1921. It is an executive agency of the Department of Justice and is charged with managing prisons in Northern Ireland. Today, there are four establishments on three sites in the prison estate. HMP Maghaberry is a high security adult male prison housing a range of prisoners from remand through to life sentenced prisoners and those convicted of terrorism-related offences. HMP Magilligan is a medium secure adult male prison, and the Hydebank Wood Secure College and Women's

Prison site houses young men under the age of 24 and adult female prison-ers, including females convicted of terrorism-related offences. The focus of today's prison service is on improving public safety by reducing reoffending through offender rehabilitation and management. However, today's service has had to overcome a difficult history. In general, prisons are considered to be some of the most stressful and extreme environments in society (Peternelj-Taylor, 2004), but in Northern Ireland during The Troubles, the stress and extremity were intensified.

Pre-Troubles, the function of NIPS was much like any other prison service, but during the Troubles, the role of NIPS became more complex, as for many years, the prison population in Northern Ireland was dichotomous. Prisons in Northern Ireland housed both "ordinary decent criminals" and terrorist prisoners aligned with republican or loyalist organisations, most of which are proscribed terrorist groups. The term "ODC" or "ordinary" (an unofficial term that was not organisationally approved) was used at the time to refer to those convicted of criminal behaviour and distinguish them from those convicted of political offences.

HMP Maze, originally established as Long Kesh Detention Centre in 1971, was the most well-known prison of the troubles. It housed loyalist and republican prisoners in its "H-blocks" and was at the centre of sig-nificant political events. Of particular note are the 1981 republican hunger strike when ten political prisoners starved themselves to death, and the mass escape of 38 republican prisoners in 1983. It also saw five years of "dirty protest" when republican prisoners refused to leave their cells, did not wash, wore only blankets instead of prison uniforms and did not "slop out[1]" but smeared excrement on the walls of their cells. At the height of this protest in mid-1978, there were over 370 men on a dirty protest within HMP Maze, and staff had to attempt to go in and clean the cells, only for them to become filthy again (Faul & Murray, 1979). These events were no doubt utterly har-rowing for all concerned. In 1997, a loyalist prisoner, Billy Wright, was shot dead inside the prison. Two guns had been smuggled into the prison. The prison system "became inextricably bound up in the political difficulties of Northern Ireland. It did not cause the Troubles, it became part of them" (BBC News, 2000a, p.1)

One republican ex-prisoner described his experience of being in HMP Maze:

> I didn't wash for three years from 1978 to 1981.... My experience was I was taken into what was the reception area of the H-block. We had already heard at that time about of reports of brutality as people were going down to the prison because, obviously, the prison authorities were trying to dissuade people from going on the protests. I was told to strip and put my clothes into a brown bag, and I stripped down to my underpants and it's bizarre because you're in the middle of this square and there are other activities going on around you, there are

prison guards and orderlies going back and forward, there's a Governor going about, and you're standing in the middle of this stripped down to your underpants and then somebody said: "Group", and a group of them gathered round and I thought there was going to be a lot of physical abuse. But there wasn't and somebody said: "We said strip. Get the fucking heap off". So, I ended up totally naked in the middle of this circle. And probably thinking back it was done to degrade you or humiliate you or whatever in some way. We had much more extreme conditions where basically you're in a cell 24/7 that was covered in excrement. We had no access to books, TV, radio, magazines, nothing.

(Reinisch, 2017)

Prison staff were deemed legitimate targets by paramilitary groups. Many prison officers dealt with threats, intimidation, riots and violence on the prison wings on a regular basis. But the threat was not limited to work. The Prison Officers' Association (POA) describe this period of history as characterised by threats and brutality: homes were firebombed, officers and their families had to move into secret safe houses, and there was a constant threat of undercar booby trap devices within the community (POA, 2024).

In total, 32 prison staff were murdered as a result of their employment. The most recent of these were the murders of David Black in 2012, who was shot dead while on his way to work, and Adrian Ismay in 2016, who died because of an under-vehicle improvised explosive device (UVIED) planted under his car. This occurred almost 20 years after the conflict was officially over. The majority of deaths, however, occurred between the mid-1970s and the mid-1980s. Many other people, including family members, have been permanently or seriously injured or have been subject to prolonged physical, verbal and psychological intimidation and abuse. This had an incapacitating impact and resulted in mental scarring for staff who lived in fear and intimidation for so long (POA, 2024). Staff were highly trained in personal security and took daily precautions during those years including checking under their cars for UVIEDs. Unlike other parts of the United Kingdom, prison officers in Northern Ireland can still choose to carry personal protection outside work.

It is not surprising then that NIPS' focus for many years was on security. At work, staff were taught how to reveal nothing of themselves to prisoners for fear that any personal information could be passed on and used to put them or their family at risk. Terrorist prisoners used a range of tactics including threatening or befriending, to try and gather information to condition or compromise staff. Relating to a prisoner in a personal way could literally cost your life or the life of a colleague. As Northern Ireland is a small place, many of the ordinary prisoners would have known, or in some cases perhaps been related to, some of the political prisoners. In fact, some prisoners and staff would have known each other and perhaps grew up together. In these conditions, prison officers had to treat all prisoners with a high degree of caution as there was always a risk that ordinary prisoners could be gathering intelligence that could be passed on for use by paramilitary organisations. I have no doubt many staff cared a great deal about the people that were in their care during those years, but the political climate and security threat forced staff and prisoners apart.

NIPS found it very difficult to recruit anyone from a Catholic background during the Troubles. Anyone from that side of the community joining the service would have been under considerable threat. The staff profile of NIPS was predominantly male and predominantly Protestant with very little staff turnover and no recruitment for many years. A review in 2011 found the service was unrepresentative of the Catholic community. Among prison managers and staff, overall 10% were Catholic, and only 8% of main grade officers were Catholic. In contrast, the 2011 review found that in all prisons there was a disproportionate number of Catholics imprisoned: around 55%, compared to 44% of Catholics in the general population according to the 2001 census (Prison Review Team, 2011). Historically, there were significant ethno-religious inequalities in Northern Ireland, with areas with a Catholic majority being more deprived, having higher unemployment, lower education and greater reliance on social housing (Flaherty & McAuley, 2023). Where there is poverty and inequality, there is often crime.

Examination of the equality and diversity data for ordinary prisoners in 2011 showed several apparent and consistent disproportionalities in treatment and outcome, in all three male prisons, in areas that depend principally on staff discretion. In comparison to their proportion in the population, Catholics were over-represented on the basic level of the incentives scheme, while Protestants were over-represented on the enhanced level. Overall, Catholics were also disproportionately represented in matters relating to prison discipline: adjudication, use of force and segregation. In Hydebank Wood and Maghaberry, Catholics were disproportionately unlikely, and Protestants disproportionately likely, to be granted temporary release for healthcare, emergencies or resettlement reasons. It also appears to be the case at Maghaberry that Catholic prisoners are over-represented in the poorer older accommodation, and Protestants are over-represented in the newer and better units (Prison Review Team, 2011). This parallels the disproportionate rates of imprisonment and the disproportionate use of lengthy sentences among people from black and minoritised ethnicities in the rest of the United Kingdom (Prison Reform Trust, 2024).

In terms of ordinary prisoners, many come from areas of social deprivation in Northern Ireland (Prison Review Team, 2011). We know that this is mirrored in other parts of the United Kingdom, and there is an over-representation of background adversity in the UK adult prison population. To illustrate, 31% of women and 24% of men in the UK adult prison population were taken into care as a child compared to 2% of the general population; and 50% of women and 40% of men in the UK adult prison population observed violence in the home compared to 14% of the general population (Prison Reform Trust, 2024).

These same deprived areas also typically experienced more civil and community unrest than more affluent areas, and a specific issue in Northern Ireland has been the long-term problem with so-called "community justice". During the conflict, policing was focused on security, and some sections of both communities in Northern Ireland did not respect the authority of the police or did not trust the police. Parts of Northern Ireland were at time "no go areas" for the police or could only be entered with military back-up. In these circumstances people sought powerful others to deal with antisocial behaviour. In Northern Ireland, this role was undertaken by various para-military groups. By punishing those accused of antisocial behaviour, para-military groups extended their power base within their local communities. Paramilitaries and local people determine what constitutes antisocial behaviour, but it typically includes drug dealing, burglary and car crime. The punishment for such behaviour includes beatings and shootings by loyalist and republican gangs, which are at times severe enough to permanently maim or kill. "Knee-capping" is a common form of punishment that involves the victim being shot through one or both knees. Between 1992 and 2001, 2,322 people were injured or died from paramilitary-style shootings and assaults (Peyton, 2002). Many young men who end up in prison or on probation in Northern Ireland have at some point been subjected to paramilitary threat, beatings and shootings, and many have been banished from their home area due to their criminality. Unfortunately, this problem persists in the present day with punishment beatings and shootings reported every year (BBC, 2023). From 1 July 2022 to 30 June 2023, there was 1 security-related death, 7 bombing incidents and 32 shooting incidents (PSNI, 2024c). Overall, 28 people were casualties of paramilitary-style assaults and there were 11 casualties of paramilitary-style shootings (Office of the Mental Health Champion, 2023). Adverse childhood experiences (ACEs) and Troubles/conflict-related adversities are still disproportionately concentrated in deprived communities, highlighting socio-economic inequalities. A recent study found that 24.4% of those in the most deprived areas reported experiencing 4+ ACEs compared with 12.8% in the least deprived areas (Walsh et al., 2025).

In 1991, NIPS employed its first psychologist as part of a strategy to address the significant impact of the Troubles on staff. As Bates-Gaston (2007), the first psychologist to be employed by NIPS, reflected, "Everything seemed to be on a 'war' footing. In the first month of my new employment a bomb went off in Crumlin Road Gaol, killing two prisoners and wounding many others including staff" (Bates-Gaston, 2007, p.36). She also recalled:

When I was hired as the Chief Psychologist there was no remit, but it was a time of great upheaval. I came from an occupational psychology background, so I used that. There was no such thing as forensic psychology then. We used the word stress, but the truth was that staff were traumatised. Staff were turning to alcohol and drugs, there were difficulties for many at home, a lot of marriages broke down, there were lots of trauma symptoms resulting from the constant assaults, the dirty protests, the hunger strikes, the bombing, the Billy Wright murder and the subsequent enquiry. They could not trust people on the outside, so an internal service was needed to try and support staff'.

(Bates-Gaston, personal communication, 11 November 2024)

In Northern Irish prisons then, there were many years when traumatised people were being managed and looked after by traumatised and threatened people. Sections of the prison population likely lived through adverse cultural and institutional experiences. Some had experienced serious Troubles-related traumas as children and adults in addition to the types of adverse childhood experiences prevalent in forensic populations.

It is beyond the bounds of this chapter to explore the wider Northern Irish context and the social and historical imprint of group-based conflict and the resulting power relations between the ingroups and outgroups at a societal level. But while any prison system cannot be fully understood separately from the broader society in which it exists, relevant lessons can still be learnt by considering what happened in Northern Irish prisons, and how the complexity of the situation in Northern Ireland arguably led to an intensified culture of "them and us".

Staff faced an active and credible threat in the workplace and in the community; there was organised and active resistance from political prisoners, external political pressure and representation issues in the prison workforce. Staff and prisoners often feared and mistrusted each other, as any alternative was simply unsafe. This resulted in battening down for both groups against each other. The relevance of this is that the them-and-us culture is something that has also been observed internationally in other criminal justice contexts (Fredriksson, 2019). It is not exclusive to Northern Ireland; we just became a more marked and exaggerated example of it. The struggle to balance security and relating is familiar to anyone working in a forensic setting. One lens through which to consider how a them-and-us culture can develop is through exploring the psychological phenomena of "Othering".

Othering and relational practice in prisons

Humans have an underlying need to be in the presence of someone

with whom one has profound reverberations of sameness in order to feel 'You are just like me, and I am just like you' … 'I am good because I know that you are good and I am just like you'.

(Riker, 2022, p.104)

Humans' ability to form co-operative groups has enabled us to thrive as a species. Finding our tribe gives us a necessary sense of belonging and safety. However, differences can trigger suspicion, threat and vulnerability (Riker,

2022). We cannot be sure how the other will behave, and we long for a predictable and secure world.

The psychology of othering refers to the cognitive and social processes through which individuals or groups are perceived as fundamentally different from oneself or one's community. Othering is ubiquitous across history and cultures and appears to be in the fabric of our nature: we experience otherness as a threat to our sense of self (Riker, 2022). Othering is likely a survival mechanism, and this may be why it appears so intractable and why, for their entire existence, humans have been intolerant of those seen as different (Riker, 2022).

Othering is not merely the opposite of sameness. Rather, it is a process by which individuals or groups see people who are different from them in a way that devalues them. It works to reinforce a sense of a "virtuous self and a lesser other" (Stabile, 2016, p.382). It is a process whereby individuals and groups are treated and marked as different and inferior to the dominant social group, and they suffer discrimination as a result (Griffin, 2017).

Othering becomes intensified when accompanied by a physical threat to our safety and can develop into tribalism. In tribalism, there is such a strong feeling of loyalty to the group that you support them no matter what they do. It may be based on shared genetics, shared cultural histories, language, music, religion, but it can lead to the objectification of others, and all too often, violence (Cottone, 2025). In Northern Ireland, there was widespread tribalism during the Troubles that permeated all aspects of life. Protestants and Catholics attended different schools, played different sports and lived in different areas. Tribal symbols marked territory, often through flags and painted kerbstones. As a child born into the Troubles, no one needed to tell me if I was in "our" part of the city or "theirs". I always knew and felt safe on our part and felt under threat on theirs. This experience has not changed significantly in the past 25 years.

The experience of working and living in the extreme and pressured environments of the Northern Irish prisons during the Troubles would have galvanised the relationships between staff and equally galvanised the relationships between prisoners, while further widening the sense of otherness of the other group. Groups of people who need empathy from one another often form around their sameness and Riker (2022) cites military veterans, alcoholics, those who share the same religious beliefs, and those that have experienced trauma as examples of groups that come together because an essential sameness is required in order for deep empathy to be experienced (Riker, 2022). Riker (2022) suggests we operate on the belief that only someone who has lived through the same experience we have can understand what we have been through.

Othering is not an intentional or conscious process, and it comes in many forms including fascism, racism, sectarianism and sexism, and it can be present in criminal justice (Peternelj-Taylor, 2004; Stabile, 2016). While othering would have been particularly evident in Northern Ireland and its prisons during the Troubles, othering arguably occurs in all justice systems.

Peternelj-Taylor (2004) argues that othering is a phenomenon revealed particularly when there is a power differential, and within criminal justice, there is always a marked power imbalance. As forensic psychologists, these are barriers to the establishment of the therapeutic relationship that we strive to create to facilitate change and support desistance.

Peternelj-Taylor (2004) explored the factors impacting on othering in the forensic and correctional milieu as they impacted on nursing staff and their practice. She notes that nurses are affected by the context in which they work, and this observation is also valid for forensic psychologists. When we work in prison, and to a lesser but still relevant extent in probation, we work in a system of power, control, enforcement and authority, where there is an inherent power imbalance.

Stabile (2016) argues that within society, there is a tendency to see people who break the law and who go to jail as "others". A key aspect of othering is that we define ourselves partly by looking at the other and understanding ourselves by what we are not: "I am not like those people who commit those terrible crimes, I am good person and they are a bad one". It does not matter what standing someone had before they went to jail; once someone is convicted and becomes a criminal, they stop being like us, and they stop mattering as much. Stabile (2016) points to the lack of resources that go into prisoner resettlement programmes and the near insurmountable obstacles ex-prisoners face on release to support this argument. Challenges with housing, employment and access to healthcare increase the likelihood of recall to prison or re-arrest, trapping ex-prisoners in an unhelpful loop. Stabile (2016) argues that the reduced focus on what happens to people after prison is because they have stopped being "us".

Society and wider culture other people who have committed crimes and examples of this can often be seen in the press. The news headlines on the landing page of one local online news outlet at the time of writing this contain the words "paedo", "pervert" and "sex pest" (Belfast Telegraph, 2024), all of which are pejorative terms that dehumanise the individual. Smith (2009, cited in Fredriksson, 2019, p. 262) describes prison as an "abject other to society" and suggests that prisoners are akin to the living dead housed in a tomb. Prison helps to keep society feeling safe because it houses the monsters and becomes the "buried, repressed, repository of social fears" (Fiddler, 2007, cited in Fredriksson, 2019, p. 262). The dehumanising aspect of othering arguably occurs on both sides of the power imbalance and is reflected in the language used in prisons. Prisoners are sometimes referred to as "cons", "roots" and "scrotes" by staff, and staff are referred to as "screws" by prisoners. While these terms and their use are sometimes accepted by both staff and prisoners, they cast individuals into the role of the other. People in prison are given a number and at times referred to as Prisoner X. In the early part of my own career, I recall asking an officer if I could speak to, for example, Alan Jones, only to be told "There is no Alan Jones here, there's only prisoner Jones".

Diagnoses within criminal justice can be problematic in reinforcing othering. Labels like "personality disorder", "psychopath" and "schizophrenic" may not be well understood by all staff working in criminal justice (Brooker & Tocque, 2023). The risk is that some staff do not see past the label and therefore dismiss the possibility that the person can change their trajectory.

Given the power imbalance in prison environments, some argue that othering may to a certain extent be inevitable, and those who are sentenced to custody are in danger of eliciting othering responses from those who work there (Corley & Goren, 1998 in Peternelj-Tayor, 2004). The systems we work in can play a critical role in either re-traumatising and reinforcing marginalisation and otherness, or, as I would argue, they can mitigate the impacts of adversity and provide opportunities for relational healing. If we are serious about effectively changing behaviour, reducing harm and protecting the public, we need to recognise and respond to the adversity experienced by the people in our care and work to ensure our systems do not contribute to perpetuating and compounding people's difficulties. And if we are not making a conscious effort to avoid othering, then we could unwittingly be contributing to it and perhaps perpetuating the problem.

To summarise, while it is likely that othering is a survival mechanism, it is a process that devalues people who are different. It can become more pronounced when accompanied by threats to our safety, which in turn galvanises loyalty within the group. It is more likely to occur when there is a power differential between the ingroup and the outgroup. Prisons have a vulnerability for othering to occur as they possess the ingredients in which it can flourish. Maintaining a "them and us" perspective is not conducive to supporting desistance; treating people inhumanely is self-defeating to the aims of rehabilitation and preparation for reentry into society (Dolovich, 2017). As professionals working in such contexts, it is important that we consider how to overcome othering.

Overcoming "othering" in practice

In 1998, the Belfast Agreement, also known as the Good Friday Agreement, brought about the official end to the conflict in Northern Ireland (The Belfast Agreement: An agreement reached at the multi-party talks on Northern Ireland,1998). Several years later, the St. Andrews Agreement, reached in 2006, led to the restoration of the Northern Ireland Assembly and the formation of a new Executive (Agreement at St Andrews, 2006). This in turn paved the way for the review of NIPS, resulting in the Owers report (Prison Review Team, 2011) and prompting a range of initiatives that improved the service.

Organisational change

Today, the core strategic aims of NIPS are the provision of safe, secure and decent custody; to reform and modernise; and reduce the risk of reoffending.

There has been a great deal of investment in creating purposeful activity and rehabilitative opportunities for those in custody. Organisationally, NIPS have introduced many mechanisms, initiatives and programmes that have brought about a seismic cultural shift and tackled othering. A voluntary exit scheme created the opportunity for staff to leave the service including those for whom change felt impossible as a consequence of their experiences. This created space for renewal and commenced the move to a different type of relationship between staff and those in custody.

To promote good relations, today each prison in Northern Ireland has an Equality & Diversity Committee overseen by a senior leader. Statistical reports are reviewed and examined for any anomalies in decision-making relating to the provision of services, discipline, drug testing, searches, complaints or adjudications, all broken down by Section 75 group.[2] The format of equality and diversity committees has recently been adjusted to include prisoner perceptions of staff treatment as a standing agenda item. Today, all prisoners have equal access to services provided within the prison.

Regular meetings are held to monitor the equality of provision of services to all prisoners, and these are attended by the Equality Commission, Chaplaincy, Probation, Independent Monitoring Board, Healthcare and the Criminal Justice Inspectorate. Prisoner Forums meet in advance of the main meeting to raise any issues prisoners may have. The prisons have sought to work in partnership with the Independent Monitoring Board to improve prisoner representation and engagement in other aspects of prison life as well. There is a complaints procedure for prisoners.

NIPS is also subject to scrutiny by the Prisoner Ombudsman, Criminal Justice Inspectorate, The Red Cross, Equality Commission, Human Rights Commission, Independent Monitoring Board and the United Nations Conventions around Human Rights. Anything these bodies raise concerns about is investigated, reported on and actioned.

In 2019, the Director General commissioned a research report from Queen's University Belfast to investigate outcomes experienced by Catholic prisoners in key areas. The resulting report found no significant difference between Catholics and Protestants when all factors (including individual, societal and prison-related variables) were considered in relation to adjudication charges, guilty adjudications, Progressive Regime Earned Privileges Scheme (PREPS) regime level and Supporting People at Risk (SPAR[3]) involvement (NIPS, 2024). NIPS has arguably made significant progress in this area, and this report clearly suggests that the initiatives NIPS introduced are working. The service provides training for prisoners and staff to raise awareness, foster good relations and provide a better understanding and appreciation of equality and diversity issues.

Whereas in the past the workforce was static, NIPS now regularly recruits new staff to the service; 177 in 2023–2024. All recruitment panel members sitting on interview panels complete Recruitment and Selection training, which includes raising awareness of unconscious bias. NIPS also uses Positive Action

Advertising Statements to encourage applications from under-represented groups and undertake outreach to universities and job fairs (NIPS, 2024).

Creating psychological safety and developing resilience

Prisons are social systems that involve intimate social contact between those who live and work in the institution. Othering can be a form of self-protection, and you cannot take away a defence unless you have something to replace it with. Stressed, anxious or threatened people have less capacity to contain the feelings of other stressed, anxious or threatened people. Physical and psychological safety is needed to reduce the impact of threatening events and the feeling of needing to protect or distance oneself from others. NIPS recognised that caring for staff had to precede staff being able to consider the rehabilitation of others. A staff survey was used to explore issues such as work-related stress, family life and staff training needs. Importantly, it also sought to understand how staff felt about their relationships with each other and with the prisoners (Bates-Gaston, 2007). The focus of psychological services in NIPS at that time became attempting to reduce the awful impact of the Troubles on staff. The staff had indicated they needed more support, but Northern Ireland is a small place, and the staff did not trust anyone outside NIPS. Staff were too afraid to tell anyone outside the service about their work for fear that terrorists might find out where they lived. An internal staff counselling and support service was established. To gain the trust of staff, the psychologists delivering the service spent time walking around the prison landings and being visible to both staff and prisoners. In the ten years between 1991 and 2001, more than 1,100 staff availed of thousands of one-to-one counselling and support sessions (Bates-Gaston, 2007). Helping staff deal with their trauma created space for compassion, hope and belief in change. Prisons of course need to attend to physical security with robust procedures, but organisations should also pay acute and sustained attention to workforce resilience and create a culture in which staff can flourish. Today, NIPS provides counselling and physiotherapy for staff. Staff in particularly stressful roles (including the Care and Supervision Unit[4] and the Prisoner Development Unit[5]) are provided with additional training through the Police Rehabilitation and Retraining Trust and Critical Incident Support Mechanism.

Like many forensic services, NIPS is finding a greater number of those in their care have mental health and addiction problems. In 2018, NIPS introduced a comprehensive system to support people at risk – the SPAR Evolution. An external review of that system in 2024 reflected positively on how people in prison are being supported. Prisoners reported that they found it responsive to their needs. The reviewers found that staff were knowledgeable about the system and invested in it. Very telling is the fact that despite the increase in the prison population, NIPS reports that this has not led to an accompanying increase in instances of self-harm or death in custody (NIPS, 2024).

Trust

Without trust, we will not have the opportunity to get to know the people we work with. In getting to know our service users, we can come to see them as people and not just as prisoners. If there is no sense of familiarity or shared understanding, trust will not develop. Recovery from difficult experiences can happen within the context of secure supportive relationships. We must establish meaningful psychological connections with those we work with by relating to them as individuals. Without trust, it is very difficult to have any genuine, meaningful communication (Dolovich, 2017). Trust is not about likability; it is the intention to accept vulnerability based upon positive expectations of the intentions and behaviour of another. It can be conceptualised as being comprised of two parts: affective trust and cognitive trust (Dowell et al., 2015). Affective trust is the interpersonal warmth you bring to conversations, the genuine interest you have and express about the life of the person that you are working with. Cognitive trust is about reliability and competence. One of the best ways to build trust is to do what you say you are going to do. Follow through, and do not work outside of your competence. If you do not know the answer or do not know how to do something, acknowledge your limitations. I have always found that if you make a mistake with a service user, owning it with honesty and integrity becomes an opportunity to develop trust.

In 2000, a review brought about the introduction of an independent parole commission in Northern Ireland (Parole Commissioners for Northern Ireland, 2025). This was hugely important as the independence of the commission increased prisoners' trust in the process. Psychologists continued to provide evidence at parole hearings but were now independently cross-examined on their evidence. (Bates-Gaston, 2024). As psychologists working in NIPS, we were never directed to follow an organisational position when it came to making recommendations. Our professional independence was respected by our colleagues, and this was important in the development and maintenance of trust by all parties involved.

An advantage of working in a small place like Northern Ireland is that it is relatively easy to work consistently with people over long periods of time. Staff often work in the same prison for many years and may see some young men come into custody on day one of a life sentence, work with them through the course of that sentence and see them released. The same staff members have been a consistent presence; staff and service users have a shared understanding, and they know what they can expect of each other. Staff maintain professional, boundaried relationships, but there is a significant degree of trust and mutual respect. While familiarity must not breed complacency, some consistency is beneficial. It provides continuity, enables the development of a secure relational base and helps service users feel that they matter.

Collaboration

I will illustrate the value of multi-disciplinary collaboration via the example of implementing Offending Behaviour Programmes (OBPs) in NIPS. Facilitator teams comprised a prison officer, a psychology staff member and a probation officer. This co-working approach helped reduce barriers between professional groups. These peer-supportive, multi-disciplinary teams lacked power imbalances as we were all doing the same job for those few hours each week. Often in prisons, it can feel like the power lies in the pervading and dominant culture carried by correctional staff. Forensic psychologists sometimes see themselves as "window dressing" rather than a core component of the system and can feel that operational staff do not understand or support their standards (Weinberger & Screenivasan, 1994). Co-delivering programmes embedded psychologists in the wider organisation and helped to reduce othering among the professions.

Practitioners should collaborate with service users at every opportunity. Historically, things were "done to", not "done with" service users. Doing things *with* service users shifts the power imbalance and builds relationships. It used to be viewed by some staff with suspicion. You must hold your professional boundaries but take every opportunity to co-produce formulations, risk scenarios and service planning *with* service users. Service users should always see a report about them and be given the chance to contribute before it goes to anyone else.

Challenge and reflective practice

It can be very difficult to challenge othering when we encounter it. I have worked in prisons throughout the United Kingdom and Ireland and can recall times when I have heard colleagues use derogatory language about prisoners. I have not always felt able to speak up. I have felt too junior to comment, sometimes I have felt like an outsider and thought it was not my place to say anything, or I have wanted to avoid conflict or avoid being seen as "soft and fluffy". Where we work can have a powerful impact on how we work. Studies have found that medical staff working in prisons change the way they provide care over the course of their employment in the prison, and this change is attributed to them learning to conform to the way the prison does things. Holmes and Federman (2003) found that negative characteristics commonly attributed to prisoners, for example, that they tell lies, manipulate, or are dangerous, came to overlay nurses' typical view of the person as a patient who needs care.

Fisher (1995) states that when non-discipline staff are working with those with a history of violence, getting on with discipline staff, who may be able to protect you if things go wrong, takes precedence over speaking up or doing the right thing. In prisons, nurses, addiction counsellors and psychologists are all "other" than discipline staff who are the majority profession.

Psychologists must find ways to maintain their professional integrity, and we cannot ignore judgemental, discriminatory or uncaring practice. As forensic psychologists, it is imperative that we see everyone as of equal worth and dignity and actively avoid assigning less worth to subsets of human beings or subsets of people who have committed specific types of offences. We need to scrutinise any thinking that rationalises us exerting control over others as contributing to some greater good to ensure we are not engaging in othering. This is where practitioners need to use professional supervision and reflection. For example, we can use supervision to discuss and rehearse ways we can challenge colleagues' use of language. We should also take the same care to understand what our correctional colleagues experience in their work and empathise with the challenges they face, and how this might affect their interactions with service users. As reflective practitioners, we need to be acutely aware of our own privilege, bias and power imbalances in our relationships and actively work to reduce them. It is encouraging that these issues are embedded in our training pathways, and they should continue to be the subject of scrutiny in our supervision throughout our careers. As a profession, Forensic Psychology should be representative, inclusive and diverse. We should be encouraging people into the profession from a wide range of backgrounds.

Become trauma-informed

One way that organisations can address these issues is to become trauma-informed. Being trauma-informed is incompatible with othering. Trauma-informed organisations are compassionate, nurturing and relationship-based and can contribute to building strong, resilient, healthy and productive people – both staff and service users (Scottish Government, 2021). Becoming trauma-informed is not a one-off activity or a standalone intervention that can be delivered in a silo. It is an organisational transformation process which requires systemic cultural change and ongoing work at all levels of the organisational hierarchy. Staff who feel supported and well-resourced feel less threatened and therefore less inclined to other for their own protection. For staff who experience critical incidents, organisational variables represent stronger predictors of post-trauma outcomes than characteristics of the incidents themselves (Clarke, 2008). Organisational factors including being dominated by high levels of bureaucracy, having internal conflicts regarding responsibility, the inflexible use of established procedures and a focus on protecting the organisation from blame or criticism, have all been found to increase the risk of poor post-trauma outcomes. Positive organisational practices, such as adoption of autonomous response systems, consultative leadership styles, training to develop adaptive capacity and allowing procedural flexibility, can all help enhance positive outcomes (Clarke, 2008).

Leadership plays a critical role. Policy makers and political leaders have a responsibility to ensure systems are not systemically biased, unfair, excluding or traumatising. The Northern Ireland Programme for Government (Northern Ireland Executive, 2024) has stated it will develop a trauma-informed public sector:

> Acknowledging the levels of trauma in our post-conflict society, we will work across the Executive to embed trauma-informed, responsive systems; systems that help people to easily navigate and access the support they need, when they need it, and for however long they need it for.
> (Northern Ireland Executive, 2025, p. 25)

The Department of Justice has a Trauma-Informed Practice working group that meets regularly to share best practices and updates on organisational changes that are happening in response to trauma. NIPS, the Youth Justice Agency and the Probation Service in Northern Ireland are all members of this working group and are committed to and actively working towards becoming trauma-informed organisations. An assessment of current practice in NIPS is ongoing with the Safeguarding Board for Northern Ireland to embed a trauma-informed approach in both policy and practice within NIPS. NIPS has commissioned a specific trauma prevalence study of the Northern Ireland prison population (NIPS Director General, personal communication, 11 June 2025). This will support NIPS' ongoing journey to become a trauma-informed organisation.

At a practice level, a "Forensic Interest in Trauma" group was created in 2018 (Byrne, personal communication, 6 August 2025). It is a platform for professionals working in a range of forensic settings who share an interest in trauma-informed approaches. It allows professionals to share knowledge, skills, experience of implementation, and relevant research. It has served to connect us to the bigger picture and to each other, reminding us that we are not alone in this.

In our workplaces, we must resist retraumatisation. We must avoid behaving in ways that replicate the events or dynamics of the original trauma and trigger the overwhelming feelings and reactions associated with them. Some behaviours that we see in our service users, such as agitation, shouting or withdrawing, might be classified as obstructive. Sometimes these behaviours occur because someone has been triggered, is feeling unsafe or they are afraid. It can be helpful to respond to those behaviours in a trauma-informed way, asking what might have happened to this person and what they might need to feel safe.

Conclusion

For years, staff and prisoners in Northern Ireland mistrusted each other, as they felt unsafe. There was a real threat to officers from prisoners and a real threat between different categories and backgrounds of prisoners. The them-and-us culture often observed in criminal justice contexts was exaggerated in the unique political climate of the Troubles. Othering, the process by which individuals or groups see people who are different from them in a way that devalues them, is one way to understand this. People do not simply conclude on their own that, as a group, they need to be afraid of another group. As Powell (2017) argues, othering is socially and culturally constructed; this therefore also implies that it is amenable to change. It is my view that organisational responses and processes can reduce the impact of othering in criminal justice. Organisational changes introduced in the NIPS have had a considerable impact on shifting culture towards a more collaborative and supportive custodial environment. Evidence indicates that this has led to better outcomes for those in custody, which one hopes will translate into reductions in recidivism. While we are not all in a position to influence organisational change, we can all take responsibility for how we choose to behave as individual practitioners. We can be the bridge that reaches across and between groups of staff and service users, and we can model the model. We should demonstrate in our language, our behaviour and in our writing that we are all inherently human, and while we have our differences, we are also very much alike. Our practice should be based on humanity and connection. Connecting with the other can be an "empowering and transformative experience" (Peternelj-Taylor, 2004, p. 132). "When we bridge, we not only open up to others, we also open to change in ourselves and actively participate in co-creating a society to which we can all belong" (Powell, 2017, para 19).

Relational hurt requires relational healing, and there is the potential for healing and recovery to occur in every interaction. We should consider the impact of othering on the behaviour we observe in both service users and staff within our organisations. And we should respond in a compassionate, nurturing and relationship-focused way.

Notes

1 The practice of prisoners emptying buckets they use as toilets during the hours their cell is locked due to not having any sanitation in their cell.
2 Section 75 refers to Section 75 of the Northern Ireland Act 1998 which places a statutory obligation on public authorities in Northern Ireland to promote equality of opportunity and good relations. There are several protected characteristics identified in the legislation.
3 SPAR & SPAR Evolution is a set of procedures designed to help vulnerable people in custody and provide support during times of crisis, with a focus on individualised care and understanding the root causes of distress.
4 The CSU is a special accommodation block for those temporarily removed from the general prison population in order to maintain good order and discipline.
5 The PDU is a multi-agency unit focused on supporting rehabilitation and resettlement.

References

Agreement at St Andrews. (2006). Accessed online 26/10/2024. https://assets.publishing.service.gov.uk/media/5a7b17bee5274a319e77cf89/st_andrews_agreement-2.pdf
Bates-Gaston, J. (2007). Forensic psychology in Northern Ireland. *Forensic Update*, 1(92), 36–38. Winter 2007/8.

Bates-Gaston, J. (2024, November, 6). *Personal communication* [In-person conversation].

BBC News. (2000a). *The Prison that served its time*. Accessed online 28/09/24. BBC News. Northern Ireland.

BBC News. (2023). *Paramilitary-style shootings on the rise in Northern Ireland*. Accessed online 16/10/2024. https://www.bbc.co.uk/news/uk-northern-ireland-67443033

Belfast Telegraph. (2024). *Sunday life*. Accessed online 6/10/2024. https://www.belfasttelegraph.co.uk/sunday-life

Brooker, C., and Tocque, K. (2023). The European survey of probation staff's knowledge of, and attitudes to, mental illness. *European Journal of Probation*, 15 (1), 71–90.

Clarke, J. (2008). Promoting professional resilience. In M. Calder (Ed.) *Contemporary risk assessment in safeguarding children*, pp. 164–180. Russell House Publishing.

Commission for Victims and Survivors. (2011). *Troubled consequences: A report on the mental health impact of the civil conflict in Northern Ireland*. Accessed online 10/10/24. https://cvsni.org/wp-content/uploads/2022/11/2011-Research-Troubled-Consequences-A-Report-on-the-Mental-Health-Impact-of-the-Civil-Conflict-in-Northern-Ireland.pdf

Cottone, J.G. (2025). Tribalism@ How to be part of the solution, not the problem. *Psychology Today*. Accessed online 21/04/25. https://www.psychologytoday.com/gb/blog/the-cube/202207/tribalism-how-to-be-part-of-the-solution-not-the-problem

Corley, M.C., and Goren, S. (1998). The dark side of nursing: Impact of stigmatizing responses on patients. *Scholarly Inquiry for Nursing Practice: An International Journal*, 12 (2), 99–118.

Department of Justice. (2024). Northern Ireland prison population 2023/24. https://www.justice-ni.gov.uk/publications/northern-ireland-prison-population-2023-24

Dolovich, S. (2017). *Prison conditions, in reforming criminal justice: Punishment, incarceration, and release 261–293* (Erik Luna ed., 2017).

Dowell, D., Morrison, M., and Heffernan, T. (2015). The changing importance of affective trust and cognitive trust across the relationship lifecycle: A study of business-to-business relationships. *Industrial Marketing Management*, 44, 119–130.

Fargas-Malet, M., and Dillenburger, K. (2016). Intergenerational transmission of conflict-related trauma in Northern Ireland: A behaviour analytic approach. *Journal of Aggression, Maltreatment & Trauma*, 25 (4), 436–454.

Faul, D., and Murray, R. (1979). *H Blocks – British Jail for Irish Political Prisoners*.

Fiddler, M. (2007). Projecting the prison: The depiction of the uncanny in The Shawshank Redemption. *Crime Media Culture*, 3 (2), 192–206.

Fisher, A. (1995). The ethical problems encountered in psychiatric nursing practice with dangerous mentally ill persons. *Scholarly Inquiry for Nursing Practice: An International Journal*, 9 (2), 193–208.

Flaherty, E., and McAuley, M. (2023). New dimensions of inequality in Northern Ireland, 1998–2020. *Space and Polity*, 27 (1), 96–115.

Fredriksson, T. (2019). Abject (M)othering: A narratological study of the prison as an abject and uncanny institution. *Critical Criminology*, 27, 261–274.

Griffin, G. (2017). *Dictionary of gender studies*. First Edition. Oxford University Press, Oxford, United Kingdom.

Holmes, D., and Federman, D. (2003). Constructing monsters: Correctional discourse and nursing practice. *International Journal of Psychiatric Nursing*, 8 (1), 942–962.

NISRA. (2022). Main statistics for Northern Ireland Statistical bulletin. *Religion*. Accessed online 10/10/24. https://www.nisra.gov.uk/system/files/statistics/census-2021-main-statistics-for-northern-ireland-phase-1-statistical-bulletin-religion.pdf

Northern Ireland Executive. (2024). *Our plan: Doing what matters most*. Programme for Government 2024–2027: Northern Ireland Executive.

Northern Ireland Prison Service. (2024). *Northern Ireland Prison Service annual report and accounts 2023–24*. Northern Ireland Prison Service.

Northern Ireland Executive. (2025). Programme for Government: Draft framework. https://www.niassembly.gov.uk/assembly-business/committees/2022-2027/executive-office/research-papers/2025/trauma-informed-approaches/

Office of Mental Health Champion. (2023). *Mental health in Northern Ireland: Fundamental facts*. Northern Ireland: Mental Health Foundation.

Parole Commissioners for Northern Ireland. (2025). *Life sentence review commissions*. https://www.parolecomni.org.uk/life-sentence-review-commissioners

Peternelj-Taylor, C. (2004). An exploration of othering in forensic psychiatric and correctional nursing. *Canadian Journal Nursing Research,* 36 (4), 130–146.

Peyton, R. (2002). Punishment beating and the rule of law. *The Lancet,* 360, s53–s54.

Police Service of Northern Ireland. (2024a). *Domestic abuse incidents and crimes recorded by the police in Northern Ireland*. https://www.psni.police.uk/system/files/2024-11/271197534/Domestic%20Abuse%20Bulletin%20Period%20Ending%2030th%20September%202024.pdf

Police Service of Northern Ireland. (2024b). *Incidents and crimes with a hate motivation recorded by the police in Northern Ireland*. https://www.psni.police.uk/system/files/2024-11/980735231/Hate%20Motivations%20Bulletin%20Period%20ending%2030th%20September%202024.pdf

Police Service of Northern Ireland. (2024c). *Police recorded security situation statistics*. Accessed online 31/12/24. https://www.psni.police.uk/sites/default/files/2024-07/Security%20Situation%20Statistics%20to%20June%202024.pdf

Powell, J.A. (2017). Us vs them: the sinister techniques of 'Othering' – and how to avoid them. *The Guardian*. Accessed online 10/10/24. https://www.theguardian.com/inequality/2017/nov/08/us-vs-them-the-sinister-techniques-of-othering-and-how-to-avoid-them

Prison Officers Association. (2024). *Our union's history – Where we are from and where we're going to – A history of the POA*. Accessed online 5/10/2024. https://www.poauk.org.uk/our-union/history/

Prison Reform Trust. (2024). *Bromley briefings prison factfile*. February 2024. Accessed online 6/10/2024. https://prisonreformtrust.org.uk/publication/bromley-briefings-prison-factfile-february-2024/

Prison Review Team. (2011). *Review of the Norther Ireland Prison Service – Conditions, and management and oversight of all prisons*. Accessed online 5/10/2024. https://www.patfinucanecentre.org/sites/default/files/2017-03/Anne%20Owers%20report%20feb%2011.pdf

Reinisch, D. (2017). Interview with former political prisoner, Irish republican activist and playwright Laurence McKeown. *A Journal of Irish Studies,* 7, 223–239.

Riker, J.H. (2022). The self and the other: Hegel, Kohut, and the psychology of othering. *Psychoanalytic Inquiry,* 42 (2), 101–112.

Scottish Government. (2021). *Trauma-informed practice: A toolkit for Scotland*. Children and Families Directorate. https://www.gov.scot/publications/trauma-informed-practice-toolkit-scotland/

Smith, C. (2009). *The prison and the American imagination*. New Haven: Yale University.

Stabile, S.J. (2016). Othering and the law. *University of St. Thomas Law Journal,* 12 (2), 381–410.

The Belfast Agreement: An agreement reached at the multi-party talks on Northern Ireland (1998). Accessed online 26/10/2024. https://assets.publishing.service.gov.uk/media/619500728fa8f5037d67b678/The_Belfast_Agreement_An_Agreement_Reached_at_the_Multi-Party_Talks_on_Northern_Ireland.pdf

Walsh, C., Bunting, L., Davidson, G., Doherty, N., McCartan, C., Mulholland, C., & Shevlin, M. (2025). *The prevalence and impact of adverse childhood experiences in Northern Ireland.* The Executive Programme on Paramilitarism and Organised Crime. https://www.drugsandalcohol.ie/42643/

Weinberger, L.E., and Screenivasan, S. (1994). Ethical and professional conflicts in correctional psychology. *Professional Psychology: Research and Practice, 25* (2), 161–167.

Part 2
Working with specific groups

5 Building and sustaining trusting relationships with children undergoing forensic evaluation and their caregivers

Louise E. Bowers

Introduction

Recent figures regarding young people in the criminal justice system indicate that during the year ending March 2023, 59,045 10–17 year olds were arrested and over 21,000 were charged with an offence and either taken to court or given a caution (Youth Justice Board, 2024). It is widely accepted that children have a greater capacity for change compared to adults (Steinberg & Scott, 2003), and this principle is enshrined in most legal systems across the world (e.g. Antonopoulos et al., 2018). Thus, there is a powerful argument for involving forensic psychologists early in the criminal justice process, so they can identify the needs of these children at a critical stage in their development (Bowers & McKeown, 2024). This ensures that appropriate support and interventions can be implemented from the outset. Yet, training on how to work effectively with children is not currently a core component of professional forensic psychological training and qualifications (Family Justice Council & the British Psychological Society, 2023).

This chapter focuses on the forensic evaluation of children (up to age 18) by psychologists for the criminal courts. These evaluations typically address key legal questions, such as whether the child is fit to plead/participate effectively in court proceedings, whether they have any cognitive impairments, mental health challenges, or neurodiversity issues, or the level of risk they may pose. The primary outcome of these assessments is a report containing expert opinion that must be valid, objective and admissible in court, serving as a critical tool in the legal decision-making process. Wherever possible, parent(s)/carer(s) are included in the assessment process. This is primarily to provide a developmental history, but their involvement can bring additional benefits, which will be examined further in this chapter.

Research has consistently shown that developing and maintaining trusting relationships is essential for a child-friendly and effective youth justice system (HM Inspectorate of Probation, 2024). However, Greenberg and Shuman (2007) caution that within the adversarial legal system, forensic evaluators must resist adopting a therapeutic approach. Instead, they argue, evaluators should remain "neutral, objective, and detached" (p. 131). This chapter

DOI: 10.4324/9781003542377-8

examines evidence indicating that, despite this need for neutrality, building a trusting relationship with both the child and their parent(s)/carer(s) during forensic evaluation is critical because it fosters engagement and helps create a safe environment where open and honest dialogue can occur. The social, psychological and legal consequences of failing to support the child and their parent(s)/carers(s) in engaging at this crucial stage of the criminal justice process can be profound and long-lasting, affecting not only the child's future but also broader public safety and protection. By examining these issues, this chapter highlights the delicate balance between maintaining objectivity and ensuring meaningful engagement in forensic evaluations of children.

This chapter begins by reviewing key evidence highlighting the importance of the relationship between children, professionals who work with them and their parent(s)/carers(s), highlighting the relational variables and personal characteristics that support the development of a positive working alliance. Following this, this chapter examines the unique psychosocial context in which forensic evaluations of children occur, identifying some potential barriers to establishing these critical relationships. Practical skills and strategies for building, nurturing and maintaining respectful and trusting relationships are then discussed, covering the stages before, during and after forensic evaluation. To enrich this discussion, this chapter concludes with reflections from two individuals with lived experience of the forensic evaluation process, Tommy (a child charged with a serious offence) and Sarah (the mother of a child charged with a serious offence).[1]

The importance of the relationship between the forensic assessor, the child and their caregivers

Therapeutic alliance refers to the quality of collaboration and connection between a therapist and client, which is strongly influenced by the therapist's personal qualities and their style of interaction (Marshall & Burton, 2010). The quality of the relationship between client and therapist is widely recognised as a critical factor influencing the outcome of psychotherapy, across various settings including inpatient mental health services (e.g. Hartley et al., 2022), correctional facilities (e.g. Marshall & Burton, 2010) and community contexts (e.g. Flückiger et al., 2018). This relationship–outcome link remains robust regardless of the therapeutic approach used, the age group of the client (adult or child) or the specific measures applied to assess it (Ardito & Rabellino, 2011).

It has been argued that therapeutic relationship variables are even more important when working clinically with children, who may enter treatment unaware of the nature of their difficulties and be resistant to change (Karver et al., 2006). Meta-analytic data relating specifically to child and adolescent therapy has identified a modest but robust association between a range of therapeutic relationship variables and treatment outcome (Shirk & Karver, 2003). Research by Hartley et al. (2022), conducted in an inpatient mental health unit, highlighted the value children place on their relationships with staff and therapists, which they saw as critical to their recovery. This is encapsulated in a key theme that emerged from this research: "Therapeutic Relationships are the Treatment" (p. 24). When working therapeutically with children, involving families in treatment is often essential. A meta-analytic study examining the therapeutic relationship variables in youth and family therapy (Karver et al., 2006), highlighted the importance of the therapist building a strong alliance with the child's family, emphasising that the family's active involvement and commitment to interventions were key factors in positive treatment outcomes for the child. Karver et al. argued that this engagement fosters the child's participation by creating a safe, supportive environment where therapy can effectively take place.

The importance of high-quality relationships extends beyond clinical settings and is equally relevant within the criminal justice system, as highlighted by the concept of therapeutic jurisprudence (Wexler, 2000, 2010). Just as the therapeutic alliance plays a critical role in fostering recovery and positive outcomes for children and families in clinical contexts, therapeutic jurisprudence emphasises the significance of supportive, respectful and empathetic relationships in legal settings. The therapeutic jurisprudence philosophy focuses on the law's impact on an individual's emotional and psychological well-being. It examines how laws, legal procedures and the behaviour of legal professionals can either contribute to or detract from the mental health and welfare of individuals involved in the legal system. By viewing the law through a therapeutic lens, this approach encourages legal professionals (e.g. judges, lawyers and other key "legal actors") to consider how their communication, actions and decisions can support positive psychological outcomes for those they serve.

Howieson (2023) advanced this philosophy by developing an evidence-based framework for evaluating and enhancing the practice of therapeutic jurisprudence. Drawing from research on the connection between therapeutic alliance and outcomes, she introduced the concept of a "legal therapeutic alliance". Howieson argues that if legal professionals actively promote the three relational pillars of therapeutic jurisprudence (procedural justice,[2] trust and self-determination) a legal therapeutic alliance will emerge. Howieson proposes that by embedding these principles into legal processes, the therapeutic impact within court settings can mirror the beneficial outcomes seen in therapy. This framework can be applied to systems, processes or individual professional practices, offering valuable guidance for creating positive relational environments in legal settings. The framework has significant implications for supporting children and their parent(s)/caregiver(s) in forensic evaluations, helping create a supportive and constructive environment that can mitigate the stress and potential trauma associated with legal proceedings.

Howieson's framework for a legal therapeutic alliance aligns closely with the findings of a recent review of the evidence base for effective youth justice services (HM Inspectorate of Probation, 2024). This report concluded that positive outcomes for justice-involved children are underpinned by "the establishment of positive, secure, consistent and trusting relationships between practitioners and children". The review identified key practitioner attributes essential for building authentic, supportive connections with vulnerable children. These attributes include empathy, trustworthiness, reliability, respect and genuineness. Positive relationships were found to significantly enhance engagement, as children who trust their practitioners are more likely to share their experiences, express their views and make use of available support. Critically, the review identified that wherever possible, the parents(s)/carers(s) of the justice-involved child should be involved in the assessment process as this was found to greatly enhance the validity and reliability of the outcome.

In therapeutic and other professional settings, psychologists typically have the advantage of time to develop a positive alliance with their clients. This alliance is essential for fostering trust, openness and the depth of communication needed for effective intervention. In contrast, forensic evaluations are time-limited interactions taking place in a high-stakes, emotionally charged context. In these assessments, the validity and reliability of the findings are heavily reliant on the accuracy and completeness of information gathered from both the child and their parent(s)/carers(s). While empirical evidence is limited, it is reasonable to expect that the quality and depth of the information provided by the child and their parent(s)/carers(s) will correlate with the quality of the relationship established with the assessor. For instance, recent evidence-based guidelines for interviewing child victims and witnesses established the critical role of rapport-building in improving the quality of communication (Korkman et al., 2024). These guidelines highlight that establishing a positive connection with the child can enhance their willingness to disclose information, reduce anxiety and help them manage negative emotions throughout the interview process. Similarly, Leach and Powell (2020) have reviewed the evidence base for eliciting reliable and complete information from children undergoing forensic risk assessment. They identified the importance of interpersonal skills and personal questioning style to build trust and engage the child. They suggest that adopting a neutral but friendly and curious stance, while avoiding confrontation, is the most effective way to enhance rapport and manage any reactance that could impact on the working alliance. McCuish et al. (2019) highlight that rapport-building is an ongoing, dynamic process, which requires more than showing initial interest and understanding. They recommend that assessors employ specific strategies to maintain and enhance rapport throughout the session, adapting their approach as needed to support the child effectively. These strategies include empathic phrasing of questions, use of encouraging body language, acknowledging frustration and distress and providing opportunities for the interviewee to demonstrate specific knowledge.

Robinson (2010) reviewed and analysed 31 studies that explored children's perspectives on healthcare professionals, which highlighted the importance of treating young patients as active participants in their healthcare, rather than passive recipients. Clear, honest and respectful communication was noted as being key to building trust between healthcare professionals and children, while a lack of empathy, respect or acceptance often undermined the relationship. Instances where children felt dismissed or patronised were found to be particularly damaging. The children expected their healthcare professionals to safeguard their privacy and confidentiality. Although this review did not include psychologists, it did include child and adolescent mental health workers, therapists, counsellors and other NHS staff who were assessing children. Notably, working with "strangers" was identified as an issue which impacted on trust and engagement for children. This highlights the challenges of building trust in forensic evaluations where prior relationships are discouraged (Davies, 2019) and there is limited time to develop a safe and supportive environment.

Overall, it can be seen that creating an assessment environment that fosters trust, respect and safety is vital for building positive working relationships between the assessor, the child and their parent(s)/carer(s), even within limited interactions. While the specific consequences of failing to establish such relationships within forensic evaluations have not been studied, this has been linked to premature treatment termination in clinical settings (Garcia & Weisz, 2002). Robinson (2010) also found that children who perceive a lack of respect or empathy from healthcare professionals were less likely to seek help in the future. This could be relevant to forensic evaluations, where a failure to build a positive relationship could result in the child disengaging from the process prematurely. Such disengagement could not only affect the accuracy of the assessment but also have long-term implications for the child's willingness to engage with forensic professionals in the future, potentially impacting their current and future legal circumstances.

Setting the context: the unique challenges of carrying out forensic evaluations with children and their caregivers

Research indicates that facing criminal charges, even without a conviction, can cause significant emotional stress and psychological trauma (Dichter, 2013; Hewitt et al., 2022). It could be argued that these impacts are even more acute for children who are psychosocially immature and may be in contact with the criminal justice system for the first time. Arrest procedures, such as strip searches, DNA testing and phone examinations, can be intrusive and frightening (Brunson & Weitzer, 2009; Simkins, 2009). Furthermore, children charged with serious offences may be remanded into custody, separating them from their home, school and friends. This experience can feel isolating, confusing and disorienting, leaving children feeling abandoned and fearful about the future (User Voice, 2023; Sugie & Turney, 2017). The slow pace of the justice system can leave young people in a prolonged state of uncertainty and anxiety, sometimes stretching over months or even years. During this time, they may be left to worry about potential outcomes, often without the support of trusted adults to guide them through the experience and alleviate their fears. This drawn-out process can disrupt their sense of stability and security, underscoring the importance of supportive systems and psychological resources for children undergoing criminal prosecution.

It is well established that a high proportion of justice-involved children have experienced previous trauma, including neglect, abuse and exploitation (e.g. Malvaso et al., 2022). These experiences can lead to mistrust, hypervigilance and dysregulation, which can interfere with the formation of a therapeutic alliance (Eltz et al., 1995). While trauma-informed approaches are essential across all age groups (Willmot & Jones, 2022), children are generally more prone to visible distress, and their coping mechanisms are typically less developed. Furthermore, a substantial proportion of children involved in the criminal justice system are known to have neurodevelopment and mental health conditions along with potential learning challenges and communication difficulties (Bryan et al., 2015; Hughes et al., 2012; Turner et al., 2020). Despite these well-documented needs, assessors may not always be fully informed about the issues and children often use "masking" to hide their difficulties. Therefore, it is imperative that forensic professionals anticipate these challenges proactively and prepare to respond effectively to the complex and diverse needs of the child clients.

The inherent power imbalance in forensic relationships is well documented (e.g. Perlin, 1991), and this can be heightened in forensic evaluations where psychologists serve the court and interviewees have little choice but to engage through fear of the consequences. This imbalance is even greater with children, who are socialised to respect adult authority. Research carried out with adults in custody has shown that they often have a poor image of forensic psychologists, seeing them as disconnected, untrustworthy yet very powerful (Shingler et al., 2020). It is unclear whether justice-involved youth share the same perceptions of forensic psychologists, but evidence suggests that children can be suspicious of specialist professionals, viewing them as strangers that they should not trust (Hill, 1999; Robinson, 2010). This dynamic necessitates careful acknowledgement and consideration when assessing children forensically, to promote safe and ethical practice.

It is clear that establishing (and maintaining) a positive relationship with children undergoing forensic evaluation requires a unique set of skills distinct from those used in adult assessments. Fortunately, forensic psychologists have now largely moved away from assessing and treating children as "miniature adults" (Steinberg, 2003, p. 25), and it is now widely recognised that specialised, child-centred, developmentally informed approaches are essential for effective forensic assessment (Bowers & McKeown, 2024). These approaches are particularly critical given the profound emotional toll that involvement in the criminal justice system can have on children.

In my experience, children undergoing forensic evaluation often present with a bewildering mix of emotions, including guilt, shame, embarrassment and fear. These feelings, as Tommy vividly describes at the end of this chapter, are not only deeply distressing but also compounded by the inherently traumatic nature of the process itself. It is essential for practitioners to recognise and validate these complex emotions, understanding that for many children, the evaluation process can feel overwhelming and isolating. Practitioners must approach their assessments with empathy and care, striving to minimise the additional harm that systemic responses can inadvertently cause. By creating a supportive and trauma-informed environment during assessment, we can help alleviate some of the emotional burden and prevent the system from exacerbating the damage these children have already endured.

Drawing on my 30 years of experience assessing over 150 children and their parent(s)/carer(s) in the context of criminal court proceedings, the next section offers practical insights and strategies for building, nurturing and maintaining respectful and trusting relationships throughout the assessment process. Rather than being a step-by-step guide to forensic evaluation, it identifies approaches that foster positive engagement with both children and their families, ensuring they feel heard, valued and supported. In my experience, creating an environment of trust allows individuals to share meaningful and relevant information, ultimately enhancing the quality and integrity of the evaluation.

Effective strategies for building positive relationships with children and their caregivers during forensic evaluations

Setting the foundations for a positive relationship prior to the assessment

Making positive pre-assessment contact

The evidence reviewed so far highlights that building rapport with the child and their parent(s)/carer(s) is essential for an effective assessment. While guidance exists on how to build rapport at the start of an assessment (e.g. Leach & Powell, 2020; McCuish et al., 2019) I would argue that forensic evaluators can begin fostering a positive relationship even before the initial meeting. For instance, I make the effort to introduce myself and my role in advance by texting or emailing the parent(s)/carer(s) and sending a letter or email to the child if they are in custody. Research shows that promoting autonomy and self-determination within the justice system fosters a "legal therapeutic alliance" (Howieson, 2023). To support this, I offer the parent(s)/carer(s) a brief introductory telephone call or email exchange based on their preferences.

Accommodating assessment needs and preferences

During this initial contact, I discuss preferred appointment times, taking into account their responsibilities, and offer evening or weekend sessions when needed. I also enquire about their preferences for location and format of the assessment, whether in-person, via videoconference, or phone, and accommodate this where possible. When the child is not in custody, I seek the views of everyone involved regarding their preferences to be interviewed together, separately or both. To promote diversity and inclusion, I inquire about any conditions that might require adjustments to the assessment, the environment or process and respect religious observances and cultural practices that may affect scheduling. By providing my contact information, I ensure families can reach out with questions or concerns. In my experience, this early, respectful communication fosters trust, promotes inclusivity and lays the foundations for a positive, collaborative working relationship, even before the first meeting.

Building rapport at the beginning of the assessment

Informed consent

Establishing informed consent involves providing clear information to help individuals make an informed decision about receiving care or services. I find that when handled with honesty and transparency, the consent process becomes a powerful way to build trust with both the child and their parent(s)/carer(s). I send a written consent form in advance, giving the parent(s)/carer(s) time to review and discuss it with their child. Robinson (2010) emphasised the importance of healthcare providers using age-appropriate language, and to ensure validity, the form must be written in accessible language that both the child and their parents can understand. I have therefore created multiple formats of the consent form following guidelines from the UK Association for Accessible Formats (UKAAF: https://www.ukaaf.org). During the assessment, I carefully explain the form, focusing on key details, including the assessment process, measures to be used, and how information will be managed. Before asking the child and their parent(s)/carer(s) to sign the consent form, I emphasise that the child is being asked to agree to participate and has a degree of choice within the legal constraints. I am honest about the benefits and potential drawbacks of engaging in the assessment and reassure them that declining consent at any stage will not impact my judgement of them. I also inform them that they could withdraw their consent at any time by notifying their solicitor. Furthermore, I explain that the child (and sometimes the parent(s)/caregivers(s)) will have the chance to review my report to identify any factual inaccuracies or misrepresentations, which I will gladly amend. I provide a copy of the signed consent form for their records. As Logan (2013) notes, consent should never be rushed; in my experience, taking the time to thoroughly discuss consent builds trust and demonstrates a commitment to the child's well-being. Done sensitively, this approach empowers the child and their family, giving them greater control over the process.

Explaining the limits of confidentiality

Allied to the consent process, it is crucial to clearly explain the limits of confidentiality in a forensic evaluation. Medoff and Kinscherff (2006) note that this includes informing the child and their parent(s)/carer(s) about how information will be used and the actions taken if any harm or risk is disclosed. Unlike therapy, where confidentiality is central, forensic evaluations require sharing information for legal purposes, and the extent of confidentiality is extremely limited. I ensure the child and the parent(s)/carer(s) understand that any shared information may be included in the report and submitted to the court. These limits on confidentiality can challenge rapport-building, as individuals may feel wary of the psychologist and hesitant to share openly. To manage expectations, I always explain to the child and their family that I will be discreet and handle what they tell me with care and respect. In my experience, being transparent about the boundaries of confidentiality helps prevent misunderstandings and builds trust by showing respect for the individuals involved and their right and capacity to understand the process.

Explaining your role and duties

To avoid misunderstanding that could undermine trust, it is essential that the child and their parent(s)/carers(s) understand the distinction between clinical examination for treatment purposes and a forensic evaluation within a legal context. As Greenberg and Shuman (2007) note, the goal of a psychologist acting as a therapist is to support individuals in making positive life changes, whereas the role of a psychologist forensic evaluator is to assess the individual for legal purposes. The outcome of the latter may, in some cases, be "the opposite of enhancing the quality of the person's life" (Greenberg & Shuman, 2007, p. 131). It is crucial to be transparent about these differences from the outset. In my experience, a clear and straightforward explanation of this distinction helps set appropriate expectations and develop mutual understanding. This is how I approach explaining this concept:

> Your solicitor has asked me to see you because they thought it would be helpful. But I need you to understand am not working for your solicitor, I am working for the court. This means that I will write a report that is honest and independent, but it might not say what you would like it to say, but I will make sure I explain why I have said these things in a way that you can understand.

Other ways to enhance the developing relationship at the start of the assessment

Names hold significance for individuals (Logan, 2013), so I always ask children and their parent(s)/carer(s) how they prefer to be addressed and ensure I pronounce their names correctly. I invite them to call me by my first name and encourage them to take breaks as needed. I make it a priority to inform both the child and their parent that we may need to discuss challenging topics during the assessment, and I encourage them to prepare for potential emotional impacts, reassuring them that experiencing emotions is a natural response in this context. I find this approach fosters autonomy, provides support and reduces apprehension about emotional reactions during the process.

Developing and maintaining the relationship during the assessment

McCuish et al. (2019) offer guidance regarding strategies that can be used to maintain and enhance rapport during forensic assessments with children. Although these recommendations were originally developed for assessing adolescent male offenders with emerging personality disorder, I have successfully used many of these techniques and others in my own practice, adapting my approach as needed to support the child effectively.

Managing time constraints

Establishing trust with a child often takes more time than with adults, as children may feel apprehensive or intimidated in formal settings. Practical constraints, such as time and fee limits imposed by the Legal Aid Agency, can add to these difficulties. These challenges can be exacerbated in custodial settings, where logistical issues often result in children being brought to interview rooms late or, at times, not at all. To address this, I begin by acknowledging the time constraints while reassuring the child of their importance in the process. For example, I might say, I might say:

> We have two hours for the assessment today. But I have read all about you and feel I understand you well. I have thought hard about the areas that I think are most important to cover today, but this is your assessment, and you will have the opportunity to tell me the things that you think are important.

If I must move things along, I explain why respectfully, for example, I might say "This has been really helpful, and I'd love to hear more, but I want to make sure we have time to cover everything that's important today". To ease time pressure, I often schedule follow-up sessions, such as video link interviews in custody or telephone/video calls in community settings. I find that including small considerate explanations helps preserve the child's sense of control and understanding while balancing the practical limitations of the assessment.

Showing an interest and sharing knowledge

I have found that allowing the child to share their knowledge can be a very helpful way to enhance and maintain rapport, particularly for those on the autistic spectrum who may have well-documented and intense special interests (e.g. Pokémon, Lego, Anime). For example, I might ask about their interest or admit my own lack of knowledge on the subject, seeking their advice. However, it has been demonstrated that justice-involved children value genuineness from their practitioners (HM Inspectorate of Probation, 2024). Therefore, it is important to only use this strategy only in an authentic way, as any hint of insincerity or patronisation has the potential to alienate the child and undermine their trust both in the practitioner and the evaluation process.

Managing frustration, resistance and distress

During my preparation for an assessment, I make a point of identifying potentially distressing topics that may need to be addressed. I approach these areas with empathy, and before introducing a challenging topic, I acknowledge its difficulty, saying something like, "I'd like to discuss something that might be hard to talk about, and I understand this may be difficult for you". I then explain, the reasons why it is necessary to explore that area, ensuring that they understand its relevance to the assessment. For example, I might say, "It's important for me to ask about this so I can better understand and help you, but please know that you are in control, and we can pause or come back to this at any time". This proactive approach helps prepare the child and/or parent(s)/carer(s), reducing the element of surprise and demonstrating my commitment to handling sensitive matters with care and understanding,

Despite this preparation, as forensic evaluations progress, they typically become increasingly challenging. These challenges may stem from the sensitivity of the questions, the duration of the assessment or the emotional demands of discussing difficult or personal topics. This can lead to frustration, resistance and/or distress in the child or parent(s)/carer(s), potentially disrupting or rupturing the working relationship if not addressed effectively. Place and Meloy (2018) provide valuable guidance on both preventing and managing reactance in a range of interview settings. Techniques include using sensitive and empathic language, demonstrating nonthreatening body language, acknowledging resistance when it arises and providing choice to empower the interviewee. If I notice that a child or parent/carer is becoming frustrated, resistant or distressed, I acknowledge their feelings in a validating and compassionate manner. For instance, I might say, "I understand that this process can sometimes feel overwhelming and tiring at times", "I can see that you are finding this difficult, and it is becoming harder to answer my questions", "I recognise that the questions I am asking are upsetting for you" or simply "I get that this process can be really hard". I would typically praise the child or parent/carer for the progress they had made so far and work collaboratively to find a solution. For instance, I might say, "you have done so well so far, let's see what we can do to make this part a bit easier". Possible options could include shifting to a neutral topic, taking a short break or stepping away from a sensitive subject altogether. To ensure my tone and body language are not inadvertently contributing to the difficulty, I also inquire if there is anything I could do to adjust my approach. For example, I might ask, "Is there anything I can do to make this process more comfortable for you?" In my experience, this empathetic and flexible approach helps maintain engagement while prioritising the well-being of all parties involved. By offering support and adapting to their needs, I ensure the child and parent(s)/caregiver(s) feel heard, respected and empowered throughout the evaluation process.

Maintaining the relationship after the assessment

Boundaried ongoing contact while keeping the child and parent(s)/carer(s) in mind

Shingler and Purvis (2024) highlight the importance of maintaining connections in forensic practice. This is especially important when working with children, who tend to value consistency and the opportunity to develop long-term relationships with professionals (HM Inspectorate of Probation, 2024; Robinson, 2010). Forensic evaluations may be a single session or span multiple meetings. Regardless of the timeframe, morally it feels wrong to delve deeply into the personal and intimate details of someone's life during an assessment, only to abruptly sever all communication once the necessary information has been obtained. Having formed a relationship in the most stressful of circumstances, it feels important not to leave the family feeling exposed or abandoned. I like to demonstrate that they matter to me and remain in my thoughts. I therefore make it a priority to email, message or write to the child and their parent(s)/carer(s) after the session to thank them for their time and participation. I will typically include a message of hope and support in this communication. I provide my work contact details, giving them permission to reach out if there is more they wish to share or feel is important. Shingler and Purvis (2024) note that providing contact details is, in itself, a gesture of trust. While children rarely contact me afterwards, one child I later assessed as an adult shared that they had kept all my emails and often reflected on them. Parent(s)/carer(s) are more likely to contact me after an assessment, typically seeking advice or requesting signposting to other professionals who can offer additional support. I have never encountered a situation where the trust extended to parent(s)/carer(s) was misused. Maintaining this approach reflects the values of connection and respect in my practice, fostering a sense of care and continuity beyond the formal boundaries of an assessment.

The experiences of Tommy and Sarah

Tommy was convicted of a serious criminal offence when he was aged 15. I was instructed by the Crown Prosecution Service to assess him when he was aged 14 and accommodated in a secure children's home. Tommy is now a young adult and was reflecting back on his experience of being assessed. Sarah is the mother of a different child who was charged with a serious criminal offence when they were aged 15. I interviewed Sarah separately from her child who at that time was detained in a secure children's home. These personal accounts provide valuable perspectives on the practical and emotional realities of forensic evaluations.

Tommy was able to describe the anxiety and fear he experienced in the early stages of his journey through the criminal justice process:

> I was terrified about what might happen to me if convicted, and this dominated much of my thinking. I was literally fighting for my life.

Sarah described the early days following her child's charges as destabilising and confusing, leaving her feeling disoriented and overwhelmed:

> I was completely clueless, in a whirlwind of unknown. There was so much happening all the time that it really was a whirlwind; a lot of panic and urgency. And no spare time to wonder whom I needed to speak to, just to accept it had to happen. I had no control in this situation whatsoever. I found myself in contact with you in the context of a dire situation, in my case quite unexpectedly, with no prior warning, involvement, or understanding of this world.

Tommy and Sarah both described their apprehension and anxiety about taking part in a forensic evaluation.

> I felt apprehensive about participating in the interview. I can now understand that the main reason for this apprehension was that I would be forced to talk about difficult subjects. Mainly my offence and my lifestyle in the build up to me committing it. I was genuinely worried that the conclusion would be that I was evil or not capable of change (Tommy).

> I was anxious, wasn't sure what you would want to know or how you would take our answers or if there was going to be enough information. So, in order to keep my sanity I had to trust that I was being introduced to a team who were genuinely keen to help (Sarah).

Tommy specifically seemed to appreciate the contact I had with him prior to the assessment, which seemed to alleviate some of the anxiety he experienced:

> My anxiety was alleviated significantly thanks to your approach. In the lead up to the interview, I remember you sent me a letter explaining the purpose of the assessment and placing a specific emphasis on the fact that the purpose of the interview was not to trip me up or paint me

in a bad light. Put simply, I was assured that the assessment would be carried out professionally and fairly.

Likewise, Sarah seemed reassured by my initial contact with her saying:

> I didn't have any reason to doubt you would not be professional with everything trusted to you. You were a lifeline of hope.

Tommy insightfully captured the tension inherent in the consent process, describing the conflicting feelings of being told he had a choice yet feeling compelled to participate in the forensic evaluation. His experience likely reflects the reality for many children in this situation, who may perceive their autonomy is limited within the confines of the legal system.

> I felt as though I had a choice in whether or not to speak to speak to you in the sense that I was not physically forced to stay in the room and could leave at any time. I remember being made aware that I was free to withdraw from the interview at any time. However, my legal team advised me that failure to cooperate with the expert witnesses would be looked upon negatively by the courts. But I was constantly aware that it was my own decision whether or not to take part.

Similarly, Sarah expressed that while she did not feel she had a genuine choice about whether to speak with me, she found reassurance in the clarity and transparency of the consent process.

> No, I didn't feel I had a choice, but I was keen to talk. I felt I had to answer anything asked of me by any/all professionals. If I didn't, it could be assumed unreasonable unconformity, which could paint a bad picture of my family and willingness to assist/ tell the truth. However, I felt assured you were there to help and this was part of the process. The consent process reassured me that that you had the best intentions for us and that you would practise very properly and respectfully. I was keen to share as much information as possible. I hoped you would be able to take our answers as pieces of the puzzle and fit them together with your own knowledge, so I gave as much detail as possible.

Both Tommy and Sarah appeared to understand the explanation I gave as to my role as an expert:

> I remember that when I met you, we had a conversation about your duty as an expert witness. I cannot remember exactly how it was explained

to me, but I do remember feeling entirely certain that I would be treated fairly by you, and I was left with no feelings of conflict or concern with regards to this specific topic (Tommy).

I understood your duty to the court, and to the truth, which was fine by me as I believed there was nothing to hide (Sarah).

Sarah seemed to appreciate the personal qualities I demonstrated during the evaluation, which helped her feel comfortable and safe enough to engage. She emphasised the importance of my responsiveness and the time I dedicated to genuinely listening to her:

You are very warm hearted, smiley, friendly, relaxed, calm, gently/ softly spoken and down to earth, which makes it very easy to relax in your presence. I feel you are very patient and good at addressing and adapting to individual needs. You really listen and genuinely care and you make time for this. Which is imperative: to feel heard, acknowledged and cared for (which during such a traumatic time faced with such unknowns really made a substantial difference to our family, feeling that they had a ray of hope that someone cares enough to help). You were so very patient and willing to lead and reassure, almost nurturing, the stark opposite of a professional with power.

Similarly, Tommy was able to identify specific aspects of my interaction that helped alleviate his anxiety. For instance, he noted:

When we met, I felt that we built up a good rapport, or at least as good a rapport as I was capable of building at the time. I felt comfortable with you, probably more than I had done with the other expert witnesses who assessed me before. I felt listened to, respected, and although I couldn't make sense of it at the time, I felt as though you showed me empathy, something the other expert witnesses, in my opinion, did not or perhaps could not do.

Despite this, at one stage of the assessment, Tommy became overwhelmed with the enormity of his situation. He recalled how he "lost control" of his emotions, smashed a telephone and threw chairs around the room. Tommy reflected on how I responded and what this meant to him:

You sat with me for around one hour. Instead of just leaving (which is exactly what I would have done) you gave me a safe space to reflect on my feelings and consider the next steps forward. This was greatly appreciated and something that I never forgot.

I wrote to Tommy after the assessment, but he did not recall this. Sarah seemed to appreciate the fact that I did not terminate our professional relationship as soon as the assessment was complete saying:

> I did feel able to reach out to you for further queries, though I do feel I need to keep it professional/appropriate/respectful. I'm aware of a boundary line, not that you set, but just because of the nature of how I came to get to know you and your involvement with my family. I trust you will help me where you can and I know you have vast knowledge and experience to draw on. I do feel that you are one of the few people who has a realistic and truthful understanding of my situation.

Summary and conclusions

This chapter highlights the essential role of building trusting relationships with children and their parent(s)/carers in the context of forensic evaluations. It argues that while neutrality and objectivity are essential, trust and engagement are equally critical for fostering an environment where open and honest dialogue can occur. This is particularly vital when working with justice-involved children, who often face complex psychosocial challenges, including trauma, neurodiversity, mental health issues and learning disabilities and challenges. This chapter outlines strategies for building rapport at each stage of the evaluation process and highlights the importance of empathy, transparency and respect in overcoming barriers such as the inherent power imbalance, time constraints and the emotional intensity of legal proceedings. Reflections from individuals with lived experience, such as Tommy and Sarah, illustrate the profound impact compassionate and empathic interactions have on reducing anxiety and distress for children undergoing forensic evaluation and their parents/carers. Ultimately, this chapter advocates for a balanced approach where evaluators maintain their professional objectivity while utilising therapeutic skills to form a legal therapeutic alliance. By doing so, practitioners will not only improve the quality of their evaluations but also contribute to a more supportive and effective youth justice system.

Notes

1 All names have been changed to protect the identities of the individuals who very generously agreed to share their experiences.
2 Procedural justice can be broadly defined as fair decision-making processes. It is underpinned by four key principles that help ensure equitable and transparent outcomes. These principles are, having a voice (can individuals express their views), neutrality (are decision made in a factual, impartial way), respect (are individuals treated with dignity and in ways that respect their rights) and trustworthiness (do the decision makers have integrity and can they be trusted to do what is right).

References

Antonopoulos, I., Dingwall, G., & Hillier, T. (2018). The continuing chronology of confusion: crime prevention, welfare and the why of youth justice. *The Journal of Criminal Law*, 82(5), 402–419. https://doi.org/10.1177/0022018318790135

Ardito, R. B., & Rabellino, D. (2011). Therapeutic alliance and outcome of psychotherapy: Historical excursus, measurements, and prospects for research. *Frontiers in Psychology*, 2, 270. https://doi.org/10.3389/fpsyg.2011.00270

Bowers, L., & McKeown, A. (2024). What works in the assessment of risk and treatment need in young people who offend. In L. A. Craig, L. Dixon, & T. A. Gannon. (Eds.), *The Wiley handbook of what works in correctional rehabilitation: An evidence-based approach to theory, assessment and treatment* (pp. 65–80). Wiley-Blackwell https://doi.org/10.1002/9781119893073.ch6

Brunson, R. K., & Weitzer, R. (2009). Police relations with black and white youths in different urban neighborhoods. *Urban Affairs Review*, 44(6), 858–885.

Bryan, K., Garvani, G., Greogry, J., & Kilner, K. (2015). Language difficulties and criminal justice: The need for earlier identification. *International Journal of Language and Communication Disorders*, 50(6), 763–775. https://doi.org/10.1111/1460-6984.12183

Davies, J. (2019). Developing a model for evidence-based clinical forensic interviewing. *International Journal of Forensic Mental Health*, 18(1), 3–11. https://doi.org/10.1080/14999013.2018.1508096

Dichter, M. E. (2013). "They arrested me-and i was the victim": Women's experiences with getting arrested in the context of domestic violence. *Women & Criminal Justice*, 23(2), 81–98. https://doi.org/10.1080/08974454.2013.759068

Eltz, M. J., Shirk, S. R., & Sarlin, N. (1995). Alliance formation and treatment outcome among maltreated adolescents. *Child Abuse & Neglect*, 19(4), 419–431.

Family Justice Council & the British Psychological Society. (2023). *Psychologists as expert witnesses in the family courts in England and wales: Standards, competencies, and expectations*. Guidance from the Family Justice Council and The British Psychological Society. https://explore.bps.org.uk/binary/bpsworks/66c8ba41e5130260/4a15919fbe9471252b3be033b99945f46099f8843252db0b9d106cf3880521ad/9781854338297.pdf

Flückiger, C., Del Re, A. C., Wampold, B. E., & Horvath, A. O. (2018). The alliance in adult psychotherapy: A meta-analytic synthesis. *Psychotherapy*, 55(4), 316–340. https://doi.org/10.1037/pst0000172

Garcia, J. A., & Weisz, J. R. (2002). When youth mental health care stops: Therapeutic relationship problems and other reasons for ending youth outpatient treatment. *Journal of Consulting and Clinical Psychology*, 70(2), 439–443. https://doi.org/10.1037/0022-006X.70.2.439

Greenberg, S. A., & Shuman, D. W. (2007). When worlds collide: Therapeutic and forensic roles. *Professional Psychology Research and Practice*, 38(2), 129–132. https://doi.org/10.1037/0735-7028.38.2.129

Hartley, S., Redmond, T., & Berry, K. (2022). Therapeutic relationships within child and adolescent mental health inpatient services: A qualitative exploration of the experiences of young people, family members and nursing staff. *PLos One*, 17(1), e0262070. https://doi.org/10.1371/journal.pone.0262070

Hewitt, J., Lewis, J., & Marsden, S. (2022, Oct 19). *The psychological effects of criminal justice measures: A review of evidence related to terrorist offending*. Centre for

Research and Evidence on Security Threats. https://crestresearch.ac.uk/resources/the-psychological-effects-of-criminal-justice-measures/

Hill, M. (1999). What's the problem? Who can help? The perspectives of children and young people on their well-being and on helping professionals. *Journal of Social Work Practice*, 13(2), 135–145. https://doi.org/10.1080/026505399103368

HM Inspectorate of Probation. (2024). *Evidence base: Youth justice services.* Retrieved November 3, 2025, from https://hmiprobation.justiceinspectorates.gov.uk/our-research/evidence-base-youth-justice/

Howieson, J. A. (2023). A framework for the evidence-based practice of therapeutic jurisprudence: A legal therapeutic alliance. *International Journal of Law and Psychiatry*, 89, 101906–101906. https://doi.org/10.1016/j.ijlp.2023.101906

Hughes, N., Williams, H., Chitsabesan, P., Davies, R., & Mounce, L. (2012). *Nobody made the connection: The prevalence of neurodisability in young people who offend.* Children's Commissioner. University of Exeter; University of Birmingham. Retrieved from https://yjlc.uk/resources/legal-updates/nobody-made-connection

Karver, M. S., Handelsman, J. B., Fields, S., & Bickman, L. (2006). Meta-analysis of therapeutic relationship variables in youth and family therapy: The evidence for different relationship variables in the child and adolescent treatment outcome literature. *Clinical Psychology Review*, 26(1), 65. https://doi.org/10.1016/j.cpr.2005.09.001

Korkman, J., Otgaar, H., Geven, L. M., Bull, R., Cyr, M., Hershkowitz, I., Mäkelä, J. M., Mattison, M., Milne, R., Santtila, P., van Koppen, P., Memon, A., Danby, M., Filipovic, L., Garcia, F. G., Gewehr, E., Gomes Bell, O., Järvilehto, L., Kask, K., Körner, A., Lacey, E., Lavoie, J., Magnusson, M., Miller, Q. C., Pakkanen, T., Peixoto, C. E., Perez, C. O., Pompedda, F., Su, I. A., Sumampouw, N. E. J., van Golde, C., Waterhouse, G. F., Zappalà, A., & Volbert, R. (2024). White paper on forensic child interviewing: Research-based recommendations by the European Association of Psychology and Law. *Psychology, Crime & Law*, 31(8), 1–44. https://doi.org/10.1080/1068316X.2024.2324098

Leach, C. L., & Powell, M. B. (2020). Forensic risk assessment interviews with youth: How do we elicit the most reliable and complete information? *Psychiatry, Psychology and Law*, 27(3), 428–440. https://doi.org/10.1080/13218719.2020.1734982

Logan, C. (2013). Risk assessment: Specialist interviewing skills for forensic practitioners. In C. Logan, & L. Johnstone. (Eds.), *Managing clinical risk. A guide to effective practice* (pp. 259–292). Routledge. https://doi.org/10.4324/9780203106433-16

Malvaso, C. G., Cale, J., Whitten, T., Day, A., Singh, S., Hackett, L., Delfabbro, P. H., & Ross, S. (2022). Associations between adverse childhood experiences and trauma among young people who offend: A systematic literature review. *Trauma, Violence, & Abuse*, 23(5), 1677–1694. https://doi.org/10.1177/15248380211013132

Marshall, W. L., & Burton, D. L. (2010). The importance of group processes in offender treatment. *Aggression and Violent Behavior*, 15(2), 141–149.

McCuish, E. C., Hanniball, K. B., & Corrado, R. (2019). The assessment of psychopathic personality disturbance among adolescent male offenders: Interview strategies and recommendations. *International Journal of Forensic Mental Health*, 18(1), 35–49. https://doi.org/10.1080/14999013.2018.1531095

Medoff, D., & Kinscherff, R. (2006). Forensic evaluation of juvenile sexual offenders. In G. P. K. S. N. Sparta. (Ed.), *Forensic mental health assessment of children and adolescents* (pp. 342–364). Oxford University Press. https://doi.org/10.1093/med:psych/9780195145847.003.0022

Perlin, M. L. (1991). Power imbalances in therapeutic and forensic relationships. *Behavioral Sciences & The Law*, 9(2), 111–128. https://doi.org/10.1002/bsl.2370090203

Place, C. J., & Meloy, J. R. (2018). Overcoming resistance in clinical and forensic interviews. *International Journal of Forensic Mental Health*, 17(4), 362–376. https://doiorg/10.1080/14999013.2018.1485189

Robinson, S. (2010). Children and young people's views of health professionals in England. *Journal of Child Health Care*, 14(4), 310–326. https://doi.org/10.1177/1367493510381772

Shingler, J., & Purvis. (2024). "It's not just words, it's something you can feel: How therapeutic relationships can support prison-community transitions. In J. Shingler, & S. Stickney. (Eds.), *The journey from prison to community: Developing identity, meaning and belonging with men in the UK* (1st ed., pp. 155–173). Routledge. https://doi.org/10.4324/9781003308171-12

Shingler, J., Sonnenberg, S. J., & Needs, A. (2020). Psychologists as 'the quiet ones with the power': Understanding indeterminate sentenced prisoners' experiences of psychological risk assessment in the United Kingdom. *Psychology, Crime & Law*, 26(6), 571–592. https://doi.org/10.1080/1068316X.2019.1708354

Shirk, S. R., & Karver, M. (2003). Prediction of treatment outcome from relationship variables in child and adolescent therapy: A meta-analytic review. *Journal of Consulting and Clinical Psychology*, 71(3), 452–464. https://doi.org/10.1037/0022-006X.71.3.452

Simkins, S. (2009). *When kids get arrested: What every adult should know*. Rutgers University Press. https://doi.org/10.36019/9780813548180

Steinberg, L. (2003). Juveniles on trial: MacArthur foundation study calls competency into question. *ABA Criminal Justice Magazine*, 18, 20–25.

Sugie, N. F., & Turney, K. (2017). Beyond incarceration: Criminal justice contact and mental health. *American Sociological Review*, 82(4), 719–743. https://doi.org/10.1177/0003122417713188

Turner, D., Wolf, A. J., Barra, S., Muller, M., Gregorio-Hertz, P., Huss, M., Tuscher, O., & Retz, W. (2020). The association between adverse childhood experiences and mental health problems in young offenders. *European Child & Adolescent Psychiatry*, 30, 1195–1207. https://doi.org/10.1007/s00787-020-01608-2

User Voice. (2023). *Youth on remand*. HM Inspectorate of Probation. Retrieved from https://www.justiceinspectorates.gov.uk/cjji/wp-content/uploads/sites/2/2023/11/User-Voice-Youth-on-Remand.pdf

Wexler, D. B. (2000). Therapeutic jurisprudence: An overview. *Thomas M. Cooley Law Review*, 17, 125–134. Available at SSRN: https://ssrn.com/abstract=256658

Wexler, D. B. (2010). Therapeutic jurisprudence and its application to criminal justice research and development. *Irish Probation Journal*, 7, 94.

Willmot, P., & Jones, L. (2022). *Trauma-informed forensic practice*. 1st edn. Routledge. https://doi.org/10.4324/9781003120766

Youth Justice Board. (2024). *Youth justice statistics: 2022 to 2023*. https://www.gov.uk/government/statistics/youth-justice-statistics-2022-to-2023/youth-justice-statistics-2022-to-2023-accessible-version#:~:text=In%20the%20latest%20year%2C%20there,which%20arrests%20of%20children%20increased

6 Effective relational practice with women in prison

Jude Kelman

Introduction

This chapter draws on the author's clinical experience of working with women in custody. It also utilises findings from qualitative research undertaken as part of the author's PhD (Kelman et al., 2022, 2024a, 2024b). These studies examined trauma-informed care within women's prisons, from the perspectives of people living and working in them. The rich narrative accounts of the way 35 staff perceived their work and 51 individuals in women's prisons experienced their imprisonment highlighted the significance of the relationships they encountered and formed. Interactions with staff and other women during their time in custody were crucial to their survival within the complex and challenging prison system. These insights have shaped and refined thinking about what effective relational practice with women in prison looks like for practitioners. This is driven largely by what those with lived experience have indicated that good relational practice *feels* like for them, and the impact it can have on their custodial experiences and their subsequent ability to engage with rehabilitative and therapeutic services.

Background

It is only since 2016 that women's prisons within His Majesty's Prison and Probation Service (HMPPS) have been grouped together and managed as their own functional team. Prior to this, men's and women's prisons in similar geographical areas were managed together, hampering the strategic coordination of gender-specific services across all women's prisons. There is now a senior leader responsible for managing the Governors of all public sector women's prisons in order to bring consistency of approach and a sense of identity to the women's prison estate. This is particularly important given that HMPPS is a male-dominated organisation where only approximately 4% of the total prison population in England and Wales are women (Prison Reform Trust, 2024). The Women's Estate Psychology Service (WEPS) team was also set up in 2016 to develop and deliver gender-specific psychological services for women in custody. Over the years since its inception, WEPS

DOI: 10.4324/9781003542377-9

has evolved and grown as a specialist group of psychologists focusing solely on the needs of people living and working in women's prisons. The WEPS team has shaped and developed effective practices in response to research undertaken both within HMPPS women's prisons and from relevant international studies. This chapter, however, does not explore the developing area of research and practice within women's prisons that reflects a recognition of the need to understand the ways in which the unique biological characteristics of women (including hormone health, pregnancy and motherhood) can impact their experiences of imprisonment. This was beyond the scope of the author's research, and none of the women with lived experience of imprisonment who participated in the research raised these factors themselves.

There is substantial evidence that the prevalence of trauma in the lives of women in prison is higher than among the general population (Corston, 2007; Messina & Grella, 2006; Stensrud et al., 2019) and higher also than for men in prison (Baranyi et al., 2018; Bebbington et al., 2017; Bevan, 2017). There is also emerging evidence that there is a gender difference in the way trauma is experienced. Women have been found to be more vulnerable to the negative impacts of trauma than men (Blanco et al., 2018) and to experience posttraumatic stress disorder (PTSD) symptoms more severely, even when exposed to similar traumatic events (Tolin & Foa, 2006). Low oestrogen levels have been found to be related to more negative impacts of trauma (Maeng & Milad, 2015), given the possible role played by oestrogen in fear-processing (Blanco et al., 2018), which might partially explain why women can experience the impact of trauma more severely than men. It is also possible that the established connection between different types of traumatic experiences and the development of PTSD (Kessler et al., 2017) accounts for some of the gender differences in PTSD rates, with girls and women more likely to experience trauma involving interpersonal violence (Hanson et al., 2008), thereby elevating their risk of PTSD.

It was this higher rate of PTSD among imprisoned people that led Baranyi and colleagues (2018) to conclude that there was a need to provide trauma-informed care (TIC) for individuals in prison. The concept of TIC arose as academic and clinical understanding about trauma and its impacts developed. While there is no universally agreed definition of what it means to be trauma-informed and no clear consensus about the essential components of TIC, there are common features referred to across studies of TIC. At the service user level, key principles consistently identified (Covington, 2015; Elliott et al., 2005; Harris & Fallot, 2001; Menschner & Maul, 2016; Substance Abuse and Mental Health Services Administration [SAMHSA], 2014) include:

- Ensuring the **safety** of individuals (whether physical, psychological or emotional safety).
- Giving **choice and control** to service users.

- Enabling service users to **collaborate** and power share in decisions about their care and/or service design.
- **Empowerment** and building the strengths of individuals accessing the service.

Additional principles identified by some authors, include being **responsive to the gender, cultural and historical context** of service users (Elliott et al., 2005; SAMHSA, 2014; Wilson et al., 2015), demonstrating **trustworthiness** (Covington, 2015; Menschner & Maul, 2016; SAMHSA, 2014), providing **peer support** (SAMHSA, 2014), and ensuring **staff are cared for** (Covington, 2018).

The language of TIC has become increasingly prevalent within HMPPS since approximately 2015 when "trauma training" for staff was rolled out across women's prisons. However, it was only relatively recently (Kelman et al., 2022) that research established the range of ways in which women experienced their imprisonment as re-traumatising or as creating additional trauma. This finding has significance for practitioners and clinicians working in women's prisons: it highlights that prison is not a neutral environment within which to provide services. In fact, as will be explored further in this chapter, the prison environment and systemic context represent a substantial barrier to undertaking meaningful and effective therapeutic and forensic work with women in custody. As a starting point, good relational practice requires exploration of the ways in which the environment/organisational context impacts the individual service user, so that efforts can be made to counteract these factors, which might otherwise significantly undermine therapeutic efforts. Although TIC and relational practice are not one and the same, the traumatic experiences of women in prison – as well as the ongoing detrimental impact of their imprisonment – necessitate relational practice which integrates TIC, in order for it to be effective.

A model derived from lived experience

The model depicted in Figure 6.1 shows what those with experience of living and working in women's prisons perceived to be the barriers and enablers to trauma-informed care. It was developed from the thematic synthesis (Barnett-Page & Thomas, 2009) of results from three separate but inter-linked research studies completed as part of the author's PhD. These studies explored how individuals in women's prisons experienced their imprisonment, given their trauma histories (Kelman et al., 2022), and the perceptions of people living (Kelman et al., 2024a) and working (Kelman et al., 2024b) in women's prisons about the barriers and enablers to giving and receiving TIC.

Within HMPPS, this lived experience-derived model of the barriers and enablers to TIC has formed the basis for the development of practical guidance describing actions for all staff to take to improve the experiences of women during their imprisonment. Within this chapter, this model will be used as a framework to structure considerations about how practitioners can engage in effective relational work with women in prison. Direct quotations

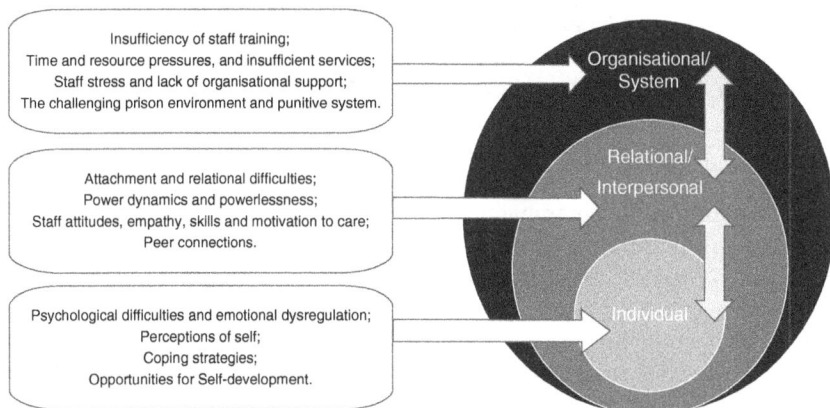

Insufficiency of staff training;
Time and resource pressures, and insufficient services;
Staff stress and lack of organisational support;
The challenging prison environment and punitive system.

Attachment and relational difficulties;
Power dynamics and powerlessness;
Staff attitudes, empathy, skills and motivation to care;
Peer connections.

Psychological difficulties and emotional dysregulation;
Perceptions of self;
Coping strategies;
Opportunities for Self-development.

Organisational/System

Relational/Interpersonal

Individual

Figure 6.1   The Holistic Ecological Model of Barriers and Enablers to Trauma-Informed Care in Prison: A Model Derived from Lived Experience (Kelman, 2024).

from staff (referred to as S followed by the participant number in parentheses after the quote) and prisoner participants (referred to as R followed by the participant number) who engaged in the research interviews are used illustratively throughout.[1] It should be noted that there is no implication that the contents of this chapter might not also be relevant to others in prison; however, they are based on the lived experiences of women.

The model shows factors at three levels: "individual", "relational/interpersonal" and "organisational/system". Although separate, these factors are also interrelated, influencing between and across levels, as well as being influenced by the other levels. Individuals in custody are situated at the heart of the model, given that they are the primary (but not only) service users within the prison context and the main intended recipients of TIC within women's prisons. The experiences of individuals in prison were both contingent upon, and contributed to, their relationships with staff and other women. Factors at the relational/interpersonal level were also impacted by the organisational/system-level factors. The prison system was not a benign presence sitting around the rest of the factors. Rather, it provided the physical and conceptual context within which everything occurred. The organisational environment, within which staff worked and people in prison lived, actively created barriers and challenges. Those living and working in women's prisons were required to improvise and navigate opportunities for TIC, often having to work against the negative influence of the organisation/system.

Individual-level factors that impact the provision of TIC for women in prison

In order to provide effective relational work with women in prison, it is first necessary to understand how they experience their imprisonment as well as how they view themselves and those around them while they are in custody. This understanding highlights both the extent of the need for trauma-informed and relational practice and the challenges for practitioners in providing TIC for women in custody.

Psychological difficulties and emotional dysregulation

Imprisonment negatively impacts the psychological health and well-being of individuals in prison: "[prison] is tiring – very, very draining, mentally and physically draining" (R7). Existing psychological difficulties, such as high levels of anxiety, are exacerbated, and the challenges of living within a prison environment contribute to high levels of emotional dysregulation: "When my anxiety is bad, sometimes.... I get stressed when there are a lot of people." (R6); "As soon as [my cell door] is opened up, my head seems to want to explode." (R35). Individuals often experience prison as traumatising and triggering in a range of ways, including the lack of clarity about how they should behave and the ever-present fear of punishment, which mirrors prior abuse experiences: "...you've got women coming into prison that have been abused ... faced with a system that also abuses." (R13). Many feel a continuous and generalised sense of threat and fear within the environment. They arrive in custody with elevated levels of anxiety arising from their preconceived ideas about prison life obtained largely from the media portrayal of prisons as dangerous places: "I only knew prison on TV ... and of course they show you the worst prisons in the world ... so coming here you think, 'Oh my God, I will not survive!'" (R1). Women describe high levels of emotional dysregulation and volatility, likely to have been contributed to by the overwhelming intensity of the environment as well as the frequent noise and sense of chaos that exists within prison: "It's horrendous ... when they open [my cell] door, you just think, 'shut the door again please – just leave me in here – at least I'm safe in here'." (R10). The restrictions on women's lives in custody mean that small incidents and events take on greater significance, and emotions can run high in response to situations which would be of little consequence to them in the community: "Little things can really set people off" (R3); "Everything is magnified.... I've seen people cry over not being able to get jam!" (R5).

Perceptions of self

Women in prison describe their indignity and shame at being dehumanised. Many feel as though they are often treated with condescension because of their crimes or status as prisoners: "...you just get treated like absolute dirt ... and [staff] think they're better than you" (R14). Others perceive themselves to be invisible or "just a number" in prison, rather than as a person with a unique identity who has value: "...any individuality, any personality ... that sort of thing ... [officers are] not interested – they don't want to hear you, they don't want to see you...." (R34). Many women identify the similarities between the way they experience their treatment by some staff in prison and their experiences of relationships characterised by emotional or physical abuse in the community: "It's very difficult for me because I don't like this power [officers] have over you." (R45). Perhaps related to prior trauma experiences, many women in prison have pre-existing poor self-perceptions and low expectations about how they deserve to be treated. However, the uncaring actions of a minority of staff compound the women's views of their low self-worth, or even worthlessness: "Sometimes you're not even spoken to like you're a human." (R39). When staff with caring responsibilities either do not demonstrate care or display active contempt towards women in prison, this exacerbates their negative self-concepts. Women feel infantilised and disempowered by the severely limited agency and control they have over their daily lives in prison and by the lack of opportunities for them to collaborate in decisions made about them, which further reinforces their low self-worth: "...especially when you get everything else taken away from you, you need people to see you as a person." (R4).

Coping strategies

The psychological distress experienced by women in prison is further compounded by their inability to use the range of ordinary coping strategies available to them in the community: "It's like another world ... because you're so contained, and you can't get away and go somewhere ... or you can't go for a walk in the park, or ... anything like natural, to go and let off steam...." (R5). Many women describe going into "survival mode" initially, to cope with the intensity of the emotional impact of their imprisonment and their profound sense that they are unsafe. Retreating to the relative safety of their rooms serves as a way of avoiding having to face the experience, with this small private space providing sanctuary from the clamour and stresses of the prison environment: "...I love that time behind my door.... You don't have to talk to anyone you don't want to. I cherish that time." (R22). Other short-term avoidance strategies include keeping their distance from staff or other women until they can determine who they can trust. Over time, as women begin to identify the staff and other women who are caring and trustworthy, they begin to make use of the support available from these individuals to help them cope: "...you build up that relationship with people, so it becomes an easier place to live in. I'm quite comfortable here now because of that." (R3). Some women use self-harm as a strategy to cope with their situation or to elicit the help they require. However, the callous way that some staff reportedly respond to self-harming behaviour only reinforces to women in prison that they are not worthy of care: "...my friend said, 'I feel like slitting my wrists' – the officer turned around and said, 'go on then, do it' – and then she went and cut herself." (R41).

Opportunities for self-development

Despite the challenges of living in an environment which actively erodes the psychological well-being of its inhabitants, substantial personal resilience is shown by many women in prison. They are resourceful and committed to self-development, making use of the range of opportunities available to learn new skills. Many are also very motivated to address their substance use or engage in talking therapies as an adjunct to the medication that most are prescribed to manage their mental health:

> I'm getting better. I think the therapy helps me because I have someone who I can talk to.... I'm actually quite lucky because I get that second chance. I get this time to go over my past traumas and understand them....
>
> (R5)

In the author's experience, women in prison often appear to want relational engagement with staff and other women, to build a social framework within which they can live as part of a community, as well as to access support from those around them.

Relational/interpersonal-level factors that impact the provision of TIC for women in prison

Much of the prior trauma in the lives of women in prison occurs within the contexts of relationships (Hanson et al., 2008). Effective relational practice with women in prison must therefore take into account the way complex trauma profoundly impacts relational functioning through issues of disordered attachment, mistrust and difficulties relating to others: "[From] what I've been through in my childhood and stuff.... I don't trust many people. It takes me a while to trust people...." (R45). While there is considerable scope for positive interactions and engagement between staff and women in prison, a range of challenges are perceived by those living and working in women's prisons. These challenges create barriers affecting the ability of staff to give and women to receive, TIC. These barriers need to be understood in order for practitioners to foster and maintain effective relational practice.

Attachment and relational difficulties

There are a range of ways in which prison creates or perpetuates barriers to the development and maintenance of trust between staff and individuals in prison: "...there was one lady I shared [a room] with and she was released and went to the press and tried to sell my story.... This betrayal was horrible.... It is so bad in here, the betrayal of the [women]." (R1). Despite struggling with attachment and relational difficulties, women express a strong desire to receive nurturance and care from staff: "just empathy and kindness – that's what a lot of women need here." (R34). Most staff are committed to providing such care for the women: "I make them feel safe by being approachable … just treat them like you would want to be treated … [to] make them feel safe." (S12).

Given the relational context of much of the prior trauma experienced by women in prison, their expectations about how they are likely to be treated by others can affect their styles of relating: "…if a male member of staff comes near my [bed] or came any further into my room, I used to hit them, I used to go mad…." (R48); "I don't like anyone putting their hands on me." (R23). While there may be a strong pull towards engagement with others in order to elicit care, this can be coupled with an equally strong desire to feel safe: this can manifest as a need to protect themselves by keeping others away: "I trust me. I don't know these people. They're not the people I choose to be around … so I never really talk about my issues." (R22).

When women in prison experience care that is consistent and makes them feel contained, they report feeling psychologically safer: "There was one lovely … officer. When I pressed the buzzer she always came to my room and would sit outside my room just to calm me down … it was really nice." (R1). Conversely, when there is inconsistency in the way staff care for individuals in prison, this creates uncertainty and a sense of unfairness: "She gave me a [behaviour warning] that day for [wearing] sliders … everyone else was wearing sliders, but she gave me a [warning]!" (R25). This undermines the development and maintenance of trusting relationships between staff and prisoners, as it mirrors difficulties in other relationships in their lives, within which they had felt unsafe. When changes occur, these are often unpredictable or poorly communicated. The anticipation or reality of an unwanted change (such as a transfer to another prison) can further unsettle women in prison, contributing to mistrust in the system and distrust of staff working within it: "…today they've woken me up – 'you're moving!' It doesn't make any sense. They're just trying to make my life a living hell." (R16).

Power dynamics and powerlessness

Women in prison describe feeling powerless within the prison system and triggered by the relational dynamics between them and staff: "They're treating us like dirt basically." (R29). Women perceive that staff hold all of the power, while they hold none: "If an officer says something, you've got to do that, whether we want to or not." (R49). Additionally, women feel that they lack control over their lives in custody due to their status as prisoners within a hierarchical and inherently coercive system: "I feel like since I've been in custody, [staff have] taken over my life." (R29). This lack of control and the imbalance of power is triggering for many women, given the similarities between these relational dynamics with staff and the dynamics within prior abusive relationships: "…it's like being in a relationship – domestic abuse – and you can't do [anything] about it, you can't go for a walk, you can't get out." (R8).

Staff attitudes, empathy, skills and motivation to care

Assistance from staff who listen, are caring and kind, and demonstrate empathy is important for women in prison, despite connections with staff being perceived as fraught with potential dangers. Staff also describe the motivation and compassionate attitude needed, as well as the complex range of skills required to enable them to be willing and able to listen, notice and respond appropriately and individually to the behaviour, emotions and needs of women in their care. The application of such skills and behaviours enables women in prison to feel heard and understood, encouraging them to trust staff and be open to receiving TIC from them: "…there are certain officers that are absolutely amazing, and they … can understand, can empathise and have compassion…. They care…" (R2).

Significantly, the willingness of staff to use what little time they have available to engage meaningfully with women in prison on an individual basis is perceived by both staff and women in prison as a crucial factor contributing to the provision of TIC. As one male officer participant explained,

> …a lot of women go through domestic abuse … by treating them with respect, by helping them, by listening to them, by being patient and understanding…. I can change their viewpoint on men…. I think it's good for women to understand that not all men are violent or abusers … that there are men out there that are good, that will help….
>
> (S30)

Staff who are willing and able to nurture positive relationships are motivated to identify, as well as create time and opportunities to engage sensitively and compassionately with women in prison. Equally, women in prison recognise that staff are time-poor and often working under pressure, which means that when staff make the effort to engage individually with them, they feel valued and held in mind, countering some of their negative perceptions of themselves as unworthy of care or attention.

Peer connections

Connections with peers are perceived as easier to navigate than interactions with staff, as well as being easier to develop. The absence of the triggering power dynamics inherent in staff/prisoner relationships, as well as the sense of solidarity from being in the same situation, means that secure attachments can be formed with peers. Thus, women feel psychologically safer and more able to cope with the challenges of imprisonment: "…I know within my little group it's safe … no one's going to cause no dramas, no one's going to breach something that I confided in them, or anything like that – we're safe." (R31). Similarly, staff appreciate the significance of their peers as a source of support to cope with the stresses of their work.

Organisational/system-level factors which impact women in prison

The prison environment is perceived by staff and women in prison as an inherently (re)traumatising context within which people live and work. Several factors at the organisational/system level impact the ability of staff to provide TIC, as well as negatively impact those women in prison with prior trauma experiences.

Insufficiency of staff training

While the use of trauma language such as "triggering" or "traumatising" is commonplace among people living and working in custody, there is a shared perception that staff trauma training needs to include skills-based components as well as awareness-raising elements. These would support staff to recognise the potential signs of trauma in the behaviour of people in prison, as well as provide them with the confidence and skills required to appropriately support women who might be experiencing a trauma response. This would enable staff to provide TIC, rather than risking escalating someone's distress.

Time and resource pressures and insufficient services

The ratios of prison officers to prisoners create a disparity between the amount of time that staff feel they have available on any given day and the large number of individuals in prison who need their time and support. Staff also feel pressured to deliver a high volume of work to meet the complex needs of multiple women for whom they are responsible:

> ...I genuinely do care about the women ... we have self-harmers ... we have women who are in crisis, we have women who are angry ... and I feel like we are doing them a disservice ... because we can't possibly spend as much time with them as they need.
>
> (S11)

The scarcity of time is a significant factor impeding the provision of TIC, even when staff have the skills or motivation to do so: "...it's so hard to have a [one to one] conversation with every inmate, and you know you have ... things to do.... We are very time limited. Time is a very big issue for us." (R18). Conversely, the availability of time creates opportunities for skilled and motivated staff to provide TIC.

The levels of services available to meet the mental health needs of women in prison can lead to them feeling uncared for and abandoned, as well as being cut off from the sources of support that existed for them in the community. Some women can be driven to behave in extreme ways in desperation to secure access to the limited support that exists: "...you need to go and cut yourself a bit and then they'll say, 'we'll see you'." (R31). Consequently, some staff might view such behaviours as manipulative, which can contribute to further problems in relationships between them and women in prison. For example, staff might be less empathetic and supportive towards women whose behaviour is perceived as disingenuous.

Staff stress and lack of organisational support

Operational staff working in women's prisons experience their job roles as emotionally and psychologically challenging: "It does get to you. It really gets you down." (S6). They perceive that there is insufficient organisational support, which has a detrimental impact on them, as they find the work mentally draining and sometimes traumatic:

> …I think [the support] should be more focused on the officer rather than the prisoner, because you can't help someone unless you're mentally stable … and a lot of [staff] have broken down on that wing – crying. I myself, first couple of months, I did start crying because I didn't know how to handle it all.
>
> (S4)

Some staff report resentment and disillusionment that they are expected to provide TIC to women in prison without being allocated the time or resources they see as necessary to do so properly, or without being supported adequately themselves: "Honestly, a lot of the staff here are just tired and worn out and unappreciated." (S5).

The challenging prison environment and punitive system

There are many ways in which the fixed, inescapable and psychologically impactful context of the prison environment affects the extent to which TIC can be provided and experienced. Prison is recognised as a challenging environment in which to both live and work. Women in prison experience many day-to-day aspects of their imprisonment as triggering given their trauma histories, and staff describe feeling powerless themselves to control, reduce or remove the triggers endemic in the environment. There are also a range of embedded and ingrained institutional symbols, such as keys and uniforms, which serve as constant reminders for people in prison of the hierarchical and punitive nature of the organisation: "…at the end of the day we're still a prison … unfortunately there's going to be loud noises … you're going to hear the jangling of keys, people being locked up, and … people have got to shout, you know?" (S29). These features of imprisonment reinforce and perpetuate the perceived power that the system has over imprisoned women.

In summary, a range of factors at the individual level, the relational/interpersonal level, and the system/organisational level create barriers and enablers to effective relational practice between staff and women in prison.

Understanding these challenges and opportunities from the perspectives of individuals living and working within prisons allows practitioners to maximise the enablers, while also striving to mitigate, reduce and remove the barriers.

Solutions for clinicians to deliver effective trauma-informed relational practice

As a starting point to working relationally in prisons, clinicians should first acknowledge the potentially detrimental impact of the prison context on the well-being of imprisoned women, as well as on the development of the working relationship with the women. It may be necessary to specifically explore this from the perspective and experiences of the person with whom you are working, as there may be opportunities to identify ways in which additional care could be taken to mitigate some of these negative impacts from the outset.

Furthermore, practitioners should be aware of how their own experiences, attitudes and perspectives could contribute to interactions with those to whom they are providing a service. These should be actively acknowledged and considered curiously either in peer supervision with another colleague or within formal supervision. Such reflexivity is particularly important in situations requiring objectivity such as risk assessments but is similarly necessary when engaging in ongoing therapy sessions with women in prison. It ensures that emotional reactions to the work and to the individual with whom the work is being undertaken can be reflexively considered and worked through. Fundamentally, clinicians should appreciate the importance of their own self-care and make use of personal therapy if required.

Planning for the work

Before beginning work of any kind (whether assessment or intervention) with any woman in prison, it is important to carefully plan the initial interaction, as well as plan the work itself. Find out what you can about their background, prison experiences and any potential triggers that might cause distress or any other negative emotional response during the course of your engagement with them. Also, seek to build a picture about strategies, which might have previously been effective with the individual in building trust with others, and identify their strengths and skills if possible.

It is important to recognise that as a member of HMPPS staff there is a genuine power imbalance between you and people in prison. This could create a barrier impacting the development and maintenance of the therapeutic relationship if you are due to engage in an intervention. Equally, a power imbalance could affect the degree to which the woman in prison might feel able to open up and disclose sensitive details about their life in an assessment interview. On a very practical level then, before embarking on the initial meeting, consider actions that are within your control that might put the person at ease and minimise or reduce the power differential between you. Consider how you might dress to create the impression you want to give, and consider the impact that this could have on the perception of the woman in prison about you and your power in the situation. Plan which location you will use for the meeting and how you might set up the room. As far as possible, choose a space which is quiet, not overlooked and within which you should not be disturbed for the duration of the session. Plan to set up the room in such a way as to facilitate the individual's comfort and to attempt to reduce their anxiety, fear or distress. Finally, think about ways that it might be possible to give choice and control to the individual – can you give them a choice about the location, or about the time or date of the session, for example? Enabling them to exercise some degree of control at the outset gives them some power in the process and could lead to them feeling more willing and able to fully engage with you.

People living and working in women's prisons recognise a number of effective strategies that minimise the power differential, or remove the power-laden positioning of "staff" and "prisoners". These include making use of opportunities for staff and women in prison to engage in conversations about ordinary subjects not associated with imprisonment, which fosters a sense of normality in the relational interactions.

At the service development level, where possible, plan delivery to meet the needs of the maximum number of clients. For example, develop interventions which can be delivered in small groups as well as individually. This enables resources to be used optimally, as well as broadening the reach of the interventions to more individuals needing them.

Establish meaningful connections and relationships to enable "work" to happen

Supporting the development of trusting therapeutic relationships should be the initial goal of any contact with women in prison. This will take time and should not be rushed. Trust cannot be assumed simply because you perceive of yourself as a trustworthy and professional practitioner. Women in prison are likely to have experienced multiple instances of prior relationships that began as trusting but became abusive, and it is therefore possible that they could be mistrustful of others as a means of self-protection.

As well as taking time, proving yourself to be trustworthy will require patience, requiring you to continuously behave consistently and follow through on your commitments. It will be important to counter suspicion and mistrust. This can be done in ways such as keeping to the time of scheduled sessions and acting exactly as you have said you will. Consider how you contract the sessions at the outset. Be open and honest about the challenges of the work ahead and collaboratively explore the roles and responsibilities you will both have in the process. Ensure that the setting of targets and goals for interventions or engagement is done genuinely collaboratively. Give time and space for questions, concerns and issues to be explored and resolved before the work begins. Where possible, give women choice and control about how the sessions will go; for example, can you be flexible about the order in which you will approach the contents of sessions to give them choice about what they tackle first and what they would prefer to leave for later? Be mindful of how you introduce yourself and describe the role you will play in the process. Try to use language which emphasises the collaborative nature of the work and, where possible, acknowledge the individual as the expert in their own life.

Trust is fragile and can be easily broken or undermined, including by circumstances or occurrences outside of your control. Prisons are busy and unpredictable environments, and occasionally sessions will be cancelled or will need to be rescheduled at short notice, or you may be genuinely unavailable for a legitimate reason that cannot be foreseen. Always be mindful of the potential impact of this on the individual and their trust in the process, or trust in you. Try to find a way to inform them in advance and communicate the reason that the session has to be rescheduled. If possible, agree on the mechanisms for this in the contracting conversation.

Use supervision or other means of reflexive (and reflective) practice to recognise and acknowledge the power that you hold as a member of HMPPS staff relative to the women in prison with whom you are working. Explore how this feels for you. Think about how the individual might seek to gain power while in prison. Consider evidence which could indicate that it has already been attempted, and how successful these efforts appear to have been. What does this evidence mean for you in terms of planning to ensure the safety of yourself and the woman with whom you are starting to work? Know and recognise the signs of trauma, and how these might contribute to behavioural presentations which could be a challenge to relationship building. Be ready to navigate the careful management of these behaviours in ways which do not reinforce or condone them, but which also acknowledge your understanding of the reasons for them. Where necessary and possible (depending on the stage of therapy) work with the client to identify and practice more suitable (i.e. less harmful) methods by which they might be able to manage their distress.

From the outset, strive to consistently and continuously demonstrate your empathy and compassion, as well as your ability to listen and really hear what is being communicated to you. Be authentic and always show a genuine interest in the women with whom you are working, in an open and non-judgemental way. The significance of unconditional positive regard (Rogers, 2004) for the development of effective relational practice cannot be overstated. Women in prison are often their own harshest critics, expecting to be viewed negatively by others due to their status as prisoners, as well as their negative self-beliefs. If practitioners consistently show up for them, in ways which do not make them feel negatively judged, this can be an important part of the process of challenging their negative self-perceptions. Self-compassion should usually be a key (early) goal in therapy, and the WEPS team frequently utilise Compassion-Focused Therapy (CFT) approaches (Gilbert, 2013, and see Chapter 12, this volume) when working therapeutically with women in prison. Equally, it is essential for practitioners to show self-compassion. This work can be demanding and difficult. Things may not always work out as planned or as hoped when we engage in assessments or therapy with people in custody. Being able to acknowledge mistakes or difficulties and creating space to discuss the challenges in an open and transparent way can be important for repairing or maintaining trust.

Maintaining connections and engagement and consistently supporting them through challenging times

There may be occasions during contact with you as a practitioner, whether for a risk assessment or for therapeutic work, when a woman wants to break off contact with you, or cease engagement in the assessment or therapy. This could be because the work is too painful, uncomfortable or challenging for them. At times this might lead to their engagement in behaviours which might be viewed as being designed to self-sabotage or in other ways interfere with the therapy – intentionally or subconsciously trying to force an end to it. Such occurrences should be recognised for what they are and potentially curiously explored with the individual (depending on whether you judge that they would be able to tolerate this, given that some individuals might perceive this as threatening if attempted too early in the therapeutic relationship). You might notice that they seem to be trying to push you away just as you are getting to the most difficult part of therapy. Crucially, this is the time when you need to maintain the consistent connection with them and demonstrate that you are there for them even when things get difficult and that you will continue to show up despite how much harder things might get. This demonstration of consistent and boundaried care is what will enable them to learn to trust you – you do not push them away even when they are distressed or behaving in ways that have led to other people abandoning them previously (see Chapter 3, this volume).

Importantly, your work with them as a practitioner is not contingent on whether you like the individual or not. Rather, it is about consistent empathy and compassionate attitudes towards the woman at the heart of the interactions, even if the behaviours they are displaying are challenging or difficult. These are the times when supervision and peer support become crucial to maintain your own resilience and motivation. Behavioural responses of women in custody can be extreme, including serious repeated acts of self-harm; their emotions can often be dysregulated. The emotional impact of working with people displaying such behaviours and emotions is significant. Many women in prison are expecting to be rejected or abandoned by those from whom they are receiving care or nurturing support and often seek to provoke rejecting behaviours in others. Ensuring that you have support throughout the work can enable you to maintain your resilience and see the work through to the end.

Planning for and managing endings

It is important to recognise that patience is a key attribute for practitioners working relationally with women in prison. All stages of work must be planned in order to anticipate, discuss and navigate any potential hurdles or difficulties. For this reason, do not rush the way endings are approached. Relationship endings might be fraught with challenges for many women in custody, especially where positive therapeutic attachments have been made (see Chapter 1, this volume). This might intentionally or unintentionally lead to an avoidance of openly discussing the upcoming ending of therapeutic contact, for fear of causing distress. But equally, you *must* plan endings – therapy cannot be endless or even particularly long-term, due to resource constraints including the high level of need across the cohort of women in custody. As with other stages in the process, such planning should be approached collaboratively, openly and honestly, giving space to the feelings that come up for the individual undertaking the therapy. Additionally, practitioners should use reflexivity to consider their own feelings and views.

The ending of contact can be an opportunity to empower the individual by providing feedback about their skills, strengths and capabilities. Narrative letters can be used to capture this feedback in a permanent way for the individual to keep and reflect on.

Demonstrating continued "mattering"

Even after the completion of therapy or other periods of engagement with women in prison, it is important for practitioners to recognise the strong need for women in prison to feel seen, heard and understood by others. This need does not end after a therapeutic or rehabilitative engagement has ceased. Evidence of the positive benefits of "mattering" to others (Flett, 2022) points towards this as one way of mediating the deleterious impact of prison on the self-concepts of women in custody. It is therefore important to consider ways that you can continue to demonstrate that you hold the person in mind. This might involve simply responding warmly when you see them while you are working around the prison. Feelings of rejection can be easily triggered in people with insecure attachments, and if someone feels ignored, this can be challenging for their sense of self-worth.

Conclusions

Working with women in custody requires resilience, tenacity and compassion. It is often establishing *how* to work effectively relationally with women that can be the most challenging aspect of the work, given that most have complex trauma histories and are further traumatised within a system that is largely designed for the male majority. Despite these challenges, motivated and creative practitioners are able to find ways to navigate the hurdles and barriers created by the context and environment of prison. The rewards of working with women in prison, who actively seek and enthusiastically engage with the therapeutic and rehabilitative services provided, are definitely worth the effort.

Note

1 The use of numbers to identify participants was agreed with the participants during the consent process. All individuals who engaged in the research knew their research numbers and understood that this would protect their anonymity, while also enabling them to identify their contributions to the research.

References

Baranyi, G., Cassidy, M., Fazel, S., Priebe, S., & Mundt, A.P. (2018). Prevalence of post-traumatic stress disorder in prisoners. *Epidemiologic Review, 40*(1), 134–145.

Barnett-Page, E., & Thomas, J. (2009). Methods for the synthesis of qualitative research: A critical review. *BMC Medical Research Methodology, 9*(1), 59–69.

Bebbington, P., Jacobowitz, S., McKenzie, N., Killaspy, H., Iveson, R., Duffield, G., & Kerr, M. (2017). Assessing needs for psychiatric treatment in prisoners: 1. Prevalence of disorder. *Social Psychiatry and Psychiatric Epidemiology, 52,* 221–229.

Bevan, M. (2017). New Zealand prisoners' prior exposure to trauma. *Practice: The New Zealand Corrections Journal, 5*(1), 8–17.

Blanco, C., Hoertel, N., Wall, M.M., Franco, S., Peyre, H., Neria, Y., Helpman, L., & Limosin, F. (2018). Toward understanding sex differences in the prevalence of post-traumatic stress disorder: Results from the national epidemiologic survey on alcohol and related conditions. *The Journal of Clinical Psychiatry, 79*(2), 17m11597.

Corston, B.J. (2007). *The Corston Report: A Report of a Review of Women with Particular Vulnerabilities in the Criminal Justice System*. Home Office.

Covington, S. (2015). *Becoming Trauma-Informed: Toolkit for Criminal Justice Professionals*. Center for Gender & Justice.

Covington, S. (2018). *Becoming Trauma-Informed: A Training Programme for Criminal Justice Professionals*. Facilitator's guide. UK women's edition.

Elliott, D.E., Bjelajac, P., Fallot, R.D., Markoff, L.S., & Reed, B.G. (2005). Trauma-informed or trauma denied: Principles and implementation of trauma-informed services for women. *Journal of Community Psychology, 33*(4), 461–477.

Flett, G.L. (2022). An introduction, review and conceptual analysis of mattering as an essential construct and an essential way of life. *Journal of Psychoeducational Assessment, 40*(1), 3–36.

Gilbert, P. (2013). *The Compassionate Mind. A New Approach to Life's Challenges*. Constable & Robinson.

Hanson, R.F., Borntrager, C., Self-Brown, S., Kilpatrick, D.G., Saunders, B.E., & Resnick, H.S. (2008). Relations among gender, violence exposure, and mental health: The National Survey of Adolescents. *American Journal of Orthopsychiatry, 78*(3), 313–321. https://doi.org/10.1037/a0014056

Harris, M.E., & Fallot, R.D. (2001). *Using Trauma Theory to Design Service Systems*. Jossey-Bass/Wiley.

Kelman, J. (2024). *Can Women's Prisons Ever Be "Trauma-Informed" and "Trauma-Responsive"? A Qualitative Exploration of the Experiences of Those Living and Working in Women's Prisons*. Doctoral Thesis, King's College London. Retrieved from https://kclpure.kcl.ac.uk/portal/en/studentTheses/can-womens-prisons-ever-be-trauma-informed-and-trauma-responsive-

Kelman, J., Gribble, R., Harvey, J., Palmer, L., & MacManus, D. (2022). How does a history of trauma affect the experience of imprisonment for individuals in women's prisons: A qualitative exploration. *Women & Criminal Justice, 34*(3), 171–191.

Kelman, J., Palmer, L., Gribble, R., & MacManus, D. (2024a). Time and care: A qualitative exploration of prisoners' perceptions of trauma-informed care in women's prisons. *International Journal of Forensic Mental Health, 23*(4), 321–332.

Kelman, J., Palmer, L., Gribble, R., & MacManus, D. (2024b). Prison officers' perceptions of delivering trauma-informed care in women's prisons. *Journal of Aggression, Maltreatment & Trauma, 33*(10), 1258–1279.

Kessler, R.C., Aguilar-Gaxiola, S., Alonso, J., Benjet, C., Bromet, E.J., Cardoso, G., Degenhardt, L., de Girolamo, G., Dinolova, R.V., Ferry, F., Florescu, S., Gureje, O., Haro, J.M., Huang, Y., Karam, E.G., Kawakami, N., Lee, S., Lepine, J.P., Levinson, D., Navarro-Mateu, F., Pennell, B.E., Piazza, M., Posada-Villa, J., Scott, K.M., Stein, D.J., Ten Have, M., Torres, Y., Viana, M.C., Petukhova, M.V., Sampson, N.A., Zaslavsky, A. M., & Koenen, K.C. (2017). Trauma and PTSD in the WHO World Mental Health surveys. *European Journal of Psychotraumatology, 8*(sup5), 1353383.

Maeng, L.Y., & Milad, M.R. (2015). Sex differences in anxiety disorders: Interactions between fear, stress, and gonadal hormones. *Hormones & Behaviour, 76*, 106–117.

Menschner, C., & Maul, A. (2016). Key *Ingredients for Successful Trauma-Informed Care Implementation*. Center for Health Care Strategies. https://www.chcs.org/media/ATC_whitepaper_040616.pdf

Messina, N., & Grella, C. (2006). Childhood trauma and women's health outcomes in a California prison population. *American Journal of Public Health, 96*(10), 1842–1848.

Prison Reform Trust. (2024). *Bromley Briefings Prison Factfile*. February 2024. Bromley Briefings. Winter-2024-factfile.pdf. Prison Reform Trust. www.prisonreformtrust.org.uk

Rogers, C.R. (2004). *On Becoming a Person. A Therapist's View of Psychotherapy*. Houghton Mifflin.

Stensrud, R.H., Gilbride, D.D., & Bruinekool, R.M. (2019). The childhood to prison pipeline: Early childhood trauma as reported by a prison population. *Rehabilitation Counselling Bulletin, 62*(4), 195–208. https://doi.org/10.1177/0034355218774844

Substance Abise and mental Health Services Administration (SAMHSA). (2014). *SAMHSA's Concept of Trauma and Guidance for a Trauma-informed Approach*. (HHS Publication No. 14-4884). U.S. Department of Health and Human Services.

Tolin, D.F., & Foa, E.B. (2006). Sex differences in trauma and posttraumatic stress disorder: A quantitative review of 25 years of research. *Psychological Bulletin, 132*, 959–992.

Wilson, J.M., Fauci, J.E., & Goodman, L.A. (2015). Bringing trauma-informed practice to domestic violence programs: A qualitative analysis of current approaches. *American Journal of Orthopsychiatry, 85*(6), 586–599.

7 Building therapeutic relationships with autistic people in forensic settings

Amy Canning and Hannah Toogood, with contributions from Jake (expert by experience)

Introduction and background

This chapter is written from the perspective of two non-autistic clinicians, based on our clinical experience of working in an NHS service for autistic people with forensic needs, in consultation with Jake, who is an autistic expert by experience and has personal experience of the criminal justice system.

There is growing recognition of the presence, and value, of neurodiversity within the criminal justice system workforce, but this chapter specifically focuses on developing therapeutic relationships between non-autistic forensic practitioners and autistic clients. As such, when we refer to practitioners in this chapter, we are referring to non-autistic professionals. We have tried to capture what we think are the most important themes to consider when developing therapeutic relationships with autistic clients. However, each client will have individual strengths, difficulties and preferences, and other aspects of identity and experience are also likely to be important, including gender identity, religion, cultural background, past experiences of relationships and trauma. We have focused on the needs of adult autistic clients who do not have a learning disability, although some of this chapter is also likely to be relevant to autistic children and young people, and autistic adults with a learning disability. We are aware that there are often very long waits for autism diagnostic assessments, so this chapter may also be helpful for practitioners working with clients who may be autistic but who do not yet have a formal diagnosis. We have considered therapeutic relationships in general terms, rather than focusing on a specific profession or therapeutic modality.

What is autism?

Autism is a neurodevelopmental condition

> ... characterised by persistent deficits in the ability to initiate and to sustain reciprocal social interaction and social communication, and by a range of restricted, repetitive, and inflexible patterns of behaviour, interests or

DOI: 10.4324/9781003542377-10

activities that are clearly atypical or excessive for the individual's age and sociocultural context.

(World Health Organization, 2022)

Every autistic person is different, but the main features of autism include:

- Difficulties understanding and responding appropriately to other people's verbal and non-verbal communication.
- Difficulties with imagining and responding to other people's emotions and perspectives.
- Difficulties with social awareness and adapting one's behaviour to fit the social context.
- Differences in non-verbal communication.
- Difficulties forming and maintaining relationships with peers.
- Difficulties with change and uncertainty.
- An inflexible adherence to routines.
- A rigid thinking style.
- Interests that are unusual in terms of intensity and/or topic.
- Repetitive and stereotyped body movements ("stimming").
- Marked sensory processing differences.

Although autism is classified as a mental disorder, it is increasingly argued that many aspects of autism should be understood in terms of differences rather than deficits, with neurodiversity being an important part of human experience (see Fletcher-Watson & Happé, 2019, for discussion). Autism often comes with particular strengths, including a logical thinking style, attention to detail, and high levels of expertise and knowledge about areas of interest. Some features of autism that may lead to difficulties in some situations may be strengths in others; for example, when autistic people do not adjust their communication according to (non-autistic) social expectations, this can be experienced as blunt or rude in some situations, but can provide valuable honesty and clarity in others.

It is estimated that approximately 1–2% of the UK population is autistic (National Institute for Health and Care Excellence, 2024). Diagnostic rates have increased over the last couple of decades (e.g. Russell et al., 2022), which is thought to be largely due to increased recognition of autism. Significantly more men than women are diagnosed with autism. The reasons for this are unclear, but may reflect both the underdiagnosis and lower prevalence of autism among women (e.g. Ratto et al., 2018).

Autistic people are at increased risk of co-occurring mental health and neurodevelopmental conditions; there are higher rates of learning disabilities, ADHD, anxiety, depression, OCD and psychosis among autistic people, compared to the general population (e.g. Lai et al., 2019). Autistic people are also at much greater risk of completing suicide than the general population (e.g. Kõlves et al., 2021). It is likely that the increased rates of co-occurring mental health conditions and suicidality are, at least in part, a reflection of the stress and challenges associated with being autistic in a society that is largely constructed around the needs of non-autistic people. Autistic people also experience high rates of victimisation, including bullying, child abuse and sexual victimisation (Trundle et al., 2023).

There is no evidence that autism is, in itself, a risk factor for offending (Chester et al., 2022). It has proved difficult to accurately estimate the number of autistic people involved in the criminal justice system, due to the lack of routine screening for autism and the limitations of those screening tools which are available (e.g. Ashwood et al., 2016); however, there is evidence to suggest that autistic people may be overrepresented in criminal justice settings (Chester et al., 2022). The reasons for this are unclear, but there is growing consensus that autism provides a very specific context for offending and that the needs of autistic people must be taken into account when designing and delivering forensic assessments and treatment programmes, and managing and monitoring risk (Al-Attar, 2018). It is also a legal requirement for public sector organisations in the United Kingdom, including those within the criminal justice system, to make "reasonable adjustments" to ensure that their services are accessible to autistic people (The Equality Act, 2010).

Why are there sometimes challenges when developing therapeutic relationships with autistic clients?

As other chapters in this book have discussed, developing therapeutic relationships with clients in forensic settings can be complex. Forensic practitioners may face particular challenges when developing therapeutic relationships with autistic clients. Historically, these have often been located in the client, with individuals being viewed as "unwilling to engage" or "unable to benefit from therapy". However, as with all relationships, therapeutic relationships involve at least two people: the client and the practitioner; many of these challenges may be better understood as a mismatch between autistic and non-autistic ways of thinking, communicating and experiencing the world. Damian Milton, an autistic author and academic, has described this as the "double empathy problem ... a breakdown in mutual understanding (that can happen between any two people) and hence a problem for both parties to contend with, yet more likely to occur when people of very differing dispositions attempt to interact" (Milton et al., 2022, p. 1901).

Mutual understanding is fundamental to any effective therapeutic relationship; practitioners must be able to understand, and attend to, their clients' experiences, thoughts and feelings; and clients must feel understood by the practitioner and understand what the practitioner is trying to convey to them. While a breakdown in mutual understanding in many contexts may be "a problem for both parties to contend with" as described above, arguably, in the context of a therapeutic relationship, practitioners bear most responsibility for ensuring that they and their client understand each other. This is particularly the case in a forensic setting, where the focus of therapeutic work is usually driven more by the practitioner than the client; there is often a need to complete tasks within a time-limited period, and the power differential is even more pronounced than in other settings. This means that, as practitioners, we have a responsibility to reflect on the non-autistic assumptions that are inherent in the ways that we work, do our best to understand what it may be like to experience the world through a different lens, and try to bridge the gap between autistic and non-autistic ways of thinking and communicating. It is also important for us to recognise that autistic clients are likely to come to us with a history of both personal and professional relationships which have been marred by a lack of mutual understanding and that many will have had the experience of their difficulties and distress being reduced to damaging labels such as "stupid", "deliberately disruptive", "an overreaction" or "callous".

Your client's view of their autism diagnosis

> Different service users have different views about things. Diagnoses can be a private thing. Some people might not think they have autism.
>
> Jake, expert by experience

It is important not to make assumptions about how your client views their autism diagnosis. Some autistic people have a positive view of autism and see it as an integral part of their identity; however, others may have a more mixed view or regard their diagnosis in negative terms. Some people may even reject their diagnosis. It is also important to hold in mind that people's relationship to their diagnosis may change over time. In forensic settings, clients who were diagnosed in adulthood may often have had a diagnostic assessment at the instigation of professionals rather than having sought this out themselves, and some will have received their diagnosis during court proceedings. This means that they may have had limited opportunity to process what being autistic means to them and may have difficult associations with the diagnosis.

People can also refer to their autism diagnosis in different ways; some people prefer to describe themselves as autistic, while others prefer to describe themselves as "on the autism spectrum" or as "having autism". Clients who received a diagnosis of Asperger's syndrome, when this was still a diagnostic classification, sometimes prefer to describe themselves as "having Asperger's", or as an "Aspie".

It is important to explore how your client feels about their autism diagnosis and what language they prefer to use to describe this, early on in a therapeutic relationship. This can help you avoid inadvertently alienating them by using terms that do not fit with their experience, as well as identify if they need more support to make sense of their diagnosis.

Different ways of processing information?

> [An autistic person] might do something and you might think "that's not rational", but to them it is, to them it might be the best way of doing things.
>
> Jake, expert by experience

An essential aspect of developing a therapeutic relationship with an autistic client is recognising that you and your client are likely to experience and therefore respond to situations in different ways. Autistic people appear to process information differently from non-autistic people, and it is thought that this may underlie the difficulties with/differences in social communication and interaction, and restricted, repetitive behaviours and interests that characterise autism. There are a number of different theories about information processing in autism. Four key theories are outlined below:

- **Theory of mind:** It has been proposed that many autistic people have difficulties with theory of mind, which is the ability to accurately hypothesise about, understand and predict other people's beliefs, thoughts, feelings, knowledge and intentions. Different situations present different levels of complexity in terms of the demands on theory of mind, so an individual might be able to accurately hypothesise about another person's thoughts and feelings in some circumstances, but find it much more difficult in others. In forensic settings, difficulties with theory of mind can often be confused with callousness or a lack of empathy; it is important to note that theory of mind relates to the cognitive aspect of empathy (the ability to *understand* other people's emotional states) rather than affective empathy (the *emotional resonance* with another person's emotional state, once this has been understood), although some autistic people who offend will have difficulties with both. It is also important to reiterate that it is not just autistic people who can find it difficult to understand other people's perspectives; non-autistic people can also struggle to understand autistic people's perspectives.
- **Weak central coherence:** It has been suggested that many autistic people have a style of information processing, which means that they tend to focus on and remember detail, rather than identifying the overarching themes or meaning in a collection of pieces of information. While a detail-focused information processing style can be a significant strength, it can also mean that people focus on less relevant details and "miss the point" or "miss the bigger picture" and find it difficult to generalise knowledge and learning from one context to another. In forensic settings, autistic clients' behaviour can sometimes be interpreted as deliberately obstructive or anti-authoritarian, when it is actually the result of a detail-focused information processing style. For example, a client's difficulties moving on from a specific detail, such as a minor error in a report, may be misinterpreted

as a delaying tactic or as deliberately antagonistic, and a failure to follow rules across different contexts due to problems generalising may be interpreted as a deliberate breach of the rules.

- **Executive functioning:** Many autistic people appear to have difficulties with executive functioning, which is an umbrella term for cognitive functions such as planning, problem-solving, initiating tasks, prioritising, sequencing, mental flexibility, working memory, impulse control and self-monitoring. Difficulties with executive functioning, combined with theory of mind difficulties and weak central coherence, may underlie the rigid, black-and-white thinking style that can sometimes be seen in autistic people. Many autistic people are very intellectually able, but still struggle with seemingly straightforward tasks due to difficulties with executive functioning. This type of "spikey profile" can sometimes lead others to overestimate or underestimate their abilities, which can lead to frustration or confusion for both the autistic person and the clinician. In forensic settings, over-estimating clients' abilities may lead practitioners to assume that issues arising from difficulties with executive functioning, such as failing to attend probation appointments on time, are a sign that the person is not taking these requirements sufficiently seriously or is deliberately avoiding them.

- **Sensory processing:** Many autistic people appear to process and experience sensory input in a different way from non-autistic people; some may be hypersensitive and find some sensory experiences extremely aversive, while others may be hyposensitive and seek out sensory input. People can be hypersensitive in one domain (e.g. touch) and hyposensitive in another (e.g. hearing). It can be very difficult for non-autistic people to fully understand how uncomfortable, or even painful, sensory overload can be for autistic people. In forensic settings, this can lead to the assumption that an autistic person is being unreasonable or over-reacting when they are struggling with sensory issues or that their attempts to control their environment to manage their sensory needs (e.g. wanting to control the lighting or where they sit in sessions) is indicative of a wider pattern of controlling behaviour.

We have referred to these theories throughout the rest of this chapter; however, it should be noted that they are open to criticism and there is continuing research exploring how autistic people process information (see Fletcher-Watson & Happé, 2019, for a review).

Autistic people can also experience, communicate and manage emotions in a different way than non-autistic people. Everyday things which may not bother most people, such as social contact, plan changes or distant noise, can contribute to high levels of anxiety and sometimes result in acute distress. In addition to this, there are high rates of alexithymia in autistic people, which means that many autistic people can find it very difficult to identify, differentiate and express their emotions. This can make emotion regulation very challenging, as they may not be aware of their distress until it becomes over-whelming. In some circumstances, acute anxiety and distress can contribute to the person becoming agitated or aggressive or lead to "shut downs", where they become entirely unable to communicate or respond to others. Autistic people may also manage their distress in different ways from non-autistic people. For example, some people need periods in a low-stimulus environ-ment in order to recover, while some may cope by stimming, which can range from movements such as rocking, to hitting themselves if they are in acute distress. All these differences can be hard for practitioners to make sense of, and in forensic settings, can lead autistic clients to be viewed as "unpredict-able", "over-emotional" and "difficult to manage".

Creating a context which facilitates the development of therapeutic relationships

> Give someone a quiet space where they don't feel threatened and they feel safe.
>
> Jake, expert by experience

Many clients (both autistic and non-autistic) find meeting with forensic prac-titioners extremely stressful. Clients are often going through a very difficult period in their lives, they are often expected to talk about extremely difficult topics, and the outcome could have life-changing consequences for them. Recognising this and, where possible, offering support and reassurance, is often an important part of building therapeutic rapport. However, there are additional stressors for autistic clients which require consideration.

As noted earlier, many autistic people have sensory processing differences, which means that the physical environment of a meeting room can in itself be stressful. Factors like noise, smells, lighting and visual clutter, which may barely be noticed by someone who is non-autistic, can be very distracting or even distressing for autistic clients. However, it is important to note that dif-ferent individuals can have very different sensory needs; we worked with one client who found the sound of ticking clocks almost painful, but worked with another who found the sound comforting, to the extent that he kept multiple clocks in his own room.

Autistic people often find uncertainty and change very anxiety provok-ing, so coping with cancelled or short-notice appointments, or not knowing what will happen in a meeting, or who will be there, can be very difficult. For example, we worked with a client who struggled to cope with the uncertainty about what would be happening in his psychological assessment, until we used a very detailed tick list to show him exactly what this would entail, and how we were progressing through the assessment. Many autistic people also find the prospect of simply meeting new people very anxiety provoking and can find meeting with groups of people overwhelming, so meeting a practi-tioner for the first time or starting a therapeutic group can be very stressful.

High levels of anxiety can make it much harder for clients to concentrate, understand and retain information and can compound any difficulties they may have with perspective taking or flexible thinking.

Forensic settings can be particularly problematic for autistic people, as they are often noisy, chaotic environments, where clients have very little control over their lives and plans can change at very short notice. However, if we do not demonstrate that we are trying to attend to our clients' needs for structure, predictability and a bearable sensory environment, there is a risk that they may interpret this as a sign that we do not understand them or, worse, do understand but are choosing not to help. We have also worked with autistic clients whose distress about sensory issues and the lack of clear and structured plans, combined with theory of mind difficulties, has led them to conclude that professionals must be intentionally trying to cause them distress. For example, we worked with one client who assumed that prison officers were deliberately trying to antagonise her by jangling their keys. All of this has the potential to be a major barrier to the development of effective therapeutic relationships and, in some circumstances, can make them unsafe. However, demonstrating recognition of how challenging adverse sensory environments, uncertainty and novel social interactions can be for autistic clients and attempting to address these can provide a context which helps clients begin to feel supported and understood.

Tips

- Review any documents laying out the specific reasonable adjustments the client requires, including criminal justice passports and/or sensory assessments.
- Consider whether there is anything you can do to control the noise, lighting, smells, temperature, visual clutter or other sensory elements of the environment in which you are meeting your client.
- Ask your client about any sensory needs. Offer them choices where possible (e.g. window open or closed, lighting on or off, seating position, etc.).
- If your client seems uncomfortable or distressed and it is not clear why, explore whether there might be an unmet sensory need. Be aware that some autistic people may not be able to fully identify or articulate their sensory needs, even when these are significant.
- If a client attempts to control an aspect of their environment, check whether there is a sensory need associated with this before making other interpretations of their behaviour.
- It can be difficult to provide a "sensory friendly" environment in many forensic settings; if it is not possible to meet the person's needs, be transparent about this and work with them to find alternative ways of problem-solving the issue.
- Consider avoiding meetings with large numbers of people, or if this is not possible, plan and structure these carefully in order to make them more

manageable, including having sufficient physical space between people and a system of clear turn taking.
- Try to reduce uncertainty/unknowns as much as possible. Try to have sessions at the same time in the same room if possible, and provide as much information as you can about your sessions in advance. For example:

  - Where will the meeting be held?
  - Who will be present?
  - The purpose of the meeting.
  - The length of the meeting.

- Give as much warning as possible if plans have to change.
- Agree a clear plan and structure for the session/piece of work. Where elements cannot be planned in advance (e.g. the number of meetings that will be necessary), discuss how best to manage this with your client.
- Agree a plan for how either of you can indicate that a break is needed or the session needs to end. Discuss how either of you would recognise if the client was becoming distressed and how best to support them if this occurs. Be aware that clients may need additional therapeutic input to help them be able to identify and communicate early signs of distress and to find ways of coping with this.

Communication within therapeutic relationships

> Even though I know the odd fancy word I'm not a clinician, I might not understand the clinical words they use. Clinicians need to be aware of who they are talking to, and make adjustments.
>
> Jake, expert by experience

Communication is at the centre of all therapeutic relationships, and most forensic practitioners will carefully consider how they facilitate discussion of sensitive topics and how they make sense of what their client is telling them. When working with autistic clients, communication requires additional thought, as difficulties (or differences) with social communication are one of the core features of autism. Many of these difficulties (or differences) may be understood in terms of the way autistic people process information. For example, difficulties with theory of mind may make it more difficult to work out what someone else is thinking and feeling during a conversation and, therefore, to judge how to respond to them. Weak central coherence can make it difficult to contextualise what the other person is saying and to work out what information may or may not be relevant to a question that has just been asked. Executive functioning difficulties can make it harder to monitor and adjust one's own behaviour during a conversation. Some autistic people have limited awareness of their communication differences, while others can be very aware of them and may try to mask them, which can be exhausting and have a deleterious effect on mental health.

Some autistic people may use very little non-verbal communication (such as eye contact, gestures and facial expressions), while others may have non-verbal communication that seems exaggerated or does not fit with their emotional state. For example, we have worked with clients who have smiled throughout their court appearances, despite being very distressed. As noted earlier, many autistic people can also struggle to identify and describe their emotions, so may not recognise or be able to communicate if they are starting to become dysregulated.

Autistic people can sometimes use language in a different way than non-autistic people, including using words or phrases in an idiosyncratic manner; for example, using the term "rest-less" to mean having slept poorly. Sometimes people may use unusually formal or technical language or express themselves in a very blunt way; for example, we have worked with clients who have described the injuries they inflicted on victims in disconcerting anatomical detail. A lot of autistic people can find managing the "to-and-fro" of conversations very challenging; this can include finding it difficult to recognise when they are expected to speak, or pause to allow someone else to speak, and difficulty knowing when and how to interrupt someone else. Some autistic people can find it difficult to judge what is wanted from them in a conversation; when they are asked a question, some may provide too little information, while others may provide too much, including information that seems unrelated to the topic. For example, when we asked one autistic client about their educational experiences, they provided detailed information about the colour of the doors and the number of windows at their primary school. All these communication differences can be challenging for non-autistic professionals to understand and adapt to.

Many autistic people can also find it difficult to make sense of non-autistic communication at times. When we reflect on how non-autistic people communicate, this is not surprising. Even though most practitioners make an effort to communicate clearly, we are often vague, littering our conversations with euphemisms (e.g. "he passed away"), metaphors (e.g. "do you have a short fuse?") and inaccuracies (e.g. "we will start in a minute"). We use phrases which require multiple levels of perspective taking (e.g. "Is there anything I should be worried about?") and sometimes say the opposite of what we mean; for example, saying that a situation is "fine" when this is definitely not the case. Rather than clearly communicating what we mean, non-autistic people tend to rely on others interpreting what we say using context and subtle cues like tone of voice and expression. This can be very problematic for autistic people, who tend to focus on the literal meaning of language. It should also be noted that the criminal justice system often uses impenetrable language that is difficult for most people to understand, whether or not they are autistic.

Practitioners, therefore, need to give careful thought about how to address the mismatch between autistic and non-autistic communication styles, as it may otherwise be difficult to have collaborative and constructive conversations, and it is more likely that there will be misunderstandings and frustrations on both sides. In forensic settings, misunderstanding our clients' communication can contribute to us making inaccurate judgements about the person and their risks; for example, interpreting the stark use of language when describing an offence as a sign of callousness, or the failure to share relevant information as a sign that the person is trying to conceal information. We have also worked with clients where communication difficulties have been a major factor in their risk to others, particularly when theory of mind difficulties have led them to conclude that the other person is deliberately misunderstanding them or communicating in an unintelligible way. However, collaboratively working with clients to find ways of making communication work well, including taking ownership of the unhelpful ways in which non-autistic people can communicate, can in itself form an important part of the development of effective therapeutic relationships.

Tips

- Check if there is any information available about how best to communicate with the client, for example, a "communication passport" or speech and language assessment.
- If the client has significant communication needs, seek advice from a speech and language therapist.
- Explore the client's communication needs and preferences with them at the outset of a piece of work. For example, check if they prefer longer or shorter sessions or find it helpful to have key information written down.
- If a client has significant communication needs but is sensitive to perceived criticism, it can help to start by focusing on the difficulties that might arise from your own communication style. For example, highlighting that you may sometimes be unclear or talk too fast, and inviting the client to make a plan about how this could be addressed. The discussion can then be extended to consider how any challenges likely to arise from their communication style could be addressed.
- Hold in mind that communication differences are a feature of autism and that autistic people can find it extremely difficult, or even impossible, to change aspects of their communication. Although it is possible to collaboratively agree on strategies to help make communication work more effectively (as described above), ultimately, practitioners hold responsibility for adapting to meet the communication needs of autistic clients. The following adaptations may be helpful.

  - Try to be as clear, concrete and explicit in your communication as possible. Short, simple sentences are likely to help.
  - Check that you and your client have the same understanding of key words and phrases, particularly in regard to terms relating to emotions, relationships and abstract social concepts such as "engagement".

- Do not assume that people with fluent speech have receptive language skills of a similar level, and vice versa.
- Be aware that autistic clients may need additional time to process information or questions before responding.
- Avoid using phrases and questions which rely on the client "reading between the lines" or rely on them interpreting your non-verbal communication; for example, you may need to explicitly state when a session is coming to an end or when you are concerned about something.
- Ask specific questions about the information you need, and do not expect the person to provide additional relevant information without being asked to do so. For example, if you ask a client whether they have ever taken an overdose, it may not occur to them to tell you about other times they have tried to harm themselves.
- When asking questions, remember that autistic people can think in concrete terms. For example, if you ask a client whether they have ever carried a weapon, it may not occur to them to tell you that they have carried items which are not designed as weapons, but could be used as such (e.g. broken glass, a screwdriver).
- Autistic people can sometimes find it difficult to provide clear narratives of past events. Consider using the "Witness-Aimed First Account", which is a technique specifically designed for interviewing autistic witnesses, to help with this (see Maras et al., 2020).
- Be very careful about drawing any conclusions from your client's communication style about them, their motivations and their risks. However, hold in mind that, as with everyone, autistic clients may sometimes attempt to conceal information or mislead others.
- Be aware that, although some autistic people use metaphorical language, this does not necessarily mean they will understand other people's use of metaphors. However, using analogies to explain concepts, particularly when they are related to the person's interest, can be very helpful; for example, warning lights on a dashboard as an analogy for signs that risk may be increasing for someone who is interested in cars.
- If the client has particular interests that they like to discuss, consider planning in time for this. This can help to reduce anxiety and provide an opportunity for you to demonstrate an interest in the client's skills and knowledge, which can be a helpful part of developing a therapeutic relationship.
- Have pen and paper available in sessions to be able to draw diagrams or pictures to illustrate key points, and be prepared to write down the key points that the client needs to remember.
- Make sure that any written communication is pitched at a suitable level for the person, including considering whether visual images would be helpful.

The social rules of a therapeutic relationship

> What was confusing for me was the doctor asking me questions about me and my mum and dad, [it meant that] I thought I could ask my OT these [sorts of] questions [about their personal life].
>
> Jake, expert by experience

All relationships, including therapeutic relationships, have social rules. Social rules are societal (largely non-autistic) expectations of how people should communicate and behave in different situations and in different relationships. They can often be very difficult to define and are heavily dependent on the context; for example, whether a joke is appropriate can depend on the setting and timing, the wider cultural context, who is present, their roles and the nature of their relationships, and what the other people are thinking and feeling, as well as the content of the joke itself and the manner in which it is delivered. Subtle changes in the context can rapidly and radically change whether a behaviour adheres to, or breaches, social rules. Although children are usually taught basic social rules (e.g. to say thank you when given a gift), in adulthood, there is generally an expectation that social rules should be implicitly understood and followed, unless someone is entering an obviously novel situation, such as going to a new country with very different customs. Despite social rules frequently being vague, changeable and rarely explained, they often elicit negative judgements when they are breached.

Everyone will breach social rules occasionally. However, understanding and operationalising social rules can be particularly challenging for autistic people, because they are often based on non-autistic ways of thinking and experiencing the world and rely not just on observing other people's behaviour but also on accurately hypothesising what they might be thinking and feeling, predicting how they are likely to perceive and respond to one's behaviour, paying attention to the wider context, drawing on relevant information from other experiences, and monitoring and adjusting one's own behaviour in response to subtle feedback (such as a minor change in facial expression). These skills are heavily reliant on theory of mind, central coherence and executive functioning, which can all be areas of difficulty/difference for autistic people.

In the previous section, we referred to some of the social rules that generally apply when communicating with others, including expectations about how people should manage the "to-and-fro" of conversations, and the type of language they should use. However, therapeutic relationships in forensic settings have additional social rules that are very different from those of most other relationships and which can seem quite contradictory. For example, clients are expected to share highly personal information about themselves, but not to ask professionals personal questions. We expect clients to talk in detail about sensitive topics such as their sexual interests when asked to do so, but do not usually expect them to raise these topics themselves. We encourage clients to become more empathic towards others, but do not expect them to enquire about or comment on our own emotional state. The relationship can feel very close, but it must not evolve into a friendship or romantic relationship. We tend to expect our clients to intuitively understand all of this and to pick up on and understand subtle cues (such as a change in our tone of voice) that indicate when they have made a mistake and to adjust their behaviour accordingly.

Not only do we rarely explain many of the social rules of our therapeutic relationships, but we also often make judgements about clients if they do not adhere to them. This can have significant implications for how the person and their risks are understood. For example, we have worked with a client whose sexualised jokes towards professionals raised concerns about sexual risk, but it transpired that this was an attempt to be friendly, as he had observed other clients making similar jokes among themselves and interpreted the professionals' uncomfortable smiles as a sign that his jokes were well received. We have also worked with a client who was thought to be deliberately trying to intimidate professionals by looking at them intently and repeatedly asking them if they were angry or scared, but it later became apparent that this was a sincere attempt to understand what they were thinking and feeling. In some circumstances, a lack of clarity about social rules can also make the therapeutic relationship unsafe; for example, if a client with a history of stalking misunderstands the nature of the relationship. Uncertainty about the social rules of the therapeutic relationship can also exacerbate the anxiety that many autistic clients will already be experiencing when meeting with a practitioner. Defining and explaining the social rules of a therapeutic relationship can therefore be an important part of establishing a safe and effective therapeutic relationship with an autistic client.

Tips

- Depending on the client, their past experiences of therapeutic relationships and your role, it can be helpful to discuss key social rules at the outset of a piece of work. It may be helpful to:

  - Highlight that therapeutic/professional relationships are different from many other types of relationships. For example, you will ask the client a lot of personal questions, but you cannot tell them about your own life, and the relationship cannot evolve into a romantic relationship or friendship.
  - Discuss how your relationship with the client may differ from their relationship with other professionals. For example, it may be appropriate for clients to talk about the details of their offences with a probation officer or psychologist, but not with a prison officer or GP.
  - Discuss what you would both do if you were to accidentally meet outside a session.

- If a client "breaks" a social rule:
  - Consider whether this may be linked to autistic ways of thinking and communicating, and whether they fully understand the social rules.
  - Consider whether the rule is important or whether it is just based on non-autistic assumptions about how people should behave. For example, it is unlikely to matter if a client makes no eye contact, but making comments about your physical appearance may impact the dynamics of your relationship, and similar behaviour could be problematic in other relationships.
  - If you need to address the breach of the social rule with your client, be prepared to clearly describe the behaviour of concern as well as explain the rationale for the rule, and why it is problematic if it is broken, rather than simply declaring that they have behaved "inappropriately".
  - Be cautious about how you interpret any breach of social rules, as it may be a consequence of autistic thinking and communication styles rather than indicating other concerns, and may or may not be relevant to risk.

Developing shared therapeutic goals

> I was quite on board with psychology, but if someone wasn't, they might get the perception that people are just keeping them locked up and not giving them their freedom for no reason.
>
> Jake, expert by experience

In order to have an effective therapeutic relationship, there needs to be some consensus between the client and practitioner about the goals of the therapeutic work. In most settings, therapeutic goals are developed collaboratively, with a focus on the client's priorities. However, in forensic settings, the agenda is usually set by the practitioner, and goals will generally relate to assessing, treating, managing or monitoring risk. Part of developing a therapeutic relationship in a forensic setting is, therefore, coming to some consensus with the client that these goals are reasonable, even if only to meet the requirements of the criminal justice system.

Sometimes, autistic clients may not believe that their offending behaviour is problematic, or their responsibility, or that there is any risk of reoffending, and therefore see no reason to engage in any risk-focused work. Although this is not unique to autistic clients, they may adhere to their views in a much more rigid, black-and-white way than non-autistic clients and may not appreciate the consequences of a lack of engagement. This can make developing shared goals particularly challenging.

These types of views about offending are also often interpreted as reflecting antisocial or anti-authoritarian attitudes or psychological defences; however, for autistic people, differences in cognitive style and processing may also be playing a significant role. For example, theory of mind difficulties can contribute to autistic clients significantly underestimating the harm they cause to victims, particularly in terms of psychological harm. We have worked with autistic clients who have believed that their victims will recover from serious violent offences in a matter of weeks, and clients who have assumed that victims have not been harmed at all by offences like threats to kill and stalking, because these did not involve any physical contact.

Weak central coherence can sometimes lead autistic clients to make sense of their offending by focusing on specific details, to the exclusion of other, more relevant factors. If autistic clients are focused on other people's actions (such as a victim behaving in what they perceive to be a provocative manner, or others not meeting their needs), they may regard this as the sole cause of their offending and be unable to see their own role in this. Sometimes, autistic people focus on relatively insignificant details as the cause of their offending; for example, we have worked with a client who was confident that he would never reoffend, because he would not be returning to the specific room where the previous offence had taken place.

Difficulties with the theory of mind may also make it difficult for autistic clients to understand why others are concerned about their risk if they themselves are not and to fully understand the implications of not addressing these concerns. They may not recognise that being perceived as a risk to others may interfere with important aspects of their lives, including future leisure, employment, housing and relationship opportunities, as well as lead to greater restrictions and monitoring from the criminal justice system. All this may be compounded if the individual has committed similar offences in the past and these have not been reported to the Police or led to prosecution, as they may interpret this as evidence that their actions were not particularly problematic or that they were not culpable for them.

In addition to all of the above, some autistic clients can find the idea and process of therapeutic change very difficult. An inflexible thinking style can make it very difficult for clients to imagine a future where they are thinking, feeling and behaving in a different way, and some autistic people find the uncertainty associated with therapeutic change, or even the idea of change itself, very anxiety provoking. Sometimes, difficulties with change can prove a significant barrier to autistic clients engaging in therapeutic work, or even core criminal justice processes. For example, we have worked with a client who concluded that there was no point engaging in further Parole Board hearings after an unsuccessful hearing, because they believed that they were unable to change and it would therefore be impossible for them to achieve a different outcome in the future.

All of this means that practitioners may need to devote the initial session(s) of any risk-focused work to helping autistic clients understand the importance of engaging in therapeutic work and manage the anxiety that they may experience in relation to this, in order to agree on therapeutic goals.

Tips

- Provide clear, concrete explanations of the rationale for a piece of work, and the potential consequences of not completing the work, at the outset.
- If a client is reluctant to engage in a piece of work, explore the reasons for this in detail, holding in mind that there may be gaps in their understanding and/or they may find the idea of change very difficult. Do not assume that a lack of engagement on the part of an autistic client is solely a consequence of factors such as a lack of empathy, anti-authoritarian attitudes or shame or assume that the client will simply become "ready to engage" over time (although this will be the case for some clients).
- If it becomes apparent that there are gaps in the client's understanding, consider how these can be addressed in a clear, logical way that makes sense to the client. They may need to complete a specific piece of work to address these issues, prior to it being possible to complete any further work with them. Be prepared to discuss issues such as:

  - Why the client was arrested/prosecuted on this occasion, if similar behaviour in the past did not result in this.
  - Why and how offending behaviour harms others; for example, why threats are harmful, if the victim was not physically harmed and the client believes that the victim knew that they did not intend to carry out the threats.
  - Why not committing further offences is in their interests, and the wider consequences of continuing to offend, including the potential impact on future relationships, housing, employment and leisure opportunities.
  - Why people may believe that the client is still at risk of reoffending, even though they may not have committed an offence for weeks/months/years.
  - More existential questions, such as why violence is legitimate in the context of war, and why sexual relationships with children under the age of 16 are permitted in some countries.

- If it becomes apparent that the person is anxious about change or does not believe that change is possible, consider how this can be addressed in a way that is meaningful to the client. In our experience, autistic clients can sometimes believe that therapeutic change means changing their whole personality, so it can be helpful to frame this in terms of learning new skills and learning how to make good decisions and to help them draw parallels with other times when they have successfully done this.

Repairing ruptures in therapeutic relationships

Understand why they are upset ... try and figure out what this person's baseline is, and when they are settled enough, calmly talk to them ... if a service user says you have upset them, it's reasonable to say "sorry I've upset you".

Jake, expert by experience

We have already highlighted some of the issues that can arise in therapeutic relationships with autistic people, and ways of addressing these, in the sections above. However, it is impossible to completely avoid any problems occurring within therapeutic relationships, and in some cases, when a rupture has occurred, autistic clients will quickly decide that the relationship is irreparably damaged, and disengage. This may be linked to a black-and-white thinking style, together with difficulties imagining that the relationship could change or that they could feel differently about it in the future, and difficulties appreciating the wider consequences of ending their engagement.

It can be helpful to pre-empt ruptures at the outset of a piece of work by explicitly acknowledging with clients that it is reasonably likely that the relationship will "go wrong" at some point, but also highlighting that relationships can be repaired. This can then provide an opening to collaboratively plan how you and your client could raise and address any issues that occur. As part of this, it can be useful to explore the client's expectations of the therapeutic relationship, as sometimes they may have made assumptions about how these work, and may find it very difficult if the relationship does not then meet their expectations. For example, we worked with a client in a secure hospital who expected that staff should always know when he was becoming upset, and understand the reasons for his distress, without him directly communicating this. When there were occasions when staff were not able to do this, he assumed that they were being deliberately neglectful. It can also be helpful to check whether there are any specific issues that would be likely to upset your client, as these can sometimes be idiosyncratic; Jake recalled a peer who would become very distressed if anyone referred to World War II.

It is also essential to ensure that clients are aware of the potential consequences of ending the working relationship prematurely; for example, that it might not be possible to find an alternative practitioner to work with them and that it could result in delays to their progress. If there is a rupture, it is important to carefully explore the client's perspective on the causes of this. We have found that one of the strengths of many autistic clients is their ability to discuss their views about therapeutic relationships in an honest and open way. However, be prepared for potentially blunt feedback about your skills and approach; at various times, we have been told by clients that our approach is "boring", "deliberately upsetting" or "pointless".

Ending therapeutic relationships

> It was difficult when X left her job, as I did a lot of work with her. I built up a lot in a short space of time, and I was lacking in a short space of time.
>
> Jake, expert by experience

Therapeutic relationships can be just as important to autistic clients as they are to non-autistic clients, and as such, the ending of a therapeutic relationship can be experienced as a significant loss. The ending of a therapeutic relationship may present further challenges for autistic clients, as endings are often associated with change and uncertainty; for example, changes to routine and uncertainty about who might work with them in the future. In addition to this, clients are often losing a relationship in which they felt understood, in the context of feeling misunderstood by many people in their lives. It is therefore often helpful to explicitly plan for the ending of a relationship in advance. This might include talking through how your client will manage the associated changes, trying to reduce uncertainty by identifying who might be working with them next and planning how you might share important information about them with other professionals; for example, through collaboratively developing a communication passport. It can also be helpful to explain how the social rules of your relationship will change once your working relationship has ended; for example, that you may have brief, general conversations if you happen to meet, but it will no longer be possible to have in-depth discussions about their personal lives and progress. For autistic clients, it can be particularly important to discuss how they can generalise the skills they have learnt within your therapeutic relationship to other contexts; for example, coping skills for difficult emotions, as well as making sure that they know who else they can go to for support.

Summary

Working with autistic clients is often very rewarding, particularly when it involves questioning non-autistic assumptions about the world and collaborative approaches to problem-solving. As practitioners, we are continuously learning about how best to work with autistic clients and are indebted to the clients and experts by experience who have helped us with this over the years. We strongly recommend that all practitioners working with autistic clients seek out the expertise of autistic people; both that of the clients they work with and that of the growing number of excellent autistic authors, speakers and experts by experience. We are very grateful to Jake, expert by experience, for helping us write this chapter, and will leave the last words to him: the best practitioners "are compassionate, reasonable, don't talk down to people and treat others as they treat themselves".

References

Al-Attar, Z. (2018). *Framework for the Assessment of Risk and Protection in Offenders on the Autistic Spectrum (FARAS): A guide for risk assessors working with offenders on the autistic spectrum.* Retrieved from http://forensicpsychiatrystudies.com/wp-content/uploads/2022/06/Framework-for-the-Assessment-of-Risk-Protection-in-Offenders-on-the-Autistic-Spectrum.pdf

Ashwood, K.L., Gillan, N., Horder, J., Hayward, H., Woodhouse, E., McEwen, F.S., Findon, J., Eklund, H., Spain, D., Wilson, C.E., Cadman, T., Young, S., Stoencheva, V., Murphy, C.M., Robertson, D., Charman, T., Bolton, P., Glaser, K., Asherson, P., Simonoff, E. & Murphy, D.G. (2016). Predicting the diagnosis of autism in adults using the Autism-Spectrum Quotient (AQ) Questionnaire. *Psychological Medicine*, 46(12), 2595–2604.

Chester, V., Bunning, K., Tromans, S., Alexander, R. & Langdon, P. (2022). The prevalence of autism in the criminal justice system: A systematic review. *British Journal Psychiatry Open*, 8(S1), S45–S46.

Equality Act. (2010). c. 15. Available at: https://www.legislation.gov.uk/ukpga/2010/15 (Accessed 05.01.25).

Fletcher-Watson, S. & Happé, F. (2019). *Autism: A new introduction to psychological theory and current debate*. 2nd Ed. Routledge.

Kõlves, K., Fitzgerald, C., Nordentoft, M., Wood, S.J. & Erlangsen, A. (2021). Assessment of suicidal behaviors among individuals with autism spectrum disorder in denmark. *JAMA Network Open*, Jan 4; 4(1). e2033565. https://doi.org/10.1001/jamanetworkopen.2020.33565

Lai, M., Kassee, C., Besney, R., Bonato, S., Hull, L., Mandy, W., Szatmari, P. & Ameis, S.H. (2019). Prevalence of co-occurring mental health diagnoses in the autism population: A systematic review and meta-analysis. *Lancet Psychiatry*, 6(10), 819–829.

Maras, K., Dando, C., Stephenson, H., Lambrechts, A., Anns, S. & Gaigg, S. (2020). The Witness-Aimed First Account (WAFA): A new technique for interviewing autistic witnesses and victims. *Autism*, 24(6), 1449–1467.

Milton, D., Gurbuz, E. & Lopez, B. (2022). The 'double empathy problem': Ten years on. *Autism 2022*, 26(8), 1901–1903.

National Institute for Health and Care Excellence. (2024). *Autism in Adults Clinical Knowledge Summary*. Available at: https://cks.nice.org.uk/topics/autism-in-adults/background-information/prevalence/ (Accessed 12.01.25).

Ratto, A.B., Kenworthy, L., Yerys, B.E., Bascom, J., Wieckowski, A.T., White, S.W., Wallace, G.L., Pugliese, C., Schultz, R.T., Ollendick, T.H., Scarpa, A., Seese, S., Register-Brown, K., Martin, A. & Anthony, L.G. (2018). What about the girls? sex-based differences in autistic traits and adaptive skills. *Journal Autism and Developmental Disorders*, May;48(5). 1698–1711. https://doi.org/10.1007/s10803-017-3413-9

Russell, G., Stapley, S., Newlove-Delgado, T., Salmon, A., White, R., Warren, F., Pearson, A. & Ford, T. (2022). Time trends in autism diagnosis over 20 years: A UK population-based cohort study. *Journal of Child Psychology and Psychiatry*, 63(6), 674–682.

Trundle, G., Jones, K.A., Ropar, D. & Egan, V. (2023). Prevalence of victimisation in autistic individuals: A systematic review and meta-analysis. *Trauma, Violence, & Abuse*, 24(4), 2282–2296.

World Health Organization. (2022). *ICD-11: International Classification of Diseases (11th Revision)*. Available at: https://icd.who.int/ (Accessed 12.01.25).

8 Working with people serving indeterminate sentences

Sophie Ellis and Emma Stevenson

Introduction: sentencing matters

Anyone who has worked with both determinate and indeterminate forensic populations may observe a distinct difference in the tone or gravity of the interaction. The relationship is very different when the person knows they are being released, compared to knowing that every interaction potentially affects their freedom.

At least 28% of sentenced prisoners in England and Wales do not know if, or when, they will be released (Ministry of Justice (MoJ), 2025a). But indeterminacy is an underexplored psychological dimension of sentencing, despite longstanding criticism of indefinite detention as illegitimate, disproportionate and psychologically harmful (Ashworth & Zedner, 2014). Indeterminacy occurs in varying forms. Of those who endure uncertainty about their release date, around 55% are serving a life or Imprisonment for Public Protection (IPP) sentence where release is purely discretionary and they may never leave prison. The other 45% are serving an Extended Determinate Sentence (EDS), under which they have an eventual fixed release date but are eligible for discretionary release two thirds of the way through their term: a more limited form of indeterminacy. There are also 4,664 restricted patients subject to criminal sanctions and detained under indefinite hospital orders (MoJ, 2025b). In total, around 25,000 people are currently subject to some form of indefinite detention: a reflection of its growing popularity as both a public protection tool and a political demonstration of tough punishment. This chapter will focus on people serving IPP sentences, though the principles will have relevance to all types of indefinite detention. We also confine our analysis to England and Wales. However, we hope its approach is also relevant to professionals working across UK justice and health settings.

Indeterminate sentences are a form of preventative justice, in which psychologists play a central role through risk assessment, reduction and management practices. Yet training often encourages a narrow clinical focus on the person while treating the sentence as background noise. This chapter begins with a simple but significant observation: the nature of a sentence (its length, structure, and release or discharge conditions) has profound psychological

DOI: 10.4324/9781003542377-11

consequences. Our core contention is that *the prison sentence matters,* yet its effects are frequently overlooked, even though they are highly significant to our clinical work. We call this *sentence blindness.*

We argue that working effectively with indeterminacy, therefore, requires an awareness we call *sentence literacy*: a working knowledge of how sentencing regimes shape beliefs, feelings, behaviour and clinical responsivity. We offer a review of legislation, policy and evidence that can enhance literacy and conclude with five guiding principles for practice. These offer practical ways to address sentence blindness, hold moral responsibility for our role in preventative detention and sustain meaningful therapeutic work in ethically complex and risk-averse systems, with people who are enduring the psychological impacts of indeterminacy.

Section 1: Indeterminacy within the changing sentencing context[1]

Determinate custodial sentences are generally distinguished by a fixed length, and a fixed release date partway through, with the remainder served on licence in the community. Life and IPP sentences lack the first two features. The sentences are potentially lifelong, and release is discretionary. People become eligible for release after serving a minimum custodial term set by the sentencing judge. They are then subject to regular reviews by the Parole Board, who direct release on licence or continued detention. Upon release, life-sentenced prisoners will remain on lifelong licence. IPP prisoners face a further review three years after release, when their sentence is either ended, or if left in place, it ends automatically after a further two years without recall. A recall resets this two-year clock, meaning a person who is persistently recalled could remain on IPP indefinitely. These routes to end an IPP were recently introduced in the Victims and Prisoners Act 2024 following a successful campaign of action led by the families of people serving IPP sentences and supported by other organisations, in which both authors were involved. Previously, the review took place ten years post-release, with no automatic end if recall was avoided.

We conceptualise indeterminacy as enduring psychological uncertainty about if, *or when*, release will occur. Uncertainty about *ever* being released is the most extreme form of indeterminacy, but in other jurisdictions, (and historically in England and Wales too) the term "indeterminate sentence" frequently refers to a fixed length sentence where discretionary release may be granted between a minimum and maximum point: a more limited form of indeterminacy (Reitz, 2012). In England and Wales, there are examples of such sentences: the Extended Determinate Sentence (EDS) and the Sentence for Offenders of Particular Concern (SOPC). These are fixed in length, with discretionary release available between the two thirds point and the end of the custodial term. We argue that recognising both "pure" and limited indeterminacy is crucial from a psychological perspective, because uncertainty about release *really matters* to prisoners, even if it is only endured for a limited time. An important prelude to this understanding is good sentence literacy, to understand how indeterminacy "shows up" in a person's experience. To that end, we now turn to a brief overview of recent indeterminate sentencing policy in England and Wales.

The Criminal Justice Act 1967 formalised the parole system, under which the Parole Board considered discretionary release for *all* prisoners after they had served a third of their sentence, making limited indeterminacy a feature of all prison sentences. The Criminal Justice Act 1991 restricted this option to prisoners serving over four years, but also introduced automatic release after serving three quarters. Then the Criminal Justice Act 2003 sharply bisected release arrangements into entirely automatic or discretionary for different sentences. Most people serving a determinate sentence were automatically released halfway through. However, people serving indeterminate sentences had no release date *at all*, only an eligibility date for discretionary release by the Parole Board. This expansion in the use of indeterminacy was achieved by the introduction of the Imprisonment for Public Protection (IPP) sentence, to sit alongside existing life sentences as a disposal.

IPP remains the "purest" form of indeterminate sentence and the most significant indeterminate sentencing experiment in English and Welsh history, owing to its expansive reach and lack of limits. The law required that an IPP *must* be imposed for a wide range of offences which fell short of the criteria for a life sentence, if the court concluded that the person posed a risk of serious further harm. However, the legislation directed judges to *presume* such risk was present if the person had committed one previous offence from that wide-ranging list, unless any other information made this presumption "unreasonable": a highly questionable method from a forensic psychological perspective, and one now recognised to have acted as a drag net.

IPP is also the only prison sentence which *may* end altogether, but *may* also be served for life, lacking the certainty of either a determinate or a life sentence (which is certainly lifelong, even though release is uncertain). IPP makes complete liberty a perpetually possible but uncertain prospect. This makes it a psychologically disastrous sentence.

IPP was abolished via the Legal Aid, Sentencing and Punishment of Offenders Act 2012, but not retrospectively, leaving 1,012 people serving it in prison today who have never been released, but who have served, on average, ten years beyond their minimum term (MoJ, 2025a), and a further 1,532 on recall. A former Lord Chief Justice described the continuing existence of IPP as "the greatest single stain on our criminal justice system" (Edgar et al., 2020). It has been the subject of a great deal of collective action (Annison & Condry, 2022), and persistent political efforts to overturn it altogether (House of Commons Justice Committee, 2022), which continue today.

For sentence literacy purposes, we believe it is also important to understand that not all life sentences are the same: they can be imposed for a single serious offence, for a combination of offences and for public protection. A mandatory life sentence is the only sentence that can be imposed for murder;

the discretionary life sentence may be imposed for a very serious offence where the person is believed to pose a serious ongoing risk of harm (Hodgson, 1967). The automatic life sentence was introduced in 1997, imposable for a second serious offence, which attracted criticism as the offence before the court may arguably not merit life. It was swiftly abolished by 2003, replaced with IPP. Upon IPP's abolition, a new automatic life sentence was introduced with much greater restrictions on when it can be imposed: only three or four are handed down per year (UK Parliament, 2021). Lastly, under a Whole Life Order, a person will serve their whole life in prison *with certainty*. Therefore most, but not all, life sentences involve indeterminacy.

Throughout the 20th century, many indeterminate sentences[2] have followed a remarkably similar trajectory. They began with political optimism about their potential as a more reformative approach than traditional imprisonment, although IPP differed in its political justification to indefinitely detain dangerous offenders, rather than rehabilitative ideals (Annison, 2015). Their introduction was followed by implementation problems, which then provoked criticisms about failure in purpose, and led eventually to abolition. Common problems included sentences being applied more widely than intended; prisons not fulfilling promises of a separate, well-resourced regime; inconsistent release decisions; and unclear effects on reoffending. These problems have been particularly pervasive in IPP, owing to its lack of a maximum end point, but they are not new. It is therefore important to appreciate that indeterminate sentences have a political and institutional life cycle and are not neutrally constructed.

Indeterminate sentencing literacy should extend to mental health disposals, because those given to people who have committed criminal offences ("restricted patients") are all purely indeterminate. The most commonly encountered disposal in forensic populations is a Section 37/41, though there are others. A court may impose a Section 37 hospital order under the Mental Health Act 1983 if the person is deemed to require treatment for "mental disorder" and a Section 41 restriction order when the court believes the person poses a serious risk. Much like the IPP, these disposals may end altogether or may last forever, governed by discretionary decision-making.

From a psychological perspective, we argue that a basic legal and procedural knowledge of sentencing is important for understanding how indefinitely detained people, as active interpreters of their own carceral circumstances, respond to their sentence. There appears to be a rather naïve political belief that people will passively respond in a way that makes it straightforward to distinguish the risky from the safe. But people are much more complicated. Indeterminacy induces anxiety, and under certain circumstances hopelessness and a pervasive sense of injustice. These emotions influence behaviour, which in turn influence the system's decisions. Section 2 turns to a review of evidence about the psychological experiences of people serving indeterminate sentences.

Section 2: The experience of indeterminate sentences: a brief review of the literature

Although crucial for understanding custodial behaviour and addressing needs responsively, the inner experience of indeterminacy has been neglected in the forensic psychological literature. We suggest that our work with indeterminately sentenced prisoners can be enhanced by understanding their sentence-related experiences in four psychosocial dimensions: uncertainty, perceived injustice, hopelessness and power.

Uncertainty

Uncertainty is generally an aversive experience, which activates the behavioural inhibition system associated with negative emotional states such as fear and anxiety, and inhibits positive states (Morriss et al., 2023). The level of uncertainty and an individual's tolerance of it are both highly related to experienced anxiety (Carleton, 2016), and with avoidant, impulsive (Sadeh & Bredemeier, 2021) and obsessive-compulsive (Xu et al., 2024) behaviours as well as substance misuse (Bottesi et al., 2021), aimed at alleviating the pains of uncertainty. Self-harm is also widely understood as a coping response when people experience a lack of control (Peel-Wainwright et al., 2021). Uncertainty can even heighten threat appraisal in situations with a potentially positive outcome by provoking loss aversion, where the fear of loss outweighs the appeal of gain (Sokol-Hesner & Rutledge, 2018). This may lead to apparent self-sabotaging behaviours because maintaining a negative position feels safer. The application of the psychology of uncertainty to prison populations has been largely overlooked, but it is crucial for understanding how people survive an uncertain length of detention.

People serving IPP have reported intense sentence-related anxiety (Harris et al., 2020). This extends beyond ordinary concern about consequences that motivates compliance. IPP prisoners and professionals working with them report uncertainty-related experiences detrimental to well-being and progression, including: deep mistrust of professionals; cynicism about prospects; substance misuse; self-isolation and withdrawal (House of Commons Justice Committee, 2022). The self-harm rate of IPP prisoners is around twice that of both life and determinate-sentenced prisoners (Ellis & Hewson, 2025), and people subject to IPP have spoken openly about using self-harm to cope with the uncertainty of their sentence (House of Commons Justice Committee, 2021).

There are sentence-specific reasons why resilience to uncertainty may be especially strained for this group. Just six people on IPP are still serving their minimum term. The rest have served *on average* ten further years of indefinite detention: an extremely prolonged period of uncertainty (MoJ, 2025a). Lengthy minimum terms endured by life-sentenced prisoners carry their own hardships, but they do offer a form of temporal certainty that IPP does not

(Hulley et al., 2016; Crewe et al., 2019). Moreover, political campaigning to overturn IPP fuels further apprehension about possible change. Together, these conditions may foster loss aversion and coping behaviours to reduce uncertainty.

Injustice

Indefinite detention has been widely criticised for violating the principle of fair punishment (Ashworth & Zedner, 2014). Detaining someone based on *what they might do, rather than what they have done,* has serious legal and ethical shortcomings, especially when imposed for less serious offences. We suggest that people serving indeterminate sentences are more vulnerable to perceived injustice and therefore to its negative effects. In other fields, perceived injustice is associated with poorer health, lower well-being and an increase in counterproductive work behaviours (Greenberg, 2010; Adamovic, 2023; Trost et al., 2024). Perceived fairness is also a crucial element of legitimacy, which influences compliance and engagement with the law (Tyler, 2006).

The social contract (the implicit agreement between individuals and society to obey and cooperate (Rousseau, 1762/2008) differs between determinate and indeterminate sentences. Under a determinate sentence, "do the crime, do the time" is a clear and widely endorsed benchmark of justice (including by many prisoners). Under an indeterminate sentence, the social contract is much more ill-defined: release at an indeterminate point, in exchange for satisfactory risk reduction. This is a hazier bargain. Prisoners consistently describe risk concepts as difficult to understand, expectations as unclear, and judgements as inconsistent (Atrill & Liel, 2007; Crewe, 2011). People serving indeterminate sentences may therefore be more likely to conclude their treatment is unjust when the benchmark for fair treatment is less clear (to both parties).

Perceived fairness of demands matters as much as fair outcomes. Indeterminately sentenced prisoners are aware that the price of their freedom is deep engagement with their life histories. Unlike determinate-sentenced prisoners, they lack the choice to simply wait out their sentence. In these circumstances, a belief that such engagement is a fair demand can mitigate the pains of coercion. People may reach the moral conclusion that, given the gravity of their crime and/or the risk they pose, working on themselves is the right thing to do. This is vastly different to feeling unjustly compelled to be painfully vulnerable in exchange for liberty. Indeterminately sentenced prisoners may therefore rely more heavily on a sense of justice to get through their punishment.

There appear to be some sentence-related differences in perceived injustice. A study of life-sentenced prisoners convicted of murder found that they engaged in a moral reckoning process, where perceived proportionality and fairness affected the kind of agency they felt over their progression, and was highly individualised (Jarman, 2020). Conversely, people serving IPP have more consistently reported strong feelings of injustice (House of Commons Justice Committee, 2022). This may be explained by IPP's broader loss of legal and political legitimacy. In other words, it is a genuine injustice, not only a perceived one. People serving IPP have reported psychological symptoms that overlap with those of people in other unjust circumstances, including wrongful conviction (Brooks & Greenberg, 2021), and politicised forms of arbitrary detention (Ferstman, 2024). In 2012, the European Court of Human Rights ruled that IPP violated Article 5(1), which prohibits arbitrary detention. More recently, the United Nations has described IPP as "wholly incompatible with the rule of law", "cruel, inhumane and degrading" (Office of the United Nations High Commissioner for Human Rights [OHCHR] 2023) and amounting to "psychological torture" (OHCHR, 2024). Arbitrary, inhumane and/or political detention can provoke extreme responses, such as hunger strikes and martyrdom (Bufkin, 2024; Farraj, 2024). We are concerned that there may be increased incidences of such behaviour from unreleased IPP prisoners as time passes. Some tragic examples have already pointed to this possibility. In 2023, a person serving IPP took his own life and left a note stating "I hope my death will change things for IPP people" (Prisons and Probation Ombudsman, 2024).

We therefore argue that it is vital to take the effects of perceived injustice seriously when working with people serving indeterminate sentences. Whether injustice is perceived or actual, its effects are real. They will be highly personal, but can also be mapped onto the legal and policy context. For sentence literacy purposes, attention should be paid to when a person was sentenced (the earliest years of implementation are usually those of greatest overreach), whether the sentence was abolished, and why, and the extent to which broader legal and political discourse is suggestive of illegitimacy.

Hopelessness

Hope is acknowledged as crucial for sentence progression and desistance (Maruna & McNeill, 2006) and more broadly is protective against ill-health and suicidality (Snyder et al., 2002). Legal scholars have argued that a "hope standard" is necessary for legitimate punishment, including being alive and capable after imprisonment and receiving reintegrative support (Brownlee, 2021). However, hope occupies a complex position in indeterminate sentencing. The theoretical existence of a route to liberty does not completely deny hope, but in practice, hopelessness is widely reported by indeterminately sentenced prisoners, particularly those who have had multiple parole knockbacks (Wright et al., 2022). This is not straightforward despair, but an ambivalent hope, where perpetual uncertainty means hope cannot straightforwardly be abandoned. Instead, people may lose the agentic aspects of hope (believing *they* can achieve release and that *they* can find ways to do it: Snyder, 2002) and find any remaining hope painful to endure. Managing the pains of hope may explain refusals to engage, apparent self-sabotaging, and learned helplessness (Senneseth et al., 2022; Marklund et al., 2020). It is also highly relevant to suicide.

The Prison Service already lists life and IPP sentences as risk factors for suicide (HM Prison & Probation Service, 2024). The rate of self-inflicted deaths among IPP prisoners spiked noticeably in 2022 and 2023, which were years of turbulent political activity in IPP reform. Although significant reforms to the IPP were secured, many hoped-for changes were rejected by the government. The raised and subsequently dashed hopes may have contributed to the rise in deaths among people serving IPP in prison. Their perpetually uncertain sentence structure also renders them particularly vulnerable to ambivalent hope. In contrast, people with very lengthy minimum terms may suffer complete hopelessness, of the kind that has been criticised in international law. This particularly occurs under "informal" life imprisonment (Penal Reform International & Life Imprisonment Worldwide Project, 2024), when age at sentencing and minimum term length mean that the person is very likely to die in prison. It is important for practitioners to sensitively consider what psychological dimensions like meaning, purpose and goal orientation may look like in this context.

Power

Ethical practice requires careful attention to power imbalances between psychologist and client. These should be minimised where possible, or else transparently discussed, with measures taken to maximise the client's voice and choice (British Psychological Society, 2017). Indeterminate sentences greatly enhance this power imbalance. In interviews with psychologists and prisoners serving indeterminate sentences, Shingler et al. (2020a, 2020b) found that the power disparity and the high-stakes nature of risk assessment placed psychologically heavy burdens on both sides. It undermined trust, increased the risks of honest disclosure and eroded the therapeutic conditions needed for effective assessment. These challenges are not insurmountable, but the structure of indeterminate sentences makes them unavoidable. It is therefore important for sentence literacy to understand how sentences change relationships through the operation of various forms of power.

"Legitimate power" occurs when one group claims the right to govern a particular domain and others acknowledge that right (Coicaud, 2002). The professionalisation of forensic psychology has proceeded in tandem with the expansion of indeterminate sentences. Psychologists offered tools to support discretionary decision-making and were therefore accorded a high degree of legitimate power with penal decision-makers. However, their legitimacy in the eyes of prisoners reduced as they came to be seen as arbiters of indefinite detention (Warr, 2020). Prisoners question psychologists' motives, the validity of their judgements, their suitability for wielding power, and the effectiveness of their methods. Specific criticisms may be familiar to readers: trainees completing risk assessments; the prevalence of young White women; mixed results from offending behaviour programmes. These are not just personal grievances but reflect broader challenges to psychologists' legitimate power and should be understood as a sociological product of power relations under conditions of indeterminacy.

"Epistemic power" is the ability to control what others "know" or accept as true, by shaping knowledge production and determining how information is shared and presented. Because forensic psychologists have cultivated legitimate power, our interpretations of people's behaviour carry a high degree of epistemic power too. People serving indeterminate sentences are sensitive to this and often feel they *must* adhere to the psychologist's interpretation in order to progress (Warr, 2019). Epistemic power can be difficult to spot when immersed in professional norms. Hacking (2006) describes the process of "making up people": the power to create classifications that rise and fall with scientific trends. Trauma and neurodiversity have gained explanatory prominence for example, displacing earlier emphases on psychopathy and cognitive deficits. Sentence-related classifications carry epistemic power too. The authors have deliberately avoided the terms "IPPs" and "lifers" which, by implying they are distinct classes of person, risk overstating their homogeneity. IPP is a particular case in point: a uniquely dangerous person did not arise between 2005 and 2012 and then disappear, a particular kind of sentence did. We should therefore exercise care with the epistemic power attached to legal disposals and not use them to "make up people".

In recent decades, forensic psychology has typically been less active in exercising its "*collective* power". However, efforts to overturn IPP in the last five years demonstrated there is a will to take action. Coordinated by the first author, a group of around 140 psychologists and allied professionals submitted evidence to parliament raising their professional concerns about IPP and supporting proposed legislative reforms (Rhodes, 2025). Originally an independent effort, it culminated in the British Psychological Society (BPS, 2023) issuing a joint statement alongside the Probation Institute, backing key changes. The BPS then backed a further set of reforms as part of a coalition of mental health bodies, human rights charities and criminal justice organisations (BPS, 2024). In 2024, the law on IPP changed. Overall, 1,800 people (almost one fifth of everyone ever given IPP) had their sentence immediately ended, and a new route off the sentence was created. This use of collective power to influence the law on indeterminate sentences was an enormous achievement and could be replicated by psychologists in future. Using our collective power may impact how we are perceived by the people we work with and our relationships with them.

Section 3: Navigating clinical relationships with people subject to indeterminacy

This section outlines a set of principles for working with people subject to indeterminate sentences (within which we include restricted patient hospital orders). We recognise that practitioners are already striving to work with humanity and compassion. Our aim is to provide proactive ways to help people address sentence blindness and strengthen therapeutic relationships. While written with psychologists in mind, these principles are relevant across forensic roles.

Principle 1: Enhance sentence literacy

> "My experience as a psychologist during the emergence of the IPP sentence was that we did not give the legalities and practicalities much thought at all. We knew the individuals who received these sentences were subject to tariffs, like life sentence prisoners, and initially that was as much thought as we gave it. I look back on this with a sense of bewilderment that I didn't pay attention; how could I have not noticed that the nature of this sentence was so significant? I pride myself on my integrity and in my strengths as a relational practitioner, and yet when I am honest it was only when others started raising concerns that I really began to think about it for myself" (Second author).

Practitioners may overlook the legal context of those serving indeterminate sentences (legal blindness) and the practical realities of these disposals (procedural blindness). These aspects of sentence blindness affect how individuals experience their sentence, perceive progression, and experience decisions made about them. People do not passively receive their sentences – they actively interpret them, and this shapes their behaviour and impacts real-world practice. Sentence blindness must be central to our learning and discussion.

Implications for practice

- Increase legal awareness of indeterminate sentences, including the context in which they are imposed, the criteria used in their application, and any retrospective or prospective changes to sentences (see Table 8.1).
- Understand how sentences work in practice.
- Reflect on the nature of the sentence being served by the person in front of you and think about how it has affected them.

Principle 2: Recognise and mitigate sentence-related biases

> "It was not uncommon for psychologists to refer to a judge's sentencing remarks that individuals were 'dangerous' as evidence for increased risk. So, let's just think about that. We took an assumption about risk without always examining how it had been reached and then used it as a double whammy to evidence why that person was indeed risky" (Second author).

Psychologists are often seen as credible and authoritative, which can obscure our susceptibility to unconscious biases (Hogue et al., 2023). Biases can influence risk assessments, treatment recommendations and social interactions (Skeem & Lowencamp, 2016). Research suggests that forensic psychologists often struggle to recognise and manage bias, relying too heavily on introspection (Neal & Brodsky, 2016). Here, we discuss the largely unexplored effects of indeterminacy on psychological judgement.

Risk perception distortions

We have outlined above the presumption of dangerousness, which underpinned by the IPP. Psychologists will recognise the limitations of binary assumptions and unstructured approaches to risk when applying this test. Despite its flaws, the label "dangerous" persists, reinforcing systemic bias, for example, where security decisions and allocation are based on sentence type rather than risk. We must be attuned to how the "dangerous" label might distort our risk perceptions. We are all prone to "fundamental attribution error": emphasising personal traits over situational factors, particularly for negatively labelled individuals. This can skew priorities: therapy is promoted while basic needs like housing and income are overlooked (Cordle & Gale, 2025). Sociologist Ulrich Beck (1992) argued that modern societies manage fear by locating risk in individuals rather than systems. For indeterminate sentences, decision-makers often ask, "what have *you* done to reduce your risk?", rather than "what have *we* done to support progress" and "what have we done to *create* risk?"

Professional and organisational bias also plays a role in risk perception (Hogue & Dernevik, 2022). Every setting has cultural narratives around risk, and high-security environments often lean towards risk aversion. Psychologists must remain alert to the "blind spot" fallacy (Dror, 2020): assuming bias exists in others but not us. We must also be cautious of the "illusion of control", the belief that professionalism alone can neutralise bias. Organisational culture shapes us all.

Desensitisation to the weight of indeterminacy

Psychologists working with people serving indeterminate sentences hold significant power. Each interaction can potentially influence liberty, and subdued compliance often reflects the quiet pressure of indeterminacy. Psychologists may not fully grasp how indeterminacy drives compliance or may recognise it, yet underestimate its emotional weight. Desensitisation and emotional detachment can lead to professionals seeing individuals as bureaucratic cases (Guthrie et al., 2016). For example, one author remembered reading an IPP dossier and seeing that the person was years and years over tariff and had no emotional reaction to it, or sense of injustice/unfairness ("I just read it like 'This is just another person who is long over tariff', and I wondered why I didn't feel anything"). Even in a compassionate and connected practitioner, the context can blind us to the impact of the bureaucracy of indeterminate sentencing.

Time blindness

Progress in the criminal justice and mental health systems is often painfully slow. Professionals can become desensitised to these delays, responding more to external deadlines than to the individual's experience. In early IPP cases, those serving IPPs were often pushed to the back of assessment and treatment queues. Today, many prisoners and restricted patients still wait months for key decisions. Bureaucratic inertia can dull our sense of urgency and obscure the psychological toll of these delays.

Affective bias

Psychologists routinely monitor any affective bias, ensuring emotions do not distort their judgement. But how often do we reflect on our emotional responses to indeterminacy?

The second author worked with a young man we will call Leon, who was subject to IPP, seven years over a three-year minimum term:

> Just prior to his parole assessment Leon was found with a mobile phone in his cell which he had been using to speak with his girlfriend. Leon had been adjudicated for the phone and when I assessed him, he was very low and full of regret and despair. I recall thinking to myself that he probably had no chance of getting parole now, even though his compliance issues were not strongly related to risk. I felt hopeless and despairing for him. I am sure this leaked out of me when we interacted.

This emotional transference illustrates how systemic injustice affects both client and clinician. Which begs the question, how might this affect psychological judgement and opinion?

Bias mitigation depends on high-quality training, supervision and reflective practice. It requires proactive strategies – not just individual insight, but a supportive culture of accountability. Reflective questions might include: What assumptions am I making? How might the system be shaping my judgement? What dynamics are at play between me and this person? Bias is not a failing but a human factor. Managing it responsibly is a core ethical task.

Implications for practice

- Engage in structured, critical self-reflection to identify personal and systemic biases when working with indeterminate sentences.
- Develop a proactive bias mitigation strategy.
- Promote systems that support reflection and growth around practitioner bias.

Principle 3: Proactively respond to indeterminacy

> We can make a difference by recognising and empathising with the impact of indeterminacy. Simple, sincere statements matter such as: "I'm sorry you've been in this situation so long … it must be hard not knowing when you'll be released or when you will get to be with your family…" (Second author).

Acknowledging sentence type as a responsivity factor

The Risk–Needs–Responsivity model has shaped forensic practice, with responsivity factors such as gender, culture, language and mental health now routinely considered (HM Inspectorate of Probation, 2023; Hart et al., 2022). We argue that sentence type, particularly indeterminacy, should also be recognised as a responsivity factor. It influences psychological state, behaviour and engagement and should be factored into formulations and treatment planning. Considerations might include sentence type, time of sentencing (relevant to the political backdrop of the sentence), sentence length, stage and age at sentencing, enabling more ethical and responsive care.

Assessing the effects of indeterminacy

No formal tools exist to assess the psychological impact of indeterminacy, and we are not suggesting that one should. While common themes emerge, people experience indeterminacy differently. Still, psychologists must explore this impact. A simple starting point is to ask, "How has this sentence affected you?" Areas to consider include the relationship between indeterminacy and:

- Psychological distress: hopelessness (ambivalent hope/complete hopelessness), trauma, depression and anxiety.
- Self-harm and suicidality
- Symptoms triggered by distress (including psychosis)
- Feelings of injustice or grievance
- Withdrawal or disengagement from interventions
- Self-sabotage
- Mistrust of professionals
- Delayed maturity due to long-term detention during formative years.

We also need to explore how indeterminacy has shaped:

- Coping strategies and strengths
- Behaviour during assessment and intervention
- Family relationships and support systems (see Hutton & O'Brien, 2024; UNGRIPP, 2023)
- Personal perceptions of injustice.

Psychological assessments should explicitly document these effects, including iatrogenic and contextual harm. This should be included in our formulations. Framing an individual's progress within this context supports more ethical and balanced formulations.

Empathising with the effects of indeterminacy

Understanding is not the same as empathising; imagining how indeterminacy shapes a person's daily life, relationships, and what is at stake. Expressing empathy builds trust and validates lived experience. Psychologists are trained to question perceptions of unfairness as potential signs of distorted thinking, such as antisocial attitudes. But in the case of IPP and other indefinite sentences, perceptions and expressions of injustice may be valid. Once, saying IPP was unjust risked being seen as collusion. Now, following widespread criticism, this view is more accepted. We must stay alert to future blind spots and remember that empathy does not mean agreement or naivety: it means holding the emotional reality of someone's experience with care.

Communicating the effects of indeterminacy

It is not enough to recognise, assess and empathise. We must also communicate these effects clearly in our reports and with other stakeholders. For example, in Leon's case described above, his response to adjudication made more sense when understood in the context of indeterminacy. That context was explicitly included in his formulation. We recommend making the psychological and behavioural impact of indeterminacy visible in assessments and care plans and visible in risk evaluations. A useful question when assessing risk is: "If the impact of this sentence were removed, how would their risk profile change?" Positive scenario planning can help communicate the impact of indeterminacy and encourages stakeholders to consider the broader context of someone's presentation.

Implications for practice

- Incorporate sentence type as a responsivity factor in clinical practice
- Assess and document the impact of indeterminacy
- Validate and empathise with the effects of indeterminacy
- Communicate the impact of indeterminacy clearly to other stakeholders.

Principle 4: Take moral accountability

"Injustice in the systems we work with really makes me angry. I hate unfairness. It also makes me cynical, judgemental of those running the systems and making the rules, and quick to make assumptions. But I must be careful because sometimes I realise I have made it all about how I feel and my indignation. I get on my high horse; this can at the expense of really understanding or listening to the experience of the individual who is the victim of injustice" (Second author).

Working with power imbalance and high stakes

For those serving indeterminate sentences, meeting a psychologist often means serious, high-stakes scrutiny. The power imbalance is significant and often unspoken but shapes the entire interaction. Psychologists should reflect on what it means to assess someone under these conditions: to be expected to disclose deeply personal information and to fear putting a foot wrong. We should acknowledge this power imbalance openly. The consent process offers a natural opportunity to do so, for example, "I know there is a clear power imbalance here, and my assessment may affect your life. I take that responsibility seriously and will be fair and respectful, but I understand it may not feel that way to you". This kind of transparency invites honest dialogue. In therapy, it can become part of the working agreement; it shows humility and helps validate the individual's experience.

Naming procedural injustice

Despite formal recognition of IPP's injustice, little redress has followed. Psychologists face tough questions: How do we acknowledge this and still build trust? How do we speak honestly without undermining other professionals? Injustice is not always as visible as in IPP. It exists on a continuum. Most psychologists will recall times when system failings blocked progress, but the burden was placed on the individual. We often avoid naming injustice, fearing damage to relationships or professional consequences. But silence makes us complicit. Take Amir; years over his minimum term, finally progressed to lower security conditions, but housed on wing with short-term determinate prisoners. For them, minor trouble meant lost privileges; for Amir, it risked significant delays to release. Others exploited this, threatening him with false accusations, which delayed his parole. Or Emil, a young man with autism inappropriately placed in a personality disorder unit aged 18 because no other service would take him. His mental health deteriorated, he assaulted staff, and he remains detained seven years later. Naming such harm matters, while continuing to assess and manage risk, holding the tension between risk and moral discomfort over how it arose.

Knowing your moral boundaries

Legal hegemony refers to how legal authority becomes so embedded in daily life that it is rarely questioned. For forensic practitioners, this raises a key ethical question: "It may be legal, but is it right?" Following years of criticism, the American Psychological Association commissioned an independent review on the role of psychologists at Guantanamo Bay (Hoffman et al., 2015). Essentially, between 2002 and 2010, the APA revised its ethics code to allow state authority to override ethical duties, enabling psychologists participation in interrogations and torture. Burton and Kagan (2007) argued that this change permitted the "Nurenburg defence" (just following orders) and undermined accountability. The APA later called this a "stain on our collective integrity" (Kaslow & McDaniel, 2015) and committed to restoring its moral compass.

Though the contexts differ, it could be argued that some conceptual parallels can be drawn between Guantanamo and the IPP in the tension between legal permissiveness and moral rightness. The United Nations' Special Rapporteur on Torture has suggested that the ongoing uncertainty amounts to psychological torture (Howard League for Penal Reform, 2025), and psychologists are part of the regime. It is important to appreciate that even egregious injustices are not necessarily viewed as such at the time. Psychologists involved in its administration must ask: Have we reflected on our role? Have we considered whether IPP is a stain on our integrity? The BPS (2023) has supported IPP reform but recognising harm is not the same as reflecting on our part in it.

While the question of what the profession should do next is complex, the importance of ethical boundaries is clear. Power shapes all organisations and questioning it can be hard, especially for early-career psychologists. But we must know where we draw the line. Our regulatory standards must guide psychologists, even when systems push against them.

Implications for practice

- Reflect on the power you hold in high-stakes decision-making contexts.
- Recognise when procedural or systemic injustice is occurring – and name it.
- Connect with others to challenge unjust practices collectively.
- Understand and critically reflect on legal hegemony.
- Define and examine your personal moral boundaries: Where do you draw the line?

Principle 5: Be open and transparent

> Richard is detained under a Section 37/41 hospital order. After two years, he was mentally stable, hoping for discharge. Instead, he was told to do offence-focused work, which he was reluctant to engage in. As his psychologist I knew that if he did not, it would remain a treatment target, and the MoJ would not authorise the stages of his progression. His real choice was "do it now or do it later". I explained this to him. It felt awful, but being honest is not always easy and I had a duty to help him make an informed decision" (Second author).

Acknowledging lived realities and constrained choices

Consent in forensic settings is inherently complex. For those serving indeterminate sentences, the idea that engagement is a free choice often rings hollow. HMPPS's "strategy of choices" (MoJ, 2020) frames engagement as voluntary, with neutrally enforced consequences. While this was designed to work with individuals holding antisocial attitudes, its application to indeterminate sentences can be problematic. Choosing between engagement and lifelong detention is arguably a *Hobson's choice*, where only one viable option exists.

We should also acknowledge limited choice during assessments. Traditionally, we may stress that the person has a choice about whether to answer the questions we ask. While this appears collaborative, it can misrepresent the reality: some omissions have consequences. It is important to explain:

> If there are topics you prefer not to discuss, and I believe these are important to the assessment, I will explain why I think they matter and also outline the possible implications of you choosing not to speak about them.

This supports informed decision-making while preserving openness and trust.

Navigating disclosure and impossible gambles

Disclosure for individuals subject to indeterminacy can feel like an impossible gamble. Honesty might support progression or trigger new concerns and delays. This should be acknowledged openly. The sense of safety and security we create in our work with people has, in our experience, led to some individuals telling us things that created further problems for them; we have been acutely aware of this when working with people serving indeterminate sentences. Take Jim, who addressed his sexually harmful behaviour in therapy. Encouraged to be honest on the basis that this would aid his risk management and his well-being, he later disclosed during parole assessment that he still experiences occasional sexual thoughts about children. While the risk assessor saw this openness as a strength, other stakeholders reacted negatively, making assumptions about his risk. This did not aid his risk management in a fruitful way. Jim was disheartened and regretted his disclosure. Would Jim have shared this had he known the consequences? We must help individuals weigh the risks of disclosure. It is about trust, but also realism. Being open about this dilemma helps protect the therapeutic relationship and respects the individual's right to informed choice, which ultimately aids risk management and protects others

Communicating realistic pathways to progression

The realities of progression must be clearly communicated beyond handing out a leaflet on the parole process or mental health rights. Richard believed mental health recovery alone would lead to discharge, but the real pathway will involve years of structured progression. This only became clear three years into his sentence, creating avoidable distress. Discomfort with delivering bad news can lead psychologists to delay these conversations. But respectful transparency strengthens trust. People have the right to understand what lies ahead, even when the truth is difficult.

Explaining options for redress

What power do people subject to indeterminacy have to raise concerns? The significant power imbalance must make it feel risky to complain about those who control decisions affecting them. Psychologists must create clear, safe avenues for redress. It is good practice to explain to individuals what to do if they have a concern. We can encourage feedback and offer to review or correct any errors. It is also important to provide information about the Health and Care Professions Council (HCPC), which regulates psychologists and handles complaints. Giving information about the right to complain should not be an uncomfortable experience if done in the spirit of genuine transparency.

Accepting and inviting scrutiny

Psychologists hold significant power, and if our work is flawed, the consequences can be profound. We must be open to challenge: not just by systems, but by the people we assess. For example, if we assess someone serving an IPP and recommend against their release, it is entirely reasonable, and psychologically healthy, for that person to challenge the conclusion. In fact, if they do not, we should be curious as to why. What barriers might prevent them from speaking up?

Implications for practice

- Acknowledge and name the structural and procedural constraints individuals face.
- Provide accessible explanations of legal processes, decisions and avenues for challenge.
- Be genuinely open to scrutiny.

Conclusion and future directions

This chapter has set out to explain the need for and outline a framework for working effectively with people serving indeterminate sentences, grounded in five interrelated principles. Together, these principles challenge sentence blindness, highlight the psychosocial impact of indeterminacy and call for more ethically attuned, reflective and responsive practice. Moving forward, forensic psychologists must deepen their engagement with the reality that indeterminate sentencing is not simply a legal category, but a lived experience with serious emotional, relational and personal consequences.

We hope that this chapter will substantially contribute to enhancing clinical practice with people serving indeterminate sentences; an area which requires more than technical skill and psychological knowledge: it requires legal and historical awareness, moral clarity, sentence sensitivity and a deeply thoughtful approach to matters of justice and punishment. The five principles outlined here offer a starting point, but the work of enacting them belongs to the profession as a whole.

Appendix

This chapter has outlined the main indeterminate sentences given in England and Wales. It has not covered all of them. As a desk reference, Table 8.1 lists the details of each sentence involving indeterminacy that we believe people will still be serving in prison. We are indebted to Nicola Padfield, Laura Janes and the Prison Reform Trust for recording the many complex changes to sentencing law.

Table 8.1 Types of pure and limited indeterminate sentence and how they operate[a]

Sentence	Age group	Criteria for imposition	Risk of harm assessment	Length	Release	Years of operation
Pure indeterminacy: no fixed end date, and release is discretionary						
Mandatory life	Adults aged 21 and over	The only available sentence for murder		Lifelong	Eligible for discretionary release after serving the minimum term set by the judge	1965–present
Discretionary life	Adults aged 21 and over	May be imposed for 24 specified offences, if the court is of the opinion that there is a significant risk of serious harm from further specified offences	The court must take into account information about: the offence, previous offences, patterns of behaviour, and any information about the offender	Lifelong	As above	2003–present in its current form, but has been available throughout the 20th century
Automatic life (old version) Sometimes referred to as life for a second listed offence	Adults aged 21 and over	1997–2000: Must be imposed for a second serious offence (of 11 offences) unless the court believed there were exceptional reasons not to 2000–2005: Court of Appeal judgements allowed greater flexibility in imposition		Lifelong	As above	1997–2005

(Continued)

Table 8.1 (Continued)

Sentence	Age group	Criteria for imposition	Risk of harm assessment	Length	Release	Years of operation
Automatic life (new version)	Adults aged 21 and over	Must be imposed for a second serious offence (of 15 offences), if the first offence had imposed either a life or IPP sentence with a minimum term of five years, or a determinate sentence of at least ten years		Lifelong	As above	2012–present
Custody for life	Adults aged 18–20	The same as mandatory, discretionary and automatic life sentences, but individuals must be detained in a Young Offenders Institution	As per the discretionary life	Lifelong	As above	1982–present
Detention for Life	Children	May be imposed for 24 specified offences, if the court is of the opinion that there is a significant risk of serious harm occasioned by further specified offences	As per discretionary life	Lifelong	As above	2003–present in its current form, but has been available throughout the 20th century
Detention at His Majesty's Pleasure	Children	The only available sentence for murder		Lifelong	As above, with the addition of eligibility for a reduction in minimum term length after serving half of it	1908–present (but with substantial changes to minimum term length)

Imprisonment for Public Protection (IPP)	Adults	2005–2008 Must be imposed for 153 specified offences if the court is of the opinion that there is a significant risk of serious harm occasioned by further specified offences 2008–2012 Became discretionary rather than mandatory, number of eligible offences reduced to 53, and equivalent determinate sentence term must be at least four years	Risk of harm was presumed if the person had been convicted of a previous specified offence (of 153 offences) unless the court considered the presumption unreasonable	Indefinite	Note that the PCSC Act 2022, restricted minimum term reviews if the person was sentenced aged under 18 (retrospectively applied to all) Eligible for discretionary release after serving the minimum term set by the judge. Eligible for discretionary sentence end three years after release. Automatic sentence end if unsuccessful but serve two further years on licence without recall. Recall resets the two-year clock	2005–2012
Detention for Public Protection (DPP)	Children	As above	As above	Indefinite	As above, but eligibility for discretionary sentence end is two years after release	2005–2012

(*Continued*)

Table 8.1 (Continued)

Sentence	Age group	Criteria for imposition	Risk of harm assessment	Length	Release	Years of operation
Limited indeterminacy: fixed length with discretionary release partway through						
Extended determinate sentence (not for terror offences where maximum penalty is life)	Adults aged 21 and over	May be imposed for 44 specified offences, if the court is of the opinion that there is a significant risk of serious harm occasioned by further specified offences, if it is not required to impose a different sentence, the person was previously convicted of a specified offence (of 20 offences), and the minimum appropriate custodial term is at least four years	As per discretionary life	Fixed length	Eligible for discretionary release after serving two thirds of the custodial term. Followed by a period of post-sentence supervision up to five years for violence, eight years for sex offences, and ten years for terrorism	2015–present
Extended Sentence of Detention (ESD)	Children and adults aged 18–20	As above, but detention must be in a Young Offender Institution or other youth custody for under 18s	As per discretionary life	Fixed length	As above	2015–present
EDS (imposed before 13 April 2015, with a custodial period of over ten years or for	Adults	May be imposed for 48 offences if the court is of the opinion that there is a significant risk of serious harm occasioned by further specified offences,		Fixed length	As above, but without special provision for terrorism	2012–2015

a Schedule 15B offence under the Criminal Justice Act 2003)		if it is not required to impose a different sentence, the person was previously convicted of a specified offence (of 48 offences), and the minimum appropriate custodial term is at least four years			
ESD (Imposed before 13 April 2015, with a custodial period of over ten years or for a Schedule 15B offence under the Criminal Justice Act 2003)	Children and adults aged 18–20	As above	Fixed length	As above, but without special provision for terrorism	2012–2015
Sentence for Offenders of Particular Concern (before the Police, Crime, Sentencing and Courts Act 2022)	Adults	Must be imposed for ten specified terror and child sex offences and another sentence is not imposed	Fixed length	Fixed length. Eligible for discretionary release after serving half if convicted of a sex offence, and at two thirds if convicted of a terror offence Followed by one year of post-sentence supervision	2015–2022

(Continued)

Table 8.1 (Continued)

Sentence	Age group	Criteria for imposition	Risk of harm assessment	Length	Release	Years of operation
Sentence for Offenders of Particular Concern (after the Police, Crime, Sentencing and Courts Act 2022)	Adults	Must be imposed for ten specified terror and child sex offences and another sentence is not imposed		Fixed length	As above, except eligibility for discretionary release is at two thirds for both offence types	2022–present
Extended Sentence for Public Protection (EPP, before 14 July 2008)	Adults	Must be imposed for 48 specified offences, but not a serious offence, if the court is of the opinion that there is a significant risk of serious harm occasioned by further specified offences, and the minimum appropriate custodial term is at least 12 months		Fixed length	Fixed length. Eligible for discretionary release after serving half. Followed by a period of post-sentence supervision up to five years for violence, and eight years for sex offences	2005–2008
Extended Sentence for Public Protection (EPP, before 14 July 2008)	Children	As above, but could be imposed for a serious specified offence if a life or DPP sentence were deemed inappropriate		Fixed length	As above	2005–2008
Standard Determinate Sentence (for terror offences)	Adults	As per the sentencing guideline for terror offences which do not meet the criteria for more severe sentence types		Fixed length	Fixed length. Eligible for discretionary release after serving two thirds	Applied retrospectively in 2020 to all eligible prisoners

| Section 85 extended sentence (for offences committed before 4 April 2005 and conviction before 3 December 2012, sentence more than four years) | Adults | May be imposed for a sexual or violent offence if the court considers that, if this sentence were not passed, the period on licence would be insufficient for crime prevention and rehabilitation | Fixed length | Fixed length. Eligible for discretionary release after serving half. Automatic release after serving two thirds. Followed by a period of post-sentence supervision up to five years for violence, and ten years for sex offences | 2000–2012 |

[a] Note that there are certain variants of sentences that usually involve pure or limited indeterminacy which diverge from the usual structure. Sentences that require serving the full custodial term are EDS for terror offences where the maximum penalty is life, the Serious Terrorism Sentence (STS), and the Whole Life Order (WLO). Sentences that permit automatic release partway through are EDS passed before 13 April 2015 with a custodial term of less than ten years and not for a Schedule 15B offence under the Criminal Justice Act 2003, and EPP passed after 14 July 2008.

Notes

1 Appendix 8.1 provides a summary of the sentences available to the courts in England and Wales which include an element of indeterminacy.
2 Readers should be aware that the sentences discussed in this chapter are only the latest in a long history of similarly constructed sentences during the 19th/20th centuries, including Penal Servitude, the Borstal sentence, the Preventative Detention sentence and the Corrective Training sentence.

References

Adamovic, M. (2023). Organizational justice research: A review, synthesis, and research agenda. *European Management Review, 20*(4), 762–782

Annison, H. (2015). *Dangerous politics: Risk, political vulnerability, and penal policy*. Oxford University Press.

Annison, H., & Condry, R. (2022). The pains of hope: Families of indeterminate sentenced prisoners and political campaigning by lay citizens. *The British Journal of Criminology, 62*(5), 1252–1269.

Ashworth, A., & Zedner, L. (2014). *Preventive justice*. Oxford University Press.

Attrill, G., & Liell, G. (2007). Offenders' views on risk assessment. In N. Padfield (Ed.), *Who to release? Parole, fairness and criminal justice* (pp. 191–201). Willan.

Beck, U. (1992). *Risk society: Towards a new modernity*. Sage.

Bottesi, G., Ghisi, M., Caggiu, I., & Lauriola, M. (2021). How is intolerance of uncertainty related to negative affect in individuals with substance use disorders? The role of the inability to control behaviors when experiencing emotional distress. *Addictive Behaviors, 115*, 106785.

British Psychological Society. (2017). *Practice guidelines*. (3rd ed.). British Psychological Society.

British Psychological Society. (2023, 26 April). *Government urged to resentence people on IPP sentences which cause psychological harms*. https://www.bps.org.uk/news/government-urged-resentence-people-ipp-sentences-which-cause-psychological-harms

British Psychological Society. (2024, 14 February). *BPS supports calls for amendments to Imprisonment for Public Protection sentences*. https://www.bps.org.uk/news/bps-supports-calls-amendments-imprisonment-public-protection-sentences

Brooks, S. K., & Greenberg, N. (2021). Psychological impact of being wrongfully accused of criminal offences: A systematic literature review. *Medicine, Science, and the Law, 61*(1), 44–54.

Brownlee, K. (2021). Punishment and precious emotions: A hope standard for punishment. *Oxford Journal of Legal Studies, 41*(3), 589–611.

Bufkin, S. (2024). The hunger strike as a biopolitical technology: Re-reading the 1981 Irish republican prison protest. *Cultural Studies, 38*(5), 1–28.

Burton, M., & Kagan, C. (2007). Psychologists and torture: More than a question of interrogation. *The Psychologist, 20*(7), 482–485.

Carleton, R. N. (2016). Into the unknown: A review and synthesis of contemporary models involving uncertainty. *Journal of Anxiety Disorders, 39*, 30–43.

Coicaud, J.-M. (2002). *Legitimacy and politics: A contribution to the study of political right and political responsibility*. Cambridge University Press.

Cordle, C., & Gale, E. (2025). *Reducing reoffending: A synthesis of evidence on effectiveness of interventions*. Ministry of Justice.

Crewe, B. (2011). Depth, weight, tightness: Revisiting the pains of imprisonment. *Punishment and Society, 13*(5), 509–529.

Crewe, B., Hulley, S., & Wright, S. (2019). *Experiencing long-term imprisonment from young adulthood: Identity, adaptation and penal legitimacy.* Ministry of Justice.

Dror, I. E. (2020). The hidden bias cascade and bias snowball effects. In T. E. Hogue, M. Dernevik, G. C. Liell, L. F. Jones, M. J. Fisher & G. C. Liell (Eds.), *Challenging bias in forensic psychological assessment and testing: Theoretical and practical approaches to working with diverse populations* (1st ed., pp. 228–244). Routledge.

Edgar, K., Harris, M., & Webster, R. (2020). *No life, no freedom, no future: The experiences of prisoners recalled under the sentence of imprisonment for public protection.* Prison Reform Trust.

Ellis, S., & Hewson, A. (2025). *Bromley briefing prison factfile: February 2025.* Prison Reform Trust.

Farraj, B. (2024). Rejecting defeat and approaching liberation: Palestinian prisoners' hunger Strikes. *Wasafiri, 39*(2), 13–23.

Ferstman, C. (2024). *Conceptualising arbitrary detention: Power, punishment and control.* Bristol University Press.

Greenberg, J. (2010). Organizational injustice as an occupational health risk. *The Academy of Management Annals, 4*(1), 205–243.

Guthrie, M. A., Ball, E., & Hargreaves, M. (2016). The impact of moral disengagement in forensic mental health professionals: Implications for practice. *Journal of Forensic Nursing, 12*(3), 149–156. https://doi.org/10.1097/JFN.0000000000000124

Hacking, I. (2006). Making up people. *London Review of Books, 28*(16), 23–26.

Harris, M., Edgar, K., & Webster, R. (2020). 'I'm always walking on eggshells, and there's no chance of me ever being free': The mental health implications of Imprisonment for Public Protection in the community and post-recall. *Criminal Behaviour and Mental Health, 30*(6), 331–340.

Hart, S. D., Kropp, P. R., & Webster, C. D. (2022). *Manual for the Sexual Violence Risk–20, Version 2: Professional guidelines for assessing risk of sexual violence.* Protect International Risk and Safety Services Inc.

HM Inspectorate of Probation. (2023). *The risk-need-responsivity model: 1990 to the present.* HM Inspectorate of Probation.

Hoffman, D. H., Carter, D., Viglucci Lopez, C., Benzmiller, H., Guo, A., Latifi, Y., & Craig, D. (2015). *Independent review relating to APA ethics guidelines, national security interrogations, and torture.* Sidley Austin LLP.

Hogue, T. E., & Dernevik, M. (2022). Individual bias in forensic practice. In G. C. Liell, M. J. Fisher & L. F. Jones (Eds.), *Challenging bias in forensic psychological assessment and testing: Theoretical and practical approaches to working with diverse populations* (1st ed., pp. 228–244). Routledge.

Hogue, T. E., Dernevik, M., Liell, G. C., Jones, L. F., & Fisher, M. J. (2023). Individual bias in forensic practice. In G. C. Liell, M. J. Fisher, & L. F. Jones (Eds.), *Challenging bias in forensic psychological assessment and* testing (1st ed., pp. 228–244). Routledge.

House of Commons Justice Committee. (2021). *Written evidence from an IPP prisoner to the Justice Committee.*

House of Commons Justice Committee. (2022). *IPP sentences: Third report of session 2022–23.* HC 266. House of Commons.

Howard League for Penal Reform. (n.d.). *What are IPP sentences?* Retrieved July 12, 2025, from Howard League for Penal Reform website: https://howardleague.org/what-are-ipp-sentences/

Hulley, S., Crewe, B., & Wright, S. (2016). Re-examining the problems of long-term imprisonment. *British Journal of Criminology, 56*(4), 769–792. https://doi.org/10.1093/bjc/azv077

Hutton, M., & O'Brien, R. (2024). *A long stretch: The challenge of maintaining relationships for people serving long prison sentences.* Prison Reform Trust.

Jarman, B. (2020). Only one way to swim? The offence and the life course in accounts of adaptation to life imprisonment. *The British Journal of Criminology, 60*(6), 1460–1479.

Kaslow, N. J., McDaniel, S. J., & APA Special Committee on behalf of the Board and members of APA. (2015). *Dear psychology colleagues in the international community* [Letter].

Marklund, L., Hansson, L., & Markström, U. (2020). Recovery-oriented practices in a psychiatric forensic setting: Perspectives of patients and staff. *International Journal of Mental Health Nursing, 29*(5), 917–926.

Maruna, S., & McNeill, F. (2006). Rehabilitation, desistance and 'what works': A critical reappraisal. In J. Muncie & D. Wilson (Eds.), *The Sage handbook of criminal justice* (pp. 279–296). Sage Publications.

Ministry of Justice. (2025a). *Offender management statistics quarterly: October to December 2024.* Ministry of Justice.

Ministry of Justice. (2025b). *Restricted patients statistics, England and Wales.* 2024. Ministry of Justice.

Ministry of Justice. (2025c). *Criminal justice system statistics quarterly: December 2024.* Ministry of Justice.

Ministry of Justice. (2020). *Piloting of motivation and engagement as a stand-alone intervention: Findings from a small-scale qualitative study.* Ministry of Justice.

Ministry of Justice & HM Prison and Probation Service. (2024, November 1). *Prison safety policy framework.* Ministry of Justice & HM Prison and Probation Service.

Morriss, J., Goh, K., Hirsch, C. R., & Dodd, H. F. (2023). Intolerance of uncertainty heightens negative emotional states and dampens positive emotional states. *Frontiers in Psychiatry, 14*, 1147970. https://doi.org/10.3389/fpsyt.2023.1147970

Neal, T. M. S., & Brodsky, S. L. (2016). Forensic psychologists' perceptions of bias and potential correction strategies in forensic mental health evaluations. *Psychology, Public Policy, and Law, 22*(1), 58–76.

Office of the United Nations High Commissioner for Human Rights. (2023, December 8). *Reform of problematic UK sentencing system welcome but bolder action needed, says UN.*

Office of the United Nations High Commissioner for Human Rights. (2024, August 8). *UN expert urges UK Government to prioritise review of indefinite prison sentences.*

Peel-Wainwright, K.-M., Hartley, S., Boland, A., Rocca, E., Langer, S., & Taylor, P. J. (2021). The interpersonal processes of non-suicidal self-injury: A systematic review and meta-synthesis. *Psychology and Psychotherapy: Theory, Research and Practice, 94*(4), 1059–1082.

Penal Reform International, & Life Imprisonment Worldwide Project. (2024). *Informal life imprisonment: A policy briefing on this harsh, hidden sentence.* Penal Reform International, & Life Imprisonment Worldwide Project.

Prisons and Probation Ombudsman. (2024). *Independent investigation into the death of Mr Sean Davies, a prisoner at HMP Swaleside, on 25 February 2023*. Prisons and Probation Ombudsman.

R v Hodgson, [1967] 1 W.L.R. 1401 (Eng.).

Reitz, K. (2012). The "traditional" indeterminate sentencing model. In J. Petersilia & K. Reitz (Eds.), *The Oxford handbook of sentencing and corrections* (pp. 270–298). Oxford University Press.

Rhodes, E. (2025, March 5). *IPP is a type of sentence, not a type of person*. The Psychologist.

Rousseau, J.-J. (1762/2008). *The social contract*. Oxford University Press.

Sadeh, N., & Bredemeier, K. (2021). Engaging in risky and impulsive behaviors to alleviate distress mediates associations between intolerance of uncertainty and externalizing psychopathology. *Journal of Personality Disorders, 35*(3), 393–408.

Senneseth, M., Pollak, C., Urheim, R., Logan, C., & Palmstierna, T. (2022). Personal recovery and its challenges in forensic mental health: Systematic review and thematic synthesis of the qualitative literature. *British Journal of Psychiatry, 8*(1), e17.

Shingler, J., Sonnenberg, S. J., & Needs, A. (2020a). Psychologists as 'the quiet ones with the power': Understanding indeterminate sentenced prisoners' experiences of psychological risk assessment in the United Kingdom. *Psychology, Crime & Law, 26*(6), 571–592.

Shingler, J., Sonnenberg, S. J., & Needs, A. (2020b). 'Their life in your hands': The experiences of prison-based psychologists conducting risk assessments with indeterminate sentenced prisoners in the United Kingdom. *Psychology, Crime & Law, 26*(4), 311–326.

Skeem, J. L., & Lowenkamp, C. T. (2016). Risk, race, and recidivism: Predictive bias and disparate impact. *Criminology, 54*(4), 680–712.

Snyder, C. R. (2002). Hope theory: Rainbows in the mind. *Psychological Inquiry, 13*(4), 249–275.

Snyder, C. R., Rand, K. L., & Sigmon, D. R. (2002). Hope theory: A member of the positive psychology family. In C. R. Snyder & S. J. Lopez (Eds.), *Handbook of positive psychology* (pp. 257–276). Oxford University Press.

Sokol-Hessner, P., & Rutledge, R. B. (2018). The psychological and neural basis of loss aversion. *Current Directions in Psychological Science, 28*(1), 20–27.

Trost, Z., Sturgeon, J., Agtarap, S., McMinn, K., McShan, E., Boals, A., Arewasikporn, A., Foreman, M., & Warren, A. M. (2024). The impact of perceived injustice on pain and psychological outcomes after traumatic injury: A longitudinal analysis. *Pain, 165*(7), 1583–1591.

Tyler, T. R. (2006). *Why people obey the law* (2nd ed.). Princeton University Press.

UK Parliament. (2021, November 30). *House of Lords written question HL4067: Life sentences statistics*.

UNGRIPP. (2023). *Written evidence from United Group for Reform of IPP (UNGRIPP)*. https://committees.parliament.uk/writtenevidence/41322/pdf/

Warr, J. (2019). 'Always gotta be two mans': Lifers, risk, rehabilitation, and narrative labour. *Punishment & Society, 21*(5), 576–594. https://doi.org/10.1177/1462474519843738

Warr, J. (2020). *Forensic psychologists: Prisons power and vulnerability*. Emerald Pubishing.

Wright, S., Hulley, S., & Crewe, B. (2022). Trajectories of hope/lessness among men and women in the late stage of a life sentence. *Theoretical Criminology, 27*(1), 66–84.

Xu, J., Ironside, M. L., Broos, H. C., Johnson, S. L., & Timpano, K. R. (2024). Urged to feel certain again: The role of emotion-related impulsivity on the relationships between intolerance of uncertainty and OCD symptom severity. *The British Journal of Clinical Psychology, 63*(2), 258–272.

9 Building professional relationships with individuals involved in terrorism

Christopher Dean and Monica Lloyd

Introduction

Forming professional relationships with those who have been involved in terrorism is a relatively new endeavour for forensic psychologists.[1] This chapter outlines the context in which psychologists first became involved in this work in England and Wales and draws on the authors' learning and experiences of developing such relationships, particularly at that time. It also incorporates more recent learning, including from national and international research.

When the whole world became aware of the Al Qaeda threat following the 2001 attack on the Twin Towers in New York, there was no blueprint for psychologists working with individuals involved in terrorism. In the UK, forensic psychologists had not been directly involved with paramilitary prisoners during the period (1969–1998) of "the Troubles" in Northern Ireland. These prisoners were held in separate H blocks in the Maze prison, where they were controlled by their own officer commanders. Moreover, the Irish Republican Army (IRA) considered themselves to be at war with the UK government and as such demanded to be treated as prisoners of war, resorting to escapes, dirty protests and hunger strikes to achieve this. A small number convicted of terrorism offences in England were held on the mainland, but it was considered neither necessary nor appropriate for prison psychologists in England and Wales to be involved in their cases.

This all changed following the 7/7 attack on the London transport system in 2005, which was carried out by British citizens on home soil. This attack was the first ever suicide bombing in the UK and it galvanised the country. In its wake, the government published its counterterrorist strategy (CONTEST) that was designed "to reduce the risk to the UK and its interests overseas from international terrorism, so that people could go about their lives freely and with confidence" (HM Government, 2023, p. 4). This strategy is still in place, and it includes the four pillars of Prevent, Pursue, Protect and Prepare, with the objective of the Prevent pillar being "to stop people becoming terrorists or supporting violent extremism … and extends to supporting the rehabilitation and disengagement of those already involved in terrorism" (HM Government, 2023, p. 30). This brought the responsibilities of the National

DOI: 10.4324/9781003542377-12

Offender Management Service (NOMS), as the prison and probation services were then named (now HMPPS) into sharp focus. These responsibilities were to protect the public and reduce reoffending by delivering the punishments and orders of the courts, help offenders to reform their lives and in doing so prevent future victims of crime (HM Government, 2006). NOMS was thereby responsible for both the management of those convicted of terrorism offences and those considered vulnerable to involvement in terrorism (Basra & Neumann, 2016, 2020).

Terrorism was defined for the first time in the Terrorism Act 2000 (Terrorism Act, 2000. Part 1(1)). The definition is generic and applies to all forms of terrorism, including the far right or other single issues. It focuses on

> The use or threat [of action] designed to influence the government or to intimidate the public or a section of the public, and the use or threat is made for the purposes of advancing a political, religious or ideological cause.

Counterterrorist (CT) legislation was also introduced that criminalised evidence of an individual's intention to commit or assist in an act of terrorism. This is an important distinction because most of those who entered custody post 7/7 were sentenced under CT legislation that sought to disrupt terrorist plotting; whereas those found guilty of advanced terrorism plotting were typically charged under mainstream criminal law, for example with murder or conspiracy to cause an explosion. The risk that the latter constituted was clearly high, whereas the risk level of CT offenders was less clear-cut, as a proportion of these, although engaged with ideology, had not necessarily crossed the threshold of intent to harm. Both groups are referred to as Terrorism Act (TACT) offenders.

There was concern about whether the prison service would be able to safely manage these prisoners, given the prospect of radicalisation in prisons[2] and their lack of experience with Islamist offenders who might also clash with serious organised criminals (Hannah et al., 2008; Pickering, 2014). It was decided that they would not be treated as political prisoners and that risk management and decision-making would remain with NOMS and the independent Parole Board, putting both organisations under significant pressure to ensure that no TACT offenders on their watch committed future terrorist offences. It was clearly understood that these offenders carried significant risks to public protection, national security and organisational and political reputations (Dean, 2024a).

Building relationships to develop an evidence-base

In 2006, NOMS established a working group to develop a strategy to manage these issues. A key recommendation was that risk assessment and intervention programmes should be developed to reduce the risk of future terrorism offences. Therefore, in 2008, a small multi-disciplinary team of forensic psychologists (including the authors), probation officers and Muslim Chaplains was established to fulfil this task (Dean, 2014).[3] Key questions were whether these offenders should work with psychologists or whether they should be managed differently from other prisoners. Initial research indicated that many in this group were not typical of the wider criminal population. There were significant differences in their criminal behaviour, how they behaved in prisons, and how they perceived those in authority, often with distrust and hostility (Dean, 2024a; Durnescu, 2024). This suggested that different approaches were required for their assessment, intervention, rehabilitation and reintegration.

Initial examination of the academic and grey literatures, and consultation with correctional services in other jurisdictions, confirmed a dearth of knowledge regarding these issues, particularly in terms of which risk and protective factors contributed to or protected against involvement in terrorism, and what interventions might effectively reduce this risk (Dean, 2024a; Lloyd & Dean, 2015). In addition, there was minimal knowledge about how to connect effectively and ethically with those we understood at the time to be directly antagonistic to government (Dean, 2012, 2024a).

It was evident that any assessment frameworks or interventions would need to be developed from scratch (Dean, 2024a). Psychologists were identified as the best placed to lead on this. It would involve dialogue with Terrorist Act (TACT) offenders and care and sensitivity to communicate safely and effectively with those who were, for all intents and purposes, enemies of the state. It was evident that we needed to listen carefully to their backstories despite the many barriers to this. With no road map, we were faced with a series of questions: How would we frame our role, build trust and agree on shared goals? How would we set about building rapport with those about whom we knew so little and to whom we were viewed as the enemy? How could we incentivise their engagement in such work? What should we say or avoid saying to build trust? How would we ensure both their safety and our own, given the uncertainties and unknown consequences of these conversations?

We were keenly aware of the importance of acting ethically in addressing these questions, and mindful that because of the public perception of their offences and their ethnic and religious backgrounds, they would likely be subject to prejudice, stigmatisation, discrimination and potentially demonisation (Bonino, 2013; Marsden, 2017). We were also aware of the potential for us to be subject to stigmatisation and rejection from those we were working with. We concluded that we needed to be transparent in our approach, open-minded and alert to our own biases, put aside preconceived ideas, invite open discussion (without being reactive or defensive) and empathise with their experiences as best we could. In the early stages, we did this just by listening to their stories without any agenda (apart from wanting to learn about their experiences) or limitations, simply to understand their experiences and build rapport. Where this was accepted, it allowed us to be more comfortable in each other's company and build trust.

On reflection, our first contact required courage on our part to approach those who were high profile in the media and subject to vitriol and contempt. TACT offenders were largely an unknown quantity at this time, and there was a risk to us of being taken hostage. The British Psychological Society were also concerned that without an evidence base for this work, we would be working beyond our competence, but it was evident that the only way to build an evidence base was to talk to these individuals to understand their drivers and goals. We were honest with them about our lack of knowledge and understanding and made no promises about the outcome. The initial offer to talk to us was rejected by more than accepted it, which was understandable as some were equally nervous about talking to us, and some were apparently being advised by their solicitors not to do so. We had to be content to sit with our vulnerability for some time until we were trusted enough for the numbers to rise.

Our use of language was critical to our acceptance. We learned through our mistakes how important it was not to label these individuals as terrorists. Our initial contact taught us that many individuals rejected the label "terrorist", arguing that it belonged only to those who perpetrated large-scale attacks against civilians on home soil. A few of those convicted under CT legislation recognised themselves in this description. It became clear that if the label "terrorist" was ascribed to them or implied in a first meeting, it would likely bring it to an abrupt end. Individual offenders varied in terms of what they were prepared to do, to whom and for what purpose, so we were careful to refer to them as "a person convicted of a terrorism offence" to avoid the presumptions that the word "terrorist" embodied. We were also conscious of the need not to pathologise violence as a means of bringing about political change, given that this was widely engaged in by state and non-state actors. Our position, if challenged, was that where there were lawful ways to express dissent, the use of violence to progress a cause was not justified.

It became clear that there had been few opportunities post-trial for these individuals to voice their experiences; such that allowing them to speak freely with our full attention proved to be key to meaningful engagement. In our early conversations, it became evident that many of those without a criminal background had been traumatised by dawn police raids and solitary confinement in police custody and needed to process this to understand how they got to where they were. Many were grieving the sudden loss of the identity, status, meaning and belonging that was associated with being part of a closely bonded group. They were faced instead with rejection, vilification, punishment and a drastic loss of status, with the prospect of having to start again from a very lonely and difficult place. We understood that to control this dialogue without acknowledging their trauma would be counterproductive.

> On reflection, we made a conscious decision not to control the dialogue, challenge their world view or religious beliefs, or to "correct" them. The team of imams and probation practitioners we worked with supported us in this by recognising the importance of "seeing the person" and connecting through compassion and understanding, though this was not always easy. In some respects, the "forensic" nature of our role was removed, and our presence in just listening and acknowledging their experiences was sufficient. For some, this allowed them to experience us as supportive and helpful, paving the way for sometimes even more challenging conversations and steps towards personal change.

We were clear that there could be no promises about how their engagement with us would shape their futures or influence decision makers. However, both parties recognised that a lack of willingness to converse and learn would inevitably prevent progress. Some had spontaneously disengaged[4] in the wake of their sudden arrest and imprisonment, and some wanted to prevent others (especially younger people) from following in their footsteps, seeing working with us as a way of achieving this. As our understanding increased so did the numbers of individuals willing to work with us, though these were self-selected and we knew there were many who chose not to engage with us at that time. We were also aware that some of the individuals we were talking to were also talking to each other, and we were unsure whether this was positive or negative, but overall, the numbers engaging with us steadily increased.

> On reflection, as we gained experience with this group, our practice matured. We were aware that contact with us might jeopardise their safety with other TACT offenders and that prison was a tough place for those who wanted to disengage from co-defendants, or who had done so, because of the pressure that was brought to bear on them. Some of those we worked with kept two "faces", one for us and one for their peers, and we were able to acknowledge this in sessions, asking them if they were safe or experienced any pressure not to engage, thereby creating an opening for them to disclose difficulties if they wanted to.

Nevertheless, some chose not to engage beyond an introductory session. Some interpreted their involvement, conviction and imprisonment as a political rather than a personal or psychological issue; some simply mistrusted us, what we represented and our agenda; and others viewed their sentences as unjust and resisted engaging with those they saw as representatives of the state. Others simply wanted to complete their sentence without drawing any further attention from the authorities, a position that would likely change as time passed and their perspectives shifted. We acknowledged and respected these decisions and their reasons for non-participation and kept the door open for them to re-engage with us or our colleagues in the future.

> On reflection, non-participation might have felt like rejection if we had not clarified at the outset that we respected a person's choice not to engage. We listened only if the person wanted to speak, and we listened whether they wanted to spend 15 minutes or two hours doing so. If they didn't want to speak at all, that was also ok, and they could change their minds at any stage if they wanted to. As forensic psychologists, we know that not everyone is at the same stage of readiness to change. This cannot be forced, and we would not do so. Forcing change through violence is what characterises terrorism and we wanted to model the opposite, not to impose ourselves but allow them to process what they had experienced and be given the space to reflect and reconsider their future lives.

Over time, it became clear to these prisoners that without clarity and understanding, it would be difficult for them to demonstrate personal change and progress through their sentences and that working with a psychologist was likely to be their best option. And so began our own journey of learning how to interact effectively and build professional relationships with this group.[5] Now, nearly 20 years on, the UK has developed a substantive evidence base to inform and guide professional practice in this field, both in the context of Prevent and through evidence-based assessment and interventions, notably the Healthy Identity Intervention and Extremism Risk Guidance assessment framework (British Psychological Society, 2018; Dean, 2014; Kenyon, 2025; Lloyd & Dean, 2015). This has been accompanied by international learning, with UK forensic psychologists in the vanguard of this, including developing guidance for effective and ethical practice (e.g. Al Attar, 2019; British Psychological Society, 2018; Lloyd, 2021; Dean & Lloyd, 2022).

The power of relationships

In the context of understanding how individuals can be drawn into terrorism, the Power, Threat, Meaning Framework (PTMF) is helpful (Dean, 2024b). It was officially launched in 2018 as a guide to how psychologists may interpret and address emotional distress, unusual experiences and troubled or troubling behaviour (Johnstone et al., 2018). It is not in the scope of this chapter to outline this framework in detail, but, in summary, it identifies how adversity and associated psychological distress can result from the misuse of power that threatens basic core needs such as justice, security, belonging and agency (Johnstone et al., 2018). Where medical models might interpret survival behaviour as symptoms of mental illness, the PTMF typically understands this in relational terms (Boyle & Johnstone, 2020; Johnstone et al., 2018).

Themes of power, threat and meaning can help explain how a relatively small number become involved in terrorist offences when most do not (Dean, 2024b; Lewis & Marsden, 2021; Sageman, 2021). The core needs for justice, security, belonging and agency are met for most people by a sufficiency of positive and protective influences that allow them to feel secure and believe in a good life. Where these are lacking, individuals can be left with feelings of shame, fear and hate and be vulnerable to seeking power and security elsewhere. This is particularly the case when individuals have experienced significant trauma in their lives (Gill et al., 2021; Lewis & Marsden, 2021). The PTMF can be used to identify sources of disempowerment and threat at a political level that resonate with these personal insecurities and that can be framed by ideologies that promise power and revenge (Dean & Lloyd, 2022; Dean, 2024b). Identifying sources of strong feelings, such as insecurity, shame and grievance can also, if used ethically and effectively, help to understand and frame the relational dynamics that take place between us and them. The following sections include some references to what we have learned about navigating power, threat and meaning in our relationships with terrorist offenders, through the PTMF lens.

A recent review of studies investigating how and why individuals disengage from terrorism identified the prison environment as a significant location for catalysing change (Morrison et al., 2021). This is contrary to the popular and persistent view of prisons as "hotbeds" for radicalisation (Basra & Neumann, 2020; Neumann, 2010). Possible explanations for this are that imprisonment provides the opportunity for individuals to physically distance themselves from past contacts, to reflect on their past and to access interventions supporting change (Morrison et al., 2021). Another consistent finding is that humane treatment in prison from those in authority (notably law enforcement and correctional staff) plays a key role in triggering, facilitating and maintaining the process of change (Axelsson & Grip, 2024; Dean, 2014; Ganor & Falk, 2013; Marsden, 2017). The impact of being treated well is expressed in various ways. For some, it motivates participation in interventions designed to reduce and end support for and involvement in terrorism (Dean, 2014). For others, it challenges beliefs about the government and those employed in its service (Abuza, 2009; Mufti et al., 2022; Sukabdi, 2015). For others it creates doubt about their involvement and triggers disillusionment and re-examination of their past (Abuza, 2009; Nawaz, 2008).

Case study: the impact of humane treatment

A young man was arrested at Heathrow airport attempting to fly to Somalia with the intention of joining Al-Shabaab, an organisation proscribed by the UK. He had no criminal background and had not anticipated that he was risking imprisonment by his actions. In conversation, he revealed how taken aback he was to be treated well by the senior officer on the induction wing when he arrived in prison. This officer discerned his vulnerability and spent time with him, checking that he had the bedding and toiletries he needed and assigning an experienced personal officer to his case. The prisoner explained that he had spent months before his arrest with a group in London discussing how they could get access to uniformed staff working for the government as human targets for a terrorist attack. This member of the prison staff who had treated him with respect and kindness was such a man, and now he found himself grateful for his kindness and professionalism. He had to accept that he would have killed this man in different circumstances. This caused him to re-evaluate everything he had come to believe about the enemies of Islam and acted as a cognitive opening for him to re-examine and reconsider his past and future actions.

The case study above exemplifies the impact of humane treatment and illustrates the power of correctional environments to promote a positive outcome (e.g. Williams & Liebling, 2023; United Nations, 2016). In contrast, inhumane treatment and negative, distant and destructive professional relationships combined with poor prison conditions and poorly managed correctional services, achieve the opposite (e.g. Amnesty International, 2017; Basra & Neumann, 2020; Dean, 2023; La Free et al., 2020; Karstedt, 1999; Williams & Liebling, 2023).

Navigating power in the relationship

While awareness of power dynamics is central to our working relationships and professional competency, it is at a premium with TACT offenders with whom there are additional barriers to establishing a working alliance (Durnescu, 2024). Acts of terrorism epitomise coercive power. Some individuals, typically leaders or those entrained in ideology with violent intent, are reluctant to relinquish this power post sentence, and remain strongly opposed to interacting with "representatives of the state" who they perceive as their enemies. Their interactions are carefully considered, strategic and "weaponised" to achieve political goals. Some may be primed and prepared for how to interact with psychologists and use strategies to preserve their position, "playing the game" to achieve their outcomes through subverting the efforts of psychologists to engage them. Some may exert power to manipulate staff (and psychologists), through "disguised compliance" (Cherney & Koehler, 2023), as was evidenced in the 2019 Fishmonger Hall terrorism attack in London (Lufcraft, 2021), or conditioning and manipulating staff, as was exposed in the 1994 escape of IRA prisoners from HMP Whitemoor (Home Office, 1994). Psychologists have not yet been implicated as targets for manipulation but we need to remain vigilant about this in our work (Durnescu, 2024).

> On reflection, one of the things we became mindful of as our experience developed was the importance of not browbeating our clients and expecting them to uncritically accept what we said. This would have repeated their radicalisation experience, and we did not want to replicate this. To mitigate this, we adopted a very transparent approach (including explaining our agenda and why we were doing what we were doing), invited self-reflection and critical questioning, and encouraged candour in our interactions and observations. Supervision also helped us by allowing us to check these areas of our practice.

Psychologists have the potential to use power in many ways to support and strengthen their professional relationships. We can use ideological power by acknowledging and respecting the meanings individuals make of their world, without seeking to impose our own. This does not mean we agree or collude with their beliefs, but that we understand the function they play in all our lives and use power carefully to encourage examination and scrutiny when an opportunity presents. We can use interpersonal power by taking measures to protect an individual's safety if they are considering ending their affiliation to a group, which could cause repercussions for them. We can also use embodied power through our body language (Durnescu, 2024) and by being inclusive, showing humanity and compassion and respecting the dignity of all, which is the antithesis of dehumanisation and demonisation (British Psychological Society, 2018).

> On reflection, one offender was anxious about the pressure being put on him by other staunch TACT offenders because he was engaging with a psychologist. To protect him, we made some changes to the way we worked, such as holding some sessions in legal visits because it obscured the nature of the session and was less suspicious. Such actions were interpreted by some as reflecting that we cared for them as people, rehumanising us, which strengthened our relationships and challenged their preconceptions of what we represented.

There are typically differences and divisions in racial and cultural heritage and religious and class backgrounds between those convicted of terrorism offences and those who assess them and make significant decisions about their lives. This remains the case in the "post-colonial" world in which asymmetries of power and intergenerational trauma continue to resonate (Dean & Lloyd, 2022; Lewis & Marsden, 2021). It is, therefore, incumbent upon psychologists to be aware of their privilege and remain vigilant about their possible misuse of power. A significant failure to do this is exemplified by two psychologists in the USA who endorsed the use of enhanced interrogation and torture of those suspected of terrorism involvement in Guantanamo Bay. It has since been acknowledged that these approaches failed to produce reliable intelligence and were rejected as unethical in an independent review by the American Psychological Association in 2015.

To navigate these issues, we must be alert to and prepared to manage the assumptions, agendas and biases that we may hold (Dean & Lloyd, 2022; Durnescu, 2024). We should be prepared to be explicit about the professional and personal values that inform our work and why we hold them – countering assumptions that we are simply agents of the state who gather intelligence (Durnescu, 2024). Our concerns about an individual should be transparent, evidenced and explicit so that we do not slip into the misuse of power. This may include discussing their motives for participating in sessions and acknowledging that actions can be driven by biases and agendas on both sides, especially in the service of causes that matter to us. Inviting individual offenders to ask questions of us and express their views on the work undertaken in sessions helped to maintain a balance of power (Durnescu, 2024).

On reflection, as we continued our conversations, aspects of a terrorist mindset became more apparent, including being rigid, absolute, presumptuous, certain and discouraging of any doubt or curiosity. In response, we actively tried to adopt and communicate a different mindset, one that was open, flexible and welcomed doubt and exploration without trying to control. Over time, some adapted to our ways of thinking, which was a significant step forward.

Power itself can also be discussed explicitly (Dean, 2024b), and we remained mindful and transparent about how we modelled power in the relationship, so that they experienced communication without coercion, force or imposition. We practised cultural sensitivity and humility, mindful of our privilege and potential biases and taking practical steps to mitigate their impact (Dean, 2012; Williams, 2017). This required us to monitor our own cultural perspective and biases, aware of how these are embedded in the science and language of western psychology.[6] Regular supervision was helpful to reflect on how current geo-political events may be affecting our attitudes towards our clients, or their attitudes towards us; and if necessary recognising when we should avoid working with those whose causes we strongly opposed (or supported) and with whom we were unable to remain impartial and/or non-judgemental (Dean & Lloyd, 2022).

Building trust

The importance of trust features in international guidance on the role of psychology in the rehabilitation and reintegration of those involved in terrorism. To quote

> …. On the part of the psychologist, treating the detainee with respect and as a fellow human being is the first step in this process. This can make a big difference, particularly because the detainees are often expecting to be treated harshly by the state. It can help create cognitive dissonance and begin to break down the inmate's rigidly held views. Psychologists should not be discouraged by detainees' unwillingness to talk or meet with them at the outset and should expect that this will be a long-term process.
> (International Centre for Counterterrorism/Hedayah, 2013, p. 1)

The importance of relational trust with these offenders has been supported by the consistent finding that a strong working alliance between practitioners and individuals is crucial in managing and preventing future terrorism offending (e.g. Corner & Gill, 2020; Durnescu, 2024; Hassan et al., 2021; Horgan, 2009; Morrison et al., 2021; Radicalisation Awareness Network, 2020, 2021; van de Heide & Schuurman, 2018). This has been established in the context of other criminal offences by many decades of research into how professionals can best support psychological change (Burnett, 2004; Lambert & Barley, 2001) and facilitate desistance and reintegration into mainstream society (Dowden & Andrews, 2004; Marshall et al., 2005; Shingler & Stickney, 2023). Now, in the context of terrorism offending specifically, openness, tolerance, collegiality, cultural sensitivity, compassion, empathy, concern, humility, respect for factual accuracy and a non-judgemental approach have all been associated with effective professional practice (see Cherney, 2018; Dean, 2016; Durnescu, 2024; Hassan et al., 2021; Horgan, 2009; Koehler et al., 2023; Salman & Gill, 2020).

> On reflection, disclosing information about our identities and lives was crucial in building reciprocity, commonality and trust. In the early days, self-disclosure was considered to be off-limits due to the risk of manipulation, but over time, its power became more apparent when used appropriately. This was possible in the context of identity-based conversations, which allowed space for sharing, vulnerability, trust and openness to be shared.

The research of Alison Liebling (one of the most experienced prison researchers in our time) and her colleagues has demonstrated what the philosopher Baroness Onora O'Neill describes as the role of "intelligent trust" in relationships with prisoners, in which professionals validate individuals by recognising their trustworthiness (O'Neill, 2018). The use of intelligent trust maintains practitioner vigilance in ensuring discretion is applied and used appropriately. This approach, combined with acting with humanity (kind regard and concern), decency (reasonably and appropriately), legitimately (transparently, responsively and morally) and fairly (impartially and proportionately) has been found to reduce what they describe as "political charge" in prisons (i.e. anger, indignation and reactivity, Williams & Liebling, 2023). Such approaches have been associated with reducing anger and alienation in those imprisoned and building their resilience against resorting to terrorism (Liebling & Williams, 2018; Williams & Liebling, 2023). These approaches endorse the effective and ethical use of power in such relationships, providing individuals with the basis for trusting correctional staff and a willingness to progress towards positive outcomes (Liebling, 2014).

These findings are also consistent with the tenets of "Procedural Justice" that guide police, judges and correctional staff at all stages of the criminal justice system (Barkworth, 2020; Tyler, 2007). These are: (1) Respect (humane, courteous treatment); (2) Voice (being heard); (3) Neutrality (openness, sincerity, fairness, transparency) and (4) Trust (empathy, support, rapport, honesty, accountability). Most of these are specifically associated with supporting a strong working alliance with those who have been involved in terrorism (Durnescu, 2024). Field studies of police interrogation (including terrorism offenders) have confirmed that applying these tenets results in greater information gain, more rapid disclosure, better cooperation, reliable admissions and compliance with the law, in contrast to coercive approaches (Goodman-Delahunty et al., 2022). These tenets also map onto the Universal Declaration of Ethical Principles for Psychologists (2008), which are Respect, Competent Caring, Integrity and Responsibility.[7]

A successful application of this approach is exemplified in the interview of a perpetrator following his arrest for a bombing and mass killing in 2011 in Norway, when police were faced with a "ticking time-bomb" scenario. The interviewee claimed that he was not alone and that further attacks were imminent from others in his army. With a defence lawyer present, the police used evidence-based questioning, built rapport, showed respect for the interviewee and used cognitive and strategic interviewing that successfully elicited the information that he was in fact acting alone (Goodman-Delahunty et al., 2022). In short, relating to individuals in ways that reduce political charge and support procedural justice are effective and ethical approaches that can build professional relationships with terrorism offenders.

Navigating threat in relationships

The misuse of power can result in real and imagined threats to our core needs for safety, security, belonging and autonomy, sometimes referred to as "relational threat" (Boyle & Johnstone, 2020). Staunch TACT offenders may demonise and dehumanise those they identify as the cause of their grievance and an existential threat (see Horgan, 2014), and we may be included in this number, perceived as agents of change sent to "reprogramme" them and change their truth. Although psychologists in correctional settings are familiar with clients who are mistrustful or hostile towards them, they do not often work with those who might class them as their enemies and denounce them because of their race, gender, sexuality, ethnicity, religion, class, nationality and/or politics. A challenge for those of us trying to build relationships is that these perceptions and feelings are inevitably subtle and hidden and therefore difficult to detect and manage.

Despite this, psychologists should be aware of these issues and prepare for sessions by developing strategies to mitigate or manage them. This might include understanding the importance of even small practical acts of support that show we are not there to make their lives difficult but to help them to meet their needs and rebuild their lives (Durnescu, 2024). While such acts might be met with suspicion, consistency in our approach can overcome this in time (Durnescu, 2020). Acknowledging commonalities and with appropriate self-disclosure, as illustrated previously, it is possible to temper feelings of threat for both parties (Dean, 2014, 2019; Durnescu, 2024).

On reflection, an individual who had been very resistant and suspicious in the early stages of our relationship said in a later session, "I've realised you and I have a lot more in common than I ever imagined we would". The power of this disclosure was in his explicit acknowledgement of our shared humanity, the challenge this posed to his previous "us and them thinking", and this reflecting a turning point in his trust of the author and his commitment to re-examining his past involvement in terrorism and his future goals and life.

In the early stages, individuals may perceive work with psychologists, consciously or unconsciously, as a means by which the state seeks to impose on them new identities and beliefs. This can include the prospect of being forced to relinquish the bonds of common identity and purpose with their group, cause or ideology (Dean, 2019). They may be mourning the loss of close relationships with their proxy family that for many displaced their biological family, and the status, belonging and security it provided (Dean, 2019). To manage this, psychologists must understand the intensity of this investment, which may still define them in part. Change on this scale accrues over time, and we needed to understand this and hold this truth for them as they journeyed from one identity to another. Without this level of understanding, we were unlikely to be able to help them change and progress. Exploring questions related to these issues validated their importance and communicated respect for them.

> On reflection, inviting individuals to express how it felt to be taken into custody without warning, with significant relationships ruptured, proved to be a powerful technique. Acknowledging and processing feelings of disconnection, change, loss and grief was challenging, but exploring these feelings sensitively raised important questions about where this left them, how we could support them and who they now believed themselves to be. This approach validated their feelings and communicated compassion and respect rather than threat.

Appreciating the value of identities and relationships is not the same as agreeing or colluding with them. Supporting an individual to develop a healthy and functional sense of identity and worth is central to their health and wellbeing, protects against feelings of threat and reduces susceptibility to terrorist ideology (Dean, 2014; Johnstone et al., 2018; Keane et al., 2023). Reducing or managing a sense of threat can be achieved through approaches that strengthen trust, such as transparency of approach. Where trust exists, it is harder for feelings of threat to remain.

Another significant paradigm is trauma-informed practice (Koehler, 2020; Lewis & Marsden, 2021; Weine et al., 2022). Such approaches are rapidly gaining traction in the supervision of TACT offenders released on licence in the community, and for supporting the reintegration of those returning from foreign fighting/nation building, notably in Syria and Iraq (Counter Extremism Project, 2022; Weine et al., 2022). Trauma-informed principles can and should inform psychological work in this area (Harris & Fallot, 2001). Trauma in TACT offenders is not confined to their experiences of dawn raids but has been increasingly identified in their childhood and adulthood lives (Lewis & Marsden, 2021). Whereas such trauma per se is not predictive of radicalisation or even proof of its relevance, the authors identify that "highly personal experiences of trauma have the potential to motivate action when reframed through a collective lens" (Lewis & Marsden, 2021). Another large study lists previous trauma as one of the jeopardies for involvement that includes mental disorders, discrimination, a sense of threat, relationship problems, unemployment, homelessness and substance misuse (Gill et al., 2021). For practitioners working in these sensitive areas, feelings of threat can be reduced and trust increased by conversations about their support and safety (Durnescu, 2024) that afford choice and voice, alongside discussion about the focus and goals of sessions (Lauland et al., 2019) and transparency, responsivity and humility in our approach.

Inviting choice and voice is inconsistent with arrogance and imposition; transparency and clarity is inconsistent with deceit and opaqueness; and practising with humility and care is inconsistent with dominance and certitude. Once again, the professional relationship can be used as a vehicle for preventing or managing a sense of threat. Below is another case study that illustrates some of the themes in this section and shows how the PTMF and navigating threats can be used to inform and guide interventions in this field.

Case study: applying the PTMF to guide psychological intervention

A young adult man was convicted of encouraging terrorism and disseminating terrorism publications. A PTMF analysis identified that negative power from a range of setbacks in his life was threatening his core needs for safety, survival and wellbeing. These included the loss of his father as a child, rejection by school friends and the withdrawal of his place in a professional football academy due to an injury. He felt shamed and humiliated, worthless, insecure and unable to trust people. His survival strategies included not trusting others, isolating himself and maintaining rigid routines and a militaristic mindset to regain a sense of control. He developed rituals and fantasies about having special powers that protected his self-image and self-worth, and he remained hypervigilant about the intentions of others towards him. Membership of a neo-Nazi online group that mocked and belittled the worth of others allowed him to boost his self-image and self-worth, and provided significance, purpose and efficacy in his life. Over time, relationships within the group deteriorated, and following his arrest and imprisonment, he reverted to isolating himself, self-injuring and threatening others to keep himself safe. In the year before his release, he worked with a practitioner who helped him make sense of his life experience in terms of PTMF principles. A shared formulation of his unmet core needs, feelings of threat and his survival behaviours allowed him to review the choices he had made in his early life to keep himself safe. This included renegotiating and examining his relationship and identification with past groups and ideologies which was personally challenging for him. With support, he was able to move forward by rebuilding his relationships with family members and old friends, furthering his education and training, and identifying and using his positive personal qualities.

Navigating meaning in relationships

Human beings are meaning-makers who actively make sense of their worlds (Boyle & Johnstone, 2020). The significance and distinctiveness of meaning-making is particularly pertinent for those whose behaviour is justified by a political, religious or ideological cause that is permeated with narratives and fictions. Such individuals are likely to have spent many hours discussing, debating and sharing the narratives that justify their violence, and some will be well-versed in the craft of ideological meaning-making. Navigating their narratives successfully involves discussing them together, which is difficult but integral to building a shared understanding of their role.

It became evident that many of those convicted of terrorism offences had different motivations for their involvement beyond the conventional understanding that this was to advance an ideological agenda through violence. They did not necessarily share the same objectives, had very diverse motivations, different views on who or what were acceptable targets for attack, and whether they would partake directly, indirectly or at all in terrorism-related violence. Being sensitive to these differences without making assumptions about them, and exploring their individual pathway and degree of engagement or disengagement strengthened their relationships with us. They needed to know that their individual trajectories were unique to them and understood by us.

Internationally, and in contrast to our practice, the approach of challenging individuals directly to reframe their beliefs has been formally adopted by many jurisdictions as a methodology for deradicalisation[8] (El-Said, 2012; Koehler, 2017). This includes confronting their theological and/or political ideological beliefs, or those that are idiosyncratic to the individual. Schema therapy has also been used to challenge ideology and offence-related beliefs (Keulen-de Vos, 2019), though the efficacy of this and similar approaches remains unclear (e.g. Hassan, 2021). Concern has been expressed about whether such approaches increase resistance, entrench beliefs or receive only superficial compliance (Braddock, 2014; Williams & Lindsey, 2014). While they have a lot of currency internationally, they may be experienced as threatening, bullying and unjust, and in practice counterproductive.

If deemed necessary, such approaches are more likely to be effective when a strong working relationship has been established and individuals have already made positive changes to their identities and lives (Dean, 2019). This provides a more robust foundation for further work with approaches that invite rather than demand individuals to explore and examine their values and beliefs openly and collaboratively.

On reflection, engaging in conversations about people's lives and specific actions in terms of what they identified with and stood for can begin a new search for meaning and dialogue about the new choices and commitments they might wish to make. The next step is to explore and, if appropriate, support them in addressing beliefs and ideologies explicitly in the light of these new goals and commitments and create new meanings to validate their new life going forward.

The process of shared meaning-making is arguably at the core of psychological intervention, and how we engage with this is likely to be a strong influence on how individuals respond and progress. For those who were indoctrinated into their ideology, experiencing the opposite in the form of explicit, explorative and supportive conversations about meaning-making can be pivotal to building trust and making progress. The imposition of rigid and absolute meanings is arguably both a misuse of power and counterproductive. Being humble in our understanding and ability to fully comprehend another's experience and how they make sense of the world is also consistent with trauma-informed practice. Inviting individuals to join you to discuss meanings with openness and humility is considered more likely to support genuine change and progress.

Conclusion and practitioner takeaways

The relationships forensic psychologists have with those who have been involved in terrorism can play a significant role in changing their lives and preventing future offending. Over almost 20 years or so we have been exploring and developing effective and ethical approaches to help those previously involved in terrorism through building strong relationships with them. The empirical evidence base for this work is relatively limited but is consistent with established approaches for addressing other forms of criminal behaviour, such as through trauma-informed practice. But there are also distinct features of terrorism offending, such as seeking to appropriate political power through violence. The professional practices described in this chapter are particularly relevant to working effectively and ethically with these individuals. They work through modelling the appropriate use of power to reduce threat, build trust and meet core needs. Importantly, they are also consistent with the Universal Declaration of Ethical Principles for Psychologists and adhere to the tenets of Procedural Justice.

Below are some key takeaways from this chapter to support psychologists in interacting with and building effective and ethical relationships with this group of individuals.

- Be self-aware about how power, threat and meaning may operate in your interactions and relationships and be prepared to discuss these explicitly with individuals.
- Take time to prepare for how an individual is likely to perceive you and respond to you, given what you know about their involvement and the implications of this for the use or misuse of power.
- Remember that efforts to form and maintain trust are likely to be central to a strong working alliance and may be the most important factor for their effective rehabilitation and reintegration.
- Openness, tolerance, collegiality, cultural sensitivity, compassion/empathy/concern, humility, respect (including factual accuracy), impartiality and a non-judgemental approach can all support reducing a sense of threat and building trust.
- Remember that your relationship, through which you act humanely and explore commonalities, can act as a vehicle for changing perceptions and

beliefs that contributed to engagement, and investing in those that facilitate desistance.
- Enacting approaches associated with trauma-informed care, procedural justice and those that reduce political charge are all likely to build effective and ethical relationships.
- Be responsive to and respectful of the potential value that identification with a group, cause or ideology affords them and manage this sensitively, which does not imply sharing or colluding with their beliefs, objectives or behaviour.
- Be cautious about directly challenging or addressing ideological or other beliefs unless a strong relationship is in place and the individual is robust enough to manage this.
- Be prepared to be humble and curious about how meanings are made and the functions they serve. The process of shared meaning-making can be a powerful way of helping individuals progress.

Notes

1 While this chapter explicitly refers to those who have been involved in terrorism (typically those convicted under counterterrorist legislation) the learning described here also applies to those for whom there are credible concerns about their potential future involvement.
2 Radicalisation referred to here means when individuals become sympathetic, motivated, and willing to be involved in acts of terrorism.
3 At this time, nearly three quarters of individuals imprisoned for terrorism-related offences were associated with Islamist groups, causes or ideologies; Islamist terrorism was considered by the authorities as the greatest threat to national and international security and Islamism was considered least well understood by the service and team. For these reasons and more, Muslim Chaplains were considered integral at this time to assist in developing our approaches.
4 Disengaged here refers to individual decisions to end or reduce their involvement in acts of terrorism often facilitated through changes in their relationships with specific groups, causes or ideologies.
5 It should be noted that this early and subsequent work included working with individuals affiliated with various groups and ideologies.
6 This was helped by working in a multi-disciplinary and multi-cultural team and guided by a multi-cultural steering group, in which discussions included checking perspectives and possible biases as best we could. Interesting discussions for example would focus on similarities and differences in concepts or ideas rooted in Western psychology compared with Islam (such as those around identity, balance and moderation) and how these could be used in a complementary way to support effective approaches. This approach has also been central to our subsequent international work.
7 Adopted by the Assembly of the International Union of Psychological Science in Berlin on 22/7/2008. https://www.iupsys.net/about/declarations/universal-declaration-of-ethical-principles-for-psychologists/.
8 Deradicalisation here refers to changing specific beliefs or ideas that contribute to sympathy, motivation and willingness to be involved in terrorism-related offences.

References

Abuza, B. (2009). The rehabilitation of Jemaah Islamiyah detainees in Southeast Asia: A preliminary assessment. In T. Bjorgo & J. Horgan (eds.), *Leaving terrorism behind: Individual and collective disengagement* (pp. 193–211). Routledge.

Al-Attar, Z. (2019). *Extremism, radicalisation and mental health: Handbook for practitioners*. Radicalisation Awareness Network. https://home-affairs.ec.europa.eu/system/files/2019-11/ran_h-sc_handbook-for-practitioners_extremism-radicalisation-mental-health_112019_en.pdf

Amnesty International (2017). *Inhuman and unnecessary: Human rights violations in Dutch high security prisons in the context of counterterrorism*. Amnesty International. https://www.amnesty.org/en/documents/eur35/7351/2017/en/

Axelsson, L. E., & Grip, L. (2024). Managing violent extremist clients in prison and probation services: A scoping review. *Terrorism and Political Violence, 36* (4), 488–511. https://doi.org/10.1080/09546553.2023.2169144

Barkworth, J. (2020). Procedural justice in prisons. In D. Meyerson, C. Mackenzie, & T. MacDermott (eds.), *Procedural justice and relational theory: Empirical, philosophical, and legal perspectives.* (pp. 63–82). Routledge.

Basra, R., & Neumann, P. R. (2016). Criminal pasts, terrorist futures European jihadists, and the new crime-terror nexus. *Perspectives on Terrorism, 10* (6) 25–40. https://www.jstor.org/stable/26297703

Basra, R., & Neumann, P. R. (2020). *Prisons and terrorism: Extremist offender management in 10 European countries*. International Center for the Study of Radicalisation. https://icsr.info/wp-content/uploads/2020/07/ICSR-Report-Prisons-and-Terrorism-Extremist-Offender-Management-in-10-European-Countries_V2.pdf

Bonino, S. (2013). Prevent-ing Muslimness in Britain: The normalisation of exceptional measures to combat terrorism. *Journal of Muslim Minority Affairs, 33* (3), 385–400. https://doi.org/10.1080/13602004.2013.853977

Boyle, M., & Johnstone, L. (2020). *A straight-talking introduction to the Power Threat Meaning Framework: An alternative to psychiatric diagnosis*. PPCS.

Braddock, K. (2014). The talking cure? Communication and psychological impact in prison de-radicalisation programmes. In A. Silke (ed.), *Prisons, terrorism, and extremism: Critical Issues in management, radicalization and reform.* (pp. 60–70). Routledge.

British Psychological Society (2018). *Ethical guidelines for applied psychological practice in the field of extremism, violent extremism, and terrorism*. British Psychological Society. https://explore.bps.org.uk/content/report-guideline/bpsrep.2018.inf313

Burnett, R. (2004). One-to-one ways of promoting desistance: In search of an evidence base. In R. Burnett & C. Roberts (eds.), *What works in probation and youth justice: Developing evidence-based practice* (pp. 180–197). Willan.

Cherney, A. (2018). Supporting disengagement and reintegration: Qualitative outcomes from a custody-based counter radicalisation intervention. *Journal for Deradicalisation, 17*. ISSN: 2363–9849.

Cherney, A., & Koehler, D. (2023). Understanding and addressing the risk of disguised compliance in CVE programming, *Behavioral Sciences of Terrorism and Political Aggression*, https://doi.org/10.1080/19434472.2023.2286966

Corner, E., & Gill, P. (2020). Psychological distress, terrorist involvement and disengagement from terrorism: A sequence analysis approach. *Journal of Quantitative Criminology, 36*, 499–526. https://doi.org/10.1007/s10940-019-09420-1

Counter Extremism Project (2022). *Alternative pathways: A trauma and countering violent extremism informed theory of change for the rehabilitation and reintegration of extremist offenders and those susceptible to radicalisation in American prisons.* Counter Extremism Project. https://4rnetwork.org/sites/default/files/2023-01/ Alternative%20Pathways_Theory%20of%20Change_092322.pdf

Dean, C. (2012). Intervening effectively with terrorist offenders. *Prison Service Journal, 203,* 31–36. https://www.crimeandjustice.org.uk/publications/psj/prison-service-journal-203

Dean, C. (2014). The healthy identity intervention: The UK's development of a psychologically informed intervention to address extremist offending. In A. Silke (ed.), *Prisons, terrorism & extremism: Critical issues in management, radicalisation and reform* (pp. 115–132). Routledge.

Dean, C. (2016). *Addressing violent extremism in prisons and probation: Principles for effective programs and interventions.* Global Center on Cooperative Security. https://www.jstor.org/stable/pdf/resrep20339.pdf

Dean, C. (2019). Good practices: United Kingdom: Translating identity theory into identity informed intervention. In M. Herzog-Evans & M. Benbouriche (eds.), *Evidence-based work with violent extremists: International implications of French terrorist attacks and responses* (pp. 161–178). Lexington Books.

Dean, C. (2023). Understanding and preventing ideologically justified violence in custodial settings: The MICO paradigm. *The Prison Journal, 103* (2), 194–214. https:// doi.org/10.1177/00328855231154598

Dean, C. (2024a). *The Application of Psychology to Prevent Extremist Violence* [published doctoral dissertation]. Cardiff Metropolitan University.

Dean, C. (2024b). The power threat meaning framework: Implications for practice in preventing extremist violence. *Journal for Deradicalization, 40,* 1–38. ISSN: 2363–9849.

Dean, C., & Lloyd, M. (2022). Challenging bias in the assessment of extremist offending. In G. Liell, M. Fisher & L. Jones (eds.), *Challenging bias in forensic psychological assessment and testing. Theoretical and practical approaches to working with diverse populations.* (pp. 423–438). Routledge.

Dowden, C., & Andrews, D. A. (2004). The importance of staff practice in delivering effective correctional treatment: A meta-analytic review of core correctional practice. *International Journal of Offender Therapy and Comparative Criminology, 48* (2), 203–214. https://doi.org/10.1177/0306624X03257765

Durnescu, I. (2020). *Core correctional skills. The training kit.* Ars Docendi.

Durnescu, I. (2024). The working alliance in practice: Navigating effective engagement with violent extremist offenders. *Journal for Deradicalisation, 40,* 265–288. ISSN: 2363–9849 https://journals.sfu.ca/jd/index.php/jd/article/view/965/495

El-Said, H. (2012). *De-radicalising Islamists: Programmes and their impact in Muslim majority states.* International Centre for the Study of Radicalisation and Political Violence. https://icsr.info/wp-content/uploads/2012/02/1328200569ElSaid Deradicalisation1.pdf

Ganor, B., & Falk, P. (2013). De-radicalization in Israel's prison system. *Studies in Conflict & Terrorism, 36* (2), 116–131. https://doi.org/10.1080/1057610X.2013. 747071

Gill, P., Clemmow, C., Hetzel, F., Rottweiler, B., Salman, N., Van Der Vegt, I., Marchment, Z., Schumann, S., Zolghadriha, S., Schulten, N., Taylor, N., & Corner, E. (2021). Systematic review of mental health problems and violent extremism. *The

Journal of Forensic Psychiatry & Psychology, 32 (1), 51–78. https://doi.org/10.1080/14789949.2020.1820067

Goodman-Delahunty, J., Corbo Crehan, A., & Brandon, S. (2022). The ethical practice of police psychology. In P. Barbosa & M. Paulino (eds.), *Police psychology: New trends in forensic psychological science.* (pp. 3–21). Academic Press.

Hannah, G., Clutterbuck, L., & Rubin, J. (2008). *Radicalization or rehabilitation: Understanding the challenge of extremist and radicalized prisoners.* RAND Corporation. https://www.rand.org/pubs/technical_reports/TR571.html

Harris, M., & Fallot, R. D. (2001). Envisioning a trauma-informed service system: A vital paradigm shift. *New Directions for Mental Health Services, 89,* 3–22. https://doi.org/10.1002/yd.23320018903

Hassan, G., Brouillette-Alarie, S., Ousman, S., Savard, É. L., Kilinc, D., Madriaza, P., Varela, W., Pickup, D., & Danis, E. (2021). *A systematic review on the outcomes of tertiary prevention programs in the field of violent radicalization* (Report No. 2021-INT-EN). Canadian Practitioners Network for the Prevention of Radicalisation and Extremist Violence. https://cpnprev.ca/systematic-review-3/

Home Office (1994). *Report of the enquiry into the escape of six prisoners from the special security unit at Whitemoor prison, Cambridgeshire, on Friday.* 9th September 1994. CM2741. HM Government Stationary Office. https://assets.publishing.service.gov.uk/media/5a7491cf40f0b61938c7e833/2741.pdf

HM Government (2006). *A five-year strategy for protecting the public and reducing reoffending.* Home Office. https://assets.publishing.service.gov.uk/media/5a7c22d0e5274a25a9140ab3/6717.pdf

HM Government (2023). *CONTEST: The United Kingdom's Strategy for Countering Violent Terrorism.* (Report No. CP903). https://assets.publishing.service.gov.uk/government/uploads/system/uploads/attachment_data/file/1186413/CONTEST_2023_English_updated.pdf

Horgan, J. (2009). *Walking away from terrorism. Accounts of disengagement from radical and extremist movements.* Routledge.

Horgan, J. (2014). *The psychology of terrorism.* Routledge.

International Centre for Counterterrorism – The Hague/Hedayah (2013). *Building on the GCTF's Rome Memorandum: Additional Guidance on the Role of Psychologists/Psychology in Rehabilitation and Reintegration Programs.* https://icct.nl/sites/default/files/2023-01/Hedayah-ICCT%20Psychology%20Good%20Practices.pdf

Johnstone, L., Boyle, M., Cromby, J., Dillon, J., Harper, D., Kinderman, P., Longden, E., Pilgrim, D., & Read, J. (2018). *The power threat meaning framework: Towards the identification of patterns in emotional distress, unusual experiences and troubled or troubling behaviour, as an alternative to functional psychiatric diagnosis.* British Psychological Society. https://www.bps.org.uk/guideline/power-threat-meaning-framework-full-version

Karstedt, S. (1999). Early Nazis 1923–1933 Neo-Nazis 1980–1995: A comparison of the life histories of two generations of German right-wing extremists. In P. Cohen, C. Slomkowski, & L. Robins (eds.), *Historical and geographical influences on psychopathology.* (pp. 85–114). Erlbaum.

Keane, C., Parkinson, V., Dower, C., & Elliott, I. (2023). *The Healthy Identity Intervention (HII): Findings from an interim outcome evaluation.* Ministry of Justice Analytical Series. HM Ministry of Justice. https://assets.publishing.service.gov.uk/government/uploads/system/uploads/attachment_data/file/1162440/healthy-identity-intervention-interim-findings.pdf

Kenyon, J. (2025). Healthy Identity Intervention: Extremism risk guide. His Majesty's Prison and Probation Service.

Kenyon, J., Carter, A. J., Watson, S., & Farr, J. (2025). Adapting risk assessments to a changing terrorism landscape: Revising the extremism risk guidance. *Journal of Forensic Sciences, 70*(5), 1–11. https://doi.org/10.1111/1556-4029.70101

Keulen-de Vos, M. (2019). A Dutch source of inspiration: Violent emotional states. In M. Herzog-Evans & M. Benbouriche (eds.), *Evidence-based work with violent extremists: International implications of French terrorist attacks and responses.* (pp. 289–312). Lexington Books.

Koehler, D. (2017). *Understanding deradicalization: Methods, tools and programs for countering violent extremism.* Routledge.

Koehler, D. (2020). Violent extremism, mental health and substance abuse among adolescents: Towards a trauma psychological perspective on violent radicalization and deradicalization. *The Journal of Forensic Psychiatry & Psychology, 31* (3), 455–472. https://doi.org/10.1080/14789949.2020.1758752

Koehler, D., Cherney, A., & Templar, A. (2023). Truth or dare? Exploring the importance of factual accuracy in different deradicalization counseling approaches, *Studies in Conflict & Terrorism, 35* (7). (pp. 1–21). https://doi.org/10.1080/1057610X.2023.2256535

LaFree, G., Jiang, B., & Porter, L. C. (2020). Prison and violent political extremism in the United States. *Journal of Quantitative Criminology, 36,* 473–498. https://doi.org/10.1007/s10940-019-09412-1

Lambert, M. J., & Barley, D. E. (2001). Research summary on the therapeutic relationship and psychotherapy outcome. *Psychotherapy: Theory, Research, Practice, Training, 38* (4), 357–361. https://doi.org/10.1037/0033-3204.38.4.357

Lauland, A., Maroney, J. D. P., Rivers, J. G., Bellasio, J., & Cameron, K. (2019). *Countering violent extremism in Australia and Abroad.* RAND Corporation. https://www.rand.org/content/dam/rand/pubs/research_reports/RR2100/RR2168/RAND_RR2168.pdf

Lewis, J., & Marsden, S. (2021). *Trauma, adversity, and violent extremism: A systematic review.* Center for Research and Evidence on Security Threats. https://crestresearch.ac.uk/resources/trauma-adversity-violent-extremism-systematic-review/

Liebling, A. (2014). Moral and philosophical problems of long-term imprisonment. *Studies in Christian Ethics, 27* (3), 258–269. https://doi.org/10.1177/0953946814530219

Liebling, A., & Williams, R. J. (2018). The new subversive geranium: Some notes on the management of additional troubles in maximum security prisons. *British Journal Sociology, 69,* 1194–1219.

Lloyd, M. (2021). *Ethical guidelines for working on P/CVE in mental health care.* Radicalisation Awareness Network. https://home-affairs.ec.europa.eu/system/files/2021-04/ran_ethical_guidelines_for_working_p-cve_mhc_2021_en.pdf

Lloyd, M., & Dean, C. (2015). The development of structured guidelines for assessing risk in extremist offenders. *Journal of Threat Assessment and Management, 2* (1), 40–52. https://doi.org/10.1037/tam0000035

Lufcraft, M. (2021). *Fishmongers' hall inquests: Prevention of future deaths report* (Ref: 2021-0362). London City Court. https://www.judiciary.uk/prevention-of-future-death-reports/fishmongers-hall-inquests-prevention-of-future-deaths-report/

Marsden, S. (2017). *Reintegrating extremists: Deradicalisation and desistance.* Palgrave Pivot.

Marshall, W. L., Ward, T., Mann, R. E., Moulden, H., Fernandez, Y. M., Serran, G., & Marshall, L. E. (2005). Working positively with sexual offenders: Maximizing the effectiveness of treatment. *Journal of Interpersonal Violence, 20* (9), 1096–1114. https://doi.org/10.1177/0886260505278514

Morrison, J., Silke, A., Maiberg, H., Slay, C., & Stewart, R. (2021). A systematic review of post-2017 research on disengagement and deradicalisation. *Centre for Research and Evidence on Security Threats.* https://crestresearch.ac.uk/resources/a-systematic-review-of-post-2017-research-on-disengagement-and-deradicalisation/

Mufti, E. A., Lisdiyono, E., Sukmariningsih, R. M., Ardyantara, D. M., & Riyanto, O. S. (2022). Correctional Institutions as a place of guidance to counter radicalism for terrorist prisoners in Indonesia. *Indian Journal of Forensic Medicine and Toxicology, 16* (3), 153–158. https://doi.org/10.37506/ijfmt.v16i3.18272

Nawaz, M. (2008). *The way back from Islamism.* Washington Institute for Near East Policy, PolicyWatch #1390. https://www.washingtoninstitute.org/policy-analysis/way-back-islamism

Neumann, P. (2010). *Prisons and terrorism. Radicalisation and deradicalisation in 15 countries.* International Center for the Study of Radicalisation. https://icsr.info/wp-content/uploads/2010/08/ICSR-Report-Prisons-and-Terrorism-Radicalisation-and-De-radicalisation-in-15-Countries.pdf

O'Neill, O. (2018). Linking trust to trustworthiness. *International Journal of Philosophical Studies, 26* (2), 293–300. https://doi.org/10.1080/09672559.2018.1454637

Pickering, R. (2014). Terrorism, extremism, radicalisation and the offender management system in England and Wales. In A. Silke (ed.), *Prisons, extremism and terrorism: Critical issues in management, radicalisation, and reform.* (pp. 183–196). Routledge.

Psychological Association (2015). *Report to the special committee of the board of directors of the American Psychological Association Independent Review relating to APA ethics guidelines, national security interrogations and torture.* American Psychological Association. https://www.apa.org/independent-review/revised-report.pdf

Radicalisation Awareness Network (2020). *Rehabilitation manual: Rehabilitation of radicalised and terrorist offenders for first-line practitioners.* https://home-affairs.ec.europa.eu/system/files/2020-06/ran_rehab_manual_en.pdf

Radicalisation Awareness Network (2021). *The role of psychotherapy in rehabilitation and exit work.* https://home-affairs.ec.europa.eu/system/files/2021-11/ran_role_of_psychotherapy_in_rehabilitation_and_exit_work_112021_en.pdf

Sageman, M. (2021). The implication of terrorism's extremely low base rate. *Terrorism and Political Violence, 33* (2), 302–311. https://doi.org/10.1080/09546553.2021.1880226

Salman, N. L., & Gill, P. (2020). A survey of risk and threat assessors: Processes, skills, and characteristics in terrorism risk assessment. *Journal of Threat Assessment and Management, 7* (1–2), 122–129. https://doi.org/10.1037/tam0000135

Shingler, J., & Stickney, J. (2024). *The journey from prison to community: Developing identity, meaning and belonging with men in the UK.* Routledge.

Sukabdi, Z. (2015). Terrorism in Indonesia: A review on rehabilitation and deradicalization. *Journal of Terrorism Research, 6* (2), 36–56.

Terrorism Act (2000). C.11. https://www.legislation.gov.uk/ukpga/2000/11/section/2

Tyler, T. R. (2007). *Legitimacy and criminal justice*. Russell Sage Foundation.

United Nations (2016). *Handbook on the management of violent extremist prisoners and the prevention of radicalization to violence in prisons*. United Nations Office on Drugs and Crime. https://www.unodc.org/pdf/criminal_justice/Handbook_on_VEPs.pdf

Van der Heide, E., & Schuurman, B. (2018). Reintegrating terrorists in the Netherlands: Evaluating the Dutch approach. *Journal for Deradicalization, 17*, 196–239. https://journals.sfu.ca/jd/index.php/jd/article/view/179

Weine, S., Bunn, M., Cardelli, E., & Ellis, H. (2022). *Trauma informed care and violent extremism prevention*. Centre for Research and Evidence on Security Threats. https://crestresearch.ac.uk/comment/moving-away-from-trauma-towards-trauma-and/

Williams, R. (2017). *Approaches to violent extremist offenders and countering radicalisation in prisons and probation*. European Commission. https://doi.org/10.17863/CAM.18616

Williams, R., & Liebling, A. (2023). Do prisons cause radicalization? Order, leadership, political charge, and violence in two maximum security prisons. *The British Journal of Criminology, 63* (1), 1–18. https://doi.org/10.1093/bjc/azab122

Williams, M. J., & Lindsey, S. (2014). A social psychological critique of the Saudi terrorism risk reduction initiative. *Psychology, Crime and Law, 20* (2), 131–151. https://doi.org/10.1080/1068316X.2012.749474

Part 3

Working with specific tasks

10 Trainee psychologists and relationships

Stepping in to bigger shoes

*Nicola Bowes, Louise Coates,
Karen De Claire and
Dakshina Raghavendra*

Introduction

This chapter considers the impact of being a forensic psychologist in training (i.e. unqualified) on the relationship between practitioners and the people they work with. The issue of unqualified psychologists (hereafter referred to as trainees) completing high-stakes work is contentious and presents challenges for both practitioners and those in receipt of forensic services (Shingler et al., 2020). Trainees hold power in making risk assessment recommendations that have potentially significant consequences, both for the lives of the people they work with and for public safety. And yet, while holding this power and responsibility, trainees are just learning, developing skills in practice under supervision. So how can trainees undertake this role safely, ethically and competently?

In this chapter, we will discuss how trainees can learn to feel confident and be authentic and human in interactions with service users and colleagues when they lack confidence and competence. We will discuss how trainees can navigate the competing demands of business needs and relational needs while also holding responsibility for complex and high-stakes decisions. We will discuss processes (including supervision and self-care) that support trainees to develop confidence to think beyond specific tasks, (while developing and demonstrating their competence in those tasks) and to develop strategies to approach those tasks in the context of developing and maintaining genuine, human relationships.

Reflection (Nicola): Trainees are under pressure from all sides and it's a steep learning curve. As a trainee myself, I remember joining a confident and competent team and I had some experience of youth work. I was new, an outsider and had no experience of working under supervision. I felt pressure to appear competent, professional and to not mess it up. So, I did what was natural to me, tried to please people and be kind. And that didn't work out so well because I couldn't please

DOI: 10.4324/9781003542377-14

everyone because everyone wanted different things from me. Then I wanted to become a builder, or a dentist, or anything much easier than being a psychologist. Thankfully, I had an excellent supervisor who helped me find my way, otherwise there is no way I would be a forensic psychologist today.

The supervision of trainees is pivotal in developing competence and navigating the complexity of relationships across the forensic context. Scaffolding through supervision can help trainees cope with many complexities inherent in forensic settings. The example above reflects a different era in forensic psychological training. Today's trainees must have significant experience before embarking on trainee roles. They will have already completed at least four years of focused, full-time education and have experience working with forensic populations, many under the supervision of a forensic psychologist. But they still face pressure to succeed, conform and progress towards their qualification without causing disruptions or placing too many demands on supervisors or their organisations. However, as a profession, we also want trainees to bring their fresh perspectives, to challenge the status quo and seek to build a broad, inclusive and dynamic profession. Our generation hasn't done so well with this (so far), so we need our next generation to do better and go further with this.

Barriers to developing relationships with service users

The trainee dilemma

Many psychological risk assessments are conducted by trainees, which understandably concerns people held in prison settings (Shingler et al., 2020). The "trainee" label can lead people in prison to question a trainee's competence or refuse to participate in the assessment. This situation presents a dilemma for supervising qualified psychologists: the need to balance the development of a trainee's competence in risk assessment with being held accountable for their work. Allowing trainees to conduct high-stakes risk assessments arguably increases the chance of errors that could endanger the public and/or harm relationships with service users, potentially affecting long-term risk management (Proulx et al., 2000). Perhaps we can understand these concerns when we look to our own experiences of people holding power over us, in medical or legal settings, for example, where we need someone else to make the right decisions that will aid us in progress or recovery. As Shingler et al. (2020) argue, when life-changing recommendations about our futures are being made, it is reasonable to want someone with skill and experience. However, effective training in risk assessments requires practical experience, meaning we need to find a way for trainees to manage this difficult balance.

Working (or being held in) forensic settings is, in itself, stressful (Gerstein et al., 1987), largely because relationships in forensic settings can be experienced as exhausting (Schaufeli & Peeters, 2000). Trainees have the additional pressures of inexperience, the need to demonstrate productivity and develop competency, working while completing a very demanding qualification, and the stressors of everyday life (including the financial challenges of a relatively low income). We can see how this stress is significant, intense and multifactorial. Stress can make individuals particularly vulnerable to errors in interpersonal skills, which are counterproductive when trying to build relationships and collaborate with service users (Shingler et al., 2018). In particular, stress can result in practice that becomes overly task focused, as trainees seek comfort from performance-related anxiety in the certainty of structure and rules. This in turn can result in depersonalisation and neglect of the relationship: a distant, impersonal style is inconsistent with the interviewing approach that psychologists and service users agree is best practice: one which achieves a human connection between psychologist and service user (Shingler et al., 2018). Distant and impersonal practice can reinforce negative views of psychologists and make difficult interactions more likely. There is a need to "get things done" but it's often *how* we get things done that is most important. Free-flowing conversation and transparency are helpful to support rapport building, but this comes with confidence, often developed through experience (Shingler et al., 2018).

> **Reflection (Nicola):** When I started as a trainee I wasn't a "blank slate": I was deeply, personally committed to a belief that people can change, recover and reconnect with community. I also had my own experiences of being a victim of crime and had been exposed to harm as a child. "Protecting the public" weighed heavier on me, probably because of this. I don't think I ever really openly acknowledged it, but it likely affected my practice and relationships. It aligned me with the harsh, cynical approach to practice rather than the compassionate approach. Something I feel some shame about now looking back.

Perceptions of psychologists

Psychologists (including trainees) are perceived by people held in prison as being experientially distant from them: being educated and privileged, never having had to struggle to survive (Shingler et al., 2020). Consequently, people in prison can feel that psychologists do not understand them, their behaviour or their lives, and this distance is detrimental to psychologists' ability to conduct a fair and complete assessment. This creates a perspective that being assessed by young, unqualified trainee psychologists undermines trust in the profession of psychology and, in turn, calls into question the legitimacy of psychological assessment (Shingler et al., 2020). The prison population in Wales and England (2024) is 96% male, with an over-representation of people from UK minoritised groups/global majority groups (Ministry of Justice, 2024). While there are assumptions being made about privilege and life experience, many trainees are young, 81% of forensic psychologists are women and 87% are white (Health and Care Professions Council, 2023). We can understand then the concerns about forensic psychologists being fundamentally different to the people they work with; this perception emerges from reality. This reality requires us as a profession to continue to make efforts to increase representation among forensic trainees. Assumptions around educational privilege also hold, with all trainees being educated to at least Masters level before taking up posts. Shingler et al. (2018) suggest that in order to address these barriers, trainees should treat service users as individuals and make human connections. Further, trainees must recognise and understand their privilege and make considerable efforts to listen to the people they are assessing in order to understand the context of their behaviours (Shingler et al., 2018). Direct action is also required to change the issue of representation within forensic psychology: we must increase the diversity of forensic psychologists as education providers and employers.

Psychologists are aware of how they are perceived. Both qualified and trainee psychologists have expressed the opinion that forensic service users view psychologists as a homogenous group of young women. They describe being stereotyped by people held in prison as either "psycho-babes", or "young, unqualified people" using people held in prison as "practice cases" (Shingler et al., 2020). There is evidence that people held in prison view psychologists with hostility and suspicion (Maruna, 2011; Warr, 2016). And so, bridging this gap of difference across domains including life experiences, privilege, gender, culture and ethnicity (along with a sense of shared suspicion between these groups) is a real challenge. The responsibility to address this challenge in the room, to bend and adapt, sits with the trainee: the trainee is the professional, who, remember, is also just learning and holding an extraordinary amount of stress.

This perception of psychologists has not developed in a vacuum. There was a tremendous shift over the 1990s and 2000s towards more rehabilitative approaches to prison. In the fallout from "nothing works" (Martinson, 1974), psychologist recruitment in prisons increased and a push towards "what works" (McGuire, 1999) replaced the pessimism of the past decades. The hope was to reform an estate that had been blighted by high levels of reconviction, peaking at around 70% in the 1970s and still hovering around 60% in the 1980s.[1] There was a focus over this time on implementing evidence-informed practice (assessments and interventions) and of developing cultures of rehabilitation instead of punishment. This is perhaps where the positions of psychologists started to shift, with more power being placed on psychological opinion and the emerging evidence base associated with psychological assessment; overt demonstrations of power were increasingly replaced by "soft", psychological power (Crewe, 2011): no less painful or restricting, but perhaps more opaque and difficult to pin down. Shingler et al. (2018) described the "pains of risk assessment" (p. 4), reflecting the immense distress that could be caused by psychological assessment. For many of us, it was on our watch that those difficulties in relating came to light. Had those difficulties in relating always existed in prison settings? Had we become more interested in evidence than people? It's not clear, but what we do know is that over this period, many of us got our relational work wrong. So now, as the supervisors of the trainees, we have a role here. How do we empower our trainees to do better than we did?

Overcoming the barriers

The job of this chapter is not to turn us into homogenised practitioners, clones of the authors, because we think we know it all. In coming together in a new relationship of writers and readers, trainees, supervisors, researchers and practitioners, we hope to inspire curiosity, share experiences, provide guidance and generate ideas for future practice and research. In the same way, the goal of supervision of trainees is not to create clones of the supervisor, but instead to create the space for the individual to develop their own identity as an authentic, autonomous and legitimate practitioner, within the broader context of a relationship-intense field of practice. As Skovolt and Trotter-Mathison (2016) point out

> One essence of practice in the helping, teaching, and healing fields is to be a highly skilled relationship maker who constantly attaches, is involved, separates well, steps away from professional intensity, then does it again with a new person.
>
> (p. 22)

Therefore, the supervisory relationship is essential in helping the trainee navigate inherent legitimacy issues and enhancing their human-to-human connections. Many of us, once we qualify, pick up the role of being someone else's supervisor, of growing them into a good psychologist. We turn our focus now onto how we might do that, recognising we may be supervising someone who is very different to us and knowing that we ourselves, are not a perfect embodiment of a forensic psychologist.

The role of supervision

The relationship between trainee and their supervisor, as they embark on their post-graduate qualification in forensic psychological practice, is likely to be different to their previous experiences. They have progressed from student to novice practitioner, aligning them more with the role of their supervisor, making the supervisor both guide and evaluator. The supervisor must recognise the impact of this shift on the trainee and the dynamics in the relationship. Supervisors need to be aware that their trainees may only have had experience of supervision as assessment and evaluation. Skovolt and Trotter-Mathison (2016) emphasise that "caring is the essential quality that must be maintained in the relationship-intense career fields, where there are high levels of need and high levels of personal connection" (p. 22). This makes it necessary for the supervisor to introduce an element of compassionate guidance to supervision. The trainee needs to feel safe, competent to engage and learn at the same time as recognising the assessment and evaluation role of supervision. If, as we said earlier, this was missing in our own development as forensic psychologists, then for us to offer it to our trainees, we need to start that shift in ourselves.

We suggest supervisors and trainees adopt a focus aligned with "therapeutic jurisprudence", which uses procedural justice principles, including developing trust, and self-determination in the client to produce therapeutic outcomes in criminal justice systems, such as positive change, healing and personal growth (Howieson, 2023). Howieson proposes a framework for practitioners that we suggest fits well with forensic psychologists' practice, regardless of where they are in their career path. The framework guides the practitioner to engage in procedural justice processes with clients that allow for voice, consideration, trust, neutrality, dignity, politeness and respect; to produce a fair, satisfying, cooperative and legitimate process. It encourages practitioners to take a "mentalising stance" with the client to build trust by understanding and respecting the person's unique experience and personal narrative and encourages self-determination to build motivation to change, by respecting their choices, autonomy, competence and decision control.

> **Reflection (Louise):** Whilst there are specific tasks required of trainees to complete their qualification, I always explore the trainee's preferences when it comes to planning their submissions. As the supervisor, I believe it is my responsibility to be responsive to the unique learning styles of the trainee, whilst also exploring with them the extent to which they can be flexible. One trainee may manage their anxiety about the process by meticulously planning each aspect of their work, while another avoids planning and takes each submission as it comes. I have my preference for how trainees approach their studies, yet it is vital I respect how they express their autonomy and competence with this, rather than have me impose my own style on them. I am explicit with them about that process, so they can choose whether it is an approach they adopt within their own practice.

Legitimacy as a trainee

To think about how the supervisor can support the trainee with this stage of their journey, it is important to understand what legitimacy looks like in this setting and how it manifests in supervision. We suggest legitimacy goes beyond the legalistic, authority-ordained permission to practice, onto an internalised sense of the practitioner as reasonable, acceptable, honest and fair. In forensic settings, legitimacy is often perceived to be related to the grade or position someone holds; rather, we argue it is rooted in the authenticity of the relationships practitioners build with those around them. As mentioned earlier, it is understandable that service users want the best-qualified person to be making decisions about their lives, and some service users articulate that need through hostility or denigration. This can leave a trainee feeling belittled and invalidated in the process, which can lead to them becoming defensive, subjugating, or authoritarian with the service user. This, in turn, can result in reinforcing the service user's expectations and leaving them feeling even more powerless in the relationship. This is where the supervisor can model the therapeutic jurisprudence approach with their trainee.

> **Reflection (Louise):** A trainee was working with someone who was hostile and reluctant to engage in an assessment. The trainee came to supervision frustrated by the lack of progress. Instead of suggesting ways of getting that person to be less hostile or telling the trainee to write the assessment report without their involvement, I took a mentalising stance. I asked them to say more about how they were left feeling about themselves and the service user, what beliefs they held about themselves, the service user and the work. The trainee explained they felt inadequate and powerless. They worried others would think they were incompetent, and they feared not meeting the deadline for their report. They dreaded seeing the service user and wished someone would take the report off them. Resisting the urge to rush to solution, I validated their perspective, then encouraged them to use the same approach to think about the service user's experience (considering their formulation) and what all of that meant for the trainee's understanding of the power in the relationship. Through this inquisitive process the trainee was able to see how the service user might experience their relationship and was using what little agency they had to take some control back. The trainee reflected on how that felt less personal and generated ways they could approach the matter with the service user. I finished by assuring them of my confidence and trust in their competence with this service user.

The supervisor has the role of creating a space for open discussions about the power imbalances intrinsic in the nature of the trainee's work, including what is perceived and what is real. By the supervisor adopting a mentalising stance to appreciate the trainee's unique story, they can model a compassionate and client-centric approach, while helping to strengthen the trainee's sense of validity in the relationship. Focusing on creating a supervisory relationship where the trainee gets to explore and develop their genuine sense of legitimacy helps them embody that in their relationships with service users and colleagues. When a trainee feels trusted and respected by their supervisor, they have a foundation from which to launch into other less-secure relationships.

As psychologists, we know the impact of modelling and learning through experience. Therefore, the supervisor can make use of the ways in which they interact with the trainee and others, to help enhance the trainee's sense of legitimacy. For example, a trainee attends a meeting with the supervisor to observe the role, and the supervisor takes time afterwards to explore with the trainee their observations of the interactions and how tricky dynamics were navigated. Of course, this does require the supervisor to have a good level of insight into their own core relational skills and be prepared for some observations they may not have been aware of. It can be helpful for the supervisor to share an example from their experience that has parallels with the challenge the trainee is facing: for example,

> I remember when I had my first trainee job and was the only female working on that unit. It felt really daunting and there were lots of comments from the male officers about women not being safe to work with male prisoners. I remember my supervisor advising me to sit in the main office with the officers and ask about their lives, so that I could start to build relationships with them as people. I also asked to shadow them in their roles so that I could get a better understanding of their jobs. Over time, those relationships started to build and I began to be invited to join in activities, be consulted for my opinion, and they supported me when prisoners were challenging. I know it can be tough when people hold preconceived ideas about you, so I want you to know that an investment in developing those relationships now <u>will</u> pay dividends in the future. Is there anything I could do to support you in doing that?

Depersonalisation

To set the context for this section, we refer to Pane (2016),who defined depersonalisation in the context of prison work as

> A negative reaction, feeling, and a kind of detachment from other people, which can often include loss of idealization. Usually it develops as a reaction to emotional exhaustion and considered as a means to protect them. But the danger is that this disconnect can .... dehumanize, losing touch with themselves, it is possible that they do not see themselves or others as valuable. The person also loses track of their personal needs. Their view of life restricts to see at the present time, and their life becomes a series of mechanical functions.
>
> (p. 2)

In their journey to become authentic, autonomous and legitimate practitioners, we suggest trainees run the gauntlet of being seen as weak, corruptible and inept by other professions and service users, due to the gendered working culture of forensic settings. For example, Harrison et al., 2024, drawing on the work of Crawley, 2004) stated:

> The working culture of the prison environment is distinctly gendered … prison work is couched firmly in the domain of typically masculine behaviours and traits. Such traits include the norm of having greater emotional self-control (Shields, 2022) with the violation of such normative displays having potentially negative social consequences.
>
> (p. 94)

Pressure can build on the trainee to emulate the ways other professionals engage with clients and in secure settings that can involve shutting off the self in favour of presenting an impenetrable persona. Trainees may find themselves shutting down their authentic selves and being drawn into inappropriate "banter" about service users, to be seen as robust enough to work in a forensic setting.

> **Reflection (Louise):** As a trainee, my supervisor told me the clothes I had worn when I worked in a bank were not considered suitable attire for working in a prison, the message from prison staff was to dress as gender neutral as possible in order to fit in and be safe. Dressing in skirt suits was considered a risk to security. As time went on I became one of the "cardigan brigade", the nickname some officers gave to psychologists who wore baggy cardigans to help cover their female form.

Louise was not alone with this sense of depersonalisation. Smith (2021) identified in her research how female prison governors were conscious of their clothing choices: "approximately half of governors described actively adapting their identity early in their careers, adopting what they thought would be viewed as more acceptable and legitimate. Overt examples referenced clothing and displays of emotion" (p. 24). Ideally, trainees would feel safe to bring this to supervision to develop healthier ways of operating. However, this is not always the case. Supervisors need to look at themselves to examine the extent to which we perpetuate that depersonalised approach. How often do we engage in "banter" to the detriment of our professional integrity? The pressure to role-model ethical practice, while also maintaining relationships with professionals who do not have the same professional standards, is immense. There is no easy fix to this; therefore, we argue that the provision of a safe, authentic supervision space is a crucial element to help trainees explore and develop new ways of operating in forensic settings without the need to resort to the inauthentic depersonalisation strategies of old. In the early days of training, the supervisor might focus on encouraging a belief in the trainee's ability to belong in the setting in which they work, focusing on what that sense of belonging looks and feels like. This must not aim to create a harsh, stoic, detached professional persona that can withstand criticism on the surface but is brittle, inflexible and highly critical of service users on the inside. Rather, it is about tapping into the curiosity that attracted trainees to the role in the first place, along with an interpersonal style that appreciates the other's experience.

> **Reflection (Louise):** The trainee talks about an interaction with a service user "*I was in the interview room with X, and there was a lot of noise outside the room, which was distracting me. I thought I'd better say something to X about it, as they might have noticed my distraction and thought I wasn't interested in them. I explained I was aware of being distracted by the noise outside the room and was concerned someone might burst in and interrupt. X then told me they thought the same, so we sat and waited for the people to move on before trying to concentrate again.*" The supervisor reflects back the ways in which the trainee applied certain skills and processes, encouraging a curious stance "*Did you notice how you thought about X's possible perspective, you quickly formulated what that might mean to them, and gave a bit of self-disclosure to help them make sense of what was going on for you? What happened because of you doing that? How did you know that was a safe disclosure to make?*"

To support a trainee to engage in an authentic way, it is useful for the supervisor to consider attachment and core relational styles and develop processes within the supervisory relationship that can help enhance the trainee's relational strengths and mitigate against the areas of vulnerability or weakness that exist within us all.

Attachment and core relational styles

It is useful to remember that psychologists and their clients did not emerge from pods into the roles they adopt within forensic settings. Both had their own unique upbringing experiences that shaped their attachment styles (Ainsworth et al., 1978) and, therefore, their core adult relational styles (Bartholomew & Horowitz, 1991). While the supervisor is not there to be therapist for the trainee, it is important they create a safe environment in which the trainee can explore their core adult relational styles and how they manifest themselves in the workplace. Coates and Bowes (2022) suggest one way to achieve this in an ethical way is for the trainee to develop their self-formulation. The trainee chooses whichever formulation method they prefer, with some guidance from the supervisor to include something about the origins of the trainee's current ways of operating. The supervisor does not need to know the origins, just the trainee's reflections on their relational styles, how they can use this to enhance their practice and what support they may need to mitigate some of their vulnerabilities. This may be through self-reflection in supervision, it may be through accessing therapy. Either way, a process of self-formulation can assist the trainee in understanding their own ways of operating in work, along with having greater insight into the client's experience of being assessed and formulated. Coates and Bowes (2022) caution the supervisor to be mindful of the impact of the power imbalance that exists between them and the trainee, as coerced self-reflection or self-disclosure can at the very least be counterproductive if the trainee does not believe it is a useful process for them. There are several reasons why the supervisor must respect that: the timing may not be right; the trainee may be anxious about being under time pressure to complete work; they may be fearful of being seen as not robust enough for the job; they may be worried or ashamed about events in their past they should not have to bring in to the workplace. They may not realise the value of self-formulation and may benefit from the supervisor sharing a little of their own self-formulation to model openness, illustrate the way in which self-formulation is used in supervision and explore some of the benefits of the approach.

Mattering

There is emerging research into mattering, or feeling significant to someone, as a fundamental psychological need that has an impact on health, well-being and success (Prilleltensky, 2020). Stickney and Lowenstein (2023) identified seven key components that make up the concept of mattering, which include feeling:

- Significant to others (Importance)
- Noticed by others (Attention)
- Important for being relied upon (Dependence)
- Emotionally invested in and able to affect others (Ego extension)
- Missed by others (Noted)
- Valued (Appreciation)
- Special and unique for who we are (Individuation)

There are several overlaps between mattering and elements of therapeutic jurisprudence, outlined earlier. Mattering is positively associated with secure attachments and negatively associated with anxious or avoidant attachments (Bowlby, 1969). Prilleltensky (2020) pointed out that a failure to feel like you matter "results in significant suffering to the person and potential damage to the people and communities surrounding the individual" (p. 6). Therefore, we can argue for the value of actively applying a mattering approach with our service users to improve their experience of their interactions with us but also support the development of healthier interactions with their communities. To demonstrate the components that make up mattering, the trainee needs to remain present with the individual and lean-in to the relationship rather than adopting a depersonalised stance. The supervisor has the role of modelling the same approach within the supervisory relationship. If trainees believe they matter to their supervisor, they are then resourced to attempt to show their service users they matter. This can be as simple as the supervisor saying they missed the trainee at a particular event or enquiring about the trainee's leave. Alternatively, the supervisor can talk about the impact the trainee has on them, for example

> I have been looking forward to telling you that since our last supervision session I have used that flowchart you developed, with a nurse. It really helped us make sense of the client's self-harm pattern. Thank you as we were quite stuck before we used your brilliant technique.

We also suggest that this mattering process does not end once the trainee qualifies. As with any healthy relationship, we hope the trainee has been able to internalise aspects of their supervisor that will help them to launch their own autonomous practice from a secure and valued foundation. In the final supervision session, the supervisor could ask the qualifying psychologist "What would you like to take away from how we have worked together? Is there anything you think I could have changed that you think you might like to do differently?"

Supervision should be a safe relationship within which a trainee can grow into a good psychologist. We hope the section above provides some guidance about how supervisors can help create this relationship, but of course trainees are the other important part of this relationship. How do trainees navigate this relationship? How do they grow? What supports and what hinders that growth? The best person to tell us about that is someone who is on the journey. We hope that this next section may help all of us, whether we are educators, supervisors or trainees, and that it might encourage and validate trainees who are on their own journey towards qualification as a practitioner psychologist.

Understanding the trainee perspective

These words are mine, a forensic trainee on my path to qualification, based on my lived experiences of training for the last three years. It documents how I have developed my relationship with myself as well as how I have developed as a practitioner. It reflects on the journey from where I started, feeling like I didn't know anything, to where I am now, where I can see how my service has benefited from my presence. It explores how we might navigate tricky dynamics in supervision: where we are required to be vulnerable, required to be wrong and required to be competent and on the ball. How do we perform as a trainee when we are also being constantly assessed and scrutinised? I offer some strategies and approaches to help navigate the challenges of training, both in terms of developing relational practice with service users and within professional relationships.

Embrace the discomfort of not knowing

It is important for us to immediately acknowledge that training is not easy. It is not meant to be. It can be uncomfortable, highly rewarding and result in a scarily accurate understanding of our own vulnerabilities, all at once. But we do not start out by knowing everything (in fact, we will never know everything, and a good practitioner will always accept that this is totally OK). Having said that, the discomfort of not knowing can get in the way when self-doubt and hesitation interfere with asking questions or seeking advice. In my experience, the discomfort is an important process in developing as a trainee, and the way to tap into its powerful potential often feels like a well-kept secret by qualified practitioners who are "in the know". The secret seems to simply (and rather anti-climatically), embrace the discomfort. But how? Good question.

> **Reflection (Dakshina):** We might be encouraged to shed the academic load and focus on the moment, but we never do, we live with both. We know that our work will be seen by an assessor and it's not perfect, it didn't go perfectly and somehow we have to roll with that.

Sometimes the only way is through, and this is also the case with training in forensic psychology. Trainees are often expected to take a leap in responsibility when they first start. This can be quite jarring and often trainees report feeling a loss of identity, particularly if we experience a constant fear of making a mistake. While this is a natural response, there are safeguards and ways in which the process of navigating this complex web of relationships and deeply challenging clinical work can be made less daunting. Our existing structures of supervision, peer support, reflection and reflective writing (practice diaries as tedious as these might seem) are helpful to scaffold our development. Another key aspect of leaning into the discomfort of not knowing is recognising limits of practice. This is a key competency that all practitioner psychologists must demonstrate (trainees included). Recognising our own limits and seeking support enables us to own our discomfort and acknowledge gaps in our understanding. This might allow us to take a more curious stance when building relationships with service users and professionals.

> **Reflection: (Dakshina)** Once during supervision, I remember feeling anxious to tell my supervisor that I did not know how to approach developing a relapse prevention plan with a service user. It seemed so basic. How did I not know this? I researched as much as I could, but my internet searching led me to multiple different approaches and I was not sure which one would best fit the needs of the service user. I felt panic and was riddled with self-doubt in my competence. I was so worried that my supervisor would judge me as lacking competence in making a simple plan. I almost considered not bringing it up in supervision. But

something told me that I needed to. When I brought this up, my supervisor helpfully (and without judgement) directed me to a few resources and even talked through a plan they had recently developed with a service user. This significantly supported my learning and development. I do not think the quality of my work with my service user would have been as rich and insightful, had I not mentioned the limits of my knowledge in supervision.

My experience above demonstrates that, to build confidence, trainees must learn to communicate the gaps in knowledge to supervisors, professionals and indeed, service users. Supervisors can support this process by observing gaps early on and gently directing the trainee's attention to them. Modelling this self-recognition is also essential to developing these skills. When supervisors or those in positions of power and experience lead by example, trainees can feel more comfortable to recognise and communicate their own limits, contributing to safer and more ethical clinical decision-making. Leading by example can also reduce the shame or anxiety for practitioners beginning their careers.

Leaning into rupture and repair

Another helpful tip when navigating complex relationships is recognising the power in the process of "rupture and repair". The complex vulnerabilities and needs of the people we work with in forensic settings are well established. This complexity contributes to the intensity of our relationships with service users. It also has a significant impact on the dynamics between professionals. An early recognition that ruptures are difficult but expected, and ultimately quite powerful, can support trainees in navigating them when they occur.

Reflection (Dakshina): The first time my therapeutic alliance with a service user experienced a rupture, I felt lost, guilty and worried. Initially, I had internalised some of the service user's beliefs that I was to blame. I felt rejected and that I had let them down. These feelings caused worry about my ability to carry out my role. Was I going to turn out to be a horrible psychologist? After some reflection and seeking guidance in supervision, I was able to think about the process of rupture and begin considering the power of repair. Reflecting on the service user's experiences of past relationships, endings and conflict allowed me to carefully think about what (from their life) was being replayed in our therapeutic alliance. These insights supported me to feel more confident leaning into the rupture and thinking about repairing the alliance. In hindsight, our rapport became stronger. Moreover, as a trainee, I felt confident in knowing that if I were to experience this again (which I would), then I would certainly be able to navigate this. I kind of wish someone had told me that this was to be expected in forensic work, it may have helped me feel more capable.

A common by-product of the rupture and repair process is realising in hindsight that this process could be quite therapeutically powerful. Now, wouldn't it be nice if we could support trainees to anticipate what a rupture could be like ahead of one happening? This could give trainees a space to reflect on what they might do when a rupture occurs, allow supervisors to share their own blunders and experiences of ruptures and help shed some of the shame or self-doubt that can arise within trainees. This will encourage trainees, when the time comes, to lean into the discomfort of a rupture, rather than shying away from it.

Good supervision can be a superpower

Trainee forensic psychologists are required to demonstrate a range of core competencies over at least 360 days of practice, all of which is rigorously supervised. Supervision, therefore, forms a fundamental part of the life of a trainee. Supervision is both a critical relationship we must navigate and a space for us to navigate other tricky relationships in our work. Specifically, this process may involve what many trainees have described as a "leap of faith" and can be best achieved within supervisory alliances which establish themselves to be non-judgemental. But what does this look like in practice, when in fact, part of the supervisor's duty is to judge competence?

Trainees share that establishing shared goals, a strong rapport and agreeing on the manner of communication play a key role in receiving critical feedback on areas of development and ways to improve practice. Trainees have also shared that they found it useful when a rapport and sense of trust were established prior to receiving critical feedback on their practice.

Furthermore, the power differences in forensic settings can seem stark. Most trainees are vigilant to the shifts in power imbalances as practitioners who hold power over the lives of service users. However, there is an odd juxtaposition when we think about the possible powerlessness experienced by trainees within supervision. Using supervision as a space to reflect on these power imbalances and the feelings that come with them is a great way of getting ahead of the challenging relationship dynamics one may come across. Here, trainees may reflect on their sense of powerlessness or feeling observed and the parallels that this might draw with the service users who feel disempowered or observed. Acknowledging this strange juxtaposition better prepares trainees for managing these power imbalances, as is a requirement of core Health and Care Professions Council (HCPC) standards of proficiency.

Ask for what is rightfully yours

> At what point do we have a voice? When do we know that we have a right to raise things? Our supervisors need to guide this.

An important aspect of managing the complexity of forensic psychology training is understanding the minimum amount of supervision a trainee should receive in order to undertake safe and ethical practice, while demonstrating essential competencies of the profession. Once this shared understanding is developed by all those involved in the training process, it is important for trainees to be empowered to ask for what is rightfully theirs. A protected space for supervision, a request for a particular type of supervision (e.g. cultural, racial, peer) are important ways in which this right can be exercised. Reasonable adjustments are also important to request when needed, as these may not be obvious to peers, supervisors or managers responsible for professionals' well-being. Due to the power dynamic that exists between trainees and other professionals within a service, asking for this can be difficult. However, supervisors should encourage trainees, where possible, to empower themselves in such ways.

Be sensitive to individual differences

Over the years, training in practitioner psychology, both forensic and otherwise, has been slow to diversify. Here, diversity refers to a variety of marginalised identities and the intersectionality of these identities, which are underrepresented in the profession. Improvements in diversity have been due to the conscious efforts of organisations and systems to recognise bias and disadvantage perpetuated by the inherent nature of their processes. This has led to the profession seeing a greater number of applications for forensic psychology training from a diversity of backgrounds (e.g. minoritised ethnicities, sexualities, genders, nationalities and a range of other protected characteristics) although these groups are still underrepresented. However, with the diversification of trainee cohorts comes the need to look into trainees' lived experiences in supervision. Given that these individuals have already faced disproportionate difficulties and disadvantage on their journey to becoming a trainee, there is a direct need for further consideration of the additional challenges faced in supervision. The evidence suggests that the vast majority of qualified forensic psychology practitioners who supervise trainees belong to a fairly homogenous group of privileged people (i.e. White, middle-class, cis-gendered, heterosexual, neurotypical females). Cross-cultural challenges are therefore common for trainees from minoritised backgrounds. These trainees are more likely to face discrimination from service users and other professionals in their work. This is unfair, and a sensitivity towards this needs to be developed by educational providers as well as clinical supervisors within organisations.

While trainees learn a great deal from their supervisors and gain the fundamental skills needed to become confident and qualified practitioners, it is also true that the interpersonal dynamics between supervisor and trainee are impacted by conversations (or the absence of conversations) around culture, discrimination and other non-clinical experiences a trainee might have during the course of work. This, in turn, may impact the trainee's trust, perception of safety, and overall well-being over the course of training. It is therefore imperative that supervisors consider challenges to cross-cultural supervision and ways of managing potential challenges faced by trainees, prior to undertaking their clinical or academic supervision.

It is the responsibility of organisations and systems to be deliberate in creating channels and safe spaces for trainees to bring unfair experiences that they face in practice. Responding in a contained and timely manner is essential. Supporting trainees, by holding space for their feelings and narratives, as well as empowering them to take action if felt appropriate, are some ways in which supervisors can respond to unfairness in practice. Ultimately, there needs to be more open conversations and a willingness for supervisors to be uncomfortable in supervision, especially relating to topics around unfairness and discrimination, both within and outside of clinical practice. This allows for a sense of empowerment and being able to ultimately carry out their work as trainee forensic psychologists, an inherently challenging job, without the added challenges of facing discrimination. When institutions and overseeing bodies fail to attend to diversity needs proactively, then they run the risk of discouraging trainees from seeking support relating to clinical practice. This not only impacts the trainee but also their navigation of complex relationships in their work. How can trainees create safe spaces when they feel marginalised and unheard?

Don't be afraid to innovate

While trainees navigate a complex web of relationships, demonstration of core competencies and academic submissions, it can sometimes be easy to forget the bigger picture. That is, trainee forensic psychologists are part of a wider system, and they have power. It can be easy for trainees to feel that they do not hold much power or authority, but the reality is that they are at the forefront of clinical practice and the cutting edge of systemic change. It is vital that trainees and those supporting trainees consciously recognise this and use this to drive innovation towards better practice.

> **Reflection (Dakshina):** During team meetings, I would always have many ideas and thoughts about service improvement. But I would feel nervous to share these with my colleagues. I was only just a trainee, right? Wrong. On the few occasions I mustered up the courage to share, my contributions were taken seriously and were fed back to be valuable insights for service improvement. This in turn validated me to share ideas more readily in the future.

Trainees contribute significantly to the services in which they work throughout training. We develop training packages, new clinical material, and consultancy projects, conduct research and interact with a host of stakeholders in the process. This places us in the perfect position to be able to note gaps in existing practice and suggest new ways of working. Trainees also sometimes undertake several placements over a short period of time and often have the advantage of taking the best from every service and sharing this knowledge with the next. While pushing new teams to innovate or try new ways of working requires courage, we recommend professionals to encourage trainees to embed this into their practice as this fuels local and wider system change for better, safer and more ethical practice.

Furthermore, being innovative includes asking questions with curiosity. This is a basic tenet of therapeutic and relational work. Curiosity supports us to build rapport and construct safe, non-judgemental spaces within which we explore, address and manage risk. This also applies to navigating relationships with professionals. Being curious, asking questions which may challenge the status quo and making innovative suggestions for how to improve the work we do, is an integral part of being able to navigate the challenges of the work. When a problem is approached with curiosity and innovation, then a sense of shared goals is developed, rather than defensiveness or further relational strain. These aspects of the training process allow practitioners to develop ways of working with others that ultimately lead to productive and progressive ways of dealing with complex systemic issues.

Relationships with people and power

Throughout the course of training in forensic psychology, a trainee learns to develop and manage relationships with a range of key players including service users, supervisors, peers within psychology, operational colleagues and other allied health professionals. At any given point in time, trainees are managing and navigating the majority, if not all, of these relationships, which come with challenges.

> **Reflection (Dakshina):** The first time I remember feeling really overwhelmed as a trainee was understandably a difficult experience. It brought on the natural feelings of self-doubt, worry about the future, and loss of faith in my own competency. After some reflection, I thought about the root of the overwhelm. It seemed to me that I felt like it was "all happening at once", and this seemed to increase my anxiety. Specifically, the high expectation both placed on myself as well as the wider system of building, maintaining, managing and navigating complex relationships with colleagues, service users, legal authorities, decision-makers and academic judges of competence, simultaneously.

It is essential for practitioners, academic bodies and supervisors to keep a check on the realities of trainees' experiences while training. It is important not to assume that because they are getting on well with training, their relationships are not causing strain. Indeed, we must hold ourselves to the high standards that we expect our trainees to strive for as well.

> **Reflection (Dakshina):** When I was a trainee, a senior member of the team made racist comments. I was expected to continue working with this individual and continue to discuss service user related matters with them. This relationship was difficult for me to navigate. They were in a far greater position of power than me and supervised some of my work, what could I do? Would I ever be able to bring up cultural context in my work without seeming like the "trainee who called race" every time? I am just a trainee, how can I raise concerns about their behaviour? Meanwhile, my internal value systems were being short-circuited.

After experiencing direct and indirect racism as well as macro- and micro-aggressions from service users, colleagues and senior practitioners (yes, simultaneously), I wondered what was keeping me going? What was protecting against total exhaustion? What was helping me cope with this daily turmoil? While it is certain that I experienced a certain degree of weathering, it was also clear that there were some aspects of my training that helped me continue to manage these difficult relationships.

- Firstly, I identify in hindsight that I had a clear goal: I wanted to be a forensic psychologist. This internal motivation and clarity helped me keep my eyes fixed on what I wanted to achieve.
- Second, an understanding of the potential risks of the job. Relational difficulties are common in forensic practice. Racist and other discriminatory behaviours are commonly experienced by professionals working with people with acute mental health difficulties, personality difficulties and a range of complex presentations. This does not excuse them, but gives them more context, which helps us to manage the impact they may have on our own well-being. The additional difficulty of managing a professional relationship that includes undertones of powerplay, racism and unfairness, is unfortunate and also a reality of many trainees.
- Third, a supervisory team that was felt to be on my side. Given all these realities, it is important to have some core people a trainee can confidently depend on to support in the exact way that is needed.
- Lastly, in hindsight, I think there is a degree of weathering that occurs when you are a trainee expected to navigate some of the most complex issues present within society, almost in a concentrated way, in forensic settings. Add racism, sexism, homophobia and some other discrimination to this, and you have a certain cause for exhaustion. When academic bodies, services and colleagues think about this more proactively than reactively, trainees will likely be better supported to achieve their goals, with minimal weathering.

Trainees also vary significantly in their experiences of training and managing the relationships that form part of training. Much like formulating service users' life experiences and current difficulties, it is important to consider the various factors which might worsen or protect against trainees' adverse experiences of navigating relationships while training. There is a resilience within trainees that can be honed through support and compassion for our roles. Pre-empting these difficulties can support us to have appropriate channels or spaces to share and legitimise our experiences. In the same way, when a trainee's role is properly identified, acknowledged and appreciated, then you have the potential for a powerhouse of growth and development for the individual, team and service as a whole.

Trust the process

Finally, a strategy that takes courage, drive and creativity is to *trust the process*. Courage and drive are two of the more obvious tools that support a trainee to apply this strategy. A way to bolster this further is for trainees to think about why they chose this profession in the first place. By tapping into the roots of their motivation, they may be able to find the courage to re-commit themselves to the process of training in the face of relational dynamics and occupational pressures that could possibly lead to compassion fatigue and burnout.

This strategy might seem like simplistic advice, but it comes from the experience of many practitioners who were once trainees. This wisdom is really valuable, and if we can encourage budding practitioners to think about this from an early stage, then we can support them to thrive in the challenges of everyday practice, rather than be riddled with self-doubt and disempowerment. Supervisors might share their own experiences of training quite early on in the process, thus modelling the normality of how overwhelming things can be for a trainee. Learning to trust the process early on can help trainees to focus on the developmental and relational aspects of the work, without feeling too bogged down by the performative aspects that come with the job. I always found it helpful to remind myself, "Training is temporary, my practice is forever".

Conclusion

In this chapter, we have set out some of the challenges facing trainees. These include the juggle of demands, the pressures and expectations to be willing to learn and also competent, considerate, compassionate practitioners. We explored how supervisory relationships can support trainees in developing and maintaining a sense of self within that journey and hopefully create safety for trainees to grow. We have also set out what that journey is like and some of the additional pressures and misuses of power that our trainees are subjected to as they try to develop as ethical, professional practitioners. We hope this chapter has offered some suggestions to people navigating this journey either as a trainee or part of the support system of a trainee. We want to encourage our profession to listen and learn from the new generation of trainees at the same time as supporting and teaching them. We hope that we will continue to have the benefit of critical friends, to call our attention to the ways in which we can do better. Together we all have the opportunity of (as Ruth Mann used to say) "doing a little bit of good today".

Note

1 https://assets.publishing.service.gov.uk/media/5a7a325340f0b66a2fc0097e/compendium-of-reoffending-statistics-and-analysis.pdf.

References

Ainsworth, M. D. S., Blehar, M. C., Waters, E., & Wall, S. (1978). *Patterns of attachment: A psychological study of the strange situation.* Erlbaum.

Bartholomew, K., & Horowitz, L. M. (1991). Attachment styles among young adults: A test of a four-category model. *Journal of Personality and Social Psychology, 61*(2), 226–244. https://doi.org/10.1037/0022-3514.61.2.226

Bowlby, J. (1969). *Attachment and loss: Vol. 1. Attachment.* Basic Books.

Coates, L., & Bowes, N. (2022). Using self-formulation in the development of trainee forensic psychologists. *Forensic Update, 1*(141), 10–14. https://doi.org/10.53841/bpsfu.2022.1.141.10

Crawley, E. M. (2004). Emotion and performance: Prison officers and the presentation of self in prisons. *Punishment & Society, 6*(4), 411–427. https://doi.org/10.1177/1462474504046121

Crewe, B. (2011). Soft power in prison: Implications for staff–Prisoner relationships, liberty and legitimacy. *European Journal of Criminology, 8*(6), 455–468. https://doi.org/10.1177/1477370811413805

Gerstein, L. H., & Tesser, A. (1987). Antecedents and responses associated with loneliness. *Journal of Social and Personal Relationships, 4*(3), 329–363. https://doi.org/10.1177/026540758700400306

Harrison, K., Mason, R., Nichols, H., & Smith, L. (2024). *Work, culture and wellbeing among prison governors in England and Wales.* Palgrave Macmillan. https://doi.org/10.1007/978-3-031-57433-7

Health and Care Professions Council. (2023). *Standards of proficiency for practitioner psychologists.* https://www.hcpc-uk.org/standards/standards-of-proficiency/

Howieson, J. A. (2023). A framework for the evidence-based practice of therapeutic jurisprudence: A legal therapeutic alliance. *International Journal of Law and Psychiatry, 89,* 101845. https://doi.org/10.1016/j.ijlp.2023.101845

Martinson, R. (1974). What works?—Questions and answers about prison reform. *The Public Interest, 35,* 22–54. https://www.nationalaffairs.com/public_interest/detail/what-works-questions-and-answers-about-prison-reform

Maruna, S. (2011). Judicial rehabilitation and the 'clean bill of health' in criminal justice. *European Journal of Probation, 3*(1), 97–117. https://doi.org/10.1177/206622031100300108

McGuire, J. (Ed.). (1999). *What works: Reducing reoffending guidelines from research and practice.* John Wiley & Sons.

Ministry of Justice. (2024). *Offender management statistics quarterly: October to December 2023*. GOV.UK. https://www.gov.uk/government/statistics/offender-management-statistics-quarterly-october-to-december-2023

Pane, M. (2016). Factor influencing depersonalization on prison employees. *European Journal of Social Sciences Education and Research, 3*(3), 161–167. https://doi.org/10.26417/ejser.v7i1

Prilleltensky, I. (2020). Mattering at the intersection of psychology, philosophy, and politics. *American Journal of Community Psychology, 65*(1–2), 16–34. https://doi.org/10.1002/ajcp.12368

Proulx, J., Perreault, C., & Ouimet, M. (2000). Proximate and long-term risk factors in the recidivism of sexual offenders. *Journal of Interpersonal Violence, 15*(5), 543–560. https://doi.org/10.1177/088626000015005005

Schaufeli, W. B., & Peeters, M. C. W. (2000). Job stress and burnout among correctional officers: A literature review. *International Journal of Stress Management, 7*(1), 19–48. https://doi.org/10.1023/A:1009514731657

Shields, S. A. (2002). *Speaking from the heart: Gender and the social meaning of emotion*. Cambridge University Press.

Shingler, J., Sonnenberg, S. J., & Needs, A. (2018). Risk assessment interviews: Exploring the perspectives of psychologists and indeterminate sentenced prisoners in the United Kingdom. *International Journal of Offender Therapy and Comparative Criminology, 62*(10), 3201–3224.

Shingler, J., Sonnenberg, S. J., & Needs, A. (2020). 'Their life in your hands': The experiences of prison-based psychologists conducting risk assessments with indeterminate sentenced prisoners in the United Kingdom. *Psychology, Crime & Law, 26*(4), 311–326. https://doi.org/10.1080/1068316X.2019.1652750

Skovholt, T. M., & Trotter-Mathison, M. (2016). *The resilient practitioner: Burnout and compassion fatigue prevention and self-care strategies for the helping professions* (3rd ed.). Routledge. https://doi.org/10.4324/9781315737447

Smith, V. (2021). The experiences of women prison governors. *Prison Service Journal, 257*, 22–29.

Stickney, J., & Lowenstein, J. (2023). "They spoke to me like I was a human, so I behaved like a human": Mattering, hope and release from prison. In Shingler, J. & Stickney, J. (Eds.) *The journey from prison to community* (1st ed., Chapter 13). Routledge. https://doi.org/10.4324/9781003308171-13

Warr, J. (2016). *Experiencing imprisonment*. Routledge. https://doi.org/10.4324/9781315764171

11 Relational issues in prison-based forensic psychological risk assessment

Jo Shingler and Jason Warr

Introduction

This chapter focuses on relational practice in forensic psychological risk assessment in prisons. The authors are informed by different perspectives, which include:

- Lived experience of risk assessment, and being a recipient of the practice of forensic psychology in prison
- Academic research on, and reflective thought around, risk assessment, relationships in forensic psychology, and the practice of forensic psychology
- A practising forensic psychologist, both within and outside the prison context

Risk assessment is central to the work of forensic psychologists in prisons. It is equally, if not more central to the lives of (particularly) indeterminate sentenced prisoners, who are dependent on favourable risk assessments to progress through their sentences. Despite significant advances, including the development of Structured Professional Judgement (SPJ) risk assessment tools, the relational element of risk assessment rarely takes front and centre. This is despite consistent evidence suggesting that relational elements shape the outcomes of assessments, that prisoners experience it deeply stressful, and that there are significant challenges in relationships between prisoners and forensic psychologists.

Informed by our empirical experiences and reflections, alongside our professional and academic knowledge, we are questioning some elements of risk assessment practice that, while may be beyond the influence of individual practitioners, affect their ability to engage in the type of relational practice that (in our view, the vast majority of) both psychologists and prisoners want. We are therefore writing this as a provocation to the profession of forensic psychology, in order to enable reflection and change, where change may be needed.

DOI: 10.4324/9781003542377-15

To ensure that both of our voices were captured equally, we based this chapter on a reflective discussion about the topic of forensic psychological risk assessment in prisons.

Firstly, we need to consider the context of risk assessment, the structural, organisational and professional context, and how these things can influence our ability, motivation or permission to engage in effective relational practice:

Jason: Firstly, and potentially most prominently in the day-to-day work-ing lives of practitioners, is the pressure of caseload: this can't be helped given the population dynamics that are occurring in prison (think of the nature of sentences, the lengths of sentences, the number of reviews in sentences that need to take place). These population dynamics create stress factors at various points in practise. But more broadly, the prison as an institution creates this kind of bureaucratic monster that has overarching power over all elements of practise within prisons. And to some degree, the person you are working with retreats and the bureaucratic need, or the need to satisfy the bureaucracy comes to the fore. That is, there are rules, systems, procedures, administration to be fol-lowed/completed to meet the needs of the organisation, and this creates a distance between the practitioner and the person they're working with.[1] This distance allows the power to operate *on* peo-ple rather than *with* people. And within that context, there is an institutional barrier to the relational work that exists outside of the discipline and practise of forensic psychology.

Jo: That's interesting. As an individual you are a representative of your profession, and a representative of the system, which creates a barrier from the start. Whilst you as an individual practitioner might have good intentions, if the person you are assessing views you as a member of a profession with bad intentions, then you as an individual can be almost irrelevant. Having said that, it can be the relationship between you and the person you are assessing that becomes the vehicle for overcoming this.

Jason: Yeah, I think it's easy to forget that when you're working in an environment where you don't have the time, you don't have the space, and your caseload is manic. And actually, the key is to remember that the work is *one person on one person*. And if that bit doesn't go right, then it creates all sorts of problems for both parties. But when the demands mean that you just get that person out the way so you can get to the next one, and the next one, and then the team meeting in the afternoon, and then the programme that you've got to run, and then all the paperwork you need to get done ... the individual and the dynamic that you *want* to focus on gets lost.

Jo: Yes, we can lose sight of the individual in that context, and get carried away with meeting organisational demands. We need to remember the person in the middle of this, and the importance of and the stress created by risk assessment for individual prisoners. Yet I believe that relational practice can still be prioritised within these very real constraints.

Jason: Yeah. And it is crucial to remember that every person you deal with is vulnerable. In clinical work, this is drilled into you. The power differential between you, the institution that you're working in, and the person that you're working with is vast. That needs to be part of your conversation both in supervision and with the individual prisoners you are working with as a practitioner. Are those conversations occurring often enough?

Jo: That's interesting, because power differentials are so explicit in prison. When somebody's wearing a uniform, or when somebody's carrying keys, you can't avoid those manifestations of power. Yet I don't think we do have those conversations enough. Or we might have them in general, but not often in relation to a specific risk assessment. And when we don't have them, we risk becoming blind to the power we hold, and, as you say, to the vulnerability of the prisoner in that situation. We need to provide a basis to enable those conversations to be had more regularly, and in relation to individual relationships in risk assessment.

Jason: I think it's an important point, the kind of reflexivity that you would operate if you were doing a piece of research: What is my positionality? What are my biases? What are my backgrounds? What are my assumptions? There is an understanding of, and focus on, the harms that can come out of your work, but I think they can get forgotten in an individual risk assessment. You might have broad discussions in supervision about these issues, but how often do you use a discussion of these issues as a starting point for a risk assessment?

Jo: In my research, I discussed the weight of expectation and the weight of responsibility that forensic psychologist felt in relation to risk assessment: the high stakes nature of risk assessment, and of their own role within it. Risk assessment is stressful for psychologists, and I wonder if this pressure makes it harder to reflect on the bigger picture, on the individual at the centre of this very challenging context, and on ourselves as a representative of the subjugating environment. I think there is something about risk assessment that brings relational challenges into the sharpest focus. I've been reading some psychotherapeutic literature about boundaries and maintaining the safe relational space. And one of the rules, when navigating therapeutic boundaries, is that all of your intervention should be for the benefit of the "client". And of course quite a lot of our work, particularly in relation to risk assessment, is not purely for the benefit of the person in front of us.

Jason: There is an argument that risk assessments, and to some extent offending behaviour programmes, are mainly serving the interests of the criminal justice system, not even really the prison that they are occurring in, but the criminal justice system more broadly. Often other stakeholders come before the prisoner.

Jo: This highlights the extent to which individual prisoners can be forgotten or sidelined in the face of the needs of a huge and complex organisation. It's important that we acknowledge that there are other stakeholders of forensic psychological work: our work is for the benefit of the public, of the organisation, of the Parole Board, for example. That is simply a fact. But within that, we should remember that there are individual people, with individual needs and difficulties who are directly impacted by us as practitioners.

Jason: In my typology of forensic psychological practice,[2] the "humanists" were nearly always focused on the individual. But all the others were focused on something beyond the individual. So for the group I call "functionalists", it was about public protection. The "retributivists" were more punitive in their ideation of practise, and it was about public protection and the institution. For the "utilitarians" it was about the idea of the greater moral good; so even though they felt they were operating from a very moral practise, they still put prisoners way down the list of priorities in terms of their practise. I think because of the context in which that work is being done and the nature of that work, not only does it create a distance, but it also creates a hierarchy in terms of who the stakeholders are. That again, I don't think is often considered.

Jo: Yes, this is a good example of an opportunity for reflection and thinking about power and thinking about our practise within its context. In supervision discussions, have a reflective conversation about not only *who* the stakeholders of a risk assessment are, but what is the relative importance of their needs in this instance? This might enable us to have those reflections on power and on the influence of the organisational context, the bureaucratic power, on our practice.

Jason: I think two things are important here: 1: is recognising that the person in front of you is vulnerable; and 2: is recognising that they know your work is often not about them. Prisoners are not stupid. They know that if you're coming to do a risk assessment that it is often not operating in their favour. Because the risk assessment may be about what the institution needs. It may be about what the Parole Board needs. It may be about what the criminal justice system needs. And the focus in risk assessment on ideas of criminogenic risk may not represent how the prisoner wants to understand himself. If you think about that, what you've got is the individual who may perceive things as "I need help with X". But "X" is not thought about as a need, more in the manner in which it represents a "risk". And that is not in the interests of the individual, and they can see that happening to them. This is another area in which forensic psychologists could engage in reflection: what is it actually like to be "risk assessed"?

Jo: I haven't had that experience, so I don't know what it feels like. At a slight tangent, I had an experience that made me think even more about this. My family was applying for funding for my father's care. It's difficult to get this specific funding, and there are criteria you have to meet to be eligible for it. We had to have a hearing in which we tried to argue the reasons why my father should qualify for this money. My mother was the representative of our side and I attended to support her, and then there were people from various agencies, social services, health et cetera. My father was too unwell to participate himself by this point. The chair of the hearing took us through a list of criteria and asked us the extent to which we felt my father met these criteria. It felt like a risk assessment. One of the people present had never met my father and had stepped in at the last minute to cover for his colleague. He kept giving incorrect information about my father's illness and how it affected him. Luckily for me, I understand these processes. I understood what was going on and I could see the power issues. I'm reasonably articulate so I could stop and say "That's incorrect. You haven't met my father. This is the correct situation". My mother was all at sea because she was anxious and stressed. And it was an unbelievably aversive, stressful, exposing situation in which somebody's greatest vulnerabilities were put on the table and argued about. And it made me think about what it feels like to be an oral hearing and to have your life laid out on the table in front of people who you feel don't really know you and whose agenda is not your welfare, it's protecting something. Do you know what I mean?

Jason: Yeah, yeah. And every part of you is rendered, for want of a better term, naked. Every element of you is being exposed to powerful vision and judgement.

Jo: And I felt utterly judged and out of control, I felt like my voice wasn't heard. And I am quite good at standing up for myself. And then I started to think "what if there'd been nobody at the meeting who understood how these things worked?" Because none of us realised what it was going to be until we got into it. And I guess that many people coming up to their oral hearing don't have a voice, don't feel heard. And I thought when you're battling all of those things, you're perhaps not that articulate, it made me think about what it must be like for people. And I realise my life or my freedom wasn't at stake, but I think the experience had some parallels.

Jason: Yes, I do think it's a comparable point because what you're experiencing is an official process where the stakes are high and you are in a position of vulnerability. And you are being judged. And things that you think are contested are being taken as writ. And you've got all of those dynamics at play but have almost no power to either effect, mitigate, or shape the process that is occurring. A lot of prisoners are in a position of what Miranda Fricker would call "epistemic injustice".[3] Prisoners are kept from the knowledge about how risk assessments operate, by necessity. So they're expected to adhere to these ideas, and represent themselves in terms of these ideas, but they are kept from understanding what all of those ideas are, and how they operate and how they link. I understand that you have to keep that knowledge separate otherwise it opens risk assessment up potentially to manipulation or inefficacy. You know, in the same way that the "powers that be" who own that pot of money? They don't want you to know that subsection B of blah blah blah means that actually your father was entitled to it. It's not in their interest for you to know that piece of information.

Jo: Absolutely, because when we said "What are the criteria that determines who gets the money?" The response was "Oh well, it's assessed on an individual basis". It was opaque; we didn't know what we had to do to push it over the line. And that's so true of people in prison, isn't it? "What do I have to do to get out?" "Well, you just have to do your best. You just have to be honest". It's opaque.

Jason: Yeah, and also you are in a context where honesty is not always going to do you a favour. And going back to the point about the information that's taken as writ, that's quite problematic. The case narrative that shapes how the institution views/understands the person is the case narrative that has been constructed by the prosecutor, given the inculpatory points of evidence that existed at the time of prosecution. But that's a story. It's not necessarily the absolute truth. And even if the individual has pleaded guilty, and admits their offence(s), there may be points of the evidence against them that they contest or see as not quite true. Yet that version of events is being imposed upon them as if it's writ. And if they counter that, regardless of what the truth is, that creates a suspicion, because of the context in which they now exist. This reflects Miranda Fricker's idea of testimonial injustice,[4] where the person, because of who they are, because of the status that they have, their testimony is untrustworthy, especially if it counters the official narratives.

Jo: Yes, and it's so important for us as a profession to bear in mind the pattern of "This is what's written down, therefore this is the truth". And in this way, a mistake can become fact. Somebody talked about that in my research. A mistake is written in your file: do you challenge it and risk being seen as difficult and obstructive, or do you accept it as truth even though it's not the truth as you understand it, and you know that's not what happened? Do you accept a lie? Where does that sit with you?

Jason: A few of the psychologists that I interviewed said that one of the things that they had struggled with was finding errors, or finding outdated theory in reports. Certainly if you've got someone who's been in prison for 20 years, some of the psychological work or some of the assessment work that was done 20 years ago may now not be valid. And the psychologists felt it was important that they corrected errors, but they still had to note the error so that they could correct it. But that meant that the error and the correction would progress into the future together. It's almost like creating a false equivalence between what was true and what was not true in the file, rather than just saying "this is nonsense, outdated theory that we no longer value, please disregard this". They could not just get rid of the error, the error and the truth needed to operate together.

Jo: And that is madness, isn't it? I did an assessment with somebody several years ago and his name was spelled in several different ways in the reports. So I asked him how he spelled his name. I used the correct spelling in my report and put a footnote to say I had clarified the spelling of his name, and the spelling I was using was correct. And despite that, everything else that was written around this time, all of the other reports, the Parole Board decision letter et cetera, all continued to use the incorrect spelling. And I thought if somebody can't even own their own name, and be the bearer of the true spelling of their own name, then where are we?

Jason: I was working with a young lad in a Young Offenders Institute who was doing a life sentence. We were running a project and we wanted him to participate, but the prison refused to allow him to attend, because they said he was a "schedule one offender".[5] We clarified that the person had not committed an offence against a minor, but the prison was insistent that he had. In fact, he was 14 when the offence happened and the victim was 17, but the system had somehow switched the ages in the file. So for years he'd been going through the system where people thought his victim had been a minor. So I physically printed off the newspaper report that had the details in it, and insisted that the authorities checked the facts, as if this person were to be transferred into the adult prison estate with this error on his file, then it could create problems. It took six months from the point that I raised it for them to make a full correction. And he had no idea that any of this was happening. He didn't know that the reason he couldn't get a red band position, the fact that he was still being assessed at a higher risk level was because of an error, because of the way things had been recorded. This is deeply problematic, and no one had checked.

Next, thinking about the interaction between an assessor and the person being assessed, how do we do this part of a risk assessment with humanity and compassion when we are working in this context?

Jo: I think despite the challenges, my sense from my research was that most psychologists really want to do risk assessment well, with respect, transparency and humanity. And most of the prisoners I interviewed, even though they had had some difficult experiences, largely identified that a supportive relationship could make the difference. But how can we even begin to create a supportive relationship in a risk assessment context?

Jason: I think firstly, strategies for criticality and reflexive practise should be systematically built into organisational structures: i.e. practice guidelines for understanding prisoners' vulnerability in terms of their interactions in risk assessment, to ensure these conversations are happening at a profession level, at a team level, and then in supervision with individual practitioners. I think once that there is a policy of best practise in terms of the vulnerability of the people you're working with, then if someone is struggling with a relationship in a risk assessment they can ask their supervisor, or they can ask other team members. There's a degree to which if they're having to do this on their own, with their own idea of what professional practise is, then that leaves them vulnerable themselves. Because if they get it wrong or if they blur the line or they don't get the dual relationship issue just right, then actually then you could end up with more problems. So I think there needs to be a strategy that allows people to have those open conversations as an expected element of everyday practice.

Jo: So the relational level element of practice has to happen as part of a system? I guess quite a lot of individual level practitioners and teams (e.g. Psychologically Informed Planned Environments[6]) are doing the things that you'd like to think people are doing in terms of humanity and decency et cetera. It is important that this is embedded in organisational culture that supports this approach.

Jason: Also, think about in concrete terms, "When you're sat in front of an individual, how do you recognise that person's vulnerability?" "How do you recognise that this is a contested context?" "How do you understand that the case narrative and their narrative may have equal weight?" How do you balance all of these elements? One of the things that I found in my work was that every forensic psychologist I spoke to operated in a different way, even from people who were in their team. So the same prisoner, in the same prison, if they get risk assessed by two different psychologists at different points in their sentence, could experience two very different forms of practise. And that can leave a person discombobulated in terms of navigating the system, because it's like, "These risk assessments are objective, but they're being done in very different ways that may produce very different results".

Jo: I think there are some really thorny issues here. I think we are striving for a level of consistency and "objectivity" that is not achievable in a human-to-human task like risk assessment, and I worry that the focus on objectivity means that we might miss attending to our own biases and influences. I also worry that the use of the term "objective" confers a level of scientific status (and corresponding precision and accuracy) to an interpersonal task. If we use a simple dictionary definition of the term "objective", we get "based on real facts and not influenced by personal beliefs or feelings".[7] However, in my view, risk assessments simply are not an objective weighing up of the evidence in front of us: risk assessment is a complex process that is influenced directly and indirectly by all sorts of things. At the most basic level, as I argue in my research, as individuals, and as psychologists, we are multiply influenced. When we start a risk assessment, we are influenced by our past experiences, by the expectations of our supervisors, by the requirements of the prison we work in, and by the directions and expectations of the Parole Board. We are influenced by any media attention there might have been in recent months, to issues of serious further offences (i.e. the reporting around John Worboys[8]). Secondly, I do not believe that an interpersonal encounter can be objective: both parties bring their past experiences, their expectations, their hopes and fears to the interview. A risk assessment interview "is more than a linear exchange of information that will be identical every time",[9] rather, it will produce something slightly different every time, as it is a unique, intersubjective experience between two unique individuals. We talked earlier about the reputation we might have as psychologists when we turn up to do an assessment: this is impacted by the prisoner's previous experiences with psychologists, but also with professionals more broadly. So the prisoner's previous experiences with psychologists will influence how he thinks, feels and behaves during the interview, and his thinking, his feelings and his behaviour are likely to be different with different practitioners, who in turn are bringing their own past experiences to the encounter. And if we go back to our earlier discussion, about key facts in many situations being contested, sometimes we do not even start from a place of agreeing on the facts. So I do not think we ever conduct an "objective risk assessment", when both ourselves and the prisoner are multiply influenced, and when facts may be contested. Being unbiased, or neutral is different: we should all be working on identifying our biases, reflecting on them and challenging them. None of us should have a stake in the outcome of an assessment: we are there to make sense of a person and a context without fear or favour. Yet if we persist with the idea that we are being objective because we have never met the prisoner before, or because we are completing an SPJ, then this could easily prevent us from attending to, reflecting on and challenging our own biases, influences etc. And equally importantly, being assessed by somebody who does not know you, and who, given the power imbalances, the (likely) trauma history, and the prison context, you may well feel does not care about you, can be deeply distressing. Like the person who appeared at my father's hearing, who had never met him, saying with authority what he could and could not do. The feeling of not being known, which might mean we can tick an "objectivity" box in our reports, creates a legitimacy problem for with the person in front of us.

Jason: Trying to mitigate the biases that exist is a very different thing from objectivity. Ontologically and epistemologically, they're very different things. There are deep problems in the way that we perceive the idea of risk and that's before we even get into whether or not we can actually measure it objectively.

Jo: How do we balance these things better? How do we produce a robust and unbiased assessment, in which the individual being assessed feels known and humanised?

Jason: I was speaking to a group of lifers recently, who are coming up to their first parole review, so they are three years before tariff. One man said that what he really liked was that the person he was now working with was someone he had worked with in a previous institution many years ago. And he said that as they've known each other at two very distinct points in time, it allows the psychologist to see how he's changed. So his interactions with them now feel very different, and much more positive. Someone else had a similar experience. He said, "Actually, I don't come away from those meetings feeling negative anymore". When I asked him why he explained that, "well, you know, we're now talking about how I was abused as a child. And actually, it's the first time I've ever been able to talk about that". For years he felt he couldn't talk about that stuff with forensic psychologists, but now he can. Now he feels that he's able to talk about these painful experiences, and I think that's more to do with the people that are working with him, than it is with him.

Jo: Interesting. Do you think that's to do with the longevity, the consistency, or the presence of somebody familiar, with whom there is a connection?

Jason: I think it might do on both sides actually. Many of the psychologists that I spoke to described a frustrating element of their work as doing quite a lot of work with someone and then not seeing any consequence to it. Either the person goes or the report goes off and they never get any feedback. And we know that having or perceiving value in your labour is dependent upon seeing the outcomes of your labour. I found a lot of the psychologists I interviewed never had that. And I do think that longevity does allow them to see the outcome of their work, and therefore see some value in it. And it's much easier to do relational work when you feel valued, and when you see the work that you're doing as valuable.

Jo: Yes, that's a really good point. My colleague has had a couple of incidents recently where she's attended parole hearings for people she's known for years. And the Parole Board has specifically commented on how helpful it's been to have somebody able to comment on a duration or longevity of relationship. But that's inconsistent with the objectivity agenda; and with the service delivery model in places, where people are "parachuted in" to complete assessments. When I interviewed psychologists several of them talked about how difficult and frustrating it is being parachuted in, both relationally and organisationally.

Jason: Yeah. You've not had the time to build relationships.

Jo: There are lots of bits of the jigsaw suggesting that longevity and consistency are really important. One of the chapters in this book is from the perspectives of people who have been through the system.[10] One of the things they talk about is how unsettling it is when the professionals working with them change. And people have repeated experiences of, "you want me to put it all on the table, and then I'm never going to see you again". And this happens repeatedly. Yet the presence of a consistent person enables the work that needs to be done to reduce risk.

Jason: Yeah. You can also have a conversation that builds on previous conversations. So you don't need to revisit things. And if you've challenged one particular element of the case narrative and the person has said "well the files say that but this is the truth", you don't need to refer to that again. Whereas when that person disappears, the next person comes in with the case narrative that is in the file and actually rather than having made progress, you're having to go backwards: you're starting again continually.

Jo: I think we, as a profession, need a narrative that acknowledges the pain of that repetition; that draws our attention to the things that cause distress in risk assessment and encourages us to discuss them openly, compassionately. You could do that in a connecting, human way or you could do it in a checkbox way, "acknowledge a pain of previous assessments, tick; acknowledge racialised trauma, tick". We need to avoid policy or practice guidelines being used formulaically to cover our backs and encourage guidelines as a means of reducing the additional trauma and stress caused by the powerlessness of risk assessment.

Jason: I was doing some focus groups with lifers. One of them said openly that he had killed a family member, they'd had a fight and the family member had died. And he said

> It is the worst thing I've ever done and the worst thing I will ever do, and I am haunted by it. But every time I speak to someone, I have to relive that haunting, and I have to relive the trauma of it over and over and over and over again.

He was at the start of his sentence, and he already felt like that. He had another 15 years to go. And so for the next 15 years, he's going to be made to talk about that over and over again. And I don't think people quite understand the trauma that that's going to have, certainly not when they're parachuted in to do a piece of work. For an individual like that, it is likely that for the next 15 years, he is going to have to deal with that regularly, at least once a year, if not more frequently. And I think people become so focused on their need to complete the task ("I have to get this report done for the Parole Board") that they do not always have time to even think about the implications of their practice. One of the things I argue in my book is that there is ethical blindness (when you become blind to the impact of your practise) and moral blindness (when you fail to see people as human). Some of the bureaucratisation makes you morally blind to people, but actually some of that delivery pressure can make you ethically blind to the impacts that you're having on people. That's nothing to do with psychologists as individuals, it is how the system operates around them.

Jo: That's such a good point. Two things spring to mind. Firstly, the people who are writing a chapter from their lived experience perspective say exactly the same about people reliving their worst moments over and over again. And secondly, I wonder if the other thing that happens is that over a period of time, people learn to cut off the feelings of that repetition, so they narrate the events without the emotion, and then that becomes part of the problem.

Jason: Well, prisons do that to you anyway. People who are in prison live in a constant state of diffidence.[11] Even if you're not in a violent prison, the threat of violence is constant. So you have to engage in the emotional labour of mitigating your emotional response to threat. It's like being in a conflict zone. Even if you're not subject to bombing raids, the fact that you know that bombing raids are going on creates a similar kind of trauma response. And we know that it deadens people emotionally. You can get a divorce between the cognitive processing of an event and the emotional processing of the same event. For example, imagine every time you walk outside your door, you see someone getting bullied. You can't feel for that bullying victim every day because that's going to become too much for you. So you have to divorce what's happening to the individual from your emotional response. And if you do that day after day, month after month, year after year, decade after decade, that will fundamentally shape the manner in which you can emotionally respond to things. And then how does that then play in terms of risk assessment, in terms of assessing "empathy" or "remorse"? Is there recognition or acknowledgement of that?

Jo: And how does that play out in an oral hearing when the panel member asks the person to give an account of their offence, and then makes some sort of judgement about their emotional response. And whilst we know that factors like "empathy" and "remorse" do not have a strong relationship with recidivism,[12] someone's emotional response in an oral hearing may well affect how they, and consequently their evidence, are perceived by the Parole Board members.

Going back to the process of risk assessment, context is everything. How does somebody construe an event in a risk assessment context when they don't see you as somebody who is there for them, which you're probably not? And as a result of their views of you and your role, you take away a contextualised understanding of the person and their risk factors, which is likely to be very different from the contextualised version that the person presents to the psychologist instructed by their own lawyers. It took me a long time to think, well, obviously, the psychologist instructed by the lawyers reaches a different conclusion because the context in which that question has been asked is different; the context creates the answer and creates the assessment and creates your understanding. And this is why we need to acknowledge the broader influences on us in risk assessment, and use reflective supervision to mitigate against them: so we can acknowledge and address our biases.

Jason: Another thing is to have a proper critical understanding that what risk is, and what risk is not. For instance, the way we conceptualise risk is often racialised. If you think about Andrews and Bonta's work[13] which shaped a lot of the conceptualisation of criminogenic risk, their population was American, white working class, drug addicted, high frequency crimes, and they were operating from a white, middle-class, educated, victimised perspective. Those conceptions of risk may not match our population, and they certainly don't match racialised populations. I've written recently on the way that young Black men in prison are often conceptualised through a colonial and racialised lens which shapes how their risks are dictated.[14] This then shapes the manner in which they have to mitigate those risks. But none of those things are related to how they self-conceptualise. So in terms of class, racialisation, gender, I think there are deep problems in the way that we perceive the idea of risk. I also think there needs to be an understanding of the institutional pressures that interfere with good relational dynamics. One psychologist I interviewed said that ideally she would meet people four times: once to introduce herself, introduce the process, what was going to happen, build rapport; then a second time to talk through the process; the third meeting would be about actually doing the risk assessment and then the fourth meeting would be about feedback. And then, she said,

> But actually in reality, I get to meet them once. And I have to do all those four sessions in one sitting. And often I'll have to do the first three in one sitting and then skip the fourth because I just don't have the time for the feedback work.

And where that reality exists, I think it's very difficult to build the relational dynamics in. But I also had a conversation with an experienced practitioner recently, and she said that one of the things that's really changed for her is that there is much more awareness around issues of racism, and much more awareness of trauma in the person's background; and there's more awareness of issues around neurodivergence. And increased sensitivity to the issues the people in front of you are dealing with results in better practice.

Jo: I would agree. I think we are better at looking at the whole picture, looking at the entirety of somebody's life and understanding their offending in that context, we are better at thinking about their trauma, their neurodiversity, their experiences of victimisation, and prejudice. I don't know if we're better at the relational element of risk assessment though. A long time ago, when I joined the service, there weren't any PCL-Rs. There weren't any HCR 20s. Those things may have existed, but nobody really used them in British practise. So our risk assessments were conversations in which we tried to make sense of things with the person, and consequently our relationships were different. Prisoners probably didn't feel checked off against a list of risk factors, because there was no list. And the fact that there was no structure or guidance to attend to meant that we attended more to the person in front of us. We moved away from this "unstructured clinical judgement" approach for good reason, as the evidence suggested that its predictions about recidivism were no better than chance.[1516] But with the shedding of unstructured clinical judgement came a prioritisation on risk assessment protocols at the expense of the interpersonal elements of risk assessment. How do we apply SPJs, and keep focus on the relational bits?

Jason: So a thing I proposed many years ago was having psychologists operate in the same way that barristers do on a "taxi rank" basis. As someone is coming up for parole, they are assigned both someone to do a risk assessment report for the system and someone to do advocacy. So like a taxi rank, you pick up the next piece of work, whatever that is. That approach could address issues of "adversarial bias" or "allegiance bias" (but would impact on the "longevity" mentioned earlier). Adversarial bias refers to the principal that people shape their evidentiary response to whoever has commissioned them in an adversarial system. So there's a very famous paper[17] where made-up case files (based on real ones, but anonymised) were sent to 108 prominent forensic psychologists and psychiatrists in the USA. The researchers flagged the files either as defence or prosecution cases, and they asked the practitioners to draw conclusions about risk. They found wide variance in these conclusions. If the practitioners thought they were operating for the prosecution they were more likely to offer higher risk scores. Whereas if they thought they were operating for the defence, they were more likely to allocate lower risk scores. These results have been replicated in other contexts, for example when asking forensic chemists to interpret drug tests, testing urine samples. So even when something is supposed to be objective, the outcome depends on the perspective of the "assessors". This is a good example of how biases can operate without our awareness.

Jo: I mean really any psychological risk assessment should not be for or against anybody: we are neither prosecution or defence, we should be neutral and unbiased. We should not have a stake in it, it is about answering the question we are asked to address.

None of us, whoever instructs us (HMPPS or a prisoner's legal representative) should set out with an agenda, we should not be taking sides, or seen to be taking sides. I think firstly, sometimes our anxiety about being held responsible for a recommendation to release that goes wrong means we do have a stake in it. We have an emotional stake in it. And secondly, I think when we get to an oral hearing, people can become wedded to their opinion and see it like "Are you going to win?" And it's not about me winning. If the Parole Board don't like my view, that's their decision. I have a view, and it's my job to explain my view. I don't even think it's about defending my view, it's about explaining my view and if they don't like it or they prefer somebody else's view, that is their job. And the sense that I have a stake in an oral hearing and if the parole board don't go with what I think then "I've lost", that's a problem.

Jason: I think this may relate to not seeing the products of your labour. I wonder if it might be related to psychologists being invested in their reports because that report is the product of their labour? So it's not what that report does, more the product becomes narrowed to the report itself. Because that's the only thing they can see as a product.

Jo: So if their report is disagreed with and a decision goes the other way, then that's a direct reflection on your skill and your professional identity?

We have talked about the history, the context and the pressures in risk assessment. Have things improved?

Jason: I think being more trauma aware, being more neurodiversity aware, being more aware of the manner in which those things impact on traditional ideas in forensic psychological practise, I think has necessarily led to an improvement. However, whilst there has been an improvement in relational practise, I think one of the toxic things that has happened over the same period is this "epistemic bleed": that is, when psychological terms such as "shallow effect" or "ideas of grandiosity" are used by non-psychologist practitioners in a non-psychologically informed way. So non-psychologists are using the same kind of language even when they may not understand the full meaning or implications of the term. You know, I've heard prison officers use the term "psychopath" as if it's not a continuum or a spectrum. When people use the term as an idea of a reified personality, like a thing in and of itself, that is problematic. This could be described as "psychological bleed" – the way that forensic psychological ideas have begun to bleed into other discourses in prisons and the criminal justice system.

Jo: Do you think that's a consequence of how dominant the psychological rhetoric is? We have talked about psychological power in prisons, how we are seen as holding power and influence, how our views and opinions carry significant weight in the parole process, for example. Perhaps our narrative/terminology is seen as carrying power and weight as well?

Jason: Yeah, and it is not necessarily promoted and promulgated by forensic psychologists, but it has been promulgated by the prison service and the Parole Board. So the more weight that they have given to those ideas, the more those ideas have spread in a way that's actually not helpful. The proliferation of true crime media is also a problem here. The concepts now have common use, common value, but they're divorced from their forensic/clinical meaning.

Jo: I discussed this in my research, as we mentioned briefly earlier, the power of the psychology report and other professionals waiting for your report before they reach their own conclusions. And actually, all professions have a different voice. And those voices should remain unique. That doesn't mean that we work in silos, but that we work together but with our own professional knowledge. When I do a piece of work with one of the occupational therapists in our team, they always see something different to me, and it is always valuable. And it's brought home to me the value of specific professional expertise as opposed to exactly the thing you say, that everything suddenly becomes a little bit uniform. And when I think about the development of forensic psychology, I think there have been periods in our history where we have devalued our specialist psychological knowledge to the point where we're seen as not having any special expertise or any special knowledge, rather it is all "common sense". I wonder if we've tried to distance ourselves from the idea of being "experts" or having expertise, to the point that we have forgotten that we do have some specialist skills and knowledge.

Jason: I think part of the problem is that some of those psychological ideas have kind of bled into the general discourse of disciplinary practise. And that's a dangerous way of thinking because it's using an idea that carries the symbolic weight of forensic psychological expertise, but with none of the substance. That may also get in the way of relational practise: I think on the one hand there's lots of good practise that's now happening in terms of relational work. But I think the discursive context in which forensic psychological practise is now operating could undermine relational practice because terms and ideas are being used wrongly by others, which has unintended consequences. Take the example of shallow affect: there may be all sorts of reasons for that, you know, from trauma to being neurodiverse, or the emotional toll of being in prison we mentioned earlier. But when someone who doesn't have that range of understanding adopts terminology or ideas, I think that becomes a problem and I think that can create issues for the way that relational work operates.

Jo: Well, I guess if you think about what we said at the very beginning about what should we anticipate reputationally when we meet somebody, if there's a context of psychological language being used in that way, and used in a way that probably hasn't benefited or hasn't served that individual well and we're associated with that as a narrative, then that's a hard place to start from.

To summarise, we have discussed some of the barriers that exist for us as forensic psychological practitioners. Here are some ideas about how we can overcome them, both systemically/organisationally, and individually:

1 **Be human:** First and foremost, remember that you are "a human being in a room with a human being".[18] It will be difficult to do anything without a connection. This means being wholly transparent about your role, your purpose, and whose needs the risk assessment is serving. It will mean seeing the person as an individual, and understanding their unique needs, experiences, fears and history. It will mean thinking hard about what they need to enable them to participate in the assessment.

2 **Contextual awareness:** When we start a risk assessment, before coming to the specific risk assessment tool, start by thinking about "What is the context in which I'm conducting this assessment?" or "What are the power dynamics in play here?", "What are this person's vulnerabilities and how do I acknowledge and work with them? How do I give them a voice in this process?" Think about starting risk assessment planning with reflections about the context.

3 **Allegiance bias:** Continually reflect on our own biases, privilege and areas of blindness in our practice; engage in reflexive thought about and within our clinical practice. Seek out advice, supervision and support from people who will **challenge** us.

4 **Reputational legacy:** What experience has the person had with (1) psychologists and (2) criminal justice professionals? What might their expectations be of you? How can you acknowledge this and, if necessary, mitigate it? How can you begin to shift the reputational legacy?

5 **Trauma history:** Understand the person's assessment history, how this may have been re-traumatising, demeaning, de-individualising. Think about the person's relational history/trauma: how might that manifest itself in the assessment context? How can we enable them to participate in the assessment, despite their history of relational trauma? Discuss

explicitly and genuinely, talk about how we can mitigate against that in this piece of work.

6 **Bureaucratic pressures:** Think about how, and in what ways, the bureaucratic pressures that we face impact on, and militate against, our relational activity and relationship building with people. Maintaining a healthy critical and reflexive stance in relation to the institution, its interests, and where and how they may clash with our practice is essential to maintaining an ethical practice and good relational work. Create and share strategies to overcome or mitigate these effects so that they become key practices within (and without or across) teams.

7 **Caseload pressures:** Think about the stress and anxiety that can be invoked by increasing and unmanageable caseloads. Reflect on the pressure of the high-stakes work, and the pressure of the responsibility we feel as forensic psychologists. How does that impact on us in our work? Develop individual, team, regional, and national strategies for recognising and mitigating these elements of the work that go beyond individualistic measures and coping strategies.

8 **Conceptual legacies:** Think about how old and outdated ideas may still exist within file data and how, in what way, where, and when, they need to be challenged or rejected. As a social scientific endeavour, the correcting of erroneous data, concepts and theory should be standard practice and not a taboo.

9 **Case narrative dominance:** Be aware that the case narrative presented at trial, and which shapes the initial file data, is but a story created from inculpatory evidence to convince a jury of someone's guilt, and we should remain sensitive to those presentational dynamics. It is not always the substantive truth of the events, motivations and causes of the index offence.

10 **Epistemic bleed:** Practitioners should be aware of, and open to challenging, and be seen to be open to challenging, the erroneous or uninformed use of specialist concepts from forensic psychology. This is not just about maintaining the rigour and explanatory efficacy of those concepts, but also trying to mitigate the unintended/negative effects of their wrongful use.

Jo: To conclude, we hope that our conversation has provided a focus for readers' own reflections on their role and their practice. Risk assessment is central both to the work of forensic psychologists in prisons, and to the lives of people serving indeterminate and other types of prison sentence. It is therefore beholden on us as psychologists to conduct this task with compassion, awareness and empathy.

Notes

1 See Weber, M. (1968). *Economy and Society*. Translated by G. Roth and C. Wittich, Bedminster Press.

2 Warr, J. (2020). *Forensic Psychologists: Prisons, Power, and Vulnerability*. Emerald Publishing Limited.
3 Fricker, M. (2007). *Epistemic Injustice: Power and the Ethics of Knowing*. Oxford University Press.
4 Fricker, M. (2007). *Epistemic Injustice: Power and the Ethics of Knowing*. Oxford University Press.
5 This is a term that was historically used to refer to people who had committed sexual or violent offences against children; it is no longer in official usage but remains a term used unofficially within prisons.
6 Freestone, M., & Kuester, L. (2024). Psychologically Informed Planned Environments. *The Wiley Handbook of What Works in Correctional Rehabilitation: An Evidence-Based Approach to Theory, Assessment and Treatment*, 327–336.
7 https://dictionary.cambridge.org/dictionary/english/objective.
8 Pollard, C., & Lucas, J. (2018, January 15th). 'Soft justice' demands. Shrink who urges leniency for pervs backed rapist Worboys' release. *The Sun*. Retrieved from https://www.thesun.co.uk/news/5348435/shrink-who-urges-leniency-for-pervs-backed-rapist-worboys-release/.
9 Shingler, J. (2019). Understanding psychological risk assessment: Exploring the Experiences of Psychologists, Indeterminate Sentenced Prisoners and Parole Board Members (Unpublished doctoral dissertation). University of Portsmouth, Hampshire, United Kingdom.
10 See Chapter 1, this volume.
11 Crewe, B., Warr, J., Bennett, P., & Smith, A. (2014). The emotional geography of prison life. *Theoretical Criminology, 18*(1), 56–74.
12 E.g., Mann, R. E., Hanson, R. K., & Thornton, D. (2010). Assessing risk for sexual recidivism: Some proposals on the nature of psychologically meaningful risk factors. *Sexual Abuse, 22*(2), 191–217.
13 Andrews, D. A., & Bonta, J. (2006). *The Psychology of Criminal Conduct*. Anderson Publishing.
14 Warr, J. (2023). Whitening black men: Narrative labour and the scriptural economics of risk and rehabilitation. *The British Journal of Criminology, 63*(5), 1091–1107, https://doi.org/10.1093/bjc/azac066; See also https://hmiprisons.justiceinspectorates.gov.uk/hmipris_reports/the-experiences-of-adult-black-male-prisoners-and-black-prison-staff/.
15 E.g., Grove, W. M., & Meehl, P. E. (1996). Comparative efficiency of informal (subjective, impressionistic) and formal (mechanical, algorithmic) prediction procedures: The clinical-statistical controversy. *Psychology, Public Policy and Law, 2*, 293–323.
16 Viljoen, J. L., Goossens, I., Monjazeb, S., Cochrane, D. M., Vargen, L. M., Jonnson, M. R., Blanchard, A. J. E.,Li, S. M. Y. & Jackson, J. R. (2025). Are risk assessment tools more accurate than unstructured judgments in predicting violent, any, and sexual offending? A meta-analysis of direct comparison studies. *Behavioral Sciences & the Law, 43*(1), 75–113.
17 Murrie, D. C., Boccaccini, M. T., Guarnera, L. A., & Rufino, K. A. (2013). Are forensic experts biased by the side that retained them? *Psychological Science, 24*(10), 1889–1897.
18 Shingler, J., Sonnenberg, S. J., & Needs, A. (2018). Risk assessment interviews: Exploring the perspectives of psychologists and indeterminate sentenced prisoners in the United Kingdom. *International Journal of Offender Therapy and Comparative Criminology, 62*(10), 3201–3224.

12 Bringing compassion to relationships in forensic settings

Kerensa Hocken

Introduction

The therapeutic relationship is understood to be a primary mediator of therapeutic success (see Norcross & Lambert, 2018), and quite rightly, significant attention is given to methods for building therapeutic relationships in research and in training for mental health practitioners. Given that the histories of people in forensic systems tend to be characterised by adversity and in particular relational adversity (Ogilvie et al., 2014), the challenges to building and maintaining a therapeutic relationship in forensic settings are understandable. However, beyond histories of relational adversity, there are additional obstacles to successful therapeutic relating that are unique to forensic settings, the dual role phenomenon (Ward, 2013) being central. This highlights the correctional role inherent in forensic practitioners' work; as figures of the state justice system, they must undertake assessments which will have significant implications for a person's future, including decisions about detainment. Not surprisingly, there is now a sound body of research which shows that people in forensic systems are distrustful of forensic psychologists (Maruna, 2011; Shingler et al., 2019). As if these challenges to therapeutic relating were not great enough, in forensic work, we are trying to build trusting relationships with another person who has caused harm, sometimes fatally. It is anathema to our basic survival instincts to do this, and thus we need to overcome our innate desire to gain distance from the person and instead move closer in. That is not an easy task, and it highlights the imperative for forensic practitioners to pay close attention to the variables that influence therapeutic relating, if we are to create safe working relationships to support rehabilitative change.

The environment of forensic work poses a unique challenge to safe relating. Rather than being supportive of relating, prisons in particular are observed to be trauma generating rather than trauma healing (Kelman, 2024, and see Chapter 6, this volume). The behavioural literature illuminates three core conditions that provoke feelings of threat: punishment, non-reward and novelty/unfamiliarity. The subsequent common responses to these conditions are emotional arousal; shut down of reward-driven

DOI: 10.4324/9781003542377-16

behaviour; and attention focused on threat (Gray, 1985). Such conditions are salient in forensic settings, particularly in secure environments such as prisons. It is no wonder then that relationships are hard to build in the presence of these threats. For many forensic practitioners, there are limited actions we can take to change the environment; however, we can look to our own behaviour to promote safe relating and ultimately behaviours that support rehabilitation. Consequently, it is incumbent on forensic practitioners to hold the therapeutic relationship as a primary aim of our work and to invest in the development of knowledge and skills that enable us to build relationships in the most challenging circumstances. Sitting at the foundation of this is the requirement to understand human relating. Attachment theory (Bowlby, 1980) is perhaps the cornerstone of evolutionary relational theory and guides practitioners to understand and create the conditions for secure attachment. However, in forensic practice, far less attention is given to the evolved psychological and physiological mechanisms that guide relating more broadly. This chapter sets out a case for the need to understand these mechanisms, to deepen our understanding of how to build and maintain successful therapeutic relationships in forensic settings. Evolutionary theory has much to offer here, as it outlines the context in which our attachment systems developed. In doing so, it orients practitioners to notice broad aspects of relating that are at play and to manage the relationship effectively.

Origins of human social relating

Humans are complex, biological organisms, with one primary imperative: survival. In the case of mammals (including humans), the challenge is to survive long enough to reproduce, and then nurture and rear offspring until they are capable of independent survival. There are multiple complex functions which support the ability for survival, including the basic in-built survival responses common to all animals: fight, flight, freeze, flop and drop (LeDoux, 1998). Mammals are group-dependent for survival, and they are heavily reliant on other members of their species. This is particularly the case for humans, where several features of our design leave us heavily reliant on the care of others. Compared with most other mammals, we are born in a relatively premature state of development, and for several years, we are entirely dependent on another human for survival. Pregnant females are dependent on group members for essential care when they are incapacitated, for example in the late stages of pregnancy, during labour and immediately after birth. This places humans in a very vulnerable position, but luckily, humans have an emotional architecture that provides us with a motivation to care for others and to nurture, and to seek out and receive care (Dunbar, 2014). Other species, such as amphibians, get along nicely without these motivations: but without them, the survival of a group-oriented species would be compromised (Sapolsky, 1990).

As well as motives to care, mammals also have motives to compete, an essential survival skill where resources are scare. These motives can lead to different types of strategies for group living and control of resources. For example, groups which are heavily motivated by care tend to have cooperative ways of relating and a "care and share" method for managing resources. Those with a competitive mindset tend to have more adversarial ways of relating and a "control and hold" approach to resources (Gilbert, 2021). For example, baboons are highly competitive, with troops being led by dominant and aggressive males (Sapolsky, 1993); bonobos, however, are highly cooperative and have a flatter hierarchy (Furuichi, 2011). Humans demonstrate both types of strategy, with the competitive "control and hold" approach being more prevalent in environments of high threat and competition for resources (Gilbert, 2021; Jetten et al., 2020).

Self-conscious emotions

Given the human dependence on others for survival, our skills for relating have some clever features to maximise the likelihood that others will care for and not harm us. It is a well-established evolutionary principle that, like other mammals, we are rank-based animals (e.g. see Social Rank Theory, Stevens & Price, 2016). We relate to others via a system of hierarchy, or rank, in which some members of a group are dominant/superior, and others are submissive/inferior (Gilbert et al., 1995; Koski et al., 2015). To live successfully in a group with rank-based structures, it is important that we are aware of where we fit in the hierarchy so we can behave accordingly and minimise within-group conflicts that are a threat to group and species survival (Breggin, 2015). In short, we need to be able to get along with those around us. Fortunately, humans are equipped with an emotional system that guides us to be sensitive to others' appraisals of us and thus our status within a group. This system is that of "self-conscious emotions" (Gilbert, 2022; Tangney & Fisher, 1995). These are emotional states, such as guilt or shame, that are more self-relevant than the primary emotions present from birth (such as anxiety). Since they rely on an ability to differentiate self from others, they do not emerge until children begin to recognise themselves as separate from others. They work by orienting us to be specifically sensitive to others' feelings and intentions towards us, and for this reason have been described as having a "sociometer" function (De Hooge, 2014). Once we notice what others think or feel about us, these self-conscious emotions motivate us to respond accordingly. If we detect possible hostility, we can fight, fly or even appease, and if we detect cues for care or mating, we can pursue or reciprocate. Mistaking others' appraisals of us could have disastrous consequences. Therefore, effective group living relies on an ability to notice, understand and care about what others think and feel about us. There are a range of self-conscious emotions that guide us to do this; the key emotions considered most relevant for forensic work are shown in Table 12.1. This is not

Table 12.1 Self-conscious emotions and their influence on social behaviour

	External shame	Internal shame	Humiliation	Authentic pride	Hubristic pride	Guilt
How we think about relationships	Competitive	Competitive	Competitive	Cooperative and caring	Competitive	Cooperative and caring
What we pay attention to	Mind of the other	Our own mind	Mind of the other	Mind of the other	Mind of the other	Mind of the other
Thoughts	They think badly of me	I think badly of me	How dare they think badly of me	I like helping others and feeling valued	I am better than others	I have hurt someone
Emotions	Anxious	Depressed	Angry	Eudemonic joy, contentment	Hedonistic joy, anxiety to retain status	Sorrow/remorse
Behaviour	Defensive	Defensive, attack self	Attack to harm and avenge	Cooperation, resource gathering	Dominance and subjugation	Reparative

exhaustive, and other examples of self-conscious emotions include embarrassment, possibly a milder version of shame (Walker & Knauer, 2011) and gratitude.

These different self-conscious emotions exert themselves over our psychology and biology and influence information processing systems such as what we pay attention to, how we think and feel about others, ourselves and our actions. They guide us to behave for group inclusion to maximise survival. For example, where there is threat because we believe others think badly of us, as is the case for external shame, we will ensure safety by defending or avoiding. Box 1 provides an example of how we might see this in forensic work.

Box 1   External shame

One of Ali's convictions includes a sexual assault as part of a burglary. He seems open and talkative about his offending but when you ask him about this conviction, he says it was his co-defendant who assaulted the woman while he was in another room. He moves the conversation back to his other offending and when you try to return to the sexual assault, he tells you he will not talk about it and will not make eye contact.

An important element here is that there are more self-conscious emotions which orient to signs of threat and rejection from others than those that orient to signs of care or admiration. This is not a coincidence: we are threat-focused animals with a negativity bias, to err on the side of caution (Gilbert, 2024). If we consider our primitive past, this makes sense: it is better to be more worried about a noise in the bushes and run or hide, than to be nonchalant and get too close, only to risk being eaten. We must remember that for approximately two million years (Hart, 2009), humans were in the mid-food chain and subject to predation. It is important to be vigilant to threats if you are likely to be eaten. In effect, humans were prey animals, and prey animals are characterised by anxiety and flight (avoidance) as the primary safety strategy. Anxiety and flight responses were likely strongly selected for by evolution as a trait that maximises survival. Traits that maximise survival become a stable feature of a species, and thus anxiety and flight remain features from our ancestral history. Of course, evolution has gifted Homo sapiens with more refined cognitive and language skills which have seen our transition from prey to predator and no doubt equipped us to be the apex predator we are today (Ben-Dor et al., 2021). However, our predisposition for anxiety remains: evolution operates slowly, and it makes little sense to discard such a strongly embedded survival skill.

This combination of a heavy reliance on others for survival, with a threat sensitivity bias, therefore primes us for self-conscious emotions weighted towards threat. When this evolutionary backdrop becomes fused with life experiences of unsafe relationships, the outcome is an individual who is necessarily highly vigilant to relational threat, well defended and reactive. In these biopsychosocial circumstances, it is not surprising that people harm people, and indeed, self-conscious emotions are shown to be highly salient motivators for harmful behaviour (e.g. Bushman & Baumeister, 1998).

Self-conscious emotions are common to all humans and give us important clues to the motivation of relating. Although they may appear similar in practice, each self-conscious emotion has its own unique motive and behaviour pattern which we should be sensitive to if we are to understand the person or people in front of us. If we understand how self-conscious emotions guide human behaviour (including our own) and if we learn to spot which self-conscious emotions are active, we can be more adept at responding in helpful ways that maximise success in safe relating. If we are not attuned to this, we risk damaging a relationship by unintentionally leaving someone feeling shamed or humiliated. There will be clients who may often feel threatened by interactions with us, particularly when past experiences have primed them to expect rejection. While we cannot eradicate this predisposition, we can behave in ways that minimise the likelihood of aggravating it. This chapter will now go on to examine the key self-conscious emotions above in more detail and consider their relevance to forensic work.

Shame

Shame is a self-conscious emotion relatively well documented in the forensic literature, largely in relation to having a role in offending (Gold et al., 2011; Proeve & Howells, 2002; Tangney, 2014). However, it can be poorly defined and not well understood, and it tends to get conflated with guilt; however, the two are very different. Shame is essentially a signal detection system for devaluation or negative appraisal and instils a sense that the self is damaged. Shame comes from a submissive mindset meaning we judge the appraisals to be valid, or we judge the appraiser as being more important than us, and we know their opinion counts in the eyes of others, even if we think it is invalid. Shame can be experienced because of something we have done, but it can also be experienced because of things we are not responsible for, such as body shape, or what others have done to us, such as bullying or abuse (Tracy et al., 2007). Strategies to stay safe centre around image repair, including denial, avoidance, withdrawal and appeasement. Shame is a painful feeling, and research shows that the pain of rejection and shame originates from the same neurophysiological pathways as physical pain (Kross et al., 2011), and thus, the motivation to ease shame-related pain is significant.

There are two types of shame that orient our thinking and subsequent behaviour very differently. External shame allows us to notice *others'* devaluing or critical appraisals of us and we are motivated to find ways to preserve safety and prevent any possible rejection because of these judgements. Basically, we notice when others do not like or value us and we care about this. Internal shame, however, enables us to notice the critical and devaluing judgements of *ourselves towards ourselves* and is characterised by a hostile, angry and critical inner relationship with ourselves. This critical voice tends to have a dominating tone and wants to punish us. The overt behaviour is similar to external shame (withdrawal, avoidance) but can be accompanied by signs of self-punishment such as self-injury or self-debasement. Box 2 shows an example of internal shame in a forensic setting. For either experience of shame, there is a strongly felt sense of disconnection and isolation from others, and the withdrawal and avoidance behaviour it motivates leads to the maintenance of disconnection.

Box 2   Internal shame

During an assessment interview with Chris, you ask about his experiences of school and learning. He looks down and tells you he has dyslexia and that he is stupid.

As a practitioner, it is essential to know if the other is experiencing shame and which type (they can co-occur) so that we can understand the function of the behaviour in context and take steps to create safe relating. The question of context has critical relevance here, since the context of forensic work carries inherent adversarial and stigmatising ways of relating (Walton, 2019). This can prime forensic staff to interpret the common shame responses of withdrawal, denial, avoidance and appeasement as signalling oppositional behaviour, resistance, deception and thus risk. Denial is one shame response that for some time was ubiquitously accepted as signalling risk in people with sexual convictions (Ware & Blagden, 2016), but research shows that it is not empirically related to recidivism (Mann et al., 2010) and is commonly motivated by desire to uphold an acceptable identity (Blagden et al., 2014), a common shame response. For many with a sexual conviction, image repair will feel out of reach, hence strategies such as denial and avoidance take hold and can prevent engagement with services. Practitioners need to be aware of their potential to pathologise normal human responses to self-conscious emotions (Walton, 2019): that is, we must remember that behaviours such as withdrawal, avoidance and denial may not reflect resistance, but rather entirely predictable responses to shame in the context of trauma and coercive environments. As noted above, this can be particularly relevant in relation to people with sexual convictions who are often targeted, isolated or treated poorly both in prison and community forensic settings (McNaughton et al., 2018).

Given the motivations towards withdrawal and avoidance, it is no wonder that shame is considered one of the greatest therapeutic challenges (DeYoung, 2019). Shame proneness is greater in people who have experienced adverse childhood experiences (ACEs) (Hassanpour et al., 2025; Karan et al., 2014). ACEs are highly prevalent in offending populations (Ford et al., 2019; Levenson et al., 2015), and as expectedly, there are elevated levels of shame in sexual offending populations (Garbutt et al., 2023a). Shame has also been shown to be a functional mediator between ACEs and causing harm to self and others (Garbutt et al., 2023b). People in forensic services then face the double stigma of having been harmed and of having harmed. Shame should therefore be a key consideration for forensic practitioners, since our interpretation of shame behaviour could pathologise and ironically create further shame. It is crucial that we can view clients as humans, reacting to humans, and to actively work to be validating, open and empathic not only in our interactions but also in our own understanding of the client.

Humiliation

Humiliation is an important self-conscious emotion that has less recognition in forensic work. Like shame, humiliation is also a signal detection system for devaluation and critical appraisal, but it has a dominant rather than submissive mindset. Whereas shame apportions responsibility for the criticism to the self, humiliation rejects the criticism of others as unjust. The concept of humiliation is subject to debate, and some authors view humiliation as a form of shame that motivates an attack on others rather than the self (Nathanson et al., 1992). Either way, the central feature is behaviour characterised by anger directed outward at the appraiser (the source of the "put down"), aimed to "down-rank" them, through attack (verbal or physical). It has a vengeful motive and is highly relevant to violence (Gilligan, 1996, 2021; Walker & Knauer, 2011) and in particular extremist violence (Abbas et al., 2025; Lindström, 2023). Allied concepts in forensic work are the risk factor of "grievance thinking" (Barnett, 2011) and the personality trait of narcissism (Grapsas et al., 2020). However, conceptualised as humiliation, it helps us to have a clearer idea about the function of the behaviour, which may be camouflaged by the primary emotion of anger. Forensic systems, such as prisons, which have a clear hierarchical structure and run on creating a dominant mindset on the part of the institution, will be very challenging for those with a mindset towards humiliation, where they will be primed for humiliated responses. Humiliation is likely to feel challenging for practitioners since anger is naturally a more threatening emotion to be faced with. A person experiencing humiliation may make deliberate moves to down-rank and create a sense of inferiority in us, including behaving in ways that feel threatening or intimidating, often as a way to restore a sense of control or self-worth. These responses are rarely about us personally, but about the dynamics of rank, power and shame. Box 3 provides an example of how we might see this in forensic work.

Box 3   Humiliation

You are undertaking a risk assessment for Susie. The first meeting is to introduce yourself, explain the assessment process and gain consent. When you explain you are a forensic psychologist in training, she becomes angry and says you are not qualified to assess her, and as someone at least 20 years younger than her, you do not have the life experience to understand her.

Pride

Pride is a self-conscious emotion discussed in forensic work, but it orients attunement to social valuation (rather than devaluation) from others. As with shame, there are two types. "Authentic pride" is noticing the admiration of others, and wanting to maintain it, and to do that in ways which benefit the group/other. It has a cooperative mindset and reflects the notions of "making good" (Maruna, 2001) and "giving back" (Perrin et al., 2018), seen as pivotal in desistance from offending. These positive appraisals become internalised to form a sense of self-worth. Authentic pride is therefore something we should facilitate in our clients.

"Hubristic pride", however, has a superior mindset and is concerned with an expectation of admiration, and a fear of losing it. This motivates behaviour to maintain admiration including by subjugation and, therefore, is a driver of harmful behaviour. Hubristic pride is a rank-based mindset which has a hierarchical view of self as superior and others as inferior. It is commonly seen alongside humiliation since those in this superior mindset are concerned with maintaining their status and will behave to promote themselves and simultaneously demote the status of others.

As practitioners, we need to be aware of these different types of pride. We need to guard against pathologising any displays of pride and misinterpreting authentic pride as impression management or even hubristic pride. This has clear implications for understanding and managing risk, particularly thinking about the value of protective factors and supporting clients to find sources of authentic pride so that we can facilitate their development. We must also be aware that, like shame, both types of pride might co-occur for the same person. Box 4 demonstrates this.

Box 4   Pride

Authentic pride

Patrick is well known for supporting other prisoners and for mentoring prisoners who are struggling with prison life. He is particularly sensitive to those with disabilities or learning needs. Patrick says he gets a sense of fulfilment and purpose from helping.

Hubristic pride

Patrick is a hard worker in the craft workshop and maintains very high standards in his work. He is a talented woodworker and brings examples of his work to your meetings. He tells you that without him, the craft shop would not operate and the staff that run it are not as skilled as he is.

Guilt

Guilt has a care-based mindset, something which motivates us to enhance the welfare of others. Guilt allows us to notice where we are responsible for causing harm to others and motivates us to repair it, in contrast to shame, which motivates concealment of the harm. Therefore, guilt is restorative, and it motivates pro-social behaviour, and it is something we should facilitate. The experience of guilt feels bad, and where restoration or repair is impossible, the guilt can feel intolerable. The reparative action motivated by guilt does not necessarily have to be in direct reparation to the victim, and in some cases, that might not be possible or feasible. However, reparations can be directed in other ways, akin to the "giving back" notion discussed by Perrin et al. (2018). These reparative actions do not need to be directed outwards however: an internal commitment to work on the self, such that harm is not caused to another person again is a reparative act. Shame can co-occur with guilt, and this can be functional: "I have hurt and I feel bad for being devalued". However, shame can risk overshadowing guilt and becoming preoccupied with the fear of judgement to the self rather than the hurt caused and the need to repair.

Responding to self-conscious emotions

There are several factors that influence which self-conscious emotions are activated. These include the social ranking of those making the appraisal, whether the appraisal is made in public or private and our judgements about the legitimacy and justness of others' appraisals (Torres & Bergner, 2010). In our role as forensic practitioners, with professional qualifications, we are automatically in a position of status and power. Added to this will be the visual cue for power such as keys in secure settings, in some cases, personal alarms and formal clothing. We will all wear some form of identification, which will include our name and our job role. Even before we speak to an individual, we are already defined in the interaction by something we have achieved (professional standing, qualifications), and in some cases, the nature of the meeting is to talk about the worst thing the person has ever done. In cases where our role is to assess risk or need relating to offending, we are automatically in a position where we must offer a public opinion of the person. These relational circumstances are primed to elicit threat-based self-conscious emotions.

Humiliation is the likely response from someone with a superior mindset who feels criticised by someone they view as having lower status. What defines "low status" from the client's perspective will vary, but it could include things like gender, age, ethnicity, qualification level, position in the organisation or team, and even perceived attractiveness. Therefore, for people who have a tendency for humiliation, our professional status may be viewed as a threat to "down-rank" them. In these circumstances, we can easily be pulled into competitive and rank-based relating without conscious awareness. Box 5 gives an example of this.

Box 5   Responding to humiliation

Susie feels we are not qualified or experienced enough to undertake her assessment. This may prompt a humiliated or shame response in us, and thus we will be pulled into a competitive way of relating. In the case of humiliation, we will be motivated to "up-rank" ourselves and demonstrate our status, leading us to showcase achievements and to prove we are capable. If we feel shame from Susie's criticism, we may find ourselves struggling to respond, appeasing (by agreeing to pass her assessment to someone more experienced), or apologising.

A more appropriate response is to adopt a care-based mind, such as recognising her concerns and exploring her fears, and explaining why we are safe to practice. It is possible Susie will retain her humiliated and competitive mindset, but importantly, we are not pulled into being competitive (either dominant or submissive), which can risk harm.

Clients who feel shame might want to demonstrate their low-ranking status to us (e.g. self-debasement), which is a form of submission, and attempt to "up-rank" us, for example by complimenting us. Box 6 is an example of how we may be pulled into competitive relating by convincing them they are wrong.

Box 6   Responding to shame

David experienced significant bullying as a child and teenager and was exploited by gang members in his neighbourhood. He continues to be bullied in prison and has a strong critical view of himself as unlikable and incapable. In our meetings, he is very complimentary of us, telling us we are good at our job, but we are wasting our time with him because he can never be helped or succeed.

We feel sympathy for him and want him to feel better. We might "down-rank" ourselves by making a joke about ourselves, or we may offer counter evidence to his view of himself to "up-rank" him. We might also ask him to tell us about the successes he has had. These are unlikely to be believed and may create a competitive dynamic in which he feels compelled to prove his failings.

In these circumstances, we should avoid minimising his compliments or contesting his view of self. These are competitive responses. We need to take a gentle approach, acknowledge his view of himself and explain that it does not influence the purpose of the interaction. We may also state the aims of our interaction and express a genuine desire to help all individuals we work with, regardless of their view of themselves or of us.

A key reflective task for us is to examine our own self-conscious emotions, to understand which are most characteristic of us, and to reflect on our life experiences which created the origins of these emotions. This can help us understand the features of the other person and the relational context that activates our different self-conscious emotions. For example, if we are prone to humiliation due to early life experiences, a client who is hubristically prideful and attempts to down-rank us may very quickly trigger our own humiliation, where we are prone to unhelpful responses. The questions in Box 7 are designed to support reflective practice here.

Box 7   Reflective questions

A client is critical towards your professional competency. What feelings does that trigger? What would they need to say or do to leave you feeling shamed or humiliated? What are you motivated to do when you feel like this?

A client is critical towards you personally. What feelings does that trigger? What would they need to say or do to leave you feeling shamed or humiliated? What are you motivated to do when you feel like this?

What are the features of a client that will be more likely to prompt a shamed or humiliated response in you? (e.g. age, gender, appearance, ethnic group)

Compassion-focused ways of working

Building effective, trusting relationships can take time, but in forensic settings, time may not be available. Brief contacts (for example, assessments) do not allow for long-term connections, but there are things we can do to ensure even brief interactions are as effective as they can be. Importantly, we must be aware of not being pulled into competitive mindsets and be vigilant to the self-conscious emotions that emerge in interactions, which will facilitate this. It is critical that we understand our reactions to these and prepare ourselves to be able to respond in the most helpful ways. Short-term assessment work, particularly around offending, carries a risk of creating shame, and while we cannot eradicate the shaming impact of this type of work, we can seek to minimise it. Taylor and Hocken (2024) propose compassion-focused ways of working in forensic settings to minimise the shaming nature of this work and be truly trauma-informed.

Compassion Focused Therapy

Compassion Focused Therapy (CFT) is an integrative psychotherapeutic approach and model of mind that has its genesis in the need to target shame. Paul Gilbert (2010), the father of CFT, working as a clinical psychologist in the 1980s using Cognitive Behaviour Therapy (CBT), noticed that clients who did not make the expected therapeutic gains had strong hostile and critical relationships with themselves. They had an inner critical voice that persistently told them how awful, useless, defective or ugly they were. In the presence of this, clients struggled to believe the alternative helpful thoughts generated by CBT and were unable to recognise and appreciate their successes. Gilbert identified the need to address the internal relationship to the self and the underlying motivation towards the self (in the case of shame, to punish self) and the resulting feelings of hostility. The aim of CFT then is to support clients to notice and understand their difficulties, and to activate their caring system to stimulate the motivation to help themselves. In CFT the two-part definition of compassion reflects these aims: Part One is *to be sensitive to suffering in self and others* (the noticing part); Part Two is *to take action to alleviate or prevent suffering* (the action part). Importantly, compassion as defined here is a motivation, not an emotion. This means that noticing suffering and doing something about it does not have to be accompanied by any given emotional state, and the beneficiary does not need to be liked. This may seem counterintuitive, but there are examples of this in our daily lives: many people working in helping professions do not know the people they help, for example a firefighter rescuing someone from a fire, or a doctor working in Accident and Emergency. Compassion can also be shown towards others who may be a threat to us. Animal welfare work involves caring for the needs of animals that might attack the workers. The obvious benefit of compassion-focused approaches is that people do not have to like themselves before they can begin to be compassionate to themselves.

A further important feature of CFT is that it is a motivation-focused psychotherapy, meaning it recognises motives, not emotions or cognitions, as the primary drivers of behaviour. Motives are systems within all animals that guide essential survival behaviour such as threat protection, resource gathering, reproduction, resting and rearing (Gilbert, 2010). In this model, emotions are secondary to motives and serve the motives by creating the body state to pursue the motive. For example, a motive to defend oneself can be served by anger or anxiety and these emotions will prepare the body for action (fight, flight or freeze). Finally, competencies come online to support the behaviours necessary to act on the motives, and these can be physical or mental. Figure 12.1 below shows how the motive to defend oneself can be served by anger and a competency in boxing will enable to the person to fight and thus defend themselves.

Many therapies target emotions, competencies and behaviours as their primary therapeutic areas for change; while CFT does this, it works first and foremost on motives, recognising that emotions and competencies can equally serve pro-social and antisocial motives. There is no point in building competencies, such as empathy and problem solving, if they are used for antisocial motives, a point made by Jones (2007) in his work on the harmful side effects of interventions to address offending. What CFT aims for is a therapeutic approach that targets the development of the caring motivational system to change the relationship to self and address shame and other self-conscious emotions. Due to its recognition of the critical nature of self-conscious emotions in driving behaviour and explicit aim to target them, CFT has been considered as a promising approach for working with self-conscious emotions relevant to harmful behaviour, such as humiliation (Walker & Knauer, 2011). The broader therapeutic benefits of CFT are significant for the risk-reducing aims of forensic work since it also develops the motive to care for others and thus promotes affiliative and pro-social behaviour (Taylor & Hocken, 2021).

A common misconception of compassion is that it is "soft" and that it is about being kind, loving and gentle. This leads to beliefs that it is weak,

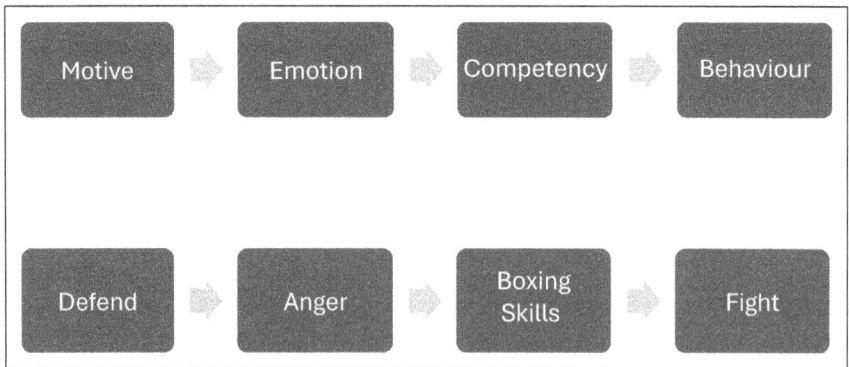

Figure 12.1 Motives as the primary guide to behaviour.

submissive and open to exploitation. Revisiting the definition of compassion, it is easy to see that a compassionate motivation could involve being kind, loving and gentle, but this is not necessary or appropriate in many cases. Returning to examples of compassion in common existence, a firefighter would not be considered loving, likely not gentle and possibly not kind. Indeed, noticing distress and doing something about it are often the most challenging things to do since it involves confronting things that feel threatening. Many of us would not feel brave enough to rescue someone from a fire or help a vicious animal. Turning away from our internal experiences because they feel too overwhelming is a common cause of mental suffering (Hayes et al., 1999). Compassion involves turning towards these experiences; it involves difficult actions for example to end a relationship, address wrongdoing or even end a life. Compassion requires courage and the wisdom to know what the most effective course of action would be to alleviate or prevent distress. This will demand a way of being that carries authority but is not dominant or punitive.

Readying ourselves

CFT places significant emphasis on the self-awareness of the practitioner, in recognition of the co-regulative nature of humans at an unconscious and physiological level. We need to be aware of what messages our own physiology could transmit to the person we are working with and exert control over it to minimise any unhelpful influences. To assist us to do this, a compassionate understanding of ourselves supports us to tune into our own state, noticing any difficulties we are having and working to alleviate that (Kolts et al., 2018). Self-awareness through reflective practice is critical for forensic practitioners (Davies, 2015), and we are perhaps used to thinking about how our ways of seeing the world (cognitions, schemas) impact our interactions with the people we are working with. However, it is less common for us to think about our physiological state in our reflective practice.

Our bodies have a nervous system that supports relating, and we are physiologically attuned to others on an unconscious level; like other animals, we pick up on signals we have no conscious awareness of. The term "gut feeling" reflects this (McCrea, 2010). The implication here is that, as practitioners stepping into a room with a person we know is harmful, or wary of us, our basic biology might give us away. These notions are captured neatly in polyvagal theory (Porges, 1995) which identifies the human necessity to be regulated by another, e.g. co-regulation, beginning from birth. Our autonomic nervous system (ANS) can detect if another nervous system is safe or not through neuroception, an unconscious process drawing on many sensors within the body. Individuals will have a bias for sensitivity to threat or safety cues, and previous adversity sets up for a threat bias (Gilbert, 2008). So, when we walk into a room with an individual our nervous systems are already working to assess that person before we even speak.

Our ANS, through the work of a cranial nerve, the vagus nerve, will exert influence over a range of physiological processes within us that are pertinent to relating. This includes voice tone, head movement and eye gaze. These things "tell" to the other person about our intentions. Our learning here is that we need to prepare our nervous systems as much as our minds for our interactions. Slow, deep breathing helps to reduce the threat response, bringing ANS into a state of regulation where we are more able to co-regulate. Adopting slow, deep breathing has been shown to improve pro-social behaviour such as cooperation and empathy (Gerbarg, 2019): it provides a grounded basis which enables access to our higher-order human skills such as self-awareness, regulation and social connectedness. Research by DeSilva et al. (2019) found that when practitioners practised slow deep breathing before delivering a therapy session with young people in custody, the sessions were considered more successful. This shows the importance of readying our biology and can be impactful in just one meeting.

Central to this is our own orientation to this work and the people we work with. Our motivations for working in forensic settings and with a particular group will set the course of our behaviour, largely on an unconscious level. How we think about the people we work with in relation to ourselves is highly relevant. CFT recognises that suffering is universal and that our unique biopsychosocial circumstances are unchosen; we didn't ask for our genes, our physical capacities, our early experiences and environments, our families, culture or race. None of those things are chosen by us, and therefore, the nature of our biopsychosocial circumstances is about chance. Someone who finds themselves in an impoverished community with a disrupted attachment experience no more chooses that than someone raised in an affluent and caring environment. Yet those circumstances will exert incalculable influence over our life course. Consequently, it makes no sense to blame people for their biopsychosocial circumstances, including their sexual urges, ways of seeing the world and ways of relating to others and their motivations. That is not equivalent to saying people should not be held accountable for their behaviour: we are all responsible for how we behave. However, the origins and predispositions for our behaviour, whether that be pro-social or antisocial are not of our choosing (Sapolsky, 2024). From this position, CFT helps us understand that fundamentally we are no different from the person in front of us, and had we lived their life, with their biology, we might be in their life position and vice versa. The evolutionary theory which sits beneath CFT also shows us that we are all capable of harm under the right circumstances, and our biopsychosocial circumstances will decide that. Once we can grasp this and genuinely appreciate it, we can have heartfelt empathy and sympathy for the people we work with, appreciating the tragic nature of life and supporting us to be humble in our relating. When we are in this position, we are better equipped to genuinely listen to our clients, understand their difficulties and take action to prevent or alleviate harm and distress. We can be compassionate. Behaving in this way will naturally support trauma-informed working increasingly recognised as vital in forensic practice (Wilmot & Jones, 2022). The reflective questions in Box 8 might support us to adopt a compassionate mindset towards our clients.

Box 8 Reflective questions

Bring to mind a client you have found challenging to work with. Imagine you have lived their life. What would have learnt to be vigilant to? What would you have learnt works to stay safe? Imagine living a day in your life if you saw the world like this. What struggles would you have? What or who could help you?

Imagine you are the client. If you were to be interviewed as them about their experience of you, what would they say? What did they notice about you? What did you do that was helpful to them? What was unhelpful?

Not only will compassion enhance our relating to our clients, but it can also enhance our own self-to-self relating and support us to care for ourselves, something that is vital in forensic work (Davies & Jones, 2024). Worries and uncertainties about capabilities, feeling frightened, angry or disconnected from people are common to therapists (Vivolo et al., 2024), but if we believe this experience unequivocally and feel frightened by them, we are likely to feel self-critical and anxious in our work. From a compassionate position, we engage with and understand our struggles, fears and vulnerabilities and view them as knowledge sources about ourselves, and we do not feel shamed by them.

To summarise, our imperative is to be self-aware. Self-awareness enables us to guide our behaviour mindfully. Key practice tips for this are:

- Understand self-conscious emotions, their evolved purpose and the function they may serve in the moment so we are able to notice what this signals on behalf of the person we are working with.
- Be self-aware and sensitive to our own self-conscious emotions, that we characteristically get pulled in to and why, and by whom.
- Ensure we are minimising cues for threat and maximising cues for safety. Some of these cues will be physiological, so we need our biology to be under our control, as far as possible. Adopting slow deep breathing practice in our lives is a simple way to do this and can be used to prepare us before meeting people.
- Behave in ways to maximise safe relating and reduce threat-based self-conscious emotions.

- Understand our motives for our work, including our broad motivations and our immediate motives with individuals.
- Understand and address our blocks to compassion.

Conclusion

We are humans, working with other humans, and ways of relating are the foundation for this work. Forensic settings pose a unique challenge to safe relating as they are contextualised by threat, a state that defaults us to our most primitive biopsychosocial operating system to achieve safety. In doing so, it blocks our access to higher-order executive skills and capacities for pro-social behaviour. As forensic practitioners, our challenge is to forge safe relationships in these contexts and to create the conditions for this from our first contact with individuals in receipt of our services. It is therefore essential that we understand the primitive biopsychosocial operating systems that are at work in threat contexts, so we can behave in ways to minimise threat and maximise safety. Evolution science offers us a means to understand our basic programming and particularly that pertaining to relating.

This wisdom directs us to the requirements to understand ourselves as much as our clients in these terms and to prepare our psychology and physiology for the task of safe relating. Compassionate ways of working offer a means to reflect on this and can be translated into actionable practice.

References

Abbas, T., McNeil-Willson, R., Boyd-MacMillan, E., & DeMarinis, V. (2025). Humiliation and perceived power loss as drivers of radicalisation vulnerability in Northwestern Europe. Behavioral Sciences of Terrorism and Political Aggression, 1–22. Advance online publication. https://doi.org/10.1080/19434472.2025.2488931

Barnett, G. D. (2011), What is grievance thinking and how can we measure this in sexual offenders? *Legal and Criminological Psychology*, 16, 37–61. https://doi.org/10.1348/135532509X480339

Ben-Dor, M., Sirtoli, R., & Barkai, R. (2021). The evolution of the human trophic level during the Pleistocene. *Yearbook of Physical Anthropology, 175*(1), 27–56. https://doi.org/10.1002/ajpa.24194

Blagden, N., Winder, B., Gregson, M., & Thorne, K. (2014). Making sense of denial in sexual offenders: A qualitative phenomenological and repertory grid analysis. *Journal of Interpersonal Violence, 29*(9), 1698–1731. https://doi.org/10.1177/0886260513511530

Bowlby, J. (1980). *Attachment and loss: Vol. 3. Loss: Sadness and depression.* Basic Books.

Breggin, P. R. (2015). The biological evolution of guilt, shame and anxiety: A new theory of negative legacy emotions. *Medical Hypotheses, 85*, 17–24.

Bushman, B. J., & Baumeister, R. F. (1998). Threatened egotism, narcissism, self-esteem, and direct and displaced aggression: Does self-love or self-hate lead to violence? *Journal of Personality and Social Psychology, 75*(1), 219–229. https://doi.org/10.1037/0022-3514.75.1.219

Davies, J. (2015). Supervision for forensic practitioners. In L. J. Clark & D. Wilson (Eds.), *Forensic psychology: Theory, research, policy and practice* (pp. 273–288). Routledge.

Davies, J., & Jones, R. (2024). *Working relationally in forensic settings.* Pavilion Publishing and Media.

da Silva, D. R., Salekin, R. T., & Rijo, D. (2019). Psychopathic severity profiles: A latent profile analysis in youth samples with implications for the diagnosis of conduct disorder. *Journal of Criminal Justice, 60,* 74–83.

de Hooge, I. E. (2014). The general sociometer shame: Positive interpersonal consequences of an ugly emotion. In K. G. Lockhart (Ed.), *Psychology of shame: New research* (pp. 95–109). Nova Science Publishers.

DeYoung, P. A. (2019). *Understanding and treating chronic shame: Healing right brain relational trauma* (2nd ed.). Routledge.

Dunbar, R. I. M. (2014). The social brain: Psychological underpinnings and implications for the structure of organizations. *Current Directions in Psychological Science, 23*(2), 109–114. https://doi.org/10.1177/0963721413517118

Ford, J. D., Chapman, J. F., Hawke, J., & Albert, D. (2019). Trauma among youth in the juvenile justice system: Critical issues and new directions. *Psychology, Public Policy, and Law, 25*(4), 381–396. https://doi.org/10.1037/law0000195

Furuichi, T. (2011). Female contributions to the peaceful nature of bonobo society. *Evolutionary Anthropology: Issues, News, and Reviews, 20*(4), 131–142. https://doi.org/10.1002/evan.20308

Garbutt, K., Rennoldson, M., & Gregson, M. (2023). Shame and self-compassion connect childhood experience of adversity with harm inflicted on the self and others. *Journal of Interpersonal Violence, 38*(11–12), 7193–7214. https://doi.org/10.1177/08862605221141866

Gerbarg, P. L., & Brown, R. P. (2019). Breathing for health: Science meets ancient wisdom. In M. S. Schwartz & A. C. Maiberger (Eds.), *Mindfulness and psychotherapy* (2nd ed., pp. 233–252). Guilford Press.

Gilbert, P. (2008). *The compassionate mind: A new approach to life's challenges.* Constable & Robinson.

Gilbert, P. (2010). Compassion focused therapy: Distinctive features. Routledge. https://doi.org/10.4324/9780203851197

Gilbert, P., Price, J., & Allan, S. (1995). Social comparison, social attractiveness and evolution: How might they be related? *New Ideas in Psychology, 13*(2), 149–165. https://doi.org/10.1016/0732-118X(95)00002-X

Gilbert, P. (2021). Creating a compassionate world: Addressing the conflicts between sharing and caring versus controlling and holding evolved strategies. Frontiers in Psychology, 11, Article 582090.

Gilbert, P. (2022). Creating a compassionate world: Addressing the conflicts between sharing and caring versus controlling and holding evolved strategies. Frontiers in Psychology, 13, Article 842447.

Gilbert, P. (2024). Threat, safety, safeness and social safeness 30 years on: Fundamental dimensions and distinctions for mental health and well-being. British Journal of Clinical Psychology, 63(3), 453–471.

Gilligan, J. (1996). *Violence: Our deadly epidemic and how to treat it.* Putnam.

Gold, J. M., Sullivan, S., & Lewis, M. (2011). Self-conscious emotions: Their adaptive functions and relationship to depressive mood. *American Journal of Psychotherapy, 65*(1), 27–41. https://doi.org/10.1176/appi.psychotherapy.2011.65.1.27

Grapsas, S., Brummelman, E., Back, M. D., & Denissen, J. J. A. (2020). The "Why" and "How" of Narcissism: A process model of Narcissistic Status Pursuit. *Perspectives on Psychological Science: A Journal of the Association for Psychological Science, 15*(1), 150–172. https://doi.org/10.1177/1745691619873350

Gray, J. A. (1985). *The neuropsychology of anxiety: An enquiry into the functions of the septo-hippocampal system.* Oxford University Press.

Hart, D., & Sussman, R. W. (2009). *Man the hunted: Primates, predators, and human evolution* (Expanded ed.). Routledge.

Hassanpour, M., & Pourmohammad, P. (2025). Associations between emotional dysregulation, repetitive negative thoughts, and a sense of self-continuity with post-divorce adjustment in divorced women. *Women's Health Bulletin, 12*(2), 79–89. https://doi.org/10.30476/whb.2025.104792.1325

Hayes, S. C., Strosahl, K. D., & Wilson, K. G. (1999). *Acceptance and commitment therapy: An experiential approach to behavior change.* Guilford Press.

Jetten, J., Reicher, S. D., Haslam, S. A., & Cruwys, T. (2020). *Together apart: The psychology of COVID-19.* Sage Publications.

Jones, C. (2007). Thinking differently about 'serious' offenders: Risk, rehabilitation and the ethics of intervention. In L. Gelsthorpe & R. Morgan (Eds.), *Handbook of probation* (pp. 369–392). Willan Publishing.

Karan, A., Tandon, M., & Singh, R. (2014). Adverse childhood experiences and their impact on mental health: A review. *Journal of Mental Health and Human Behavior, 19*(2), 89–95. https://doi.org/10.4103/0971-8990.152773

Kelman, J., Palmer, L., Gribble, R., & MacManus, D. (2024). Prison officers' perceptions of delivering trauma-informed care in women's prisons. *Journal of Aggression, Maltreatment & Trauma, 33*(10), 1258–1279. https://doi.org/10.1080/10926771.2024.2371860

Kolts, R. L., Bell, T., Bennett-Levy, J., & Irons, C. (2018). *Experiencing compassion-focused therapy from the inside out: A self-practice/self-reflection workbook for therapists.* Guilford Press.

Koski, S. E., de Vries, B., Kraats, L., van Vugt, M., & Sterck, E. H. M. (2015). The evolution of laughter-like vocalizations: Emotional expression and social function in chimpanzees. *Emotion, 15*(5), 528–537. https://doi.org/10.1037/emo0000068

Kross, E., Berman, M. G., Mischel, W., Smith, E. E., & Wager, T. D. (2011). Social rejection shares somatosensory representations with physical pain. *Proceedings of the National Academy of Sciences, 108*(15), 6270–6275. https://doi.org/10.1073/pnas.1102693108

LeDoux, J. E. (1998). *The emotional brain: The mysterious underpinnings of emotional life.* Simon & Schuster.

Levenson, J. S., Willis, G. M., & Prescott, D. S. (2015). Adverse childhood experiences in the lives of female sex offenders: Implications for trauma-informed care. *Sexual Abuse, 27*(3), 254–273. https://doi.org/10.1177/1079063214548019

Lindström, J., Bergh, R., Akrami, N., Obaidi, M., & Lindholm, T. (2023). Who endorses group-based violence? *Group Processes & Intergroup Relations, 27*(2), 217–237. https://doi.org/10.1177/13684302231154412

Mann, R. E., Hanson, R. K., & Thornton, D. (2010). Assessing risk for sexual recidivism: Some proposals on the nature of psychologically meaningful risk factors.

Sexual Abuse: A Journal of Research and Treatment, 22(2), 191–217. https://doi.org/10.1177/1079063210366039

Maruna, S. (2001). *Making good: How ex-convicts reform and rebuild their lives.* American Psychological Association. https://doi.org/10.1037/10430-000

Maruna, S. (2011). Why do they hate us? Making peace between prisoners and psychology [Editorial]. International Journal of Offender Therapy and Comparative Criminology, 55(5), 671–675.

McCrea, S. M. (2010). Intuition, insight and the right hemisphere: Emergence of higher sociocognitive functions. *Creativity Research Journal, 22*(1), 68–73. https://doi.org/10.1080/10400410903579501

McNaughton Nicholls, C., & Webster, S. (2018). *The separated location of prisoners with sexual convictions: Research on the benefits and risks.* His Majesty's Prison and Probation Service Analytical Summary. https://assets.publishing.service.gov.uk/media/5bc74704ed915d0ae30b91fe/separated-location-prisoners-with-sexual-convictions-report.pdf

Nathanson, D. L. (1992). *Shame and pride: Affect, sex, and the birth of the self.* W. W. Norton & Company.

Norcross, J. C., & Lambert, M. J. (Eds.). (2018). Psychotherapy relationships that work III (special issue). *Psychotherapy, 55*(4), 303–315. https://doi.org/10.1037/pst0000193

Ogilvie, C. A., Newman, E. L., Todd, L., & Peck, D. (2014). Attachment and violent offending: A meta-analysis. *Aggression and Violent Behavior, 19*(4), 322–339. https://doi.org/10.1016/j.avb.2014.04.007

Perrin, C., Blagden, N., Winder, B., & Dillon, G. (2018). "It's sort of reaffirmed to me that I'm not a monster": Sex offenders' movements toward desistance via engagement in humanitarian work. *International Journal of Offender Therapy and Comparative Criminology, 62*(13), 3841–3863. https://doi.org/10.1177/0306624X17740014

Porges, S. W. (1995). Orienting in a defensive world: Mammalian modifications of our evolutionary heritage. A Polyvagal Theory. *Psychophysiology, 32*(4), 301–318. https://doi.org/10.1111/j.1469-8986.1995.tb01213.x

Proeve, M., & Howells, K. (2002). Self-conscious affects: Their adaptive functions and relationship to depressive mood. *American Journal of Psychotherapy, 65*(1), 27–41. https://doi.org/10.1176/appi.psychotherapy.2011.65.1.27

Sapolsky, R. M. (1990). Adrenocortical function, social rank, and personality among wild baboons. *Biological Psychiatry, 28*(10), 862–878. https://doi.org/10.1016/0006-3223(90)90568-M

Sapolsky, R. M. (1993). The physiology of dominance in stable versus unstable social hierarchies. In W. Mason & S. Mendoza (Eds.), Primate social conflict (pp. 171–204). SUNY Press.

Shingler, J., Sonnenberg, S. J., & Needs, A. (2020). Psychologists as 'the quiet ones with the power': understanding indeterminate sentenced prisoners' experiences of psychological risk assessment in the United Kingdom. Psychology, Crime & Law, 26(6), 571–592.

Stevens, A., & Price, J. (2016). *Evolutionary psychiatry: A new beginning* (Routledge Mental Health Classic ed.). Routledge.

Tangney, J. P. (2014). The self-conscious emotions: Shame, guilt, embarrassment, and pride. In J. D. A. Parker & D. H. Saklofske (Eds.), *Handbook of emotional intelligence* (pp. 541–568). Wiley.

Tangney, J. P., & Fischer, K. W. (Eds.). (1995). *Self-conscious emotions: Shame, guilt, embarrassment, and pride.* Guilford Press.

Taylor, J., & Hocken, K. (2021). Hurt people hurt people: Using a trauma sensitive and compassion focused approach to support people to understand and manage their criminogenic needs. Journal of Forensic Practice, 23(3), 301–315. https://doi.org/10.1108/JFP-08-2021-0044

Taylor, J., & Hocken, K. (2024). Illuminating the dark side: Life story and formulation work to understand criminogenic capacities and human harmfulness. *Abuse: An International Impact Journal, 5*(1), 46–50.

Torres, W. J., & Bergner, R. M. (2010). Psychological consequences of torture: A critique of the concept of learned helplessness. *Journal of Social, Evolutionary, and Cultural Psychology, 4*(3), 213–228. https://doi.org/10.1037/h0099283

Tracy, J. L., Robins, R. W., & Tangney, J. P. (Eds.). (2007). *The self-conscious emotions: Theory and research*. Guilford Press.

Vivolo, M., Owen, J., & Fisher, P. (2024). Psychological therapists' experiences of burnout: A qualitative systematic review and meta-synthesis. *Mental Health and Prevention, 33*, 200325. https://doi.org/10.1016/j.mhp.2022.200325

Walker, L. E. A., & Knauer, S. (2011). Shame and compensatory aggression. In R. G. Geen & E. Donnerstein (Eds.), *Human aggression: Theories, research, and implications for social policy* (pp. 113–131). Academic Press.

Walton, J. S. (2019). The self-conscious emotions and the role of shame in psychopathology. In M. Lewis (Ed.), *Handbook of emotional development* (pp. 311–350). Springer. https://doi.org/10.1007/978-3-030-17332-6_13

Ware, J., & Blagden, N. (2016). Responding to categorical denial, refusal, and treatment drop-out. In T. Ward & S. Maruna (Eds.), *Forensic psychology: Treatment, intervention and the management of risk* (pp. 76–94). Wiley-Blackwell.

Ware, J., & Blagden, N. (2016). Prison climate and rehabilitating men with sexual convictions. In B. Blagden, H. Winder, & B. Hocken (Eds.), *Challenges in the management of people convicted of a sexual offence* (pp. 173–189). Palgrave Macmillan. https://doi.org/10.1007/978-3-030-80212-

Ward, T. (2013). Addressing the dual relationship problem in forensic and correctional practice. *Aggression and Violent Behavior, 18*(1), 92–100. https://doi.org/10.1016/j.avb.2012.10.006

Willmot, P., & Jones, L. (Eds.). (2022). *Trauma-informed forensic practice* (1st ed.). Routledge. https://doi.org/10.4324/9781003120766

Afterword
Beyond compliance: centring relationships in forensic psychology

Andi Brierley

"Psychologists hold the authority to determine whether someone is progressing or has 'changed.' Yet, this power often feels disconnected from an understanding of what it is truly like to live within the system".

(Tassie)

Among the many profound insights within these pages, this particular statement struck me most deeply, giving rise to a reflection of my own understanding of psychological interventions in custodial settings. Once upon a time, many moons ago, I found myself attending a Prisons Against Substance Related Offending (PASRO) group while I served a two-year prison sentence in HMP Lindholme. It was facilitated by three trainee forensic psychologists. I was 22 years old with a tragic biography, facing my fourth prison sentence post the care experience, heroin addiction and grappling with the daunting question of how I would exist in the world beyond prison walls that kept me contained and controlled. I was entangled in self-doubt, unsure of who I was, what I stood for, and, crucially for desistance from crime, where I was heading. I had no sense of a self-narrative, no script that explained how I'd come to be known as a repeat offender and "junkie", and whether that story could ever be rewritten, reshaped and reworked into something that would create a new direction for a young man crippled by the combination of social adversity and poor personal choices.

PASRO, despite its limitations in the evidence base, was a Cognitive Behavioural Therapy (CBT) programme designed to enhance motivation for change, build self-control, develop relapse prevention strategies and promote healthier lifestyles to reduce the risk of reoffending. The curriculum itself was sound; I have now been trained to deliver CBT courses in my professional life, as two years after leaving HMP Lindholme, I became a Youth Justice Practitioner. However, back when I was sitting in this group setting, in the prison, I rejected the content – not because of what it stated, but because of how it was delivered and received. The relational foundation between facilitators and participants was on shaky ground. As this book and work outlines, the "who" matters just as much as the "how". When I challenged aspects of the theory or questioned the frameworks being presented to us as prisoners, my curiosity and critique weren't welcomed. Instead, I was labelled as "too challenging" and referred to undertake Enhanced Thinking Skills (ETS) on licence upon release to the community. How dare a prisoner question the positivist ideas of forensic knowledge?

Today, as someone undertaking a PhD and working as a University Lecturer, I look back and realise that my critical thinking would now be celebrated within my academic social world and understood as standard academic critique. I would be unlikely to pass my transfer viva if I had not engaged with critiquing theory and methodology within research. On the contrary, back then, my intellectual engagement was misinterpreted as "non-compliance". My passion for seeking truth, for asking difficult questions, was viewed as a threat within the hierarchy of knowledge, placing me, a criminal and junkie, as an individual who should simply accept the course material as fact. After all, I was a prisoner, and they were indeed psychologists. I wasn't seen as a critical thinker, but as a dangerous risk in their assessment. My risk level was increased: not because of what I did, but because of who I was perceived to be. This, in many ways, speaks to the legitimacy crisis within prison-based psychological practice and echoes a sentiment shared by many who have served time: that psychologists in prison often hold power quietly, but profoundly.

At first glance, this edited volume may appear to the untrained eye to focus solely on therapeutic relationships in custodial settings. However, this perception would be mistaken; this work is so much more. For those of us who know the reality of professional relationships behind prison walls, on landings, in cells, classrooms, group rooms and faith spaces, this book is deeply grounded in redemption, humanity, attachment and social connection.

Each chapter invites forensic psychologists and related professionals to reflect, develop, be curious, investigate and ultimately grow from the evidence provided and ask, "what else could I do?" It confronts essential issues: how to centre intersectionality in forensic practice; how to support LGBTQ+ prisoners and women who arrive at the prison doors already bearing the weight of multiple disadvantages and "trauma histories", navigating a prison built for their male counterparts. Additionally, the text offers valuable insight into how staff can manage both soft and hard power through frameworks such as The Holistic Ecological Model, a Trauma-Informed Care (TIC) approach grounded in the lived experiences of incarcerated women. This model places these women firmly at the centre of all forensic interventions and rightly so: these are often incredibly resilient women who have faced life challenges that most people can only grasp in theory. The authors outline how to treat all prisoners, including those convicted of terrorist and sexual offences, with dignity and compassion in environments that are often hostile, hypervigilant and complex. This book is grounded in the premise that professionals working in forensic settings must learn to sit comfortably with uncertainty: a challenging realisation, given that they are typically recruited and valued for their knowledge and academic expertise.

Having lived experience on both sides of the prison and criminal justice system for three decades, I see this book as a much-needed guide and call to move beyond "good enough", to an expectation of a "gold-standard" level of forensic care in a landscape fraught with difficulty. I know, perhaps better than most, that relationships, whether in prisons, probation services, youth justice or social care, are built on the professionals' ability to provide presence, attunement, connection, trust and the ability to work within the professional boundaries of the criminal justice system without losing sight of our humanitarian understanding of power and position when we encounter those who linger within our overcrowded and understaffed prison services.

This volume underlines the critical importance of listening to the voices of those who are incarcerated. The contributors urge forensic professionals to embrace co-production, cultivate trust, operate within trauma-informed principles, recognise neurodiversity and deeply appreciate everyone's abilities, potential and the impact of their social context on their journey into – and out of – criminality. This work provides a specific focus and pre-sents critical "tips" for forensic staff on the developing area of understanding the sensory, relational and functioning needs of autistic clients. Possibly, for me, most importantly due to the incorporation of all the above, it calls for compassion: to humanise risk assessments, confront power imbalances and restore legitimacy to a criminal justice system that all too often overlooks the coercive use of authority. There is a shared hope within each chapter – that it is indeed possible to maintain security, hold individuals accountable for their actions and still act as professional advocates. This advocacy is vital for building a rehabilitative environment that promotes and supports desistance pathways, regardless of one's crime, race, sexuality, capacity, background or religion.

Yes, it is ultimately up to the person who offended to take ownership of their life circumstances and choose to desist from crime and become positive contributors to society. However, this edited volume and the contributors who gave their time clearly demonstrate that even in the darkest corners of the carceral system, the forensic workforce can construct psychological safety and, as a result, play a significant role over the process and outcomes within a trauma-informed and relational context. It is worth saying that if you have taken the time to read this book, you are certainly on a journey of learning and able to recognise and understand our limitations as all-knowing criminal justice practitioners, lived or learnt knowing, or indeed both. To ensure we centre the most important voices within our collective journey, before I sign off and thank you for your time and commitment, let's hold onto Arabella's statement: "You never know the difference you might make. But know this: it could be everything".

Andi Brierley
Senior Criminology Lecturer in the School of Criminology,
Investigation and Policing at Leeds Trinity University

Index

Note: **Bold** page numbers refer to tables; *italic* page numbers refer to figures and page numbers followed by 'n' refer to notes.

For Product Safety Concerns and Information please contact our EU
representative GPSR@taylorandfrancis.com
Taylor & Francis Verlag GmbH, Kaufingerstraße 24, 80331 München, Germany

www.ingramcontent.com/pod-product-compliance
Lightning Source LLC
Chambersburg PA
CBHW050337270326
41926CB00016B/3493

9 7 8 1 0 3 2 8 9 3 5 4 9